FROM KNOWLEDGE MANAGEMENT TO STRATEGIC COMPETENCE

Measuring Technological, Market and Organisational Innovation

Series on Technology Management

Series Editor: J. Tidd (Univ. of Sussex, UK)   ISSN 0219-9823

Published

Vol. 1   Engines of Prosperity
          Templates for the Information Age
          by G. R. Ungson *(Univ. of Oregon, USA)* & J. D. Trudel *(The Trudel Group,
          USA)*

Vol. 2   The Knowledge Enterprise
          Implementation of Intelligent Business Strategies
          edited by J. Friso den Hertog *(MERIT, Maastricht University and
          Altuïtion bv, 's Hertogenbosch, The Netherlands)* &
          E. Huizenga *(Altuïtion bv, 's Hertogenbosch, The Netherlands)*

Vol. 3   From Knowledge Management to Strategic Competence
          Measuring Technological, Market and Organisational Innovation (2nd Edition)
          edited by J. Tidd *(Univ. of Sussex, UK)*

Vol. 4   Japanese Cost Management
          edited by Y. Monden *(Univ. of Tsukuba, Japan)*

Vol. 5   R&D Strategy on Organisation
          Managing Technical Change in Dynamic Contexts
          by V. Chiesa *(Univ. degli Studi di Milano, Italy)*

Vol. 6   Social Interaction and Organisational Change
          Aston Perspectives on Innovation Networks
          edited by O. Jones *(Aston Univ., UK)*, S. Conway *(Aston Univ., UK)*
          & F. Steward *(Aston Univ., UK)*

Vol. 7   Innovation Management in the Knowledge Economy
          edited by B. Dankbaar *(Univ. of Nijmegen, The Netherlands)*

Vol. 8   Digital Innovation
          Innovation Processes in Virtual Clusters and Digital Regions
          edited by G. Passiante *(Univ. of Lecce, Italy)*, V. Elia *(Univ. of Lecce,
          Italy)* & T. Massari *(Univ. of Lecce, Italy)*

Vol. 9   Service Innovation
          *Organisational Responses to Technological Opportunities and
          Market Imperatives*
          edited by J. Tidd *(Univ. of Sussex, UK)* & F. M. Hull *(Fordham Univ., USA)*

SERIES ON TECHNOLOGY MANAGEMENT – VOL. 3

FROM KNOWLEDGE MANAGEMENT TO STRATEGIC COMPETENCE

Measuring Technological, Market and Organisational Innovation

Second Edition

Editor

Joe Tidd

SPRU, University of Sussex, UK

Imperial College Press

ICP

Published by

Imperial College Press
57 Shelton Street
Covent Garden
London WC2H 9HE

Distributed by

World Scientific Publishing Co. Pte. Ltd.
5 Toh Tuck Link, Singapore 596224
USA office: 27 Warren Street, Suite 401-402, Hackensack, NJ 07601
UK office: 57 Shelton Street, Covent Garden, London WC2H 9HE

British Library Cataloguing-in-Publication Data
A catalogue record for this book is available from the British Library.

First published 2006
Reprinted 2007

FROM KNOWLEDGE MANAGEMENT TO STRATEGIC COMPETENCE:
Measuring Technological, Market and Organisational Innovation
(2nd Edition)

ISBN-13 978-1-86094-638-7
ISBN-10 1-86094-638-0

Typeset by Stallion Press
Email: enquiries@stallionpress.com

Printed in Singapore by World Scientific Printers (S) Pte Ltd

Preface to the Second Edition

There continues to be much interest in the business and academic communities in the concept of strategic competencies or core capabilities, that is, how organisations define and differentiate themselves. More recently, this movement has fragmented into a number of related fields with subtle differences in focus: knowledge management — concerned with how organisations identify, share and exploit their internal competencies, in particular the knowledge of individuals; organizational learning — on the relationship between individual and organisational knowledge and how organisations "unlearn" past competencies and acquire new competencies; strategic management — how competencies can be assessed, and how these contribute to performance; and innovation management — on how such competencies are translated into new processes, products and services.

We believe that this fragmentation and increasing specialisation of academic research is counterproductive, and makes it more difficult to provide clear guidance for managers on how to identify, measure, build and exploit strategic competencies. This book attempts to re-establish the links between strategic competencies, knowledge management, organisational learning and innovation management, in an effort to establish a more coherent and integrated framework for future academic research and business practice. We adopt a practical, but rigorous, approach to the subject. Contributors include leading researchers and consultants from the field. We focus on the measurement, management and improvement of organisational, technological and market competencies and, where possible, identify the relationships with strategic, operational and financial performance. Innovation is about creating, capturing and combining knowledge — creating new possibilities through combining different knowledge sets. These can be in the form of knowledge about what is technically possible or what particular configuration of this would meet an articulated or latent need. Such knowledge may already exist in our experience, based on something we have seen or done before. Or it could result from a process of search — research into technologies, markets, competitor actions, etc. And it could be in explicit form, codified in such a way that others can access it, discuss it, transfer it, — or it can be in tacit form, known about but not actually put into words or formulae (Tidd *et al.*, 2005).

In Part 1, we begin with a review of the relationships between strategic competencies, innovation management and organizational learning, and argue that we need to re-integrate these fields in order to better understand and manage organisations. Specifically, we need to be able to operationalise or measure competencies and knowledge before we can model learning and innovation. Richard Hall follows with a review of the resource-based view of the firm and breaks down strategic competencies into four component capabilities: regulatory, positional, functional and cultural. Regulatory capabilities include contracts, patents and licences. Positional capabilities include reputation, distribution and supply chains and external networks. Functional capabilities include employee and supplier know-how and skills in R&D, operations, marketing and finance. Cultural capabilities include the ability to work in teams, a tradition of customer service and the ability to manage change and innovation (Isaksen and Tidd, 2006). In each case, he makes the distinction between tangible and intangible assets. Based on his own experience and a survey of firms, he argues that it is the intangible resources which contribute most. This provides a link between strategic competencies and knowledge management. Peter Hiscocks and Dan Riff identify some common pitfalls in implementing an innovation strategy and provide some practical advice for translating strategy into action. They propose a systems approach to implementation, which incorporates a range of measures of critical performance indicators. The power of the framework is illustrated with a case study from financial services.

In Part 2, Tony Clayton and Graham Turner describe the PIMS (Profit Impact of Market Strategy) approach to measuring and improving market-based competencies, and provide empirical evidence and case studies of the significance of brand development and maintenance. Ciaran Driver and I extend the analysis and develop a model to link measures of technological and market competencies with financial performance based on an analysis of 40 firms. We demonstrate that whilst there appears to be no significant relationship between innovation and profitability at the level of the firm, there is strong evidence that measures of technological and market innovation have a significant affect on both short-term financial measures — such as value-added — and longer-term measures of financial performance, such as the market to book value. Next David Tranfield and co-authors use an empirical study of four firms to link the fields of knowledge management and innovation. They develop a framework which comprises eight generic routines: search, capture, articulate, contextualise, apply, evaluate, support and re-innovate. This can be applied to external sources of knowledge, including customers and collaborative organisations.

In Part 3, we examine the role and measurement of technological competencies. Pari Patel reviews the range of measures available and discuss their relative merits, including R&D spending, patents, product announcements and innovation surveys. He assesses the relationship between firm size and technological performance, as well as the impact of technological activities on firm performance. He concludes by presenting an analysis of the technological specialisation and performance of a sample of 440 firms based on patent activity. Francis Narin continues the assessment of technological competencies by bibliometric (publication) and patent analysis, specifically by means of the Tech-Line® database of more than 1,000 leading firms, universities and agencies in 26 industry groups in 30 technology areas, over 10 years. For each organisation, the assessment is based on nine technology indicators, including the number and quality of patents and technological and science strength. Donald Hislop completes this section, with a study of how communities of practice and innovation processes interact in the implementation of organisation-wide technological process innovations such as ERP (Enterprise Resource Planning), based on seven case studies.

In Part 4, we focus on the assessment of internal and external organisational competencies. Dorothy Griffiths and Max Boisot begin with a review of different notions of core competencies and identify some of the problems associated with measurement. They present their own framework, C-Space (culture space), which consists of two dimensions: codification, that is, the extent to which the knowledge is structured; and diffusion, that is, the extent to which the knowledge is shared by a given population. They argue that knowledge moves around this C-space through a social learning cycle of problem-solving, diffusion, absorption and scanning. They demonstrate how this framework can be used in practice to map and identify linkages between technological elements by means of workshop facilitation, and they illustrate this with case studies of three companies. Jonathan Sapsed develops the notion of "knowledge bases" which applies to complex, multi-technology companies. He uses this to explore the classic tension in organisations between the needs of functional specialisation and project co-ordination. He examines attempts to re-organise in two high-technology firms, and concludes that firms should challenge simplistic prescriptions of organisation design, and need to consider likely losses as well as the potential benefits. In the final chapter in this section, Richard Lamming traces the historical development of supplier relations and assessment from adversarial to partnership. He reviews the range of selection and appraisal criteria available against which suppliers are assessed, including price, quality, delivery and responsiveness, as well as the more formal methodologies used in the defence, aerospace and automobile sectors. He argues that differences in supply markets will demand different supplier relations and assessment criteria and, therefore, recommends a flexible approach to exploiting supplier competencies.

In Part 5, we explore how organisations can improve their existing capabilities and, where necessary, develop new competencies. Pervaiz Ahmed and Mohamed Zairi review various methods of benchmarking performance by focussing on benchmarking innovation processes. Finally,

John Bessant provides a practical guide to organisational learning by describing the organisational routines which support the process of continuous improvement: experimentation, experience, reflection and conceptualisation. Throughout, there is a strong emphasis on formal, documented processes and measurement. Based on his research, he presents a reference model against which an organisation can benchmark, as well as a developmental model to enable an organisation to improve its performance.

Joe Tidd
SPRU, University of Sussex
Brighton, UK
January 2006

Contents

Preface to the Second Edition................................. v

List of Contributors 1

Part 1 — Strategic Competencies   3

Chapter 1 5
The Competence Cycle: Translating Knowledge Into
New Processes, Products and Services
Joe Tidd

Chapter 2 26
What are Strategic Competencies?
Richard Hall

Chapter 3 50
Making Strategy Happen
Peter Hiscocks and Dan Riff

Part 2 — Market Competencies   75

Chapter 4 77
Brands, Innovation and Growth: The Role of Brands in
Innovation and Growth for Consumer Businesses
Tony Clayton and Graham Turner

Chapter 5 94
Technological and Market Competencies and
Financial Performance
Joe Tidd and Ciaran Driver

Chapter 6 126
Building Knowledge Management Capabilities
for Innovation Projects
David Tranfield, Malcolm Young, David Partington,
John Bessant and Jonathan Sapsed

Part 3 — Technological Competencies   151

Chapter 7 153
Technological Indicators of Performance
Pari Patel

Chapter 8 179
Assessing Technological Competencies
Francis Narin

Chapter 9 220
The Complex Relations Between Communities of Practice
and the Implementation of Technological Innovations
Donald Hislop

Part 4 — Organisational Competencies   247

Chapter 10 249
Are There Any Competencies Out There? Identifying and
Using Technical Competencies
Dorothy Griffiths and Max Boisot

Chapter 11 279
The Organisation of "Knowledge Bases"
Jonathan Sapsed

Chapter 12 309
Assessing Performance in Supply
Richard Lamming

Part 5 — Improving Competencies 335

Chapter 13 337
Innovation: A Performance Measurement Perspective
Pervaiz K. Ahmed and Mohamed Zairi

Chapter 14 375
Learning and Continuous Improvement
John Bessant

Bibliography 401

Index 435

List of Contributors

Pervaiz K Ahmed
Chair in Management
Wolverhampton Business School
University of Wolverhampton
Shropshire Campus, Telford, Shropshire
TF2 9NT, UK
pkahmed@wlv.ac.uk

John Bessant
Chair in Innovation Management
Tanaka Business School
Imperial College London
South Kensington Campus, London
SW7 2AZ, UK
j.bessant@imperial.ac.uk

Max Boisot
Professor of Strategic Management
ESADE, PO. Box 144
08870 Sitges, Barcelona, Spain
max.boisot@retemail.es

Tony Clayton
Former Director, PIMS Asoociates
15 Basinghall Street, London
EC2V 5BR, UK
tonyclayton@cix.compulink.co.uk

Ciaran Driver
Professor of Economics
Tanaka Business School
Imperial College London
South Kensington Campus, London
SW7 2AZ, UK
c.driver@imperial.ac.uk

Dorothy Griffths
Professor of Human Resource
   Management
Tanaka Business School
Imperial College London
South Kensington Campus, London
SW7 2AZ, UK
d.griffiths@imperial.ac.uk

Richard Hall
Professor of Strategic Management
Durham University Business School
Mill Hill Lane, Durham City
DH1 3LB, UK

Peter Hiscocks
Integral Europe, Suite 2,
Quayside, Bridge Street, Cambridge
CB5 7AY, UK

Donald Hislop
Lecturer in Organizational Behaviour
The University of Sheffield
   Management School
University of Sheffield
9 Mappin Street, Sheffield, S1 4DT, UK
d.hislop@shef.ac.uk

Richard Lamming
Professor, Director of School
   of Management
University of Southampton
Highfield, Southampton
SO17 1BJ, UK
R.C.Lamming@soton.ac.uk

Francis Narin
ipIQ, 1 North LaSalle, Ninth Floor
Chicago, Illinois 60602, USA
Info@ipIQ.com

David Partington
Senior Lecturer in Project Management
Director, Management Research
    Programmes
Cranfield School of Management
Cranfield University
Cranfield, Bedford
MK43 0AL, UK
d.partington@cranfield.ac.uk

Pari Patel
Senior Fellow
SPRU (Science and Technology Policy
    Research)
University of Sussex
Freeman Centre, Falmer
Brighton, East Sussex
BN1 9QE, UK
P.R.Patel@sussex.ac.uk

Jonathan Sapsed
Senior Research Fellow
CENTRIM (Centre for Research in
    Innovation Management)
University of Brighton
The Freeman Centre
    (University of Sussex campus)
Falmer, Brighton
BN1 9QE, UK
j.d.sapsed@brighton.ac.uk

Joe Tidd
Professor of Technology and
    Innovation Management
SPRU (Science and Technology Policy
    Research)
University of Sussex
Freeman Centre, Falmer
Brighton, East Sussex
BN1 9QE, UK
J.Tidd@sussex.ac.uk

David Tranfield
Professor, Director of Research
    and Faculty Development
Deputy Director, Cranfield
    School of Management
Cranfield University
Cranfield, Bedford, MK43 0AL, UK
d.tranfield@cranfield.ac.uk

Malcolm Young MBE
Research Fellow
Cranfield School of Management
Cranfield University, Cranfield, Bedford
MK43 0AL, UK
m.young@cranfield.ac.uk

Mohamed Zairi
Professor, Best Practice Management
European Centre for Total
    Quality Management
School of Management,
    University of Bradford
Emm Lane, Bradford, BD9 4JL, UK
M.Zairi@bradford.ac.uk

PART 1

STRATEGIC COMPETENCIES

Chapter 1

The Competence Cycle: Translating Knowledge Into New Processes, Products And Services

JOE TIDD

In this chapter, we introduce the central concepts examined in this book and identify some of the key issues to be addressed. Specifically, we discuss the relationships between strategic competencies, innovation management and organisational learning — what we refer to as "the competence cycle": first, we need to be able to identify core competencies; second, we must be able to translate these competencies into new processes, products and services; and, finally, we must learn from successful and unsuccessful projects, and to use this experience to improve existing competencies and, where necessary, develop new competencies.

The most influential proponents of the notion of "core competencies" have been Gary Hamel and C.K. Prahalad (1990). According to Hamel and Prahalad, the concept of the corporation based on core competencies should not replace the traditional one, but a commitment to it "will inevitably influence patterns of diversification, skill deployment, resources allocation priorities and approaches to alliances and outsourcing" (1990: 86). The strength of the approach proposed

5

by Hamel and Prahalad is that it places the cumulative development of firm-specific competencies at the centre of the agenda of corporate strategy. In essence, they argue that:

(i)   The sustainable competitive advantage of firms resides not in their products, but in their *core competencies*: "The real sources of advantage are to be found in management's ability to consolidate corporate-wide technologies and production skills into competencies that empower individual businesses to adapt quickly to changing opportunities" (1990: 81). This approach to strategic management is also known as "resource-based" or "capabilities-based", although there are subtle differences in focus and interpretation.

(ii) Core competencies feed into more than one core product which, in turn, feed into more than one business unit. They use the metaphor of the tree, where core competencies are the roots and the end products and services are the leaves, flowers and fruits. This suggests that the most appropriate level of analysis and investment is neither the product nor the market, but the core competencies.

(iii) Core competencies require *focus*: "Few companies are likely to build world leadership in more than five or six fundamental competencies. A company that compiles a list of 20 to 30 capabilities has probably not produced a list of core competencies." (1990: 84). This suggests that competencies represent a coherent cluster or aggregation of assets, knowledge and skills, and are much more than organisational "strengths" or "weaknesses". They suggest three acid tests for a competence: it adds value to end products; applies to a range of different markets; and is difficult to develop and imitate.

(iv) The identification and development of a firm's core competencies depends on its *strategic architecture*, defined as: "a road map of the future that identifies which core competencies to build and their constituent technologies...should make resource allocation priorities transparent to the whole organisation...Top management must add value by enunciating the strategic architecture that guides the competence acquisition process" (1990: 89). This begs the question of how an organisation identifies which competencies will be relevant to the future and how it might develop or acquire them.

This approach suggests a number of questions (Tidd *et al.*, 2005):

(i) *Definition.* How are competencies identified and measured?
(ii) *Innovation.* How are competencies translated into new products, services and processes?
(iii) *Learning.* How does an organisation acquire new competencies?

These three activities or processes can be combined into what we call the "competence cycle" (Fig. 1.1).

Definition: Identifying and Measuring Competencies

There is no widely accepted definition or method of measurement of competencies, whether technological or otherwise. One possible measure

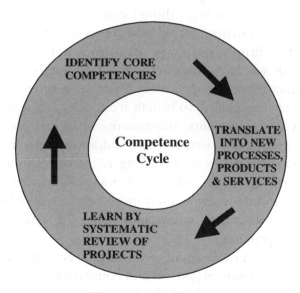

Fig. 1.1. The competence cycle.

is the level of *functional performance* in a generic product, component or sub-system, such as the performance in the design, development, manufacture and performance of compact, high-performance combustion engines. As a strategic technological *target* for a firm like Honda, this obviously makes sense. But its achievement requires the combination of technological competencies from a wide variety of *fields* of knowledge, including mechanics, materials, heat transfer, combustion and fluid flow. Furthermore, over the last 20 years, competencies in other fields have become necessary, such as ceramics, electronics, computer-aided design, simulation techniques and software.

A functional definition of competencies bypasses two central tasks of corporate strategy: first, to identify and develop the range of disciplines or fields that must be combined into a functioning process, product or service; second (and perhaps more important), to identify and explore the new competencies that must be added if the functional capability is not to become obsolete. This is why a definition based on the measurement of the combination of competencies in different fields is more useful for formulating innovation strategy.

Recommendations that firms should concentrate resources on a few fundamental (or "distinctive") world-beating competencies are potentially misleading. Large firms are typically active in a wide range of fields — in only a few of which do they achieve a "distinctive" world-beating position. In other related or supporting fields, a *background* competence is necessary to enable the firm to benefit from outside linkages, especially with suppliers of components, sub-systems, materials and production processes (Granstrand & Pavitt, 1997). In addition, firms are constrained to develop competencies in an increasing range of technological fields, such as IT, new materials and biotechnology — in order to remain competitive as products become even more "multi-technological". This is certainly not a process of concentration, but of diversification in both technology and product.

The most common measures of technological activity are expenditure on research and development, patents and counts of technical publications and citations (Narin *et al.*, 1987). Each measure has its advantages and disadvantages. Hence, in practice, some combination of measurements is desirable. Patents and technical publications have an inherent advantage in that they allow disaggregation by technical field and are, thus, of particular relevance for measuring technological diversity. Clearly, differences in the propensity of firms to patent or publish will affect such measurements. For example, research suggests that on the one hand, American firms tend to patent less in the US than their Japanese counterparts. On the other hand, Japanese firms are under-represented in English language technical journals compared to equivalent American firms (Frumau, 1992). In an effort t o limit such biases, a combined measure of technological activity should be used which includes patents and publications.

Similar problems are encountered when attempting to measure product activity. The most common measures of market diversity are continuous measures based on standard industrial classification (SIC) codes and categorical or strategic typologies, although both types of measure can be combined (Hall & St. John, 1994). Product count measures based on SIC codes tend to underestimate the extent of product diversity because of the assumption that products within the same SIC code must be more closely related than those in a different SIC code. Conversely, measures of market diversity based on strategic typologies must, to some extent, be subjective. Nevertheless, they appear to have a stronger relationship with performance (Rumelt, 1991). Therefore, a hybrid measure of product diversification is desirable.

Innovation: Translating Competencies into New Products, Processes and Services

Having identified some of the problems and measurement, we now turn to how such competencies might be related to processes, products and services. The "tree" metaphor provided by Hamel and Prahalad is attractive, but provides little detail of the precise relationship between competencies and processes, products and services. We make two observations based on our research (Tidd & Bodley, 2002):

(i) Across different sectors, technological and commercial opportunity affects the rate and success of innovation.

(ii) Within a sector, firm-specific competencies and organisational processes will affect the rate and success of innovation.

Early research on strategic management placed great emphasis on the role of technologically advanced industries and diversification (Chandler, 1966; Channon, 1973). The historical success of the chemical and electrical industries has not been based on a single product, process or market. They are good examples of what Chandler refers to as "extensible technologies". The chemical industry extended into textiles and pharmaceuticals; the electrical industry into consumer electronics and machine tools. In contrast, the steel industry is an example of non-extensible technology which has focussed on cost reduction and product improvement rather than diversification. This suggests that the scope of the technology is an important factor in diversification, and that this will affect the effectiveness of the multi-divisional organisational structure.

Much of the research on the management of innovation has attempted to identify some "best practice", irrespective of sector, but industries differ in the amount of resources devoted to R&D and in the rate of technological advance — what is sometimes called and referred to as "technological opportunity" (Geroski, 1994). We know that different sectors are characterised by different levels of innovation inputs and outputs — investment in R&D, process innovation, patents and new products (Tidd et al., 1996). Although difficult to measure and model, three potential sources of technological opportunity have been identified (Klevorick et al., 1995): advances in scientific understanding; technological advances in other related industries; and positive feedback from prior technological advances.

The relative importance of these different mechanisms varies by sector. For example, the pharmaceutical and semiconductor sectors both have strong links to basic science; the former to a narrow range of scientific fields and the latter to a much wider range of fields. In the food and electronics industries, material suppliers and equipment manufacturers are important sources of innovation. Customers are important sources of innovation in the machinery, electrical equipment and medical instrument sectors. Pavitt (1990) develops a similar taxonomy based on the primary sources of innovation:

(i) Science-based, such as pharmaceuticals.
(ii) Supplier-dominated, such as agriculture.
(iii) Specialised suppliers, such as machinery.
(iv) Scale-intensive, such as automotive.
(v) Information-intensive, such as finance.

However, the relationship between innovation inputs and outputs is much stronger at the sectorial level than at the firm level (Silberston, 1989). The economic impact of "spillover" of knowledge from other sectors can also be significant (Geroski, 1994). Within any sector, there is significant variance in the innovative performance of firms. This suggests that firm-specific competencies are as important as technological and commercial opportunity (Hay & Morris, 1990).

For example, we identified significant differences in the technological and commercial opportunity of different sectors (in terms of R&D spending and the new products introduced, respectively), as well as the innovative efficiency (in terms of the R&D spending per new product) of firms within the same sector (Tidd *et al.*, 1996). With such measures, the food and drink industry is characterised by high levels of technological and commercial opportunity and the chemical industry, relatively low levels. However, within each industry, there is a wide range of firm efficiencies to translate technologies into new products. For example, the average R&D spending per new product for firms in the food and drink industry varies from £2m to £26m and in the chemical industry, from £3m to £19m.

Almost by definition, technological and organisational competencies are firm-specific, being based on experience and accumulated over time (Tidd *et al.*, 2005). However, not all firms have the same level of skill to deploy these competencies, particularly searching the technological and market environment and managing inter-organisational relationships for knowledge acquisition (Bessant *et al.*, 1996). At the level of the firm, we need to distinguish between the affect of firm-specific competencies and investments in complementary "assets", or knowledge, from those tools, methodologies and processes which allow a firm to exploit these competencies through innovation.

The relationship between competencies and end products is likely to be most evident in the concept generation and selection stages of new product development. There is a well-established debate in the literature about the relative merits of "market pull" versus "technology push" strategies for new product development, but a review of the relevant research suggests that the best strategy to adopt is dependent on the complexity or novelty of the new product. For incremental adaptations or product line extensions, "market pull" is likely to be the preferred route as customers are familiar with the product type and will be able to express their preferences easily. However, there are many "needs" that the customer may be unaware of or are unable to articulate. In these cases, the balance shifts to a "technology push" strategy. Nevertheless, in most cases, customers do not buy a technology; they buy products for the benefits that they can receive from them (Wind & Mahajan, 1997). The "technology push" must provide a solution to their needs. Thus, some customer or market analysis is also important for more novel technology (Bacon, 1994; Murphy & Kumar, 1997), but there is a difference in emphasis.

We would expect fit with existing competencies to be a critical factor in the screening and selection of product concepts prior to development. There are two levels of filtering. The first is the strategic or aggregate product plan, in which the new product development portfolio is determined. The strategic plan attempts to integrate the various potential projects to ensure that the collective set of development projects will meet the goals and objectives of the firm, as well as to help build the capabilities needed. The second level of filters are concerned with specific product concepts. The two most common processes at this level are the development funnel and the stage-gate system. The development funnel is a means to identify, screen, review and converge development projects as they move from idea to commercialisation. It provides a framework in which to review alternatives based on a series of explicit criteria for decision-making. Similarly, the stage-gate system provides a formal framework for filtering projects based on explicit criteria. The main difference is that where as the development funnel assumes resource constraints, the stage-gate system does not.

In practice, firms use a range of criteria to screen projects prior to development. Besides financial criteria such as payback, return on investment (ROI) and net present value (NPV), firms use a range of non-financial criteria to screen and select development projects. The most common criteria are the probability of technical and commercial success, as well as the predicted market share (Table 1.1). Given how subjective estimates of probability can be, the widespread use of such criteria is surprising. However, there are significant differences in the usefulness of criteria for assessing high complexity projects (Tidd &

Table 1.1. Use and usefulness of non-financial criteria for project screening and selection. (Tidd & Bodley, 2002)

	High Complexity		Low Complexity	
	Usage (%)	Usefulness	Usage (%)	Usefulness
Probability of technical success	100	4.37	100	4.32
Probability of commercial success	100	4.68	95	4.50
Market share*	100	3.63	84	4.00
Fit with core competencies*	95	3.61	79	3.00
Degree of internal commitment	89	3.82	79	3.67
Market size	89	3.76	84	3.94
Competition	89	3.76	84	3.81
Gap analysis	79	2.73	84	2.81
Interactive techniques	68	4.23	58	3.91
Strategic clusters*	42	3.63	32	2.67

*Denotes that difference in usefulness rating is statistically significant at 5% level.

Bodley, 2002). For complex projects, market share, core competencies and strategic clusters are all believed to be more useful than for low complexity projects. We might expect that the more strategic criteria, such as fit with competencies or other development projects, would be more relevant to the high complexity projects. However, the reliance on predicated market share is more difficult to interpret. Perhaps this is a function of the higher cost and perceived risk of such projects. Therefore, in most cases, the fit with existing competencies is an important consideration when determining new product development strategy. This is particularly so for more novel or complex products. Clearly, then, a development project is usually driven by the wish to exploit existing competencies. Alternatively, it may drive the development of new competencies. These two opposing motives — leverage or learning — have very different structural and managerial implications (Tidd & Taurins, 1999).

Learning: Acquiring New Competencies

The competence-based approach is concerned with the identification, development and exploitation of core competencies based on prior experience. However, it fails to address how firms cope when existing competencies become obsolete, or how firms acquire new competencies. As Dorothy Leonard-Barton (1990) has pointed out, "core competencies" can also become "core rigidities" in the firm when established competencies become too dominant. In addition to sheer habit, this can happen because established competencies are central to today's products, and because large numbers of top managers may be trained in them. As a consequence, important new competencies may be neglected or underestimated (such as the threat to mainframes from mini-computers by management in mainframe companies). Perhaps more interesting, established innovation strengths may overshoot the target. A focus on the structures and processes which facilitate learning at the level of the organisation, rather than the level of the individual, may provide a useful means of examining such issues (Tidd, 1997).

The importance given by Hamel and Prahalad to top management in determining the "strategic architecture" for the development of future technological competencies is debatable. As *The Economist* (1994) has argued:

> "It is hardly surprising that companies which predict the future accurately make more money than those who do not. In fact, what firms want to know is what Mr. Hamel and Mr. Prahalad steadfastly fail to tell them: how to guess correctly. As if to compound their worries, the authors are oddly reticent about those who have gambled and lost."

The evidence, in fact, suggests that the successful development and exploitation of core competencies does not depend on the management's ability to forecast, accurately, long-term technology and product. Instead, the importance of new technological opportunities and their commercial potential emerge not through a flash of genius (or a throw of the dice) from senior management, but gradually through an incremental corporate-wide process of trial, error and learning in knowledge-building and strategic positioning. This is how Ericsson's new competence in mobile telephones first emerged (Granstrand *et al.*, 1992). It is also how Japanese firms like Canon developed and exploited their competencies in opto-electronics (Miyazaki, 1994).

However, traditional conceptualisations of learning in the field of technology management, such as the experience curve or learning by doing, focus on the improvement of some narrow expertise or process, rather than the acquisition of new competencies. Conversely, research on organisational development (OD) and change has focused on wholesale organisational change. Therefore, it is useful to distinguish between learning "how" and learning "why" (Edmondson & Moingeon, 1996). Learning "how" involves improving or transferring existing skills, whereas learning "why" aims to understand the underlying logic or causal factors with a view to applying the knowledge in new contexts. Neither form of learning is inherently superior, and each will be important in different circumstances. For example, learning "how" is more relevant where speed or quality is critical, but learning "why" will be necessary to apply skills and know-how in new situations.

Much of the research on technology management and organisational change has failed to address the issue of *organisational* learning. Instead, it has focussed on learning by *individuals* within organisations: "...it is important to recognise that organisations do not learn, but rather the people in them do" (Bessant *et al.*, 1996: 67); "an organisation learns in only two ways: (i) by the learning of its members; or (ii) by ingesting new members..." (Simon, 1996: 176). Clearly, individuals do learn within the context of organisations. This context affects their learning which, in turn, may affect the performance of the organisation. However, individuals and organisations are very different entities, and there is no reason why organisational learning should be conceptually or empirically the same as learning by individuals or individuals learning within organisations (Cook & Yanow, 1996). Existing theory and research on organisational learning has been dominated by a weak metaphor of human learning and cognitive development, but such simplistic and inappropriate anthropomorphising of organisational characteristics has contributed to confused research and misleading conclusions.

A clear distinction needs to be made between individual learning and organisational learning, and there is a need for a clearer conceptual framework at the specific level of organisational learning. For example, Chen (1997) compares how publishing firms and software firms have diversified into multi-media markets. The publishing firms have tended to exploit their existing assets, such as intellectual property rights and sales and distribution networks, but have so far failed to develop the new skills and processes necessary for the rapid development and commercialisation of multi-media products. In contrast, the software firms already possess the appropriate skills and processes, and have simply had to purchase the relevant intellectual property. Therefore, it is useful to distinguish three distinct components of organisational learning:

knowledge acquisition, information distribution and organisational memory (Huber, 1996).

Knowledge acquisition

Organisations can acquire knowledge by experience, experimentation or acquisition. Of these, learning from experience appears to be the least effective. In practice, organisations do not easily translate experience into knowledge. Moreover, learning may be unintentional or it may not result in improved effectiveness. Organisations can incorrectly learn, and they can learn that which is incorrect or harmful, such as learning faulty or irrelevant skills or self-destructive habits (Huber, 1996). A competency trap can occur when an inferior procedure provides favourable performance. This leads an organisation to accumulate experience with it, but prevents it from gaining sufficient experience of a superior procedure to make it rewarding to use (Levitt & March, 1996).

Experimentation is a more systematic approach to learning. It is a central feature of formal R&D activities, market research and some organisational alliances. When undertaken with intent, a strategy of learning through incremental trial and error acknowledges the complexities of existing technologies and markets, as well as the uncertainties associated with technology and market change and in forecasting the future (Tidd et al., 2005). The use of alliances for learning is less common and requires an intent to use them as an opportunity for learning, a receptivity to external know-how and partners of sufficient transparency (Hamel, 1991). Whether the acquisition of know-how results in organisational learning depends on the rationale for the acquisition and the process of acquisition and transfer (Tidd & Trewhella, 1997). For example, the cumulative effect of outsourcing various technologies on the basis of comparative transaction costs may limit future technological options and reduce competitiveness in the long term (Bettis et al., 1992).

Information distribution

The concept of core competence is useful at the corporate level, but it becomes more difficult to apply to the multi-divisional firm. Are the core competencies of a multidivisional firm simply the sum of the competencies of its divisions, or does the architecture of the firm create additional competencies? For example, the development of new products may demand new technology-product-market linkages and, therefore, require close collaboration between different divisions (Tidd, 1995).

Information distribution is the process by which information from different sources is shared and, therefore, leads to new knowledge or understanding. Greater organisational learning occurs when more of an organisation's components obtain new knowledge and recognise it as being of potential use. However, in practice, organisations often do not know what they know. Many firms now have databases and groupware to help store, retrieve and share information, but such systems are often confined to "hard" data. Tacit knowledge is not easily imitated by competitors because it is not fully encoded, but for the same reasons it may not be fully visible to all members of an organisation (Hendry, 1996). As a result, organisational units with potentially synergistic information may not be aware of where such information could be applied. The speed and extent to which knowledge is shared between members of an organisation is likely to be a function of how codified the knowledge is (Boisot *et al.*, 1996).

The problem of information distribution is likely to be more common in large, multi-divisional firms. The multi-divisional structure emerged because the volume and complexity of information placed strains on the traditional functional structure. The structure is particularly appropriate to firms adopting a strategy of product-market diversification where different markets, products and technologies demand different expertise, but has become the normative model for large commercial organisations. Market focus and technical efficiency are the main benefits associated with the multi-divisional structure. In terms of financial performance, research suggests that performance at the level of business units is of much greater significance than that at the corporate level: "corporate returns will differ because their portfolios of business units differ...there is no evidence of 'synergy'" (Rumelt, 1991: 182).

This suggests that the multi-divisional structure may discourage innovation: managing product divisions by short-term financial performance limits the scope for long-term or high-risk projects; and decentralising research and development reduces the scope for exploiting the interrelatedness of technologies. However, multi-divisional firms can be efficient innovators just as the more focussed firms are, measured in terms of patents and new products per unit of research and development expenditure (Cardinal & Opler, 1993). Measured in these terms, the multi-divisional structure may facilitate efficient innovation within specific product markets, but may limit the scope for learning new competencies: firms with fewer divisional boundaries are associated with a strategy based on capabilities-broadening, whereas firms with many divisional boundaries are associated with a strategy based on capabilities-deepening (Argyres, 1996). As Table 1.2 shows, the notion of core competencies suggests that large and multi-divisional firms should be viewed not only as a

Table 1.2. Two views of the corporation: core competencies versus strategic business units. (Tidd & Bodley, 2002)

	Strategic Business Unit	Core Competencies
Basis for competition	Competitiveness of today's products	Inter-firm competition to build competencies
Corporate structure	Portfolio of businesses in related productmarkets	Portfolio of competencies,core products and business
Status of business unit	Autonomy: SBU "owns" all resources other than cash	SBUis a potential reservoir of core competencies
Resource allocation	SBUs are unit of analysis. Capital allocated to SBUs	Competencies are unit of analysis. Top management allocates capital and talent
Value added of top management	Optimising returns through trade-offs among SBUs	Enunciating strategic architecture and building future competencies

collection of strategic business units, but as bundles of competencies that do not necessarily fit tidily into one business unit.

For example, in the case of home automation, a combination of competencies is required to develop and deliver new products and services, including construction, energy, electronics controls and "white"

Table 1.3. Technological and market dispersion of electronics companies. (Tidd, 1995)

	Technological Diversification (USpatents) (A)	Market Diversification (USSales) (B)	Leverage of Competencies (B/A)
Bosch	58	52	0.90
Philips	69	78	1.13
Siemens	74	87	1.17
Thomson	66	68	1.03
Fujitsu	59	63	1.07
Hitachi	75	78	1.04
Matsushita	65	70	1.07
Mitsubishi	68	64	0.94
NEC	61	80	1.31
Sharp	57	61	1.07
Sony	53	35	0.66
Toshiba	72	86	1.19
AT&T	66	22	0.33
GE	73	59	0.81
HP	59	58	0.98
Honeywell6	3	39	0.62
IBM	62	34	0.55
Motorola6	0	75	1.25
RCA	59	69	1.17
TI	59	60	1.01

Note: The diversification measure is a percentage of the activity outside the core field, that is, a low score indicates high concentration and a high score, a broad range of activities.

and "brown" consumer products. No single company is active in all the relevant fields, but a handful are active in two or more. An analysis of the technological activity and product diversity reveal different combinations of competencies and different approaches to the development of products for home automation (Tidd, 1994, 1995). Table 1.3 summarises the data on technological and market activity. Technological diversification is estimated by the proportion of patents a company produces outside its core technological field, and the market dispersion by the proportion of revenue outside the main product market. For the sake of clarity, data on technical publications is not included. However, use of bibilometric data from the INSPEC database of technical publications produces similar results to the measure of patent activity. The ratio of the market to technological diversity provides a crude indication of the firm's ability to leverage its technological competencies across a range of different markets. If a nominal threshold of 70% is applied to both technological and market diversification, only a handful of firms emerge as being highly diversified in both technology and markets (Fig. 1.2).

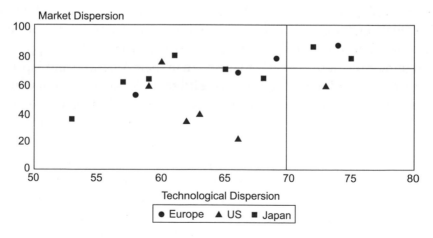

Fig. 1.2. Technological and market diversification of electronics firms. (Tidd, 1995)

By these measures, General Electric of the US, Siemens of Germany, and Hitachi and Toshiba of Japan have high levels of technological diversification. In addition, Motorola of the US, Siemens and Philips of Europe, and Hitachi, Toshiba and NEC of Japan have a high level of market diversification. Combining the measures of technological and market diversification gives us some idea of the firm's ability to leverage its technological competencies across markets. By this measure, of the technologically diversified firms, only Siemens, Philips, Hitachi and Toshiba score highly. Significantly, no American firm in the sample satisfies both criteria. Relaxing the 70% threshold for technological diversification allows comparisons to be made between the organisational structures of the highest scoring American, European and Japanese firms. These differences may be the result of the fashion for highly focussed strategies in the 1980s. Alternatively, it may be a result of the measures used. Clearly, the data and method of aggregation may have introduced some bias to these findings. For example, the use of patent activity as a measure of technological diversification may overstate the diversification of Japanese firms due to their higher propensity to patent. However, substituting data on technical publications provides consistent patterns of technological diversification.

Comparisons of the organisational structures of the companies reveals some consistent differences. All are large, multi-national and multi-divisional organisations, but they differ in how focussed the business units are. The product divisions of the two European firms appear to be significantly more narrowly focussed than their American and Japanese competitors. In Philips, at least six different divisions are relevant to home automation products and services: consumer electronics, domestic appliances, lighting, communication systems, components and semiconductors. Similarly, in Siemens, there are six divisions which are relevant: industrial and building systems, automation, private communications, semiconductor, audio-visual and lighting (Osram). In contrast, the divisions in the Japanese companies appear to be much broader, which may facilitate better co-ordination of product development and commercialisation. For example, in NEC, two divisions are most relevant — Home Electronic Products and Communications Systems and Equipment — perhaps with the addition of the Electron Devices division. Similarly, in Toshiba, only two divisions are involved: Consumer Products and Information and Communication Systems. Interestingly, the structure of the two American companies appears to be closer to that of the Japanese companies than it is to the Europeans. Motorola has just four major divisions, of which three are relevant to home automation: electronic devices, radio communication products and computer equipment. General Electric has a multitude of product divisions, but only three of these are of direct relevance to home automation: appliances, lighting and electrical distribution and control.

Clearly, more detailed case studies are necessary before any firm conclusions can be reached. However, it does appear that in the case of home automation, the Japanese and American companies have fewer, more broadly defined divisions than their European competitors, and this facilitates the exploitation of competencies across divisions. However, two qualifications must be made. First, the emphasis has been on the horizontal component of diversification, rather than on issues of vertical integration and positions in value chains. It may be significant that almost all of the firms examined are active from semiconductors to final consumer products. Second, the focus has been on structural characteristics, rather than on processes. It is possible that firms which have similar divisional structures, or organisational "hardware", may have different organisational processes or "software" to integrate the various product divisions.

Organisational memory

Organisational memory is the process by which knowledge is stored for future use. Such information is stored either in the memories of members of an organisation or in its operating procedures and routines. The former suffers from all of the shortcomings of human memory, with the additional organisational problem of personnel loss or turnover. Bessant *et al.* (1996) argue that competencies are made up of abilities which, in turn, are the result of behavioural routines. Over time, these routines create and are reinforced by artefacts such as organisational structures, procedures and policies. In these terms, competencies become highly firm-specific combinations of behavioural routines and artefacts. This specificity questions the validity of the current fashion for benchmarking "best practice" processes and structures: what works for one firm may not work for another. Conversely, the difficulty in anticipating future needs means that much non-routine information is never stored in this way.

Hall (1994) goes some way towards identifying the components of organisational memory. His main purpose is to articulate intangible resources and he distinguishes between intangible assets and intangible competencies. Assets include intellectual property rights and reputation. Competencies include the skills and know-how of employees, suppliers and distributors, as well as the collective attributes which constitute organisational culture. His empirical work, based on a survey and case studies, indicates that managers believe that the most significant of these intangible resources are the company's reputation and employees' know-how, both of which may be a function of organisational culture. Thus, organisational culture, defined as the shared values and beliefs of members of an organisational unit, as well as the associated artefacts, become central to organisational learning (Cook & Yanow, 1996).

Nonaka and Takeuchi (1995) argue that the conversion of tacit to explicit knowledge is the critical mechanism underlying the link between individual and organisational learning. They argue that all new knowledge originates with an individual, but that through a process of dialogue, discussion, experience sharing and observation, such knowledge is amplified at the group and organisational levels. This creates an expanding community of interaction, or "knowledge network", which crosses intra- and inter-organisational levels and boundaries. Such knowledge networks are very different from the concept of the virtual corporation, in which a firm exploits the knowledge of its suppliers, customer and competitors. In contrast, knowledge networks are a means to accumulate knowledge from outside the organisation, to share it widely within the organisation, and to store it for future use (Nonaka *et al.*, 1996). This process is underpinned by "communities-of-practice", which are groups of people related by processes or need to solve a problem, rather than by formal structural or functional relationships. Within communities-of-practice, people share tacit knowledge and learn through experimentation. Therefore, the formation and maintenance of such communities represent an important link between individual and organisational learning.

Conclusions

We have identified three issues which must be addressed if the competence approach to strategic management is to be successfully implemented. First, competencies must be clearly defined and measured in order to distinguish them from generic organisational "strengths" or more routine activities and tasks. We advocate that competencies be disaggregated into distinct clusters of technological and market know-how, which are then deployed by means of organisational competencies or processes. Second, competencies represent a *potential* and, therefore, cannot contribute to competitiveness or performance unless they are successfully translated into new processes, products and services. This is the role of innovation management. Finally, organisational learning demands the systematic review of successful and unsuccessful projects and the dissemination of experience throughout the organisation. This process helps to refine and develop existing competencies and to detect when new competencies might need to be acquired. These three processes constitute the "competence cycle".

Chapter 2

What are Strategic Competencies?

RICHARD HALL

Introduction

Prior to becoming an academic, the author spent 14 years running a company manufacturing consumer products. For 12 years, the company was successful. Then it took two years to die. Whilst it was dying, it was perfectly obvious what was wrong; when it was successful, the management team did not ask, let alone answer, the question: "What are the sources of our success?" This experience was responsible for the intellectual curiosity regarding the sources of sustainable competitive advantage which has resulted in the research activity reported here.

The concept of strategic competencies, sometimes referred to as distinctive capabilities, has received much attention from academics and practitioners in the last 10 years, especially since the publication — in 1990 — of Prahalad and Hamel's (1990) seminal article, *The Core Competence of the Corporation*. This article suggested that the most critical task for management is to create new products which customers need, but have not yet imagined, and that they should do this by creating competencies which enable the new, unanticipated products to be conceived.

Suppliers have competencies and customers have needs. Products are, from time to time, the embodiment of the means by which suppliers' competencies fulfil customers' needs. This "inside out" perspective does not replace the previous "outside in" perspective which was concerned with products and markets; it compliments it. This approach, which was triggered by the Prahalad and Hamel article, broadened the strategic manager's field of view to include corporate resources as well as markets, and the approach became known as the "resource-based view" of strategy. The essence of the resource based approach can be captured in the following apocryphal tale:

Box 2.1

> A small British company in the 1970s decided that it was time to start exporting to Europe. The CEO called a meeting of his management team and asked if anyone could speak any language other than English. One manager said he could speak Spanish. "Right", said the CEO, "We will start exporting to Spain".

The resource-based view is concerned essentially with identifying and building on strengths, preferably those which, for whatever reason, are unique to the firm.

One major consequence of the need to focus on competencies concerns organisational structure. An organisation which is structured around strategic business units (SBUs), each of which is product/market-focussed, may be inappropriate because such an organisational structure could inhibit the development of the core competencies shared by all the SBUs. For example, if surface chemistry is a core competence common to all the divisions of Proctor & Gamble, it may be that the development of this core competence is hindered by a divisional structure based on toilet preparations, drugs, detergents and so forth. This is because each division will jealously guard the resources (competencies) which it should be sharing and developing with the other divisions. This train of thought leads us to the conclusion that companies ultimately compete with competencies, not with products.

Strategic competencies produce competitive advantage. Before we explore more fully the nature and characteristics of strategic competencies, it is necessary to examine the concept of competitive advantage.

Competitive Advantage

The early writers on business strategy suggested, not unreasonably, that any organisation which operates in a competitive environment needs a competitive advantage in order to survive and prosper.

For most organisations, the competitive environment exists in the "downstream" sales market. However, it can sometimes apply in the "upstream" supply market where, for example, an ambulance service may be in competition with a fire brigade for limited financial resources.

In his book *Competitive Advantage*, Michael Porter (1985) suggested that the product of a successful strategy was a competitive advantage which could be sustained in the marketplace. Porter suggested two generic types of competitive advantage: cost leadership and differentiation. The proposition that there are only two generic types of competitive advantage was widely accepted, and taught, for many years. It was held that companies had a basic choice: a strategy of cost leadership or a strategy of differentiation; any attempt to do both was not to be encouraged!

Cost leadership was not necessarily meant to result in selling price leadership, although it was assumed that in most cases the lowest cost producer would also be a low price seller. It was argued that the large volumes which usually go with low selling prices would result in a cost leadership company continually reinforcing its advantageous position by virtue of the learning curve effect (the more one does, the better one gets at doing it) and by virtue of its superior recovery of fixed costs. While there is strong evidence that companies with above average market shares do enjoy above average return on investment (Buzzell & Gale, 1987) the causal "trail" from low price to high market share to high return on investment is by no means established as a universal law; indeed, there are many examples of once dominant companies being overtaken by new entrants.

Differentiation was defined as offering a uniqueness in the marketplace with respect to features which were widely valued by customers. To be commercially advantageous, this uniqueness has to be rewarded with a premium on the selling price which exceeded the extra costs associated with producing the differentiation.

Porter suggested that it was dangerous to attempt to pursue both cost leadership and differentiation at the same time as this would result in the company being "stuck in the middle". This claim is now largely discounted as there are examples of companies which manage to differentiate their product offerings whilst at the same time selling at low prices. One example of such a company is the John Lewis Partnership (JLP), a chain of department stores in the United Kingdom. This company manages to differentiate the products it trades by the level of service it gives to its customers — the latter being due arguably to the profit-sharing arrangements made for all its employees/partners. As well as offering a differentiated product, JLP also sells at competitive prices. Indeed, it broadcasts its selling price policy with the slogan "Never knowingly undersold".

A more pragmatic view on the nature of competitive advantage was advanced by Coyne (1986) whose argument starts with the observation that any company which is making repeat sales in a competitive market must enjoy an advantage in the eyes of the customers who are making the repeat purchases! He went on to argue that for a *sustainable* competitive advantage to exist, three conditions must apply:

(i) Customers must perceive a consistent difference in important attributes between the producer's product/service and the attributes offered by competitors.

(ii) This difference is the direct consequence of a capability gap between the producer and its competitors.

(iii) Both the difference in important attributes and the capability gap can be expected to endure over time.

This approach echoes the statement made in the introduction to the effect that suppliers have capabilities and customers have needs. In Coyne's terms, customers recognise the attributes which will satisfy their needs and these attributes are the direct consequence of the supplier's capabilities. We are now getting closer to concepts which we can operationalise because it is now possible to ask the question, "What is the nature of the package of product/delivery system attributes which customers value?", and to go on to ask the question, "What is responsible for producing the valued attributes?". The product/delivery system attributes will include factors such as price, quality, specification and image. Selling price is one, albeit important, attribute in a package of attributes. It may be paramount if customers are constrained by the price they can afford to pay, or it may be subordinate to availability if demand exceeds supply. Coyne also points out that having a low cost base — and, in consequence, higher margins — only results in a competitive advantage in the marketplace if the extra margin is used to produce new valued attributes. If the margin is reflected in higher dividend payments to shareholders, then no competitive advantage results. It is the application of resources, not their accumulation, which results in competitive advantage.

Coyne suggests that there are four — and only four — types of resource capability:

(i)   *Regulatory.* The possession of legal entities, such as patents and trademarks.
(ii) *Positional.* The results of previous endeavour, such as reputation, trust and value chain configuration.
(iii) *Business systems.* The ability to do things well, such as consistent conformance to specification.
(iv) *Organisational characteristics.* This includes the ability to manage change.

This categorisation of resources has been included in the author's technique for analysing the role of intangible resources in business success which will be presented in this chapter.

Strategic Competencies

The essence of the resource based view of strategy is neatly captured by Nooteboom (1996):

Box 2.2

"...the firm is made up from a number of competences, based on resources, embodied in a configuration of various forms of capital (financial, human, social), which to a greater or lesser extent is idiosyncratic to the firm. It is such unique capabilities of firms that allow them a basis for profit."

Every firm is unique by virtue of its history, value chain configuration, organisation culture and so forth. The challenge is to make the firm's uniqueness the source of its sustainable competitive advantage. The factors which constitute a firm's uniqueness are "path dependent"; they will have taken time to acquire. Mole, Griffiths and Boisot (1996) express the point well:

Box 2.3

"...strategic assets are built up over time and defy imitation because they have a strong tacit content and are socially complex. Their development is so tied to the history of the firm in terms of previous levels of learning, investment and development activity that these aspects of firm resources are non-tradable. Would-be imitators are thwarted by the difficulty of discovering and repeating the developmental process and by the considerable time lag involved in attempting to do so."

In describing strategic assets, Mole *et al.* use expressions such as "tacit" and "socially complex". These are concepts which are not usually subject to the scrutiny of accountants; they are intangible resources. In this chapter, tangible assets are identified as those which are normally represented on a balance sheet and intangible assets are those characteristics of a firm which usually cannot be represented on a balance sheet, but which are held to be the source of the firm's future earning capability. If, as is often the case, a firm's market capitalisation is a multiple of five, or even 10, times its balance sheet net worth, this means that the stock market's assessment of the value of the company places between four-fifths and nine-tenths of the value "off balance sheet". This is held to represent the company's future earning capability. The point is well-expressed by Baxter (1984):

Box 2.4

> **"A simple mind could hardly entertain the notion of intangible assets. In a child's tale, wealth is castles, land, flocks, gold — i.e., physical things. It is a long step forward to realise that the essence of wealth is the prospect of benefits, not their physical source."**

From the foregoing, we can see that the important characteristics of strategic competencies are as follows:

(i)   They are responsible for delivering a significant benefit to customers.
(ii) They are idiosyncratic to the firm.
(iii) They take time to acquire.
(iv) They are sustainable because they are difficult and time-consuming to imitate.
(v)   They comprise *configurations* of resources.
(vi) They have a strong tacit content and are socially complex — they are the product of experiential learning.

This chapter will explore these characteristics and discuss how strategic competences may be identified, sustained, enhanced and leveraged.

"Find the Hero Inside Yourself"

This section will describe the technique for analysing intangible resources which the author has developed and validated. It is based on the identification and development of the strengths in the key product/delivery system attributes and the intangible resources which produce them.

The valued attributes

As Coyne has pointed out, any company which is making repeat sales in a competitive market has an advantage in the eyes of the customers who are making the repeat purchases. The nature of the advantage may be defined in terms of a package of product/delivery attributes. The identification of the key attributes and their relative weighting can be done by market research or by Delphi panels of relevant executives. Examples of product/delivery system attributes are shown in Table 2.1.

It may be necessary to identify different rankings for different categories of customers, such as new versus long-standing customers and retailers versus end users. In carrying out this analysis of attributes, it is appropriate to seek consensus between the relevant executives with respect to questions such as:

(i) Can executives agree on an importance weighting for each attribute?
(ii) Can executives agree on a benchmark score for each attribute compared with the competition?
(iii) Can executives agree on the *sustainability* of the advantage represented by each attribute?

The degree of congruence, or dissonance, in executives' perceptions of these issues can in itself be illuminating. In addition to identifying the current strengths in the marketplace, it is also appropriate at this stage to identify known deficiencies in the product offering.

In the research carried out to date, the firms which dealt directly with end users tended to emphasise availability — buses must run to time, retail outlets must be in the right location and stock the products which customers expect to find; firms engaged in manufacturing tended to emphasise quality — is the product "fit for purpose", and do the products consistently conform to specification?

Table 2.1. Typical product/delivery system attributes which define sales advantage.

Image. What is the image of the product range? Is it important?

Price. Is a low selling price a key buying criterion?

User-friendliness. Is it important for the product to be user-friendly?

Availability. Is product range availability crucial?

Rapid response to enquiry. Is it important to produce designs, quotations and so forth very quickly?

Quick response to customer demand. Will sales be lost to the competition if they respond more quickly than you?

Width of product range. Is it important to offer a wide range of products and/or services to customers?

New product to market time. How important is the product development time?

Quality — the product's fitness for purpose. Does the product, or service, deliver exactly the benefits which the customers want?

Quality — the consistent achievement of defined specification. Is constant conformance to specifications vital?

Safety. Is safety in use a major concern?

Regulatory requirements. Does meeting regulatory requirements earlier/better than the competition give a competitive advantage?

Degree of innovation. Is it important for the product or service to represent "state of the art"?

Ability to vary product specification. Is it important to produce product or service modifications easily and quickly?

Ability to vary product valume. Is it important to be able to increase, or decrease, production volume easily?

Customer service. Is the quality of the overall service which customers receive a key to winning business?

Pre- and after-sales service. Is the supply of advice, spares and so forth a key aspect of winning business?

The intangible resources which produce the valued attributes

While it is possible for a valued product/delivery system attribute to be the result of a tangible asset, such as a building or a specialist manufacturing capability, the majority of the executives participating in the research have to date identified intangible resources, such as product reputation, employee know-how and so forth as the factors most often responsible for producing the attributes which are valued by customers.

The resources which produce product/delivery system attributes may be placed in a framework of capabilities derived from Coyne's work. This framework places resources into four categories as shown below:

(i) *The regulatory capability.* Resources which are legal entities:

   (a) Tangible, on balance sheet, assets.

   (b) Intangible, off balance sheet, assets, such as patents, licences, trademarks, contracts and protectable data.

(ii) *The positional capability.* Resources which are not legal entities and are the result of previous endeavour, that is, with a high path dependency:

   (a) Reputation of company.

   (b) Reputation of product.

   (c) Corporate networks.

   (d) Personal networks.

   (e) Unprotectable data.

   (f) Distribution network.

   (g) Supply chain network.

   (h) Formal and informal operating systems.

   (i) Processes.

(iii) *The functional capability.* This comprises resources which are either individual skills and know-how or team skills and know-how, within the company, at the suppliers or distributors.

   (a) Employee know-how and skills in operations, finance, marketing and R&D.

   (b) Supplier know-how.

   (c) Distributor know-how.

   (d) Professional advisors' expertise.

(iv) *The cultural capability.* This comprises resources which are the characteristics of the organisation:

(a) Perception of quality standards.
(b) Tradition of customer service.
(c) Ability to manage change.
(d) Ability to innovate.
(e) Teamworking ability.
(f) Ability to develop staff, suppliers and distributors.
(g) Automatic response mechanisms.

The identification of the intangibles responsible for each key product attribute results in a summary, such as that shown in Table 2.2.

The resources which occur frequently in the body of the matrix are those which, either by themselves, or in combination with others, are the company's strategic competencies.

Table 2.2. An example of the matrix of attributes and resources.

Key Product/ Delivery Attributes	The resources which produce, or do not produce, the key attributes:			
	Regulatory Capability	Positional Capability	Functional Capability	Cultural Capability
Strengths				
1. e.g. availability		Value chain configuration	Forecasting skills	
2. e.g. quality				High perception of quality
3. e.g. specification	Patent "abc"		Technology "xyz"	
etc.				
Weaknesses				
1.				
2.				
Summary of the key resources				

Development scenarios

Having identified the key intangible resources, it is appropriate to examine development scenarios in terms of protection, sustenance, enhancement and leverage. Some of the results of the empirical work which has been carried out using this approach by Hall (1992, 1993) are summarised in the next section.

The Results of Empirical Work on the Role of Intangible Assets

A national survey into the contribution which intangible assets make to business success

Ninety-five CEOs answered the question, "What contribution does each of the listed factors make to the success of the business?" The six most important factors are shown below, the first five being intangible assets:

Rank	Intangible Asset
1	Company reputation
2	Product reputation
3	Employee know-how
4	Organisational culture
5	Personal networks
6	Specialist physical resources

The ranking was independent of sector and company performance. The value in this finding is not that successful companies rate "reputation" as being important while unsuccessful companies do not; the value is in the wide acceptance of the important contribution which "off balance sheet items" make to corporate success.

The section of the questionnaire relating to employee know-how contained a sub-section regarding the most important area of employee know-how. The ranking of each area of employee know-how, analysed by sector, is shown in Table 2.3.

It should be stressed that the question relates to the most important area of employee know-how, *not* the most important function. It is possible that this ranking reflects the tacit knowledge content needed for practitioners to be effective in the different areas. For example, "Operations" may have been ranked as an important area of employee know-how by executives in four of the six sectors because its high tacit knowledge content takes a considerable time to acquire and is difficult for competitors to replicate.

Table 2.3. Ranking of the "Most important area of employee know-how".

	Operations	Sales, and Marketing	Technology	Finance	Others
Manufacturing consumer products	Second	First	Third	Fourth	Fourth
Manufacturing industrial products	First	Third	Second	Fourth	Fourth
Retailing	Third	First	Second	Third	Fifth
Other trading	First	Second	Fourth	Second	Fourth
Services	First	Fourth	Second	Fourth	Third
Diversified	First	Second	Third	Fourth	Fifth

The results of six case studies using product attributes and the four capabilities framework

The most important product/delivery system attributes quoted by the six case study companies are shown below.

Company	*Most Important Attribute*
Motor Manufacturer	Quality (Fitness for purpose and conformance to specification)
Packaged Food Manufacturer	Quality
Outdoor Clothing	Quality
Retail Baker	Availability (outlet location)
Bus Company	Availability (routes)
Supermarket Chain	Availability (outlet location)

Quality was identified as the most important attribute by the manufacturing companies whereas availability was the most important attribute for those companies dealing directly with the public.

The key intangible resources identified in the case studies were similar to those identified in the national survey:

(i) In the *Cultural Capability*: Perception of high quality standards, ability to manage change
(ii) In the *Functional Capability*: Eleven different areas of employee know-how
(iii) In the *Positional Capability*: Reputation
(iv) The *Regulatory Capability*: Was not held to be of great importance.

When executives have identified the key intangible assets, it is pertinent to ask questions concerning *protection, sustenance, enhancement* and *leverage*. Examples of such questions are found in Table 2.4.

Examples of the analysis of product/delivery system attributes, intangible resources and development scenarios are given in Appendix 1. These examples relate to classroom work carried out on the specialist UK car manufacturer, The Morgan Car Co. Ltd.

An advantage of using the "four capability framework" is the emphasis it gives to the importance of *positional capability*, an importance which other strategic analysis techniques may not emphasise sufficiently.

The benefit which participating executives have reported from the use of this approach to the analysis of intangible resources is the acquisition of a new perspective and language that enable them to codify the tacit

Table 2.4. Issues with respect to the development of intangible resources.

With respect to protection:

  (i) Do all concerned recognise value of this intangible resource to the company?

 (ii) Can the resource be protected in law?

With respect to sustainability:

  (i) How long did it take to acquire this resource? Is it unique because of all that has happened in creating it?

 (ii) How durable is the resource? Will it decline with time?

(iii) How easily may the resource be lost?

(iv) How easily and quickly can others identify and imitate the resource?

 (v) Can others easily "buy" the resource?

(vi) Can others easily "grow" the resource?

(vii) How appropriable is the resource? Can it "walk away"?

(viii) Is the resource vulnerable to substitution?

With respect to enhancement:

  (i) Is the "stock" of this resource increasing?

 (ii) How can we ensure that the "stock" of this resource *continues* to increase?

With respect to exploitation:

  (i) Are we making the best use of this resource?

 (ii) How else could it be used?

(iii) Is the scope for *synergy* identified and exploited?

(iv) Are we aware of the key linkages which exist between the resources?

knowledge which they have of their companies. In particular, executives have welcomed the, sometimes new, emphasis placed on issues, such as:

  (i) How can the key resource of reputation be protected, enhanced and leveraged?

 (ii) How can management ensure that every employee is disposed to be both a promoter and custodian of the reputation of the company which employs him/her?

(iii) What are the key areas of employee know-how? Can they be codified? How long do they take to acquire?

(iv) Is the business organised so that working and learning are the same?

Every turn of the business cycle should result in an increase in the "stocks" of intangibles, such as employee know-how and reputation, because the intangibles account for the bulk of the worth of most companies.

The Knowledge-Based View of Strategy

In the light of the views presented above, the reader will not be surprised to learn that the "resource-based view" of strategy is beginning to develop into the "knowledge-based view" of strategy. The essence of this new perspective is described by Grant (1997):

Box 2.5

> **"If individuals must specialise in knowledge acquisition and if producing goods and service requires the application of many types of knowledge, production must be organised so as to assemble these many types of knowledge while preserving specialisation by individuals. The firm is an institution which exists to specialise in developing specialised expertise, while establishing mechanisms through which individuals co-ordinate to integrate their different knowledge bases in the transformation of inputs into outputs."**

A model which helps our understanding of the issues concerning the knowledge-based view of strategy is shown in Fig. 2.1. This model, and much of the recent work on knowledge management, come from Boisot (1995) and Nonaka (1994).

The characteristics of the model of knowledge space are as follows:

(i) *Regions A and D.* These comprise tacit knowledge. Tacit knowledge is not codified; it is concerned with knowing *what* things work. It is characterised by confusion with respect to cause and effect and, consequently, it is usually difficult to communicate other than by time-consuming observation, imitation and shared experience.

Fig. 2.1. The learning cycle in "knowledge space".

(ii) *Regions B and C.* These comprise explicit knowledge. Explicit knowledge is concerned with knowing *why* things work. It is concerned with the creation of taxonomies and the establishment of cause-and effect-relationships. The codification of the knowledge means that it is more easily communicated than tacit knowledge and, for this reason, it is usually desirable to create explicit knowledge by *externalising* the tacit knowledge.

The codification axis is described in this paper as "*Consciously* Codified" and "*Not Consciously* Codified" rather than simply

"*Codified*" and "*Uncodified*". This is because once knowledge has been codified, it cannot lose its codification. Instead, the complete learning cycle results in a practitioner ceasing to rely consciously on the codification of the knowledge. This is because, for the expert, the knowledge has become second nature. It is possible to achieve expert status by the transfer of tacit knowledge only, such as a child gaining verbal fluency in its first language. Alternatively, expert status can be achieved by the acquisition, initially, of explicit knowledge — such as an English child learning French grammar at school — followed by a process of *learning by doing*, or *internalisation*, during which the reliance on the codification becomes less and less. There are, therefore, two types of tacit knowledge: tacit knowledge which has never been codified; and tacit knowledge which is the internalised explicit knowledge of the expert who no longer needs to refer to the codification because the application of the knowledge has become second nature.

The diffusion axis may represent the transfer of knowledge from one person to another, from one to many, or from many to one; the diffusion may be to a team, a department, or from a society to an individual. An example of the latter transfer is when an individual joins a new company; (s)he is not given a manual which codifies the organisation's culture — its diffused tacit knowledge — but the individual will usually have little difficulty in assimilating the culture.

The dynamics of the learning cycle are described below:

(a) *Externalisation.* Nonaka describes "externalisation" as usually involving the use of metaphors to articulate individual perspectives and release trapped tacit knowledge. This is the stuff of social science research!

(b) *Education.* The codified nature of the knowledge which is being diffused enables this process to involve many participants at large distances.

(c) *Internalisation.* Nonaka describes "internalisation" as representing the gradual loss of the need for the codification of the knowledge. It is evidenced by the learning curve phenomenon and may be described as "learning to *do things better*". It is the *"single loop learning"* described by Argyris and Schon (1978).

(d) *Socialisation*. Nonaka suggests that tacit knowledge is transferred by a process of "socialisation" which usually involves shared experiences and the creation of trust.

(iii) *Discontinuous learning*. It is about "learning to *do better things*". It results in a change in mindset, a paradigm shift.

It is possible to relate the four types of capabilities described earlier (regulatory, positional, functional and cultural) to the model of knowledge space. This is because each capability has different types of knowledge associated with it. The identification of the differing natures of these knowledge bases is crucial if we are to manage the capabilities effectively.

The regions of the knowledge space illustrated in Fig. 2.1 relate to the four types of capability as shown in Fig. 2.2.

Continuous and discontinuous learning

Prahalad and Hamel (1996) have advanced the proposition that operational efficiency, by itself, is not enough to win sustainable competitive advantage on the grounds that operational efficiency is relatively easy to replicate. They suggest that operational efficiency, like quality, is a hygiene factor, and that discontinuous learning which produces fundamentally new ways of doing things is the key to future success. This is because fundamentally new operations *are* difficult to replicate.

Continuous learning may involve four of the stages described in the learning cycle: externalisation, education, internalisation and socialisation. Discontinuous learning is concerned with learning to do better things; it may be "triggered" by major threats or opportunities. In view of the fact that one man's step change may be another man's incremental change, there is no clear divide between continuous and discontinuous learning. For the purposes of this paper, we will assume that discontinuous

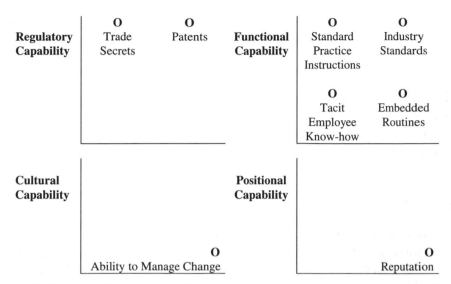

Fig. 2.2. Example of the regions of knowledge space occupied by the knowledge which underpins the four capabilities.

learning involves fundamental change and will require significant *unlearning.* This unlearning is difficult, for as Sir Francis Bacon (1620) wrote:

Box 2.6

"The human understanding, when it has once adopted an opinion, draws all things else to support and agree with it. And though there be a great number and weight of instances to be found on the other side, yet it either neglects and despises, or else by some distinction sets aside and rejects, in order that by this great and pernicious predetermination, the authority of its former conclusion may remain inviolate."

Stacey (1993) recognises the fact that human organisations are complex non-linear dynamic systems with both positive and negative feedback loops. He suggests that such *self-adaptive systems,* like most eco-systems, are at their most flexible when they exist in a state of bounded instability where positive, as well as negative, feedback operates. He argues that the formal organisation, by definition, cannot be self-adaptive and that it is usually the informal (self-adaptive) organisation which produces discontinuous learning. He argues that by nature and training, most managers strive for predictability and stability by practising negative feedback in order to eliminate variances from the desired norm. A consequence of this is that the lead indicators of required change may be damped out. He describes two styles of management:

Box 2.7

> "Ordinary management is practised when most of the managers in an organization share the same mental models or paradigm. Cognitive feedback loops then operate in a negative feedback manner so that shared mental models are not questioned. Ordinary management is about rational processes to secure harmony, fit or convergence to a configuration, and it proceeds in an incremental manner."

Box 2.8

> "Extraordinary management involves questioning and shattering paradigms, and then creating new ones. It is a process which depends critically upon contradiction and tension. Extraordinary management, then, is the use of intuitive, political, group learning modes of decision-making and self-organising forms of control in open-ended change situations. It is the form of management that managers must use if they are to change strategic direction and innovate."

It seems, from this argument, that where discontinuous learning is required, confrontation and conflict are not only likely, but they are also desirable. It seems that we need to practise "ordinary (command and control) management" in order to "sweat the assets" — to achieve the operational efficiency which is hygiene. However, we also need to practise "extraordinary management" in order to facilitate discontinuous learning. Are the two management styles mutually exclusive?

Conclusion

This chapter has reported research which suggests that the sources of corporate success are the intangible, off balance sheet resources, such as employee know-how and reputation, and it has been argued that companies should try to organise their affairs so that every turn of the business cycle results in the "stocks" of the intangible resources increasing.

The research has suggested that the most important intangible resources are company reputation, product reputation, employee know-how, organisational culture and personal networks. In view of the nature of these resources, it is not surprising that the management of knowledge is currently receiving increasing attention.

The management of knowledge involves an understanding of the different types of learning, particularly the dichotomy between continuous and discontinuous learning. The former is needed for operational efficiency, the latter for fundamental change. Is it possible to organise one's corporate affairs so that the formal organisation sweats the assets whilst the self-adaptive informal organisation produces the fundamental changes which will be required to create new strategic competencies?

Appendix 1

The Morgan Car Company Analysis

	The Morgan Attributes (%) Importance Weighting
1. Specification — High performance	20
2. "User" statement — Image	20
3. "Family" feeling — Morgan car clubs	20
4. Conformance to specification — Reliability	15
5. Value for sterling pound — Low depreciation	15
6. Appearance	10
TOTAL	100

The Competitive Advantage

	Comparison with Competitor
A. Positive Attributes	
A1. Specification	+
A2. "User" statement	+
A3. "Family" feeling	++
A4. Conformance to specification	+
A5. Value for sterling pound	++
A6. Appearance	+
B. Negative Attributes	
B1. Availability	–

-   Worse than competitor
-   Much worse than competitor
- + Better than competitor
- ++ Much better than competitor

The Sustainability of the Advantage

	Competition's Ability to Replicate		
	Easy	Medium Difficulty	Difficult
1. Specification			✓
2. "User" statement		✓	
3. "Family" feeling			✓
4. Conformance to specification	✓		
5. Value for sterling pound			✓
6. Appearance	✓		

The Intangible Resources Related to the Key Product/Delivery System Attributes

Key Product Attributes	Regulatory Resources	Positional Resources	Functional Resources	Cultural Resources
1. Specification			Design capability	
2. User statement	"Morgan" TM	Reputation		
3. Family feeling		Clubs		
4. Conformance to Specification			Craftsmanship	Perception of quality
5. Value for sterling pound		Overhead structure		
6. Appearance			Design capability and craftsmanship	

Development Scenarios

Actions/Key Intangibles	Protecting	Sustaining	Enhancing	Leveraging
1. The trademark	Worldwide registration			Licence in California
2. Reputation		Damage limitation plans	Promote by word of mouth	
3. Product development	Succession?	Succession?		
4. Craftsmanship		Recruitment	Train in JIT, etc.	
5. Perception of Quality		Be careful with organisational culture		

Chapter 3

Making Strategy Happen

PETER HISCOCKS and DAN RIFF

Introduction

Within even the best-run firms, strategic planning remains a periodic exercise that is plagued by uncomfortable compromises and informed by inconsistent and inadequate information. Innovation management takes place in *ad hoc* forums and passageway conversations, and day-to-day management operates by reacting to threats that are often noticed too late.

In this chapter, we build a bridge between strategic vision and operating reality. This bridge is achieved by articulating an innovation strategy, by pursuing the project actions that deliver strategic goals, and by putting in place a performance measurement system that apprises the leadership team of progress towards these goals.

Background

"If we don't know where we are going, then how will we know when we get there?" This quote from *Alice in Wonderland* crystallises the management dilemma faced by today's business leaders. To try to resolve this dilemma and to define "where we are going", leaders articulate visions and mission statements that intend to galvanise the corporate organisation. Unfortunately, a lot can be lost in translation. The picture of what a firm will look like "when we get there" can be different for everyone you ask.

This is the case because heads of business areas deploy somewhat crude "vision" roadmaps with a degree of license. Sometimes, interpretations merely fall out of alignment. At other times, differing perspectives can leave a firm wandering aimlessly or even in conflict. The consequence is often that one business head can imagine the firm has succeeded while another is struggling to drive his resources towards somewhere else entirely.

Clearly, this is inadequate. To ensure that a firm knows where it is going requires more than platitudes about growth and market success. The firm's leadership must have clarity about purpose, objectives and the actions necessary to deliver these.

Corporate strategy should take lessons about planning action from warfare. Sun Tzu's brief tome, *The Art of War*, is as applicable to a multinational's pursuit of global presence as it was to the hopes of conquest in 500 BC. In warfare, a proclamation of the desire to defeat the enemy does little to direct troops to achieve desired ends. Rather, "battle plans" must translate strategy into concrete actions for the whole of the corporate-acting troop.

Notions of what constitutes a sound strategy have consumed senior managers' time since Alfred Chandler's book of 1962, *Strategy and Structure*. John Kay has written an interesting review on strategic thinking called "A Brief History of Business Strategy" in his book, *The Foundations of Corporate Success* (1993). In this, he identifies different approaches that have been developed during the past 35 years to address this problem of how to achieve that elusive "perfect strategy". He covers rationalist, emergent and organisational perspectives.

The rationalist approach to strategy assumes that a study of the environment of a business, its customers, suppliers, competitors and its own resources will enable the formulation of a strategy that will achieve success. This approach usually involves the steps of:

(i) Assessing the environment.
(ii) Formulating the strategy.
(iii) Implementing the strategy.

When the strategy does not achieve the aims expected, then the weak link is usually tracked down to its implementation. While this is often the case, it is important to have formulated a strategy that is more than just a vision or set of unachievable objectives. To quote John Kay, "one might say that Saddam Hussein had a fine strategy — defeat the United States army in pitched battle and so conquer the oil reserves of the Middle East — but there were failures in implementation". Strategy must be achievable and this means that it must be capable of implementation. In addition, the business must have the skills, processes and capabilities to successfully carry out that implementation.

Subsequent critics of the "rationalist approach" have looked for "emergent strategy". This theory was proposed by Mintzberg in the early 1980s and assumes that strategy is "the result of reactive solution to existing problems — the adaptive organisation makes its decisions in incremental, serial steps". While this is an obvious description of how businesses work, it assumes that planning can have little role, that destiny is already cast, and that having a clear strategy can have little effect. If this were the case — and there are new schools of thinking that argue against it — then it would still be in the effectiveness of the response to changes in the environment, that would determine success or failure. While strategy may be incremental and adaptive, there is no reason to assume that it cannot be analysed, managed and controlled. This is especially the case in the difficult steps of making it happen within the firm and adapting to changing circumstances during, or as a result of, implementation.

The school of thought on strategy deriving from organisational behaviourists is the contingency or resource-based approach. This states that there is no overall best strategy or organisational structure, but that the business needs to respond and adapt to their environment (Burns & Stalker; Woodward). This approach has been further developed recently by Prahalad and Hamel's work on core competencies, leading to the view that it is the development and maintenance of distinctive differential capabilities that is at the core of a successful strategy.

It is our premise in this chapter that a new brand of strategic thinking is required for fast-moving innovative companies to succeed. It adds little to suggest that it is not enough to have a vision and a mission statement. It contributes less to suggest that only pieces of rationalism, emergence and organisationalist thinking can be of help. In the pages that follow, we suggest that there is a way to put strategy and plans into action. We also indicate how this process can be adaptable to changes in the increasingly turbulent business environment and can be made to operate real-time in your organisation.

This chapter follows a structure designed to help you drive improvements in your organisation immediately:

1. We characterise the common pitfalls in making strategy happen.
2. We introduce the principles that underpin strategy.
3. We *define* the notion of an innovation strategy and identify how such a strategy can bridge vision and reality.
4. We frame how to make choices that translate strategy into actions.
5. We detail how the right measures can show the impact of the strategy.
6. We provide case studies about firms that do this right.

As you read this chapter, keep in mind its title, *Making Strategy Happen*. Throughout these pages, you should find the answers to:

(i) How can we ensure that people all across the firm understand the vision?
(ii) How can we translate the vision into a set of planned actions?
(iii) How can we make choices among the ideas that compete to pursue planned actions?
(iv) How can we monitor actions as they impact upon operations?
(v) How can we measure operations as they migrate towards our vision?

Common Pitfalls in Making Strategy Happen

Do too many of your innovation projects arrive late, over budget or not at all? Do you face a wide chasm between your organisation's creative ideas and your strategies? Do you face too many projects fighting for too few resources? Do you struggle to balance projects delivered by teams and pay cheques delivered by functions? Are you unable to respond to market and competitive challenges? Do you struggle to capitalise on emerging opportunities? Do missed milestones and under-delivery result in finger-pointing and unclear accountability?

If you have answered "Yes" to the questions above, you are not alone. Too often, firms lack the information they need to connect events in the marketplace, data from day-to-day operations and plans for new product development. Strategies remain static, leaders miss opportunities and innovation is driven from the bottom-up rather than from the top-down. In short, firms cannot become nimble and responsive to changing conditions.

To become a high performer, a firm must make strategy actionable, map the actions that will deliver it and put in place the measures that monitor progress real-time.

Principles that Underpin Strategy

Based on our experience working with innovative firms, we have found that the high performers adhere to a set of principles that underpin the way they manage their business. The rest of the chapter reinforces why the principles matter and what a firm can do to ensure it adheres to them.

The sum of individual actions must equal strategy

Only rarely do firms find themselves moving in the direction that their strategies suggest that they want to. Vision is translated differently by

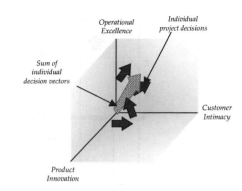

Corporate strategy as defined by
the corporate leadership

Sum of individual decisions equates
to an implicit direction for the future
of the company

Fig. 3.1.

each operating area and day-to-day pressures and realities intercede. By translating strategy across and downwards into local actions, a firm can ensure that all areas align (see Fig. 3.1).

High performers can be assured that the CEO's vision of future direction can be disaggregated into the incentives that trigger process improvements on the shop floor. The best firms cascade vision downwards through the firm as a set of shared goals, targets and measures — measures that inspire the individual actions that make all actors aligned with strategy.

Less is more

Firms often imagine that if they push more into the front-end new product development pipeline, they are bound to get more new products to market and more value from their investments. This could not be less true. A pressure cooker approach to new product projects "dehydrates" and devalues the best ideas as too many concepts fight for too little available sustenance. In our experience, we see firms overload their innovation pipeline by a factor of at least 2–3X. Our research has

Fig. 3.2.

demonstrated that by reducing work demand to bring it into line with the resources available, a firm can increase output by up to 50% (see Fig. 3.2).

High performers focus their resources on a balanced set of strategic initiatives and even leave 10%–15% of capacity free for unforeseen glitches. When a firm is overloaded, the innovations that "make it" tend to be quick-wins launched for visibility rather than value-providing solutions. The best firms take the long view and opt out of "swinging at every pitch".

Management must pay attention up-front

Our research has shown that management attention often comes as "too little, too late". Managers respond adeptly to tangible prototypes, but only in passing to new project proposals. It is not on the final prototype that the manager should be focussing his energies; a manager's hands can shape the initial concept far more readily than the prototype (see Fig. 3.3).

This is best illustrated by an example from the American automobile industry in the early 1980s. One of the big three auto-makers at the time used to employ what was referred to as the "Golden Butt" test.

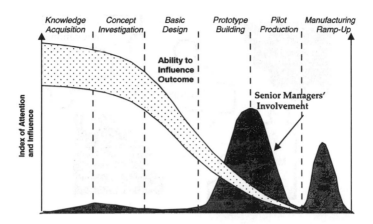

Source: Gluck & R. Foster (1975) *Harvard Business Review*, September/October.

Fig. 3.3.

The CEO would personally inspect the first car off the production line for each new model. In one case, the CEO insisted that the slope of the dashboard was too steep. His 35 years in the business meant far more to him than the myriad focus group tests and successful prototypes. The changeover that this late stage examination inspired cost the firm 18 months in re-development time and a re-work investment in excess of US$150 million.

High performers avoid this plight by ensuring that senior management has access to clear, consistent information about major change efforts at their beginnings. Each investment in fiscal and human resources is assessed against strategy in measurable terms before the tangible output is discovered to be radically out of line with expectations.

Accelerate innovation through a system approach

Choices about change action cannot be made in a vacuum. Projects deliver strategy, change, organisational culture and impact on

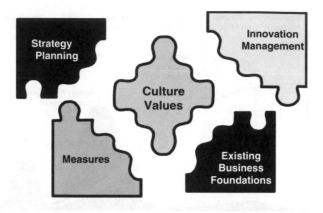

Fig. 3.4.

day-to-day operations. These links and relationships must be visible and measurable.

High performers tie together the disparate management processes of strategic planning, innovation management and day-to-day operations by taking account of culture and aligning actions with consistent measures (see Fig. 3.4). Without this coherence, strategy remains a wish-list, innovation management a wasteland of poor focus and minimal accountability, and day-to-day operations a set of efforts with an undirected life of their own.

Bridging Vision and Reality:
What is an Innovation Strategy?

An innovation strategy translates vision and mission into the goals and targets that define what the organisation must look like. It takes a vague hope of "market leadership in core business segments" and suggests that four minor product launches in Segment A and three major launches in Segment B over the next three years are what are required to get you there. It articulates the levers to pull that drive the bottom line. And it tells you how people work within processes to satisfy customers.

From the outset, an innovation strategy must determine whether a market/industry is propelled more by scope/feature/function change or by discernible pace or timing. That is, do market windows open and shut with regularity (driven by a dominant firm or customer demands) or do the composition of given launches prop up the competitive windows? Can you afford a delay of a major strategic launch or should you go ahead with the ugly flaws exposed?

Firms such as Sony have dominated their markets by pursuing rigorously timed project launches. Professor Steven Wheelwright of Harvard Business School has likened this to Aiwa, Panasonic and others trapped in a violent surf, crushed down by impending waves of launches each time they stand up with their own competitive response. In contrast, a firm such as Silicon Graphics can afford to be a bit slower because their customers will wait for their unique product combinations. In these examples, both a machine gun and a B1 bomber win in their respective markets.

To develop an innovation strategy, a firm must assess a market's rhythm and timing. To do this, it requires that they answer the following core questions:

(i) *Pace of industry change.* How long are product life cycles in our core markets? Do firms pursue planned obsolescence and cannibalise themselves? How frequently is market news needed? How much change can various sectors of the market absorb?

(ii) *Pace of customer change.* How are customer needs and expectations evolving? To what degree are customers cost-focussed, feature-focussed and service-focussed?

(iii) *Pace of technology change.* How are core technologies evolving? At what stage are the primary elements (inception, growth and maturity)? How is the make/buy equation shifting? How are dynamics between allies, vendors and suppliers being altered?

(iv) *Competitor characterisation.* How do our competitors drive and/ or react to these change cycles? What can we do to foreclose on their emergent opportunities?

The answers to these questions certainly differ by industry, and probably by regions within industries as well. To complete the picture, a firm must also look inward:

(i) *Strategic positioning.* How does a current leader approach the market? What about an aspiring leader? And a committed fast follower?

(ii) *Pace of capability change.* What is our ability to climb the learning curve? Are we sufficiently flexible and responsive? Are we at the top with our innovation/development resource? On the ground, in the landing/implementation sphere?

(iii) *Pace of innovation.* How fast can we move? What are current and potential future cycle times for major and minor innovations in key markets?

(iv) *Skill gaps.* Where have our innovations been most successful in the past? Is this where our strategy and external opportunities indicate that we should play in the future?

Taken together, the views of external market cadence (rhythm and timing) and internal pacing can suggest both broad positioning and untapped niche opportunities. An examined view of these issues imbues one's strategies with a sense of realism as well.

Once a firm defines "what" and "where", it aims to innovate; it needs to determine "how". Five steps facilitate this process:

(i) Ensure that innovation strategies are buttressed by measurable goals and targets, such as to grow market share in the consumer products segment "A" by 20% in two years.

(ii) Determine how much you are able and willing to invest to deliver goals and targets (capital expenditure, operating expenditure and people resource) and to allocate investment money to opportunity areas, such as 20% of capital and half my people to achieve goal "A".

(iii) Define co-ordinated sets of actions that optimise available investments. Outline ideas and concepts and use these as placeholders that will serve as magnets for good ideas in the future. An example would be customer satisfaction initiative in call centres that improves response time by 50%.

(iv) Determine expected paybacks from each investment in a set of co-ordinated actions. Assess whether actions are likely to deliver goals and targets and iterate on architectures and/or strategies, such as a 10% increase in retention from improved response time delivers $100 million per annum.

(v) Put in place a process to communicate the strategic plan and its associated actions. Establish forums and measures to track progress.

This last item may be the most important. Processes and forums ensure that the management dialogue addresses the key drivers of business performance and the lexicon of shared, balanced measures permeates the organisation.

Making Choices: Translating Strategy Into Action

To migrate from a firm's current state to a future state that realises strategic aspirations requires more than just a long-range blueprint. Much of the blueprint remains only a plausible translation of strategy into *potential* actions until real choices among alternatives are made and funding and resources are allocated. It is not enough to hope that if you build a clear plan, results will come.

As we noted above, many firms permit too many ideas to compete to deliver a set of strategic solutions. This Darwinian approach to managing innovation and change is wrong-headed. Senior management must commit upfront, often with imperfect information, to the right sets of projects and actions to deliver goals. To remove some of the inherent subjectivity and discomfort associated with this, many firms put in place a process of portfolio screening and selection.

A number of lenses provide unique views into the sets of project actions being considered. No single view provides the "right" answer to guide project selection and sequencing. Rather, assessing the different views together helps to ground an otherwise subjective, and often fruitless, debate in a consistent language along multiple dimensions of business value.

Strategic impact and alignment

Firms assess competing ideas relative to one another based on:

(i) Benefit to clients.
(ii) Benefit to internal processes.
(iii) Internal technology change.
(iv) Internal process change.
(v) Alignment with core objectives (financial, customer, business process and human resource.)

Ideas are assessed against one another for the benefits they promise and the change that they portend (see Fig. 3.5). More concretely, strategic impact "lenses" permit views of:

(i) Impact of projects on the marketplace.
(ii) Mix of portfolio.
(iii) Active list of projects.
(iv) Trade-off decisions among projects.

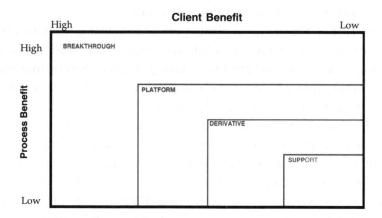

Fig. 3.5.

Risk and return

Firms weigh management, implementation, technical and other risks against potential paybacks. The definitions of each category of risk and the tolerance for risk in core strategic areas are unique to each firm. Taken together, these risk dimensions provide more than a single figure per project indicating risk-adjusted returns. Instead, they offer multiple perspectives on risk set against prospective returns (see Fig. 3.6).

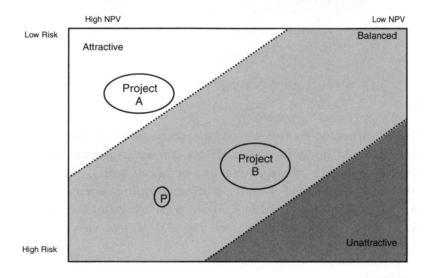

Fig. 3.6.

Resource analysis

Firms assess resource capacity against demand to ensure that the set of project actions being pursued does not exceed available staffing. Resource demand is measured in terms of the number of innovators required to complete a project successfully. This figure should be unconstrained by available staffing or skill sets. Resource supply is measured in terms of the staff available (and capable) to work on projects

Time in months

Fig. 3.7.

of various difficulty. Factors such as day-to-day and administrative work demands should be factored out. Firms can assess demand and supply by line level (senior management to operations staff), functional area (marketing, finance and R&D), skill set (coding, focus groups and prototyping) or some combination of these three elements.

A resource mountain chart (see Fig. 3.7) offers views of:

 (i) Availability of resources to undertake the proposed portfolio of projects.
(ii) Magnitude and timing of resource constraints.
(iii) Timing of resource availability for future projects given current portfolio.
(iv) Proportion of time spent on non-project activities.
 (v) Ratio of own staff to outsource resources.

Again, it is important to note that firms should use these three screening "lenses" in unison without weighting one over any other. Used together, the lenses permit focussed choices to be made between alternative routes to strategy realisation. A firm's portfolio planning process should be guided by a set of core principles:

(i) Review, select and sequence projects in aggregate relative to strategy.
(ii) Review projects at the maximum level of transferable resource only.
(iii) Managing portfolios is different from managing projects.
(iv) Design the project portfolio selection process for rigid structure, flexible execution and content.
(v) Incent ownership of portfolio and ensures group objectives are addressed.
(vi) During the portfolio analysis sessions have the right people with the right information involved at the right time.

Measuring the Progress and Impact of Action

Once a firm articulates its innovation strategy, frames measurable goals, details investment allocations, maps co-ordinated future actions and begins to make choices among project options, it must monitor the progress and impact of its decisions.

Too often, even a well-chosen strategy falls prey to poor management decision-making. Senior managers continue to make decisions based on what has already happened rather than what the future holds. Corporate leadership is *reactive* to financial end results rather than *proactive* based on early warnings such as "customers are unhappy", "processes are broken" or that "staff is incompetent".

Strategies, project actions that deliver them and the operational environment that evolves as projects impact on it must be more tightly linked. As projects land in the operating environment, their contributions can be measured far earlier than the bottom line. Project actions operate on the business drivers of financial return and be measured as they hit these — the customers, the processes and the people.

To realise an innovation strategy and sustain the changes that it provokes, a firm must put in place a management performance metrics system. A balanced and integrated metrics system often works best. This type of system offers a network of early warning and end result metrics which focus and guide individuals and groups towards shared goals. Balance ensures that cause-and-effect is linked from the staff working

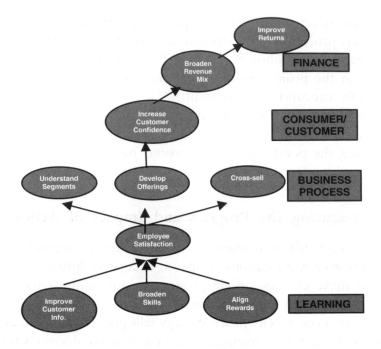

Fig. 3.8.

within a process to serve a customer that contributes to the bottom line (see Fig. 3.8). Integration ensures two things:

(i) That the language at the top — strategic business objectives — is translated downwards into corporate measures, core process measures, innovation measures and even project team measures.
(ii) That the measures which articulate strategy are connected to the metrics that monitor innovation and then onwards into the targets that guide operations. A common measurement language informed by the levers and drivers of successful business performance should unite these three distinct processes.

To ensure success at creating a meaningful measurement system, a firm must take care to answer four questions for each measure selected:

(i) *What?*: What is the measure? What is its purpose? What is it related to?
(ii) *Who?*: Who measures? Who analyses? Who makes decisions?
(iii) *How?*: How is data collected? How is data represented? How is data analysed? How is data interpreted?
(iv) *Where?*: Where is it reviewed? Where are decisions made?

Too often, firms overload their managers with too many measures. Sometimes, they even emphasise contradictory or conflicting measures that pull performance in two or more directions. In selecting measures for one's metrics system, it is best to focus on the critical few measures, keep it simple and timely and make measures a natural part of the staff's job.

Typically, a "dashboard" of critical performance indicators provides the greatest visibility of progress and the need for management input and action (see Fig. 3.9). The dashboard puts all critical information in a central, easily viewable repository. Measures that are related to one another can be assessed together. Also, causal relationships can be seen easily.

Fig. 3.9.

Who does this Right and Why?

Many firms profess to excel at innovation. Too often, what they really mean is that they are moderately proficient at project management. Clearly, this is not sufficient. Firms must move upstream of individual projects, to become expert at selecting among project ideas that compete to delivery strategy, and then further to communicate the roadmap that translates strategy and draws out the ideas before they are generated. Top firms in these arenas include BankCorp, Ltd.

Leading Financial Services Concern

Overview

BankCorp, Ltd., a leading financial services firm in South Africa, developed a technology-enabled planning and management tool for its Retail Banking Division. This tool was to serve four purposes:

(i)   To *translate* vision and strategy into meaningful goals and targets.
(ii) To *map* the actions that will change current operations to deliver these goals and targets.
(iii) To *provide* real-time verified data feeds into the decision-making forum.
(iv) To *embed* measures and decision-making processes to ensure that operation migration happens.

BankCorp sought an end-to-end solution — connecting strategy to day-to-day action and making change happens everyday. In their original organisation they found planning, innovation and operations management to be disconnected processes. While these processes engaged a common set of actors, divergent languages divided them. The technology-enabled planning and management tool sought to unite these processes around a common language of critical performance data, balanced measures and analyses.

To better understand BankCorp's needs, imagine the CEO as an air traffic controller (see Fig. 3.10):

TODAY ———————————————▶ POTENTIAL FUTURE

- Planes with different cockpits
- Pilots with different objectives
- No co-ordinated flight plan or in-flight contact
- Sporadic crashes

- Standardised cockpit read-outs
- Aligned pilot team
- Central flight plan and in-flight early warning measures
- Flawless execution of plan

Fig. 3.10.

Let us decompose this metaphor further. As in many firms, BankCorp had a group direction and a number of business units that were briefed to drive their areas towards this direction. Unfortunately, not all business units shared the same basic "read-out" of how they were performing. Some had state-of-the-art measurement and indicator systems to track their progress towards group goals. Others had poor or disjointed financial data that told them little about where they were going or why. As a first step, then, this effort sought to put in place a "common cockpit" for different leadership teams in the organisation.

Next, the business units at BankCorp were often torn by divided objectives. Their leaders (or pilots) understood what they had to deliver to meet group goals, but at the same time were sometimes caught up in infighting with their colleagues over resources, "turf wars" and other such issues. Business units sought to ensure that their area shined brightest, sometimes at the expense of the other areas — and therefore at the expense of overall group goals. A second step, then, was to bring the pilot team together to define how all would contribute constructively in the interdependent pursuit of group direction.

Third, the group direction tended to be a static statement of hopes and wishes rather than a dynamic migration plan within which all managers shared evolving roles. It simply wasn't clear who owned what explicit sets of actions to move towards group goals. In some cases, it was not even clear what the collective set of actions was. And, possibly most damaging of all, was the lack of regular, consistent and rigorous contact between the control tower (group leadership) and the pilots (business unit heads). The result was that this challenged the control tower's efforts to co-ordinate all the planes in the air and speak to each of them in a common language to determine positioning and status.

The price of this infrequent and inconsistent contact can be an occasional in-flight collision. Business units can pull the organisation in competing or conflicting directions. Without sufficient means of early warning indicators, the control tower may only find out about the danger once it is too late — when reaction and damage control is the only option.

The problem

BankCorp, Ltd. faced several challenges in the early and mid-1990s. As South Africa's economy emerged from apartheid, the pool of "bankable" consumers multiplied threefold. Without adequate customer management, delivery channel and segmentation approaches in place, BankCorp's Retail Banking Division (RBD) found itself in the unenviable position of having fewer than 20% of its clients delivering nearly 85% of its profits.

BankCorp needed to focus on its more profitable customers, improve satisfaction, expand delivery channel variety and penetration and revitalise core product lines — all at once, for a burgeoning consumer population. They demanded something more than static strategy documents and quarterly innovation reviews.

Existing technology and consulting solutions were inadequate. Simply bringing all the data into one place (Data Warehouse, SAP) was not enough. Even the paring down of the list of measures and linking them was insufficient, such as in the "Balanced Scorecard". What was needed was a way to *make strategy happen everyday*. This required two things that off-the-shelf tools lacked:

(i) A planning and management space that provided access to critical data, analysis and insight.

(ii) A connection between key performance measures and action — what actions are in the arsenal to respond to a threat or to capitalise on an opportunity? What financial and human resources are required to pursue these actions?

The approach

The task was to deliver a way "to make strategy happen everyday" and "get rid of all the consultants". With this in mind, the bank's leadership team faced four questions:

(i)   *The future.* Does our team share a common vision and strategy?
(ii) *The present.* Does our team share a common view of how Operations perform?
(iii) *Closing the gap.* Does our team agree on how strategy will transform Operations?
(iv) *The actions.* Does our team agree on what levers to pull and actions to invest in?

BankCorp discovered that the Executive team could restate vision statements and current financial indicators with ease. When the time came to draw a picture of how the shared vision would transform Operations, perspectives diverged. And when probed on where to invest scarce people and money to deliver the vision, no one agreed.

Given these responses, we took a three-tiered approach to defining the right solution:

(i)   *As Is Audit.* What do current strategies suggest? Where do current innovation plans focus? What do existing management reports say? What supplemental data is out there?
(ii) *Should Be.* What are the gaps in current management metrics — strategy, innovation and operations? How should Executives interact with data to make better decisions faster?
(iii) *Technology.* What is needed to move from the "As Is" environment to the "Should Be" vision?

The solution

BankCorp's planning and management tool is a physical space that links strategic planning, innovation management and day-to-day operations through a set of related measures. These measures represent a common language that ties together otherwise disconnected data sets and management processes (see Fig. 3.11). The solution:

 (i) Puts the right data at decision-makers' fingertips.
 (ii) Displays information graphically using multiple video monitors.
(iii) Captures reliable operational and strategic indicators of financial, customer, process and HR performance.
(iv) Helps to plan project-based actions by allowing executives to construct and evaluate scenarios.
 (v) Assesses cause-and-effect between related measures and events.
(vi) Permits easy navigation and decomposition of aggregate data along financial (General Ledger) and geographic (branch table) hierarchies.

At the heart of the solution is a flexible platform for the viewing, publication and exploration of management information — the Workbook.

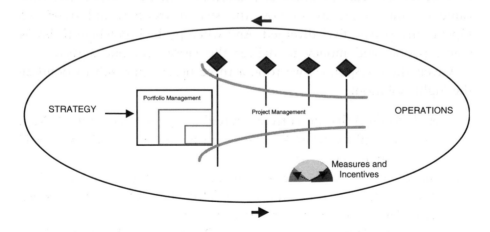

Fig. 3.11.

Workbooks offer the ability to connect measures to the bank's data systems, to explore data easily and to capture the decisions and actions taken in Executive forums. Below is a schematic of the solution:

The results

The solution helped BankCorp to:

(i) *Triage*. Over 1,000 management metrics have been pared back to the 50 most critical views.

(ii) *Align*. Each executive has been provided with unique views of the business tuned to his/her decision-making responsibilities.

(iii) *Accelerate*. Decisions that once took three months now take a week, without the blind data searches and caveats of the past.

SITUATION: Recently, ATM fees were raised. Our staff expected price insensitivity among profitable clients who liked technology. Recently, these clients have migrated to branches, angered over fee increases.

You want to know three things:

1. What will happen to branch queues and customer service as branches fill up?

2. What financial impact am I exposed to based on this ripple effect?

3. What can I do to correct the problem and please branch and electronic customers?

BankCorp's planning and management tool is designed to provide the answers.

Fig. 3.12.

As an example, BankCorp was able to stem customer dissatisfaction before it negatively impacted the bottom line using this decision system (see Fig. 3.12). In this instance, they discovered fee price sensitivity which they had not expected and were able to measure cause-and-effect and take corrective action to stem real harm.

BankCorp has invested in:

(i) Clearer plans translated downwards.
(ii) Instant feedback on threats and opportunities:

    (a) What happened?
    (b) Why did it happen?
    (c) What could happen next?
    (d) What could I do to fix it?

(iii) Reliable risk/return data to measure trade-offs.

With this, they can achieve:

(i) Flexibility.
(ii) Responsiveness.
(iii) Revenue growth.
(iv) Cost reduction.
(v) Higher share of wallet.
(vi) Speed: "scale or kill" market moves.

BankCorp has set its own explicit targets for business benefit as well:

(i) Extend planning horizon for project actions from 18 months to five years.
(ii) Shift management discussions from reviews of financial end results to balanced strategic dialogues.
(iii) Improve core banking performance ratios by 10%.

PART 2

MARKET COMPETENCIES

Chapter 4

Brands, Innovation and Growth: The Role of Brands in Innovation and Growth for Consumer Businesses

TONY CLAYTON and GRAHAM TURNER

Benchmarking Business Performance

For over 20 years, a programme of business measurement and comparison has been in operation, capturing data on the markets, operations and performance of thousands of businesses, in companies across all sectors of the economy. If invented today, this work would carry a name including the word "benchmarking". It is called PIMS, which stands for Profit Impact of Market Strategy. Its purpose is to quantify and compare for client companies the key differences between successful and unsuccessful businesses, and to advise them what aspects of "winners," behaviour and marketing strategy are likely to pay off in the long run.

PIMS was originally born at General Electric (GE). The company developed, by the early 1970s, a consistent framework for measuring and comparing business units and understanding the differences between those which were consistently profitable and growing, and those which were not. In 1973, GE decided to move this framework outside its own markets and involve many other North American companies. PIMS

Table 4.1. Examples of PIMS "profit driving" measures.

Measures of:	Example
Competitive Position	
• Scale	Share of target or "served" market
• Relative scale	Relative share = business share/share of top three competitors
• Relative quality	Weighted preference score versus major competitors
• Relative value	Preference score set against relative price positioning
• Innovation investment	R&D spend as a percentage of sales
• Innovation output	Percentage of revenue from products/services under three years old
Market Attractiveness	
• Customer price sensitivity	Importance of product to buyer budget
• Customer buying power	Amount negotiated in one contract/transaction
• Customer Complexity	Number of key customers, customer communication cost
• Seller power	Share of top four sellers into the market
Productivity	
• Investment intensity	Net assets as a percentage of business value added per annum
• Capital flexibility	Gross fixed assets as a percentage of value added
• Labour productivity	Value added per employee
Human/organisation capital	
• Culture	Measured attitude to problem resolution
• Training/time management	Balance of top management time on tasks
IT capital	
• Strategic fit	Balance between IT spending and strategic goals
• Change investment	Percentage of IT investment in change related projects

was created as an independent organisation to hold confidential information under secure conditions from a range of companies, and to develop the measurement and applications approaches for quantitative comparison.

The framework used in PIMS comparisons has evolved and expanded over time, with key components added as new research is completed. Over 200 variables are captured and tracked in constituent parts of PIMS, with the most extensive range of experience still focussed in the core areas of competitive position, market attractiveness, cost structure and productivity. The key measures used for comparison are summarised in Table 4.1.

The early research results from PIMS, based on the original measurement parameters covering competitive position, market attractiveness and productivity, made a significant impact on business planning concepts and practice. Evidence generated on links between non-financial measures and financial results shaped a generation of thinking. The importance of quality, share and customer value for business unit profits, and the damage caused by fixed capital intensity, are covered in a range of PIMS publications (Buzzell & Gale, 1987).

Benchmarks for Growth

PIMS' early focus on the determinants of profit margins or return on assets as performance measures quickly broadened to include the drivers of growth. Benchmarking profit and growth plans became the core of work for contributing companies.

In 1994, the Industry Directorate of the Europran Union (EU) approached PIMS, on the recommendation of its clients, to advise on the key determinants of business growth. The study they commissioned was designed to test the relative importance of "intangible" business measures, alongside "hard" measures such as costs and productivity. It looked at the role of such business measures — quality, innovation, intellectual property and marketing investment — in driving growth, value added, employment and profits. We chose these indicators because they measure:

(i) The ability to compete for customers preferences.
(ii) The ability to create value and jobs.
(iii) The ability to compete in markets for capital — an essential for growth.

Our findings were no surprise to companies that had worked with PIMS. But they were sufficiently different to be published in the Commission's Panorama of EU Industry (EU, 1996). The three main findings — all proven from the businesses we observed — were that:

(i) "Intangibles" are not necessarily difficult to measure and they are powerful growth drivers for individual businesses.
(ii) Innovation and intellectual property are the key determinants of growth in competitive markets.
(iii) Quality, innovation and intellectual property are more effective as creators of wealth and jobs than investment in fixed assets.

The 1997 EU "Competitiveness" White Paper accepted this PIMS evidence on the key role of intangibles, including quality, innovation and intellectual property, in driving business and employment growth.

Do Brands Help Growth?

The earlier work outlined above, although highlighting the importance of intellectual property, did not say anything specific about brands. Brands represent an important part of intellectual property for businesses, sometimes more than the technical know-how behind product or service advantage.

The European Brands Association, therefore, commissioned the research described below to examine behaviour and performance in branded consumer markets. The purpose of the study is to test whether the competitive forces that drive individual businesses are the same as those which create consumer value and economic growth, and if brands play a measurable part in turning new product ideas into growth.

Scope of the Study

We look at how branded fast-moving consumer goods (fmcg) businesses grow by:

(i)   Winning market share in the battle against competitors for customer preference.
(ii) Creating additional value added — their contribution to growing the economy.
(iii) Achieving Return on Capital Employed (ROCE) above the cost of capital so that they can compete for investment capital — essential for any business wanting to grow.

We also look at job creation, which is closely related to business growth.

Evidence comes from over 200 businesses in the PIMS database, mainly in the EU and NAFTA, which are clearly fmcg operations. Each is tracked in detail over a minimum of four years on financial and non-financial measures. Most are branded, but the sample contains some businesses which are "unbranded" or which do not support their brands, and these provide some interesting comparisons. The conclusions we show from this data have been separately tested on both sides of the Atlantic, and over time.

The Role of Brands

The economic case for branding is dynamic. A brand should be a means of communication to facilitate innovation and to help realise benefits from R&D investment. There are at least two ways in which this can happen:

(i)   Known brands can help consumers recognise trusted suppliers in changing markets, that is, brands aid the process of consumer choice.

(ii) Brands can help producers gain trust for new approaches to meet consumer needs thus providing access to market for innovation.

If this case is real, we should expect to see the processes of choice work more responsively in branded markets. Branded businesses should be sensitive to "value for money" pressures and are more likely to compete through innovation.

What the Evidence Shows

The data shows that branding in fmcg markets does boost competitive innovation. Branding is associated with more dynamic response by producers to consumer needs and competitive activity. Branded businesses do invest more in innovation, strongly associated with business and employment growth. Successful brands must deliver improving value to consumers through innovation — otherwise, they cease to prosper.

Earlier PIMS work showed that quality, innovation and intellectual property drive business and employment growth in the wider economy. We can now show that the links from investment in innovation, quality and value to business growth are stronger for branded consumer products than for other sectors.

Competitiveness and Growth

We begin with an analysis of the ability of a business to grow "relative market share", defined as share of the target market divided by the sum of shares of its top three competitors.

In the branded fmcg sector, more than any other, the drivers of business growth are dynamic; to win the competitive battle for market share, businesses must be able to:

 (i) Offer improving quality and increasing value for money to consumers.
 (ii) Move faster and more successfully than competitors on innovation.
(iii) Sustain a strong market reputation.

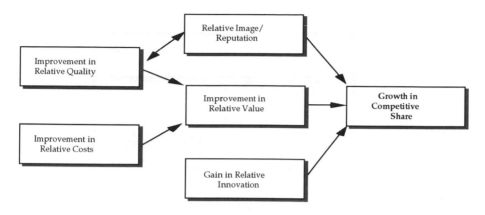

Fig. 4.1. The key growth drives.

Just "being good" isn't enough (Fig. 4.1).

In the charts which follow, we show the impact of value, innovation and reputation on share change versus competitors for branded fmcg businesses. To do so, we must first establish and allow for the starting share position of a business — since for very high share operations, there is nowhere to go but down!

Improving value for money is an important way for high share businesses to limit share loss and for low share businesses to grow (Fig. 4.2). A business can boost its value position either by improving the relative quality of the offer or by reducing the relative price. When it comes to sustaining growth, "intangible" quality is a more powerful driver than price.

Innovation advantage is essential for businesses with high shares to maintain their position. Again, simply maintaining high rates of new product introductions isn't enough; what matters is increasing success in innovation versus the competition (Fig. 4.3).

Reputation, or brand image, can give a huge boost to the share prospects of small share businesses (Fig. 4.4). Reputation is a key enabler for share growth; without it, businesses are less likely to get new products tested in their markets or quality/value improvements appreciated. At

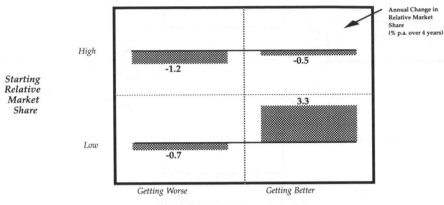

Source: PIMS branded FMCG database.

Fig. 4.2. Better value for money helps share retention or growth.

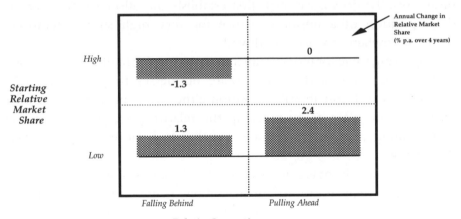

Source: PIMS branded FMCG database.

Fig. 4.3. Staying ahead on innovation helps drive share gain.

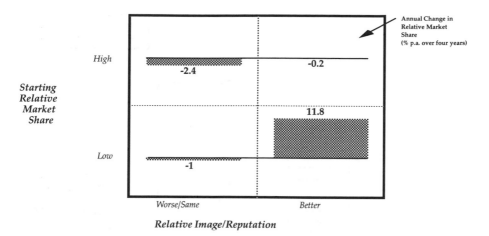

Source: PIMS branded FMCG database.

Fig. 4.4. Superior reputation helps market share.

the same time, failure to maintain a strong brand reputation by a market leader can bring rapid erosion of share position. There is little chance of a "quiet life" for high share branded produces — if their competitions innovate or match them on image, they can lose customers quickly.

For each of these key relationship, we can track the driving forces of growth back to investment in product and process R&D, to advertising and promotion, and to key capabilities in intellectual property, speed to market and service to distribution channels. These linkages are:

(i)   R&D and intellectual property investment in consumer businesses boost successful product innovation and, thus, relative quality.
(ii) Process innovation reduces competitive costs and improve value to consumers.
(iii) Innovation, good service to retailers and investment in commercial communication enhance brand image and company reputation.

The entire set of relationships combines to present a dynamic mode of competitive growth more explicit and powerful than in other types

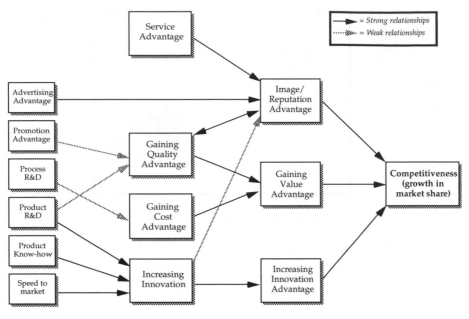

Source: PIMS branded FMCG database.

Fig. 4.5. From intangible investment to business growth.

of business. It is a model (Fig. 4.5) which responds rapidly to changes in consumer requirements and gives branded businesses a major incentive to invest in new products to meet them. Each of the relationships in this model can be demonstrated in multi-variate regression and by simple statistical relationships.

Evidence on value added growth shows a very similar set of relationships (Fig. 4.6). Innovation, the ability to deliver superior quality products and services and to reduce costs are the key drivers of real value added growth at the business level. Not only do businesses which win on these factors gain share of their markets, they also make the biggest contribution to the growth of the economy. And, as we shall see later, innovative branded businesses grow employment and, at the same time, achieve the highest level of productivity.

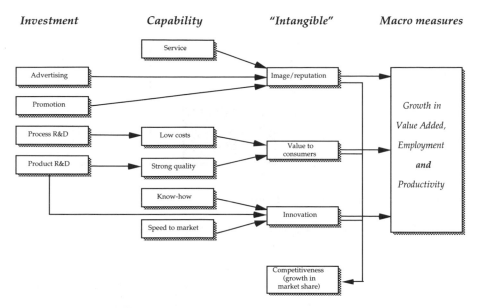

Source: PIMS branded FMCG database.

Fig. 4.6. From business investment to economic growth.

Brands and Innovation

Not surprisingly, given this set of relationships, branded businesses undertake more innovation in the consumer products sector than unbranded producers (Fig. 4.7). They spend more on product and process R&D as a percentage of their sales revenue. New products, defined as the percentage of products with significantly new characteristics introduced in the last three years, also represent a much higher proportion of their sales.

For jobs, after stripping out the impact of market growth (clearly a strong driver of employment creation), innovation matters a great deal. Innovative branded businesses in growing markets are where new jobs are created faster. This is because meeting new consumer needs creates new employment oppportunities (Fig. 4.8). Of course, some of this growth is at the expense of other firms, but the message for

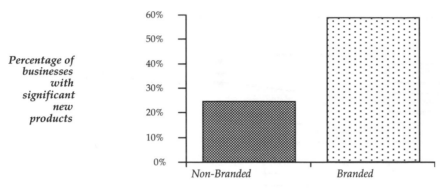

Source: PIMS branded FMCG database.

Fig. 4.7. The majority of branded businesses innovate.

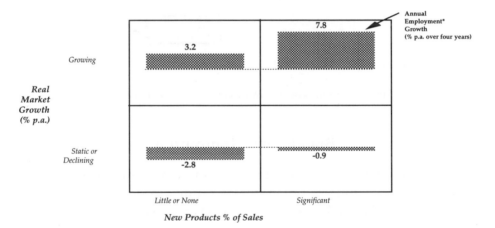

Source: PIMS branded FMCG database.

Fig. 4.8. Innovation is linked to new jobs.

European businesses competing in a global context is that successful innovation is the key to growth.

But what about the costs and benefits of innovation to business profits? Evidence shows that strong brands are an essential part of sustainable innovation. Preferred brands help manufacturers to invest

Source: PIMS branded FMCG database.

Fig. 4.9. Preferred brands make innovation profitable.

in innovation successfully and profitably; without brand preference, the costs of innovation are substantially higher (Fig. 4.9). Innovation is, in turn, essential to keep strong brand positions ahead of the competition — without it, they fall behind.

Competition, Innovation and Growth

This research on first moving consumer goods is mirrored by work we have done elsewhere on durables markets. This is further evidence that branded consumer businesses have a strong profit incentive to innovate behind good brand positions to keep their offering to consumers fresh and ahead of competition. Competitive forces raise the pressure for innovation and they increase the rewards for "doing it right". There is a virtuous circle of incentives that should encourage EU branded businesses to compete in global markets through innovation.

If the economic case for branding set out at the start of this paper is real, we would expect to see branded businesses achieving a significantly

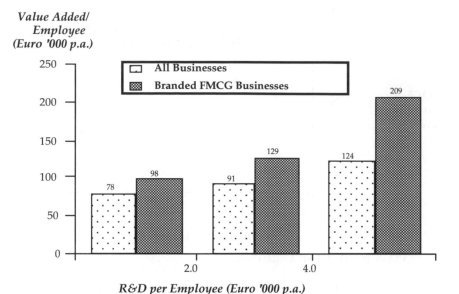

Source: PIMS database.

Fig. 4.10. Brands boost value from R&D.

better "return" on innovation. If we do the "accounting" in terms of value added, we find that branded fmcg businesses show a strong correlation between R&D and business value added (Fig. 4.10). Looking at the relationship between R&D spending and value creation per employee, typically an extra Euro of R&D spending in this sector is associated with an extra two to 2.5 Euros in value added. In the rest of the economy, the ratio is typically 1:1.3. This suggests that branding does increase the effectiveness of businesses in creating value from R&D investment.

These business level incentives help explain the higher innovation in branded markets. And, at the "macro" level, we can also show a strong relationship between innovation and market growth (Fig. 4.11). It is not possible, from data on individual businesses, to "prove" the direction of the relationship between innovation and market growth.

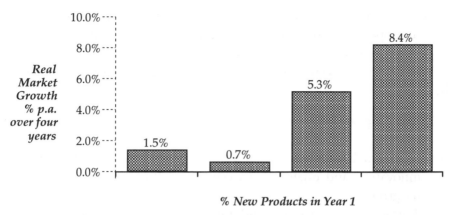

% New Products in Year 1

Source: PIMS branded FMCG database.

Fig. 4.11. Innovation is strongly associated with market growth.

However, it is clear that the markets where our observed businesses have little or no new product revenue are those which do not grow.

Conclusions

PIMS evidence shows that the ability of branded consumer businesses to win the battle for consumer preference is best explained by three interrelated factors:

(i) The abiliy to improve value to consumers through better products and more competitive price.

(ii) The ability to get new products to market faster and more effectively than competitors.

(iii) A sustained advantage in consumer and trade reputation, without which it is unlikely that value advantage will be seen by consumers or that innnovation will reach the market.

We have also examined fmcg producers who focus on unbranded or " unsupported" products. They are much less innovative and invest less effort in key drivers of growth.

The evidence, from real businesses operating in real markets, shows that:

(i) Branding is essential for innovation and growth in consumer markets in competitive economies.
(ii) Successful brands deliver ever improving value to consumers through innovation and quality improvement; if they fail in this, they fail to grow.
(iii) Policies on competition and intellectual property should take as much account of branding in "everyday" products (where the bulk of this evidence comes from) as they do in the more conspicuous "hi-tech" areas of the economy, where much of the debate on intellectual property protection has focussed.

Our results show that branding helps producers to innovate and consumers to choose. The economic case for brands stands up; the importance of marketing communication in promoting innovation and growth is proven.

Implications for Policy and for Management

Partly as a result of this study, EU policy-makers have increased efforts to make the single market in commercial communication a reality. European firms suffer the disadvantage in that while they can move products around the single market, the marketing to support them is still seriously limited by national regulations. Restrictions on promotional offers in Italy and bans on advertising toys in Greece are examples.

American companies — in addition to their advantage of a having a single language for their domestic market — suffer fewer restraints on marketing and the use of brands. This helps to explain why US businesses have historically been better able to capitalise on quality advantages in their markets and have been more innovative. It is not always appreciated by policy-markets that the commercial communication costs associated with innovation can be greater than the costs of technical development. Therefore, restraints which push up marketing costs can stifle new product launches. Europe needs more than a single market in physical products to compete on equal terms in innovation markets.

There are lessons, too, for branded business managers. A brand is not, as some have suggested, a device to "tax" consumers. Successful brands justify themselves through innovation and improving value to consumers. If they fail in this, leaving themselves with nothing to communicate, they die. PIMS evidence shows that branding sharpens the operation of competitive forces. Any brand owner who ignores this does so at his or her own peril.

Chapter 5

Technological and Market Competencies and Financial Performance

JOE TIDD and CIARAN DRIVER

Introduction

In this chapter, we summarise and review the range of technological, market and organisational measures of innovation discussed in this book and elsewhere, and examine the relationship between these measures and financial performance. The chapter consists of three sections. First, we review the range of technological, market and organisational measures of innovation discussed in this book and elsewhere. Second, we examine a range of financial measures of performance, as well as the relationship between these and our measures of innovation. Finally, we develop a simple — but, we believe, comprehensive — model of innovation based on selected indicators of innovation at 40 companies in the United Kingdom (UK), representing all key sectors, and identify the relationships between different measures of innovation and the financial performance of these companies.

Measures of Innovation

The aim of this section is to identify a range of measures of technological, organisational and market which can be used to construct an innovation scoreboard. By definition, the study of innovation is multi-disciplinary.

However, to date, most studies have been conducted within a single, narrow discipline, principally economics. Therefore, the literature review presented here is broad and covers relevant research in the economics, finance and strategic management literatures. We focus on measures based on data in the public domain, rather than survey data, as these are more readily accessible and comparable across different companies, sectors and nations. For a recent review of survey-based studies, see Smith (1992) or Crepon and Mairesse (1993).

The most established, and still the most commonly used, indicators of innovation are technology-based, including capital expenditure, expenditure on research and development, and patent activity. The respective strengths and weaknesses of technological indicators, such as expenditure on research and development and patent, are well-documented (see, for example, Chapters 6 and 7). These indicators have the advantage that definitions are relatively consistent and data is collected on a routine basis. However, previous research suggests that such indicators may be more reliable indicators at the national and sectoral levels than at the firm level. The review that follows identifies the advantages and drawbacks of different technology-based indicators of innovations.

Innovation can be viewed as a set of outputs responding to inputs, that is, the so-called "linear" model. Although this view does not command unanimous support — and we will point to some limitations — it is convenient to use this framework and there is no obvious alternative. R&D expenditure or R&D capital stock is usually taken as an input. Data is available on expenditure, but we generally have little idea what depreciation rate to use to construct capital stock estimates. Hence we can let the capital stock be represented by a weighted sum of previous R&D expenditures, where the weights can either be estimated or imposed. There is a further problem as to whether we should deflate the R&D expenditures. If we do, we are trying to deal with a technical or production relationship. If we do not, we are simply looking at relationships in monetary terms.

As for the outputs, this is often taken as deflated production (assuming that the R&D figures are deflated), usually adjusted first to take account of other inputs such as labour, fixed capital or materials. However, as we will discuss later, some studies look at profitability instead — perhaps because of the restrictive assumptions needed for production function estimation. Other possible output measures are patents, innovation counts and the diffusion of innovations. Griliches (1990) reviews the use of patent statistics as indicators of innovation. He makes the important observation that the standard of novelty and utility for granting patents is not very high, and that is varies greatly over time and across different countries. Archibugi (1992) provides a comprehensive list of the advantages and disadvantages of patent statistics as indicators of innovative activity. The main advantages of patents are:

(i)   Patents represent the output of the inventive process, specifically those inventions which are expected to have an economic benefit.
(ii) Obtaining patent protection is time consuming and expensive. Hence applications are only likely to be made for those developments which are expected to provide benefits in excess of these costs.
(iii) Patents can be broken down by technical fields, thus providing information on both the rate and direction of innovation.
(iv) Patent statistics are available in large numbers and over very long time series.

The main disadvantages of patents as indicators of innovation are:

(i)   Not all inventions are patented. Firms may chose to protect their discoveries by other means, such as through secrecy. It has been estimated that firms apply for patents for 66% to 87% of patentable inventions.
(ii) Not all innovations are technically patentable — for example, software development.
(iii) The propensity to patent varies considerably across different sectors and firms. For example, there is a high propensity to patent in the pharmaceutical industry, but a low propensity in fast-moving consumer goods.

(iv) Firms have a different propensity to patent in each national market, according to the attractiveness of markets.

(v) A large proportion of patents are never exploited, or are applied for simply to block other developments. It has been estimated that between 40% to 60% of all patents issued are used.

In order to determine whether patents measure anything of relevance, it is necessary to look for correlations with other indicators, such as R&D expenditure, productivity growth, profitability or the stock market value of the firm. For example, there is quite a strong relationship between R&D and the number of patents at the cross-sectional level, across firms and industries. However, at the level of the firm, the relationship is much weaker over time. More promising are econometric studies of the relationship between patents and financial performance. An example is the use of patent numbers as a proxy for "intangible" capital in stock market value of firm regressions.

Econometric techniques can be used to assess the impact of innovation inputs, specifically the, expenditure on research and development, and on some measure of performance, typically productivity or patents. The work of Griliches (1984) and Stoneman (1990) suggests that product R&D is significantly less productive than process R&D according to the estimates. Studies by Geroski (1991, 1994) use the usual production function framework, but include significant innovations (SPRU databank) categorised by the producer sector and the user sector at three-digit SIC level. The greatest significance was found for innovations used (nearly four times as much as for innovations developed). A further breakdown showed that innovations used originating in the engineering industries had the strongest effect. The study noted that the productivity increases took 10–15 years to be fully effected. The fit between inputs (R&D) and outputs (patents) improves the broader categorisation used in the study. At the national level, patents and R&D are correlated and, also, to some extent at the sectoral level. As Pavitt (1988) notes, however, the extent of unexplained variation is high at the level of cross-company analysis (see also Silberston, 1987) which gives a ranking of patents and R&D by activity heading using the UK standard industrial classification. It is clear from his figures that the correlation is far from perfect. Furthermore, he suggests that important patents are likely to be located in high R&D industries.

Part of the difficulty in obtaining stable relationships between patents and R&D lies in the fact that firms have different propensities to patent their discoveries. This partly reflects the ease of protecting the gains from innovation in other ways, such as secrecy and first-mover advantages. Furthermore, the effectiveness of patents may vary across industries as Levin *et al.* (1987) have shown. R&D statistics also display industry-specific bias with some sectors classifying their development work as design or production (Pavitt & Patel, 1988). The fact that weaker relationships between outputs and inputs are observed at the firm level, rather than at the industry level, suggests that there is a lot of variability in the productivity of technological inputs, and that there may be some point in studying the particular conditions under which the inputs are used most effectively. The most likely explanatory factors are scale, technological opportunity and management (Hay & Morris, 1990).

The evidence on scale is mixed. There are two linked hypotheses — that the size of the R&D effort counts, and that the size of the firm makes R&D more effective, say, because of economies of scope between projects (Cohen & Levin, 1989). Studies suggest that the scale of R&D effort is important only in chemicals (Hay & Morris, 1990) and pharmaceuticals (Jensen,). Firm size is a more difficult issue to study because the interpretation of R&D and patents differ between class sizes of firms. A recent study (Blundell *et al.*, 1993) compared over 600 manufacturing firms between 1972 and 1982 in the UK, matched to the SPRU database of significant technical innovations. It suggests that large firms tend to innovate more because they have a higher incentive to do so: a doubling of market share from the mean of 2.5% will increase the probability of innovation in the next period by 0.6%. This result is qualified by noting that less competitive firms (higher concentration and lower import ratios) innovate less.

Technological opportunity at the industry level is surveyed by Levin *et al.* (1987) in the context of their study of appropriability. Technological opportunity also exists at the firm level via the spillover effects from other firms (Jaffe, 1986). Geroski (1994) reaches similar conclusions. The classic study of the managerial efficiency of R&D inputs is project SAPPHO, best summarised in Freeman (1982). Not surprisingly, commitment to the project by senior management and good communications are crucial to success. Chusil (1978) shows that growth markets are less favourable to overspending than stable or contracting markets.

A major problem with measuring inputs and outputs is: how do we take account of the "spillover" of innovation benefits or information to other firms or industries? For example, if we are looking at a particular sector's industrial output or productivity in relation to its R&D spending, how do we take account of spillover from other sectors or non-industry R&D? (Mansfield, 1984). The question really relates to the appropriate level of investigation — is it the company/or industry/or entire economy?

Freeman (1982) discusses the question of spillover, arguing that the appropriate connection to make is not so much company R&D and productivity as industry R&D and productivity. For example, the whole electronics industry benefitted from Bell's work on semiconductors, and only a small part was recovered by Bell in the form of licensing or sales. There may also be a different kind of spillover internal to the firm. Some products fail, but their R&D is still useful. For example, the large sums spent by IBM on the (failed) Stretch computer in the 1960s (only a few were sold) led to the successful 360 series.

Geroski (1991) notes that the spillover from innovations between closely related sectors is not as great as previous research has suggested with regard to R&D spending (Jaffe, 1986). Rather, there is spillover between producers and users. This is presumably because the innovation itself is too firm-specific to show much spillover effect, whereas the information shared with R&D spillover is less firm-specific. Although firms are increasing, drawing upon external sources of innovation, few have yet to systematically scan outside their own sector (Tidd & Trewhella,

1997). A particular form of spillover occurs when the economy, as a whole, benefits more from an innovation than is appropriated as profits. A difference, then, occurs between the private rate of return and the social rate of return (Mansfield, 1990).

The limitations of R&D and patents, as surrogates for innovation, have led to more recent studies turning to less robust but market-based measures, such as new product announcements and innovation counts. Jensen (1987) related the number of new chemical entities discovered in the US pharmaceutical industry to constant price R&D and other variables. A non-linear (convex) relationship with R&D was discovered and there was some indication that when R&D was interacted with sales in a large firm, it was more effective. The study by Devinney (1992) reports the strength of the relationship from patents to innovations in order to judge whether patents can be used as an innovation indicator. Innovation is measured by a count of citations in the *Wall Street Journal*. The results are striking in that at the four-digit industry level, there is a strong relationship. This disappears when the firm level data is analysed. Indeed, the best predictor of a firm innovation is the patent intensity of the industry it is in.

The collection and analysis of innovations in the "product news" columns of trade journals has three advantages over company surveys. First, data can be collected without contacting companies. This reduces the resources required and places no additional burden on industry. Second, data can be collected relatively cheaply by scanning trade journals and databases. Third, the data set can be extended into the past to allow comparisons over time. The main drawback of this approach is that it fails to capture process innovations. Few, if any, firms choose to make public announcements of their process innovations. However, official statistics focus on factor productivity — labour and capital. Hence this may not be a major shortcoming.

The use of product announcements to measure innovation first took place in the US in the early 1980s (Edwards & Gordon, 1984). This pioneering study, commissioned by the US Small Business Administration, developed a database of product announcements in 100 technology, engineering and trade journals. Firms were classified by size and the four-digit SIC code. The innovations were then classified according to a four-point scale of significance.

A subsequent study analysed innovations announced in all major US publications in the year 1982 (Acs & Audretsch, 1988), but more recent studies have restricted the scope to leading financial publications such as the *Wall Street Journal* (Chaney & Devinney, 1992). These studies indicate that innovation tends to be concentrated in larger firms, in less concentrated industries and is strongly affected by joint investment in advertising and R&D. At the industry level, patent intensity and new product announcements are strongly related, with 60% of the variance in the new product sample being explained by patent intensity. However, at the level of the firm, the relationship is very weak, and only 2% of the variance of individual firm level new product activity appears to be explained by patenting activity (Devinney, 1993). As use of the absolute number of patents or new products would introduce bias towards large firms, the measures used were a proportion of total patents and a proportion of new product total announcements. What also stands out from Table 5.1 is that firms introducing new products tend to be large and R&D and advertising-intensive.

Table 5.1. Patenting versus non-patenting firms.

	Patenting Firms		Non-Patenting Firms	
	No New Products	New Products	No New Products	New Products
Assets ($ millions)	882	3,328	1,705	3,960
Advertising/sales (%)	1.0	2.9	1.4	4.2
R&D/assets (%)	2.3	4.8	2.1	6.3
Debt/market value (%)	39.2	33.5	43.4	29.2
Return on sssets (%)	6.6	6.0	5.9	0.0
New products (number)	0.0	4.5	0.0	1.8
Patents (number)	156	592	0	0

Source: Derived from Devinney (1993).

A growing body of research on product announcements emerged in the 1990s. Various studies in the US, the Netherlands, Austria, Ireland and the UK have refined and validated the methodology. Most recently, the use of product announcements as an indicator of innovation has been the subject of a number of studies in the UK. The Technology Policy Unit at Aston has examined the relationship between the expenditure of R&D, patents and new product announcements in the pharmaceutical industry (Steward, 1994). A study by UMIST (Coombs, Narandren & Richards, 1994) applied a similar methodology to the Dutch study. The researchers examined product announcements in 35 trade and industry journals over a period of three months in 1993. The unit of analysis was the product announcement rather than the firm. The study identified almost 1,000 product announcements originating from a similar number of companies.

The Dutch study (Kleinknecht & Reijnen, 1993) is of particular interest because it developed a detailed scheme of classification which has been adopted by many subsequent studies. The research, supported by the Ministry of Economic Affairs, examined all product announcements in the 1989 volumes of 36 trade and industry journals. Data was collected on each of the following:

 (i) The identity of the firm and the four-digit SIC code.
 (ii) The product name and a brief description of the innovation.
(iii) The degree of complexity of the innovation (see below).
(iv) The type of innovation (see below).
 (v) The properties of the innovation (see below).
(vi) The origin of the innovation.
(vii) The main market of the innovation.

The study distinguishes three levels of complexity:

 (i) *High*. A system consisting of a larger number of components, often from different disciplines, such as a new car or aircraft.
 (ii) *Medium*. A unit consisting of a smaller number of components, such as a new machine tool.
(iii) *Low*. A single innovation, such as an improved component.

In addition, the research distinguishes five types of innovation:

(i)   A *completely new* or decisively changed product or service, such as a mountain bike or electronic banking.

(ii) A *modestly improved* product or service, such as a more energy-efficient machine or improved safety protection of credit cards.

(iii) A new or improved *accessory* product or service, such as a safer child's seat for a car or improved life assurance connected to a mortgage.

(iv) A product or service *differentiation*, such as new packaging;

(v)   A *process* innovation.

It is important to note that in this scheme of classification, the complexity and the type of innovation are independent of each other. A highly complex product may only be a modest improvement or conversely, a product of low complexity can be totally new. The distinction made between incremental innovation and product differentiation is also important. The test used involves checking a product announcement against a list of 14 innovation properties, such as greater efficiency, longer life and easier maintenance. If a product announcement does not satisfy any of the properties listed, it is classified as a product or service differentiation.

Significantly, the EUROSTAT pilot questionnaire for the EC innovation survey specifically excludes product or service differentiation. However, research suggests that more than a quarter of all innovations are product or service differentiation (Coombs *et al.*, 1994). Other studies also indicate that product differentiation is one of the main drivers of profitability (Luchs, 1990). Therefore, the inclusion of product and service differentiation is a significant benefit of using product announcements as indicators of innovation. There are a number of additional reasons for choosing this methodology:

(i)   It is a useful measure of innovation output and allows comparison with more conventional input indicators, such as R&D and patents.

(ii) It provides a direct measure of product differentiation, which is not captured by other indicators.

(iii) It can be aggregated to compare the performance of different firm sizes, sectors and regions.

(iv) It provides a direct measure of the flow of innovations into the UK.

 (v) By adopting a common methodology, it allows direct comparison with similar databases overseas.

(vi) It identifies new product and service development for subsequent in-depth case studies.

Measures of Innovation and Financial Performance

Many traditional accounting and financial indicators concentrate on short-term measures of profitability and, therefore, may undervalue innovation. However, measures based on value added, market to book value and price to earnings multiple may be better indicators of innovation. A recent study of accounting practice suggests that traditional financial performance measures, such as return on capital employed, earnings per share and cash flow projections, are being replaced by performance indicators based on the highest level of the firm, such as strategic benchmarking or, at the very detailed level, activity-based costing (CIMA, 1993). Rappaport (1986) lays down some "fundamental criteria" which measures of financial performance should attain:

 (i) *Valid.* Consistent with basic economic theory of value.

(ii) *Verifiable.* Calculated unambiguously from readily available data.

(iii) *Controllable.* The person being measured must be able to control performance.

(iv) *Global.* Applicable everywhere.

 (v) *Communicable.* Easily explained.

The most common measures of stock market performance are earnings per share (EPS) and the price to earnings multiple (P/E). In particular, it is commonly assumed that provided a company achieves a satisfactory growth in its EPS, the market value of its shares will increase. However, an increase or decrease in earnings may not result in a corresponding increase or decrease in shareholder value. This is because, first, earnings do not take into account the level of financial and business risk. Second, earnings do not include the capital and fixed investment needed to achieve the anticipated growth. Third, the time value of money is ignored.

For these reasons, return on investment (ROI) has become a more popular measure of financial performance. The assumption is that if the ROI is greater than the cost of capital, shareholder value will be increased. However, in practice, this is highly misleading as ROI is an accrual accounting-based measure, whereas the cost of capital is the economic return demanded by shareholders. ROI tends to overstate the economic or discounted cashflow (DCF) return for a number of reasons: capitalisation policy; depreciation policy; and the lag between investment outlays and subsequent cash flows. As a result, ROI tends to understate the economic rate of return during the early stage of an investment, and overstate rates at later stages as the undepreciated assets base decreases. Unfortunately, the effects are rarely self-correcting. A further objection to the use of ROI to evaluate performance is that it ignores the residual value of the business after the period in question. Clearly, the true change in shareholder value must take into account the present value of future cashflows and the residual value of the business.

Rappaport (1986) proposes a practical means of assessing changes in shareholder value. He identifies a number of value drivers: sales growth rate, operating profit margin, working capital investment, fixed capital investment, forecast duration, cost of capital and rate of tax. These factors can be used to calculate the present value of forecast cashflows. However, for most businesses, the cashflow over the next five or 10 years represent only a small proportion of the change in value. In most cases, the residual value of the business is the largest proportion of the change in value. This is particularly so where a business attempts to increase market share by increasing expenditure on production capacity, new product development and marketing. Typically, such businesses may experience negative cashflows for several years, but may enhance value in the long run.

Therefore, the estimate of the residual value of a business is critical. However, there is no agreed method of calculating residual value and, to a large extent, it depends on the assumptions made for the forecast period. One commonly used method is based on perpetuity value. The perpetuity method assumes that after the forecast period, the business will earn, on average, the cost of capital on new investments. In other words, after the forecast period, the business will invest in strategies which will, on average, have a zero net present value. This assumption can be justified by the behaviour of most competitive markets. If a company is able to earn returns above the cost of capital, it will eventually attract competitors who will, in turn, drive down return to the minimum acceptable or cost of capital rate.

There are a number of alternative methods of estimating residual values, such as those based on the market to book (M/B) value or price to earnings (P/E) multiple. Using the M/B ratio, the residual can be estimated by multiplying the book value of equity by the projected M/B ratio at the end of the forecast period. However, the book value is affected by earnings calculations rather than actual earnings and, in practice, it is difficult to forecast future M/B ratios. Similar objections exist for using P/E multiples. The residual value can be estimated by multiplying the earnings at the end of the forecast period by the forecast P/E. However, in practice, average P/E multiples vary significantly over time, making them difficult to forecast. Conceptually, use of either M/B and P/E is unsatisfactory because both use accounting data to estimate the residual value, whereas the present value of cashflows is used for the forecast period.

A practical implication of shareholder value analysis is the concept of a threshold margin. This is defined as the minimum operating profit margin a business must achieve in order to maintain shareholder value. In other words, it represents the operating profit margin at which the business earns exactly its cost of capital. The threshold margin can be expressed either as the margin required on incremdntal sales or the margin required on total sales.

The view frequently taken is that the Stock Exchange consistently undervalues shares of the firms which spend on R&D because expensed (as opposed to capitalised) R&D reduces Earnings Per Share in the year of expenditure — one of the two major performance criteria used by analysts. The fact that analysts use fundamentals such as EPS was confirmed by Arnold and Moizer (1984). Some industrialists believe that this approach systematically undervalues long-term research and development and capital expenditure. This is, because, first discounting reduces the value of expected future revenue. Secondly, it is difficult to value the future options which research and development may create. The fact that there is a weak correlation between company valuations, in terms of the price to earnings, and expenditure on R&D suggests that the problem of undervaluation is industry-specific, if it exists at all. The problem appears to have more to do with a lack of communication between industry and its investors.

The financial community relies heavily on various financial ratios and scoring methods to evaluate company performance. Both Altman (1971) and Taffler (1991) have used ratios to help create an index to predict corporate failure, although the third seminal author (Argenti, 1976) prefers a taxonomy of events/factors to a multi-variate approach. Altman (1983), in the US, and Taffler, (1982) in the UK, have used multiple discriminant analysis to identify what factors differentiate financially successful companies from those which fail. Multiple discriminant analysis involves attributing weights to each variable such that the distribution of scores for each group has the least overlap. The reliability of these models has proven to be high, being able to predict company failure with 95% accuracy.

However, such indices are difficult for managers to interpret. Therefore, we prefer specific financial ratios which have some relation to long-term performance. For example, Kay (1993) places great emphasis on the value added by a firm as a measure of corporate performance. He argues that there can be no long-term rationale for a firm which does not add value. There is no agreed definition of value added, but essentially it is simply the difference between the market value of outputs and the cost of inputs. This contrasts with operating profit, which is the difference between the value of output and the value of material and labour inputs. The assessment of value added must also take into account the cost of capital inputs — depreciation and a provision for a reasonable return on the capital invested. The most simple definition of value added is turnover less depreciation and bought in materials and services. This definition has the advantage that it is simple to calculate and interpret; it enables comparison to be made between companies with very different activities and cannot be manipulated to the same extent as accounting profit.

Walker (1979) uses a R&D/Value Added ratio as a proxy for innovation output in his study. In his justification for the measure, he points out that identical R&D expenditures in different industries do not necessarily indicate identical innovation activity. He also argues that R&D thresholds will be different for different industries, some being far more capital-intensive than others. Budworth (1993) proposes a related but more complex ratio. He develops an "innovation ratio" based on the ratio of cash outlay to cash return, as well as the ratio of development time to market life of specific development projects. The idea is that when, or if, a company with a portfolio of different products reaches steady state, the innovation ratio will be equivalent to the ratio of innovation spending to value added. On this basis, it is possible to calculate an innovation ratio for specific sectors and companies. For example, Budworth calculates the ratio for the UK mechanical engineering sectors to be around 14%. As the value added for that sector is some 50% of turnover, this suggests that at least 7% of revenue should be devoted to innovation in order to sustain intangible assets. Conceptually, this ratio is similar to the depreciation charge for tangible assets.

Peters and Waterman's (1982) bestseller, *In Search of Excellence*, provides a good example of the application of financial ratios to company evaluation. The authors use average return on equity, return on capital and return on sales as measures of success. Perhaps more promising, they also use the average ratio of market value to book value as a measure of the long-term innovative potential of a company. The reasoning behind this is that the difference between the two methods of company valuation represents the contribution of future earnings above and beyond the tangible assets. This element of "goodwill" can be substantial and may be a useful proxy for innovativeness. It may be possible to disaggregate this into components, such as the value of brands, levels of staff training, R&D and other intellectual assets.

Geroski (1994) shows that the profit margin of innovators — using matched data from the SPRU database and company accounts — is higher than non-innovators, controlling for other influences. However, the effect was rather small, suggesting that benefits may have been captured by users. Innovating firms are also more protected from cyclical downturns. Scherer and Revenscraig (1982) looked at the relationship between profitability and lagged indicators of capital input, marketing expenses and R&D. The main conclusion was a rate of return to R&D of about 33% with an average lag of about five years. Process R&D had four times the rate of return as product R&D, but was more risky with a more variable return.

The impact of R&D on the stock market is more difficult to judge as one needs a prior position on the efficiency or, otherwise, of financial markets before setting up a testable hypothesis. Some key papers are Pakes (1985), who observed a significant (though noisy) effect, and Hall (1993). The latter paper raises an important worry about whether stock market valuations of innovation are consistent. The valuation of R&D capital collapsed from a value of unity to a quarter over the 1980s, a result that is robust to measurement and specification tests. The market valuation of R&D does not appear to be affected significantly by accounting policy. The revenues accruing to any particular project might be many years removed from the time of the development costs. This has led firms onto capitalise their expenditures until the revenue arrives. Surveys suggest that analysts, as a whole, are able to "see through" this kind of capitalisation and, in consequence, do not treat such companies any differently from those which write off the expense. The same research suggests that analysts even prefer R&D spending to increasing the productive base of the firm through asset acquisition.

Countering the view that analysts are short-sighted is the fact that analysts in the UK graded the importance of R&D information with a 2.32 some on a scale of seven (with one as the "best"), making it the fourth most important with product development coming in third at 2.36 (Pike *et al.*, 1993).

The use of stock market value as an output indicator has a major advantage over other financial measures. Other indicators, such as profits or return on investment, are likely to reflect the effect of innovation only slowly. In contrast, developments which cause the market to re-evaluate the future output of the firm should be recorded immediately. The simplest market value model assumes that the market value of the firm is proportional to its physical, or tangible, capital and intangible capital. This can be written as

$$V = q(A + gK) = qA(1 + gK/A),$$

where V is the market value of the firm, A is the current replacement cost of its tangible assets, K is its level of intangible assets, g is its relative shadow price, and q is the current premium or discount of market value over the replacement cost of tangible assets. The contribution of innovation to the value of the firm, net of expected dividend and investment policy, can be written as the sum of three components:

$$qV = w + n + u,$$

where q is the rate of return on stock holding, V is the total market value of the firm's assets, w corresponds to the change in the firm's R&D position arising from news associated with current patent applications, n reflects a re-valuations of past patents and u reflects all other sources of fluctuations in the value of the firm.

Research suggests a significant, independent effect of patents on the market value of firms, beyond the R&D expenditure, but fluctuations in patents account for only around 1% of the total fluctuations in market value. Griliches *et al.* (1991) examined the relationship between patents and the market value of the firm and found that with the exception of the pharmaceutical industry, changes in market value due to changes in the patent rate were not significant. Product announcements may be a more generic indicator of product innovation. A benefit of using product announcements as a measure of market innovation is that it lends itself to an event-study methodology to link product announcements with the market value of a firm. This is an extension of the rational expectations/efficient market assumptions of financial economics, that is, the share prices in an efficient stock market will instantaneously reflect all available information on the firm. For example, a study (Chaney, Devinney & Winer, 1991) of more than 1,000 product announcements in the *Wall Street Journal* found that these had a positive effect on the share price of the originating firm. The impact of the announcement on share price will depend on two factors: first, an assessment of the probability of success of the new product; second, an evaluation of the level of future earnings from the product.

The study found that firms introducing new products accrue around 0.75% excess market return over three days, beginning one day before the formal announcement. The average value of each new product announcement was found to be $26 million (in 1972 dollars). Of course, the precise return and value of each product announcement depends on the industry sectors: the highest returns were found to be in food, printing, chemicals and pharmaceuticals, computers, photographic equipment and durable goods. Excess returns due to new product announcements suggest that past and current accounting data have little predictive value. However, the P/E ratio may be a better predictor. The study found that the average P/E ratio of the firms making new product announcements was almost twice that of the firms which made no new product announcements (Table 5.2). This implies that the stock market is valuing the long-term stream of future earnings generated by the innovative firms at a much higher rate than the non-innovators.

So far, little attempt has been made to relate innovation to company performance. The PIMS (Profit Impact of Market Strategy) database attempts to do this. PIMS was established in 1972. Since then, some 3,000 business units representing 450 companies have contributed data. For each business unit PIMS collects data on market conditions,

Table 5.2. Firms making new product announcements versus non-announcers.

	Total Expenditure ($m)	
	Firms Announcing New Products	Firms Not Announcing New Products
Asset	532.57	95.84
Sales	2119.68	467.88
Advertising	45.58	6.39
R&D	56.50	11.55
Capital exp.	178.77	32.24
P/E	x15.82	x7.95

Source: Derived from Chaney, Devinney & Winer (1991).

competitive position and financial and operating performance. The measure of performance used in each case is profit as a percentage of sales (that is, profit margin or return on sales — ROS) and profit as a percentage of investment (return on investment — ROI). Of the two measures, is superior to ROS as it relates results to the resources used to achieve them. By analysing such data using multiple regression, PIMS attempts to identify common patterns of relationships between different factors. The factors listed in Table 5.3 explain about 40% of the difference in performance between businesses. A more complete statistical model, which includes market and other conditions, can explain over 70% of the difference.

The product life cycle model suggests several measures of market characteristics:

(i) The age of products, that is, how long ago the product were developed.

(ii) The stage in the life cycle, that is, introduction, growth, maturity or decline.

(iii) The real rate of growth of the market, that is, excluding price inflation.

Table 5.3. Measures of strategy dimensions and impact on performance.

Strategy Dimension Measure		Impact on Roi/Ros
Competitive position	Market share	Positive
Product policy	Relative quality	Positive
	New products % sales	Negative
Marketing	Marketing as % sales	Negative
Investment	Plant % sales	Negative
	Newness of plant	Positive
	Labour productivity	Positive
	Inventory %sales	Negative
Vertical integration	Value added % sales	Positive
Research & development	R&D as % of sales	Negative

Source: Derived from Buzell & Gale (1987).

Generally, profitability declines as the market evolves over time for a number of reasons. First, product and service differentiation tend to be reduced. Second, competition tends to shift to price and rates of return fall. Third, at least in the manufacturing and production sectors, capital intensity tends to increase, driving returns down even further. More specifically, the real rate of market growth is associated with profitability. At the extremes, a real annual rate of growth of 10% or more has a ROI four points higher than markets declining at rates of 5% or more. High rates of market growth are associated with:

 (i) High gross margins.
 (ii) High marketing costs.
(iii) Rising productivity.
(iv) Rising value added per employee.
 (v) Rising investment.
(vi) Low or negative case flow.

Market differentiation measures the degree to which all competitors differ from one another across a market. Therefore, market differentiation is related to market segmentation and is a measure of market attractiveness. Customers in different market segments will value different product attributes. The joint effect of relative quality and market differentiation is significant. Markets in which there is little differentiation and no significant difference in the relative quality of competitors are characterised by low returns. High relative quality is a strong predictor of high profitability in any market conditions. Nevertheless, a niche business may achieve high returns in a market with high differentiation without high relative quality. A combination of both high market differentiation and high perceived relative quality yields very high ROI, typically in excess of 30%.

The importance of market share varies with industry. Intuition would suggest that share would be most important in capital-intensive manufacturing and production industries, where economies of scale are required. However, PIMS suggests that market share has a much stronger impact on profitability in innovative sectors, that is, those industries characterised by high R&D and/or marketing expenditure. For the R&D and marketing-intensive businesses, the ROI of the market leader is on average 26% points higher than the average small share business. In the manufacturing-intensive businesses, the corresponding difference is only 12 points. This suggests that scale effects are more important in R&D and marketing than in manufacturing.

It appears that the same factors which affect short-term ROI have a similar effect on long-term value enhancement. However, there are some important differences between factors which affect performance over the short- and long-term. These factors are rate of new product introduction, R&D expenditure and marketing expenditure. All three factors are central to innovation and long-term performance, but may depress performance in the short run. As shown earlier, high rates of product introduction and high expenditure on R&D and marketing all reduce ROI in the short run. However, all three factors are positively related to the long-term value enhancement of the business.

Towards a Synthesis of Measures

There are three difficulties in constructing a model of the effects of innovation on the financial performance of the firm.

First, at the firm level, the relationships between inputs and outputs is much weaker than at the industry level. The weakness in the relationship may be caused simply by the random unpredictability of innovation. If this were the case, then firms spending more on inputs could be said to be more innovative in a probabilistic sense even if they did not actually innovate strongly. However, if firms differ in their technological opportunities, it may not make sense for one firm to innovate more than another — it would mean a misallocation of resources. Even if spillover was believed to be particularly strong so that innovation was likely to be sub-optimal in general, it would not be clear, without looking at the specifics of a firm, whether it was over- or under-investing in R&D. Any comparison must, therefore, be across homogenous firms and this may be difficult to arrange.

Secondly, the reporting behaviour of firms may change in respect of any variable that is monitored to be used in an index of innovation. This reflects the so-called "Goodhart" law phenomenon whereby monetary indicators devised by the government became subverted as behaviour changed in response to measurement.

Thirdly, an objective of the indicators may be to influence financial markets and lending behaviour. However, these markets at present give a lot of attention to the management and efficiency of technological inputs which are assessed almost entirely by track record. It is not clear that any index of innovation activity is likely to supplant this. Furthermore, financial markets will concern themselves only with the gain appropriable by the firm itself.

As noted earlier, it is convenient to conceptualise innovation as a set of outputs responding to inputs — the linear model. We fully appreciate the limitations of this model from both a theoretical and an empirical perspective (see, for example, Tidd *et al.*, 2005), but it allows technological, market and financial indicators to be incorporated in the scoreboard.

To help assess the relative perceived importance of the various measures available, we consulted 25 organisations and, where possible, at the level of the chief executive or other person responsible for assessing the company's performance. The scope of consultation was sufficiently broad to include all the relevant communities: industry, finance, media and academia. We found that there was general support for better measures of innovation and its contribution to financial performance. Managers frequently linked innovation with the broader issue of competitiveness, which they associated with a range of non-price factors, such as product quality and product differentiation. Therefore, few of the practitioners we consulted were interested in improved measures of technological inputs, such as R&D expenditure, capital expenditure or patent activity. Rather, there is a demand for measures of the *efficiency* and *effectiveness* of the innovation process: efficiency in the sense of how well companies translate technological and commercial inputs into new products, processes and services; effectiveness in the sense of how successful such innovations are in the market and their contribution to financial performance.

We have chosen to use expenditure on research and development and capital investment as indicators of technological innovation and inputs into the innovation process. The ratio of research and development to sales is a proxy for product innovation, and the ratio of capital expenditure to sales is a proxy for process innovation. Despite their limitations, both measures are well-understood by both academics and managers. Data on patents have not been included in the trial Scoreboard, but may feature in the final version. Research suggests a significant independent effect of patents on the market value of firms, beyond the R&D expenditure, but fluctuations in patents account for only around 1% of the total fluctuations in market value. In addition, there is the practical problem that data on UK patents are not as accessible as data on US patent activity.

Product announcements made in trade and industry journals are included to provide a better indicator of innovation outputs at the firm level. As noted earlier, this approach has three advantages over company surveys. First, data can be collected without contacting companies. This reduces the resources required and places no additional burden on industry. Second, data can be collected relatively cheaply by scanning trade journals and databases. Third, the data set can be extended into the past to allow comparisons over time. The main drawback of this approach is that it fails to capture process innovations as few firms choose to make public announcements of their process innovations. However, the Scoreboard does include data on capital expenditure, which may act as a proxy for investment in process innovation.

Clearly, it is not sufficient to simply count new product announcements. It is necessary to classify and weight the raw data to get a better idea of the relative importance of the innovations. In this pilot study, we were not able to adopt the method of classification proposed by Kleinknecht and Reijnen (1993) and used by Coombs *et al.* (1994) and others. For the purpose of the feasibility study product announcements were extracted from the Predicasts *F&S Index* database of 1,000 journals. However, in most cases, the database does not abstract sufficient information to classify the innovation by type and complexity. Future work will be based on more detailed product announcements received direct from the companies.

To give an idea of the potential of product announcement data, we interrogated the Predicasts *F&S Index plus Text* database. This commercial database contains abstracts compiled from 1,0000 trade and industry journals worldwide. More importantly, it allows analysis by company, country, product and event. Products are classified down to a seven-digit level. For example,

36	Electrical & Electronic equipment
365	Consumer electronics
3651	Audio & TV equipment
36511	Radios
365111	Household radios
3651111	Table radios

Events include market information, people, resources, management procedures and products and processes. Events are identified by a single-digit code and sub classes, by two digits:

3	Products & processes
30	Products dictionaries
31	Science & research
32	Manufacturing processes
33	Products design & development
34	Product specification
35	Product

For the purpose of the trial Scoreboard, event code 33 — Product Design & Development — was used to identify product announcements. The initial search revealed more than 20,000 entries in the year examined. By restricting the search to the 15 sample companies, the number of citations were reduced to a manageable level. The raw data were checked for errors and duplications, which reduced the total number of recorded new product announcements to 228. In most cases, the database provided an abstract of the original article, but these were found to be insufficient to determine the type and complexity of the innovation.

The trial Innovation Scoreboard also includes three financial indicators of innovation: value added, price-to-earnings multiple and the ratio of market to book value. We included value added because of the emphasis managers and recent management texts place on it as a key measure of corporate performance (Kay, 1993). In addition, intuitively we would expect some relationship between innovation and value added. We chose the price to earnings multiple (P/E) because it remains one of the most common measures of stock market performance. It also reflects future potential rather than past performance. The other financial indicator included is the market/book (M/B) value. The average ratio of market value to book value would appear to be some measure of the long-term innovative potential of a company. The reasoning behind this is that the difference between the two methods of company valuation represents the contribution of future earnings above and beyond th tangible assets. This element of "goodwill" can be substantial and may be a useful proxy for innovativeness. The trial Scoreboard shown in Table 5.4 includes indicators of technological, market and financial

Table 5.4. An innovation scoreboard.

	R&D/ Sales[1]	Capex/ Sales[2]	R&D/ Value Added[2]	Value Added[2]/ Sales	New Prod Count[3]	R&D mil/ New Prod[3]	Sales mil/ New Prod[3]	Price/ Earnings[2]	Market/ Book[2]
1. Chemical									
Chem. A	5.4	6.8	39.6	15.8	63	10.3	191	24.8	1.2
Chem. B	2.9	10.9	6.8	38.4	7	11.6	462	15.9	2.4
Chem. C	1.9	5.6	6.2	30.7	12	3.1	171	12.2	3.4
Chem. D	2.8	6.9	36.6	34.8	2	18.9	971	21.5	3.9
Chem. E	1.2	16.4	3.7	42.3	1	7.2	254	20.3	5.5
Chem. F	1.7	4.6	5.7	29.4	2	3.0	261	19.1	2.9
Chem. G	1.6	10.0	5.3	28.7	1	5.2	328	16.4	1.7
Chem. H	2.2	3.4	6.2	34.9	0	n.a	n.a	11.9	5.4
2. Electrical									
Elec. A	7.2	3.5	17.6	42.2	55	7.6	102	17.2	2.7
Elec. B	4.2	3.8	13.4	42.7	10	7.6	127	11.5	1.3
Elec. C	0.7	10.2	1.8	28.2	23	1.1	194	23.4	5.5
Elec. D	3.2	2.9	5.2	61.0	3	4.4	139	25.1	4.4
Elec. E	5.0	4.6	13.7	35.9	2	6.2	126	60.6	4.8
Elec. F	8.7	2.9	14.1	47.8	3	3.4	40	14.7	9.4
Elec. G	3.4	7.2	6.3	53.4	0	n.a	n.a	23.7	6.8
Elec. H	7.8	3.3	20.3	39.8	3	2.7	34	21.6	2.9
3. Engineering									
Eng. A	5.7	4.4	8.0	51.2	0	n.a	n.a	20.2	5.0
Eng. B	3.4	4.1	7.1	48.0	8	4.9	144	28.2	6.6
Eng. C	1.1	5.4	57.1	39.7	10	9.3	977	21.3	6.6
Eng. D	3.3	3.6	9.8	34.1	2	12.0	360	n.a	3.2
Eng. E	1.8	5.5	5.8	30.8	2	10.1	570	31.9	3.1
Eng. F	1.2	3.2	2.9	42.3	1	12.8	1035	19.8	2.3
Eng. G	1.8	5.9	4.1	43.2	0	n.a	n.a	19.2	3.6
Eng. H	1.2	1.5	3.8	30.8	13	0.8	73	n.a	1.4
4. Food and drink									
Food A	0.9	4.5	8.3	22.6	18	25.6	1372	16.5	1.0
Food B	0.6	5.2	2.1	30.1	3	5.9	934	22.4	1.8
Food C	0.4	5.7	1.2	29.4	5	2.4	674	18.3	1.9
Food D	0.4	3.3	1.7	25.6	0	n.a	n.a	n.a	2.0
Food E	0.4	1.5	3.3	12.1	1	13.4	3395	35.7	2.6
Food F	0.2	2.3	1.2	20.5	0	n.a	n.a	12.8	n.a
Food G	0.2	1.7	2.3	9.9	0	n.a	n.a	14.2	n.a
Food H	1.2		n.a		0	n.a	n.a	n.a	2.1

Table 5.4 (*Continued*)

	R&D/ Sales[1]	Capex/ Sales[2]	R&D/ Value Added[2]	Value Added[2]/ Sales	New Prod Count[3]	R&D mil/ New Prod[3]	Sales mil/ New Prod[3]	Price/ Earnings[2]	Market/ Book[2]
5. Services									
Service A	n.a	12.8	n.a	58.3	2	n.a	161	n.a	1.5
Service B	n.a	9.7	n.a	50.9	9	n.a	625	38.1	1.8
Service C	n.a	n.a	n.a	11.1	3	n.a	2928	24.0	2.4
Service D	n.a	n.a	n.a	24.3	8	n.a	1348	n.a	2.0
Service E	n.a	n.a	n.a	39.3	7	n.a	853	19.6	2.6
Service F	n.a	n.a	n.a	n.a	2	n.a	252	n.a	n.a
Service G	n.a	n.a	n.a	4.1	1	n.a	2818	31.2	n.a
Service H	n.a	n.a	n.a	33.5	2	n.a	1145	n.a	2.1

[1]From 1993 UK R&D Scoreboard.
[2]Derived from Datastream and accounts.
[3]Derived from Predicasts database.

Source: Tidd, J., Driver, C. & Saunders, P. (1996).

performance for 40 companies, representing five different sectors. The companies were chosen to provide a range of R&D intensity in each of the five sectors. Analysis of the data confirms the findings of previous research, but it also reveals relationships which warrant further study.

The data confirm that expenditure on research and development, as a proportion of sales, has a significant positive effect on value added (regression not shown) and the number of new product announcements made (Table 5.5). This suggests that research and development activities contribute both to increasing the number of new products introduced as well as their value. The use of sales revenue as a proxy for firm size indicates that the number of new product announcements made may also be a function of the size of the firm. This finding is consistent with the work of Devinney (1993) and Chaney *et al.* (1991). Absolute expenditure on research and development also has a significant positive effect on the number of new product announcements (third column in Table 5.5). The introduction of a term to represent the interaction

Table 5.5. Regression analysis of new product announcements.

Dependent Variable: Number of New Product Announcements

	(1)	(2)	(3)
Intercept	−7.33	−3.54	1.50
	(−1.33)	(−0.99)	(1.38)
Sales	0.002***	0.002***	—
	(3.59)	(3.63)	
R&D/Sales	2.72***	2.60***	—
	(2.82)	(2.80)	
Capex/Sales	0.65	—	—
		(0.93)	
R&D	—	—	0.00131***
			(7.53)
R&D*Sales	—	—	−0.0000003*
			(−1.91)
N^1	32	32	32
R^2	0.40	0.39	0.87
Mean	8.06	7.81	7.81
S.E. of regression	12.02	11.78	5.51

*$p < 0.10$
**$p < 0.05$
***$p < 0.01$
[1]The number of observations were reduced as data on R&D expenditure were not available for all firms.

Source: Tidd, J., Driver, C. & Saunders, P. (1996).

of research and development with sales indicates diminishing efficiency with firm size (fourth column). In short, larger firms make more product announcements, but not in proportion to their size. This is consistent with the findings of Jensen's (1987) study of new chemical entities in the pharmaceutical industry. The inclusion of industry dummy variables had no significant effect. This is something of a surprise given the importance of technological opportunity, but firm size may proxy to the industry effect.

Table 5.6 explores the relationship between various inputs and market
-to-book value. Three variants on the relationship are reported, with
the highest R^2 obtained for the specification in the third column. First,
the data confirm that research and development, as a percentage of
sales, has a significant positive effect on the market-to-book value. This
supports the findings of previous work (Sciteb/CBI, 1991). The results
suggest that the financial markets do value expenditure on research and
development. The coefficient of about 0.3 on R&D/Sales may be used
to estimate an elasticity of the dependent variable at the mean value

Table 5.6. Regression analysis of market to book value.

Dependent Variable: Market/Book Value			
	(1)	(2)	(3)
Intercept	2.04	2.54	3.10
	(2.13)	(4.38)	(5.12)
R&D/sales	0.33*	0.33**	0.29*
	(1.97)	(2.13)	(1.92)
Capex/sales	0.12	—	—
	(1.02)		
New prod/R&D	—	10.91*	9.35*
		(1.88)	(1.70)
Sales	—	—	−0.001**
			(2.12)
N^1	29	29	29
R^2	0.14	0.21	0.33
Mean	3.63	3.63	3.63
S.E. of regression	1.97	1.88	1.76

* $p < 0.10$
** $p < 0.05$
*** $p < 0.01$

[1] The number of observations were reduced due to the
absence of data on expenditure on R&D and capital
expenditure.

Source: Tidd, J., Driver, C. & Saunders, P. (1996).

of R&D/Sales of 2.9. A 1% rise in R&D/Sales would translate into a 0.08% rise in the market to book value. This suggests that the market may somewhat undervalue R&D expenditure, but a larger sample would be needed to confirm this result. Secondly, ths use of the ratio of new product announcements to absolute R&D as a proxy for research efficiency indicates that the efficiency of research also has a significant positive affect on the market-to-book value. This suggests that the market values the past *efficiency* of research and development (that is, track record), as well as the *expenditure* on research and development. Clearly, this analysis does not take into account the time lag between research and product launch. Nevertheless, product announcements may be a useful indicator of research productivity in those cases where research expenditure is relatively stable, such as the automotive and chemical industries, or where product development cycles are short, such as the electronics and food industries. In other cases, the effect of lags would need to be incorporated.

Conclusions

In this chapter, we presented the results of a study on the feasibility of developing an Innovation Scoreboard to measure and track the performance of companies based on data in the public domain. The statistical relationships identified suggest that there is sufficient empirical support to develop such an Innovation Scoreboard. However, two aspects demand further development.

First, a more detailed model of the drivers of innovation in different circumstances must be developed. At present, the effect of factors such as the size of the firm, sector and market structure are ill-understood. Our analysis confirms that both expenditure on research and development and the number of new product announcements increase with firm size. However, there appears to be diminishing returns to scale. Previous research suggests that the sector has a significant effect on the firm, but the fact that weaker relationships between outputs and inputs are observed at the firm level, rather than at the industry level, suggests that there is a lot of variability in the productivity of technological inputs, and that there may be some point in studying the particular conditions under which the inputs are used most effectively. Research suggests at least three explanatory sets of reasons: scale, technological opportunity and management. Scale has received a disproportionate amount of attention in the literature, although more recent studies have begun to examine technological opportunity (Geroski, 1994). However, there is still a need to unravel the effect of *technological* opportunity, essentially a supply-side factor, and *market* opportunity, essentially a demand-side factor. In addition, the effect of different organisational structures and processes needs to be incorporated into our model.

Second, the quality of data on new product and service announcements must be improved. A number of problems remain with the use of data on product announcements. The first and most fundamental shortcoming is that product announcements do not capture process or organisational innovations. It is difficult, if not impossible, to capture such innovations using data in the public domain. The collection of primary data from firms, as used by PIMS (Buzell & Gale, 1987) and other benchmarking methodologies, would appear to be the only option. Moreover, although analysis of product announcements does not capture all forms of innovation, we hope we have demonstrated that it represents an important addition to the existing indicators of innovation, such as R&D and patents. Of particular benefit is the ability to capture product differentiation and service innovations.

The more practical problem is the collection of sufficient data to ensure that all product announcements are captured. For example, there are more than 4,000 specialist trade and industry publications in the UK. For the purpose of the feasibility study, product announcements were extracted from the Predicasts F&S Index database of 1000 journals. However, in most cases, existing commercial databases do not abstract sufficient information to classify the innovation by type and complexity. More robust sources of data will be necessary for the Innovation Scoreboard. Thus, it may be necessary to restrict the search to selected journals and a representative sample of UK companies. However, the quantity of data is likely to present less of a problem than the quality. Specifically, the editorial policy of the specialist press is likely to be influenced by factors other than the technical merit of an innovation, such as advertising revenue or company sponsorship. For these reasons, it may be preferable to short-circuit the specialist publications and, instead, receive announcement direct from companies. Therefore we are currently developing a database of product announcements made by UK companies based on their press releases. Combined with data on research and development, patents and financial performance, this should provide further insights into the links between innovation and firm performance.

Chapter 6

Building Knowledge Management Capabilities for Innovation Projects[*]

DAVID TRANFIELD, MALCOLM YOUNG,
DAVID PARTINGTON, JOHN BESSANT
AND JONATHAN SAPSED

Background — Innovation and Strategic Advantage

Innovation is widely recognised as a core renewal process within organisations. Unless managers continuously look for ways to change or at least improve offerings (product/service innovation) or create and deliver those offerings (process innovation), organisations risk becoming increasingly vulnerable to hostile and turbulent environments (Bowen, 1994). For this reason, growing attention has been paid to the challenge of innovation management in trying to understand the generic and firm-specific issues surrounding the problem of dealing with this challenge (Tidd *et al.*, 2005). A number of issues related to this have emerged from previous research:

[*]This chapter results from EPSRC Grant GR/M72869, Teamworking for Knowledge Management: Building Capabilities in Complex Environments, Tranfield D. R., Bessant J., Partington D. First published as a paper, Knowledge Management Routines for Innovation projects: Developing an Hierarchical Model, *International Journal of Innovation Management*, 2003, 7(1), 27–50.

- Organisations need to be prepared for innovation — that is, to be capable of picking up signals about change threats and opportunities in internal and external environment, remain receptive to those signals as triggers for change, and be capable of processing their information content (Christenson, 1997; Utterback, 1994).
- Managers need to share an understanding of the nature of innovation, and in particular the way it operates as a process. Moving from a loosely articulated possible response to trigger signals through to an implemented and diffused innovation requires the creation of structures and procedures and the disposition of scarce resources within a series of time-based stages (Freeman, 1982; Van de Ven *et al.*, 1989; Rothwell, 1992).
- Organisations need to develop a strategic portfolio of innovation projects, covering the spectrum from incremental "do what we do better" improvements through to more radical "do different" options across both product and process innovation fields. These must be matched with the existing internal and accessible resources which the organisation can deploy (Tushman & O'Reilly, 1996; Day & Schoemaker, 2000; Hamel, 2000; Leifer, 2000).
- Central to this strategic process is the question of knowledge, particularly in terms of technologies, products, markets, etc. and the ways in which organisations can mobilise this knowledge (held in tacit as well as codified form) to create advantage through innovation (Nonaka, 1991; Leonard-Barton, 1995).

From these perspectives, a key management task is one of enabling and managing the knowledge creation and deployment processes associated with innovation. This development of "dynamic capability" has been highlighted by a number of writers who see the challenge as being more than the simple accumulation of technological competence. In their studies, Teece and Pisano suggested that firms demonstrating sustained competitive advantage exhibited "timely responsiveness and rapid product innovation, coupled with the management capability to effectively co-ordinate and redeploy internal and external competencies" (Teece & Pisano, 1994). A central feature of this model is its dynamic nature. Overall, the argument is that there is a need to create and deploy different responses to meet differing environmental challenges. The model also places emphasis on the conscious role which can be played in shaping and configuring the organisation and its competencies to meet these challenges, what Teece and Pisano term "managerial capability".

In other words, what distinguishes a firm and gives it competitive advantage is not so much its size or position nor its depth of knowledge (competence), but rather its ability to respond and lead in the continually shifting environment described above. In the dynamic capability model, three factors determine the strategic nature of the firm: its position, path and processes. Position refers to the current endowment of technology plus other assets such as relationships with key customers or suppliers, in other words what many writers call the "core competence", which must, in turn, be supported by the firm's specific "strategic architecture" (Kay, 1993; Prahalad & Hamel, 1994; Bogner *et al.*, 1999). Technological competence of this kind can be built in many ways, ranging from internal R&D (learning by experimenting) through to transferring technology, which emphasises acquiring solutions developed elsewhere and learning through a process of using. Such competence is firm specific, or, often, in the case of large firms, division-specific (Brown, 1998), because it results from a cumulative learning process and cannot easily be replicated through acquisition.

The second element, path, refers to the strategic direction which a firm chooses to follow. Again this is firm-specific but is also shaped by the prior experience and activity of the firm, the so-called technological trajectory (Dosi, 1982). This path-dependent view argues that whilst history matters strongly in influencing future search for new strategic opportunity, it also opens the firm up to the risk of doing "more of the same". In such cases, "core competencies" become "core rigidities" and constrain the firm from seeing and taking on new strategic directions (Leonard-Barton, 1992). This explanation is advanced by Christensen (1997) for the otherwise paradoxical observation that many highly successful firms fail in trying to move into new technological fields. Thus a key capability here is to see, and if necessary reframe, the emerging patterns of technological opportunity and environmental demand, and to follow or switch trajectories (Pavitt, 1990).

Processes are essentially concerned with the particular ways in which an individual organisation has learned to behave, and include the routines which characterise the "culture" of the organisation (Schein, 1984). How the firm searches for opportunities, how it hears and processes the signals from the environment about threats and opportunities, how it mobilises creativity and innovative behaviour amongst its employees, how it manages the learning and knowledge accumulation activities, are all activities made up of organisational routines. They may become embodied in particular structures or procedures but underpinning them is a set of organisational behaviour patterns which are highly firm-specific. They constitute the firm's problem-solving capability in dealing with the puzzles outlined above, and have strategic value because they are difficult to replicate. Routines of this kind evolve over time and cannot simply be copied (Nelson, 1991).

Our interest in this paper is to identify and understand how knowledge is managed to drive innovation within a variety of organisations and across a range of projects. In this sense, our aim was to investigate and understand those knowledge processes on which dynamic capability depended. Specifically, this paper reports on the development of a process model of innovation constructed from a synthesis of innovation literature from which we derived the overall conceptual framework, and knowledge management routines resulting from our fieldwork conducted across a variety of sectors.

The "D-R-N" Process Model of Innovation

Models of innovation take a number of forms, each of which is helpful in highlighting particular aspects and enabling better understanding and practice (Abernathy & Utterback, 1978; Van de Ven et al., 1989; Angle & Van de Ven, 1989; Rothwell, 1992; Jelinek & Litterer, 1994; Utterback, 1994; Dodgson & Rothwell, 1995; Bellon & Wittington, 1996; Pavitt, 2000; Tidd et al., 2005). For our purposes in this paper, we are interested in looking at innovation as a staged process within the firm. In dealing with the challenge of renewing products/processes, our research has identified three distinct phases of activity from the literature which we have termed discovery, realisation and nurture.

Discovery emphasises the need to scan and search environments (internal and external) and to pick up and process signals about potential innovation. These could be needs of various kinds, opportunities arising from research activities, regulative pressures, or the behaviour of competitors. In total they represent the bundle of stimuli to which the organisation must respond if it is to survive and grow (Millett & Honton, 1991; Coombs et al., 1992; Thomas, 1993; de Geus, 1996; Tidd et al., 2005).

The realisation phase is concerned with issues surrounding how the organisation can successfully implement the innovation, growing it from an idea through various stages of development to final launch as a new product or service in the external market place or a new process or method within the organisation. Realisation requires selecting from this set of potential triggers for innovation those activities to which the organisation will commit resources. Even the best-resourced organisation cannot do everything, so the challenge lies in resources activities which offer the best chance of developing a competitive edge (Adler, 1989; Dodgson, 1989; Roussel et al., 1991; Ford & Saren, 1996; Cooper, 2000; Tidd et al., 2005).

Nurturing results from the organisation having chosen an option. Here, organisations need to provide resources, developing (either by creating through R&D or acquiring through technology transfer) the means for exploration. This might be a simple matter of buying off-the-shelf or exploiting the results of research already carried out, or it might require extensive search to find the right resources. It involves not only codified knowledge formally embodied in technology, but also tacit knowledge in the surrounding social linkage which is needed to make the innovation work. The nurture phase involves maintaining and supporting the innovation through various improvements and also reflecting upon previous phases and reviewing experiences of success and failure in order to learn about how to manage the process better, and capture relevant knowledge from the experience. This learning creates the conditions for beginning the cycle again, a pattern which Rothwell and Gardiner (1984) term "re-innovation". Activities in this phase include learning through diffusion, and user-involvement in the innovation, as well as other learning effects (Arrow, 1962; Rosenberg, 1982; Rogers, 1984; von Hippel, 1988; Herstatt & von Hippel, 1992; Moore, 1999).

In different ways organisations build structures and procedures to enable progress through these phases, and there is enormous contingent variation depending on factors like firm size, sector, market, etc. Prescriptions for structuring the process abound, for example, in the area of product innovation management (Booz Allen & Hamilton, 1982). Many variations exist on this theme, for example, Cooper's (1994) work suggests a slightly extended view with "gates" between stages which permit management of the risks in the process. Similar models have been advanced for managing process innovation (Davenport, 1992).

Of course, in practice this apparently straightforward linear process rarely emerges. Most innovation is messier, involving false starts, recycling between stages, dead ends and jumps out of sequence, etc. Various authors have tried different metaphors, for example, seeing the process as a railway journey with the option of stopping at different stations, going into sidings or even, at times, going backwards, but most agree that there is still some sequence to the basic process (Van de Ven *et al.*, 1989).

Research Methodology

Unit of analysis — The organisational routine

Levitt and March describe routines as involving established sequences of actions for undertaking tasks enshrined in a mixture of technologies, formal procedures or strategies, and informal conventions or habits. Importantly, routines are seen as evolving in the light of experience that works. They become the mechanisms that "transmit the lessons of history" (Levitt & March, 1988). In this sense, routines have an existence independent of particular personnel. New members of the organisation learn them on arrival, and most routines survive the departure of individual organisational members. Routines have been argued to represent "effortful accomplishments", the more formal and codified aspects of organisational life, and also "automatic responses", the more uncodified or taken-as-given aspect (Pentland & Reuter, 1994). It has also been postulated that these routines have within them cognitive, behavioural and structural aspects (Tranfield & Smith, 1998) which are constantly being adapted and interpreted such that formal policy may not always reflect the current nature of the routine, as Augsdorfer points out in the case of 3M (Augsdorfer, 1996). Our purpose, therefore, was to identify and understand the various aspects of knowledge management activity prevalent in the innovation projects of the collaborating organisations, and by synthesising organisational practices across cases, investigate the possibility of developing a set of "generic routines" which might inform the theoretically derived D-R-N process model.

Approach

We adopted an inductive approach to the research programme, which we believed would be most likely to surface appropriate data. At the core of our approach we placed the fundamental principle that the key characteristics of an organisation would be revealed by identifying how managers and others allocate their scarce attention (March, 1998). We further surmised that within these characteristics we would discover their priority knowledge needs. These needs would initiate management action to find knowledge sources which would satisfy the needs. However, those same characteristics would also represent (internal) knowledge sources to meet other needs. Viewed holistically then, management action would scan both internal and external knowledge sources to satisfy knowledge needs (see Fig. 6.1). Finally, we made the fundamental assumption that the key knowledge management routines and practices

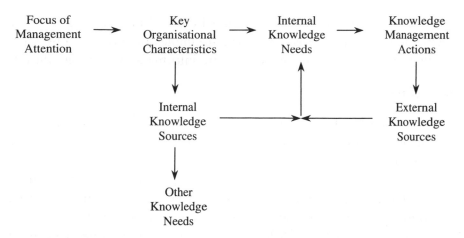

Fig. 6.1.   Sequential model of management attention and knowledge management action.

within an organisation would be revealed by the way in which informants described their actions.

Sample

We engaged in a programme of research which included a total of 11 dissimilar organisations across nine sectors: health, food packaging, whisky distillation and bottling, highway maintenance, software development, simulation, advanced electronics and aerospace. Our aim was to surface as large a spectrum of idiosyncratic activities as possible, then to make comparisons across sectors, to discover whether or not "generic routines" existed and if so to identify their nature and characteristics.

The innovations chosen for investigation were defined by four categories bounded by the dimensions, incremental-radical and product-process. Thus we investigated examples of radical product, radical process, incremental product and incremental process innovations. Because of the difficulties of definition, we chose not to differentiate between goods and service in the category of "product". In each of the four cases below, generic routines are exemplified by actual practices signified by specific activities. Each case ends with examples of broader contextual enabling and blocking activity which the informants saw as significant.

Data collection

Working towards what Partington refers to as a "grounded theory of management action" (Partington, 2000), and following the methodology of Glaser and Strauss (1967), we used as the prime data source in-depth open-ended interviews with key managers and operators in the collaborating organisations, supplemented by archival data in the form of written procedures, etc., and observation of operations. In all, data was collected from 123 interviews from all levels in the organisation. Interviews were of variable length but with a mean of approximately 1.5 hours. Where possible interviews were tape recorded and transcribed for analysis. Where this was not possible or inappropriate extensive field notes were made immediately after the interview. These were validated by respondents and also transcribed in order to become part of the final data set. We eschewed any attempt to render a fundamentally new definition of knowledge at the outset but, following the grounded theory concept, we chose to derive our final notion of knowledge mainly from our informants. During the fieldwork therefore, we chose to operate by the simple minimalist explication of knowledge as the capacity to act in a context. In the event, our data also agreed with the many explications of knowledge in common parlance which connote the ability to make decisions and to act on those decisions, both having contextual significance.

Validating the data

We started from the fundamental principle that the key characteristics of an organisation would be revealed by identifying how managers and others allocate their scarce attention (March, 1998). Our view was that these characteristics would be revealed by how respondents described their work. We surmised that collecting data in this way would reveal temporally significant knowledge needs. We used detailed analysis of in-depth open-ended interviews with key managers and operators in a broad cross-sector collaborator group, supplemented by theoretical archival and observational data. Throughout, by continually feeding-back our results and emerging theory to our collaborators both individually and in open workshops, we were able to achieve a high level of consensual validity (Gouldner, 1970). This practitioner-based approach allowed us to identify firm-specific knowledge management activities which, on closer examination, camouflaged more generic groupings of routines which exhibited clear, cross sector resonance.

Case 1 Radical Product Innovation — Computer-based Training Solutions

Innovation narrative

Organisation A (Org A, see Table 6.1) is a provider of customised simulators and training solutions to military and civilian markets. These high value, complex products require the integration of various engineering disciplines; software, electrical, electronic, mechanical as well as specialist knowledge of the applications such as image generation or user-end knowledge such as the behaviour of artillery in the field. The workflow is project-based and the firm has adopted a functional matrix organisation for familiar product lines, but deploys cross-functional project teams where applications are novel and more project management is required. Org A therefore has built up capabilities in new product areas different from their customary business. In the 1990s civil aviation companies ceased the practice of flying actual aeroplanes in the "type conversion" of their pilots. There was a considerable cost advantage in the use of flight simulators when compared with real flight training. Concurrently, lesser devices were being developed to fulfil some training requirements. In particular microcomputer-based training (CBT) was proving to be an effective and low-cost alternative to high-end customised simulators.

The trend towards PC-based solutions had lowered barriers to entry in the simulation and training industry, meaning that Org A faced competition from new entrants exploiting the relatively small investments

Table 6.1. Organisation A: Radical product innovation.

High-level Phase (Theoretically informed)	Generic Routine (Synthesised from data)	Organisational Activities (Empirically derived)
Discovery	Search	Establish trends through regular customer contact. Scan published information sources. Attend academic and industrial conferences. Specify responsibilities to staff.
	Capture	Incorporate trends and other data in working paper.
	Articulate	Circulate working paper to provoke discussion. Present ideas to key actors.
Realisation	Contextualise	Connect idea to invitation to tender for large MOD contract. Demonstrate need for change of mindset. Demonstrate primary computer based training (CBT) as solution to nature, scale and cost structure.
	Apply	Make customer training need analysis (TNA) a core contracting procedure. Match technology to need parsimoniously.
Nurture	Evaluate	Monitor customer satisfaction.
	Support	Recruit TNA specialists and educational psychologist to exploit novelty and diversification opportunities.
	Re-innovate	Create training needs and courseware department. Contribute to industrial standardisation.

needed for PC-based CBT. Increasingly, the lower cost solutions were proving attractive to military customers. Key individuals in the company believed that its people needed to move from a position of thinking that they provided simulators which were large, high-cost pieces of equipment, to a position where they provided solutions to training needs, involving whatever technologies were appropriate. This change of mindset has progressed to the extent that it is characterised here as a radical product innovation. The company now has a qualitatively different competence to support new product offerings that are of themselves quite different from its traditional products.

Enabling activities

The relatively small size of the customer base means that close relationships are maintained through regular face-to-face contact and through formal visits. Such regularity of contact and familiarity with the customer is helpful to become aware and apprehend new thinking about customer requirements. The company champions of CBT were helped in their cause by the fact that the company had produced prior work that they argued, was a form of CBT package. Champions could point to such work as effective computer based training of the type they were advocating. The area seemed less of a "brave new world" given these previous developments. The recruitment of an experienced technology champion from outside the company was seen as more efficacious than an insider in mobilising people to think seriously about the emerging trends. Other recruits were from backgrounds that were new and fresh to the company and bore no preconceptions. This was seen as a key complement to the body of industry specialists already in the firm.

Blocking activities

The overarching hindrance to this innovation was the culture of the industry and the company. Traditionally ITTs specified simulator equipment and technology, containing no guidance as to training needs. The company had therefore adopted this mindset over time, and it was difficult to change. The champions of CBT also had to challenge the idea that the existing software engineers in the firm could develop the Computer Based Training applications. In the early stages there was no general appreciation of the qualitatively different nature of what was proposed. Existing Quality Assurance procedures were inconsistent with the new Training Needs Analysis procedure and this required some time and effort to co-ordinate and implement.

Case 2 Radical Process Innovation — Reorganisation of Psychiatric Services

Innovation narrative

Organisation B (Org B, see Table 6.2) is a psychiatric unit within the NHS renowned for its innovative approach to issues of old-age psychiatry, which usually means patients over 60 years of age. Specifically the condition "dementia" is usually age related and indeed most evident in ages over 60. Services are therefore generally optimised for delivery to this age group. However, through continuous review of both parochial and more general information, Org B identified an unsatisfied need for

Table 6.2. Organisation B: Radical process innovation.

High-level Phase (Theoretically informed)	Generic Routine (Synthesised from data)	Organisational Activities (Empirically derived)
Discovery	Search	Track and share clinical experiences across departments. Scan professional information sources. Liaise with research facility.
	Capture	Make sense of information flow. Isolate inadequacies. Identify emerging realities.
	Articulate	Explore options in open forum. Challenge orthodoxy.
Realisation	Contextualise	Focus on demand not supply. Make community care the primary delivery mechanism. Prioritise work by need not departmental specialism. Compare needs of old and young.
	Apply	Reorganise social workers (ASW) and community psychiatric nurse (CPN) as integrated teams. Establish common resource pool. Appoint head of service. Make in-patient out-patient and

(*Continued*)

Table 6.2 (*Continued*)

		community care a continuum. Provide a "drop-in" facility.
Nurture	Evaluate	Establish a "research forum". Share experiences in open forum.
	Support	Co-locate staff. Amalgamate care report media. Provide professional and personal counselling across team.
	Re-innovate	Appoint knowledge and practice leaders in differentiated but complementary fields.

the provision of dementia related services to an emerging population of patients well under the age of 60, including some in their teens.

This led to the development of a range of in-patient, out-patient, community care and "drop-in" services which could span this enlarged age range by bringing expertise in dealing with old age dementia, the results of leading edge research and a highly innovative style to bear. This initiative currently stands as unique in the field of the provision of dementia services.

Enabling activities

The key enabler was a charismatic, maverick tendency in the lead clinician (consultant) and the willingness to develop service "out of the gaze" of the formal organisation. This has led to the development of open internal communications with high levels of informality. There is broad visionary sweep and a willingness to challenge health service orthodoxy.

Blocking activity

This unit works within an unharmonised Department of Health and Department of Social Security milieu. These departmental frictions (differentiated budgets, staff conditions, statutory requirements, etc.) coupled with hierarchical, command and control orthodoxy and an element of need blindness at high levels make progress labourious.

Case 3 Incremental Product Innovation — Use of Global Positioning System

Innovation narrative

Organisation C (Org C, see Table 6.3) is a wholly-owned subsidiary of a major construction group with a large in-house labour force. Org C provides road maintenance and management services to the Highways Agency and to several local authorities in the south and west of England. The company employs around 800 production staff and 200 support staff.

Table 6.3. Organisation C: Incremental product innovation.

High-level Phase (Theoretically informed)	Generic Routine (Synthesised from data)	Organisational Routine (Empirically derived)
Discovery	Search	Manage and facilitate exchange of ideas through cross-functional forums. Gain access to people known to think in different ways.
	Capture	Remain open to the genesis of new ideas. Develop ideas for presentation. Showcase ideas at divisional innovation forums.
	Articulate	Appoint champion to identify short- and long-term advantages of proposed innovation.
Realisation	Contextualise	Investigate and develop ideas in specific context. Prototype application in advance of formal launch.
	Apply	Develop operational model from prototype application. Launch initiative on limited geographical scale. Deploy initiative across operations.
Nurture	Evaluate	Reflect self-critically on process and application. Identify lessons learned. Identify modifications.
	Support	Encourage and publicise innovative applications.
	Re-innovate	Identify additional applications. Encourage alternative suggestions.

Road maintenance contracts are renewable, typically over a four-year term. Contracting practice in the sector has moved beyond pure short-term price considerations. There is a new and important emphasis on partnering with local authority clients and the provision of "best value". Technological and administrative innovations which support these aims present significant opportunities to demonstrate efficiency gains and other advantages to clients which their rivals in the contract renewal process cannot match. Innovations thus enable Org C to work towards continuity and a longer term prospect. A notable recent example of the innovative use of technology for mutual benefit is HiMaSSS (Highway Maintenance Satellite Support System). HiMaSSS is a vehicle-mounted system which uses differential Global Positioning System (GPS) technology interfaced with a communication link via mobile telephony. The system provides detailed, accurate records of the location and condition of client assets including street lighting, gullies and manholes, at the same time allowing geographical and temporal monitoring of road maintenance vehicles, and reducing paperwork.

HiMaSSS is an interesting case since it can be interpreted as both a product and a process innovation. It constituted a process innovation since it changed the ways in which the company operated in this particular task area, but it was also a product innovation since it involved adapting and reconfiguring an existing product on the market to suit a specific set of conditions for the firm.

Enabling activities

Org C had an understanding client, sympathetic to the fact that doing things differently might need some initial investment.

Blocking activities

There is a local government direct labour organisation tradition with no incentive to innovate exacerbated by the pressure of day-to-day work and the difficulty in finding energetic champions within the business.

Case 4 Incremental Process Innovation — Work Breakdown Structure

Innovation narrative

Organisation D (Org D, see Table 6.4) is a supplier of high-end technology screen displays and structures for a wide range of visualisation applications. These include corporate presentation and broadcasting, training devices such as simulators and a growing range of applications in virtual reality, which involve visualisation in education and engineering, as well as in entertainment. The firm is organised around three core cross-functional teams that specialise in specific product lines. Although

Table 6.4. Organisation D: Incremental process innovation.

High-level Phase *(Theoretically informed)*	Generic Routine *(Synthesised from data)*	Organisational Activities *(Empirically derived)*
Discovery	Search	Appoint development manager (DM) with specific search responsibilities. Develop product architecture to focus search.
	Capture	Match information to product architecture. Embody in work breakdown structure (WBS).
	Articulate	Publicise emerging WBS and iterate through formal and informal feedback.
Realisation	Contextualise	Pilot WBS in a specific project and adjust as necessary.
	Apply	Launch WBS. Establish (progressively) as standard procedure for all projects.
Nurture	Evaluate	Monitor (DM) use of WBS and amend as necessary.
	Support	Link WBS to enterprise resource planning (ERP).
	Re-innovate	Link to WBS and ERP through management information system (MIS). Encourage alternative applications.

this promotes a degree of standardisation, the workflow is project based and involves considerable customisation for each client. The firm has been growing at a steady rate of around 20% for 10 years and is entering a stage of consolidation and maturity, as distinct from its early period as an entrepreneurial start-up.

Managers thought that the firm needed more structure and control over its work processes. In its early days as a technology-centred start-up, there was little rigour and transparency in the projects. Project and team managers planned in different ways with no standard framework for comparison of data. As a result there was little understanding of where excess costs were incurred on projects and where efficiency gains were available. As part of a drive to improve profitability, the company decided to develop and implement a Work Breakdown Structure to apply across the organisation. The resulting structure is now used on every bid and on every project. This enables consistent booking to projects and measurable information on each part of the business process. The company knows the real cost structures of projects and this is reflect in much more accurate bids.

Enabling activities

The protracted period of consultation enabled broad involvement and agreement with the aims of the WBS. It ensured that all interested parties were compliant and contributing to the structure. This improved its accuracy and utility in projects. Another enabler was introducing the WBS concurrently with a Project Management software package, the adoption of each supported the other.

Blocking activities

The culture of Org D was primarily technology and engineering-centred, as opposed to project management and processes. People were not used to collecting data, and booking time and resources in all their activities. It is still taking time to implement the WBS comprehensively to operate as a matter of routine. A source of conflict in the process was the level of detail stipulated in the WBS, the concern of the PMDM and Directorate was that the level should be high enough to apply across all product teams, otherwise the benefits would be lost. Criticism was constructive throughout the process of developing the innovation. However, this was insisted on in the consultation process.

Discussion

Synthesising a process approach to managing knowledge for innovation

Achieving synthesis from the diverse data sets represented by the empirical data from the projects posed a challenge, for it is always problematic to generalise findings from a series of projects which are unique. Indeed, the organisations involved are unlikely to carry through such innovations again and therefore even within the confines of any of our collaborating partners, the opportunity to identify, articulate and codify specific behaviours remains limited. In order to ensure confidence in the generality of our findings, synthesis of data from our fieldwork required, therefore, an explicit and replicable methodology based on a transparent set of assumptions and philosophy. Here we were helped considerably by taking an action perspective on research synthesis.

In line with Pentland and Reuter's (1994) notion of "grammars of action", we made a detailed analysis of the reported data to isolate significant verbs (e.g., seek, select, shape, envision, advocate, champion, redefine) and the context within which they were expressed. In this way we were able to identify the organisational activities to which they referred. Where one verb could be used generically to cover a range of reported activities, we referred to this as "a generic routine". Hence we created "natural groupings" of verbs, labelling them appropriately and arriving at synthesis through harmonisation of the lists of verbs. Finally, we identified whether, where, and how the labelled groupings of "generic routines" aligned with the D-R-N framework. The identification of "generic routines"

Fig. 6.2. Hierarchical process model of knowledge management for innovation.

made the link between the theoretically informed high-level process model and the empirical data on idiosyncratic activity in the cases. As we will describe, what emerged were eight "generic routines", based on the knowledge management activities in the cases. These "generic routines" were labelled search, capture, articulate, contextualise, apply, evaluate, support and re-innovate (SCACAESR — see Fig. 6.2).

Definitions and descriptions of generic routines can be seen in Table 6.5, together with examples of specific knowledge management activities from the research data.

The innovation cases provided a ready and rich source of examples. As the four empirical examples given above indicate, organisations develop and enact a suite of superficially idiosyncratic routines and practices most relevant to the needs of their projects, retaining and developing those which confer advantage and discarding those which lack efficacy. These successful innovations were highly performative, based on the timely sharing (knowledge flows), rather than the secured custody (knowledge stocks), of organisational knowledge. However, even from this small sample, the idiosyncratic knowledge management activities exhibit common themes and purposes inherent

Table 6.5. Hierarchical process model linking innovation phase to knowledge management activities.

Phase in the Innovation Process	Generic Routines	Description	Examples of Detailed the Knowledge Management Activities
Discovery	Search	The passive and active means by which potential knowledge sources are scanned for items of interest	Active environmental scanning (technological, market, social, political, etc.) Active future scanning. Experiment — R&D, etc.
	Capture	The means by which knowledge search outcomes are internalised within the organization	Picking up relevant signals and communicating them within and across the organisation to relevant players
	Articulate	The means by which captured knowledge is given clear expression	Concept definition — What might we do? Strategic and operational planning cycles — From outline feasibility to detail operational plan
Realisation	Contextualise	The means by which articulated knowledge is placed in particular organisational contexts	Resource planning and procurement — Inside and outside the organisation Prototyping and other concept refining activitie. Early mobilisation across functions — Design for manufacture, assembly, quality, etc.
	Apply	The means by which contextualised knowledge is applied to organisational challenges	Project team mobilisation Project planning cycles Project implementation and modification —"Cycles of mutual adaptation" in technological, market, organisational domains Launch preparation and execution
Nurture	Evaluate	The means by which the efficacy of knowledge applications is assessed	Post-project review Market/user feedback Learning by using/making/ etc.

(Continued)

Table 6.5 (*Continued*)

Phase in the Innovation Process	Generic Routines	Description	Examples of Detailed the Knowledge Management Activities
	Support	The means by which knowledge applications are sustained over time	Feedback collection Incremental problem solving and debugging
	Re-innovate	The means by which knowledge and experience are re-applied elsewhere within the organisation	Pick up relevant signals to repeat the cycle Mobilise momentum for new cycle

in which lay the potential for them to be grouped into more generic categories. When taken together with the remainder of the empirical data (which yielded a further 24 case examples), this phenomenon became progressively more apparent. By detailed analysis of the data for each case, collapsing actions and practices into routines in the manner indicated in the example cases, we were able to identify generic routines which organisations enact, to a greater or lesser extent and with greater or lesser effectiveness, in managing organisational knowledge.

These generic routines represent a class which captures the fundamental essence of a spectrum of activity camouflaged by the superficial idiosyncrasy of particular projects and programmes. Such a taxonomy of processes represent a synthesis across the range of projects studied, for it is by using these "generic mechanisms" that innovation and improvement is delivered rather than by the projects themselves (Pawson, 2001).

There was evidence to suggest that there was sequential significance at both the phase (D-R-N) and routine (SCACAESR) levels. However, within each level were discrete, essential elements to be addressed. The relationship between these elements could be interpreted as thematic, in the musical sense of prominence or recurrence, and only contingently sequential (Scholes, 1974). It can therefore be more important to understand in which thematic category current activity is located, rather than being prescriptive about strict temporal sequence. Indeed, all informants agreed that they frequently iterated between the generic routines, without the need continually to re-initiate the process in toto, while driving innovations. This echoes the findings of Van der Ven *et al.* (1989) in their analysis of a wide range of innovation cases.

Knowledge management — A description and definition

Taken together, the outcomes of this research indicate that knowledge management is the process by which the capacity to act is facilitated or enhanced. By extension from our fundamental principle of the focus of management attention and action, this is achieved by the matching of knowledge sources to knowledge needs. This suggests that knowledge management is a performative competence which, for the most part, privileges the flow and sharing of knowledge over the custodial role of storage and security. In turn, knowledge and knowledge management are value rated by their contextual efficacy. Given these insights we can now propose a new description of knowledge management, that is:

> "The process by which the capacity to act is facilitated or enhanced, matching knowledge sources to knowledge needs, using performative competencies which privilege the flow and sharing of knowledge over simple custody, and which is value rated by its contextual efficacy."

Conclusions — Implications for Theory and Practice

In addition to this synthesised description, we believe that we have established a link between the theoretically-informed phases of knowledge management and the organisationally idiosyncratic knowledge management activities which can be represented by the hierarchical process model shown in Table. 6.5. This hierarchical process model has a number of implications for both theory and practice.

From a practitioner perspective, it offers a conceptual framework for knowledge management in innovation, a map of the territory rather than a prescriptive route. It offers managers a framework within which they can initially locate, and then subsequently monitor, their innovation activity. Second, it enables managers to audit their knowledge management processes, either off-line as a review of past procedures or on-line during a current innovation, to assess the presence or absence of routines, to exploit those at which they are adept and to improve on those at which they are less so. Third, this synthesis and generic model is both theoretically and empirically grounded in evidence from widely dissimilar organisations. It therefore provides a basis for cross sector transfer of learning and practice. It can, for example, be used to identify and develop communities of practice in similar knowledge management contexts which may transcend superficial organisational and project dissimilarities.

Finally, our work has implications for the understanding of the theory of innovation, particularly in project based environments. For example, in mass production environments, generic operational routines are relatively easy to identify and understand since there is sufficient repetition to enable learning and improvement. But work on project-based innovation, for example in complex systems, suggests that although each project may be unique, many projects share similar characteristics and can also be mapped on to a generic process model of the kind developed in this paper (Rush *et al.*, 1997). As mass production environments seek to use projects to "customise" to gain advantages of serviceability and tailoring, and "stranger" or "one-off" production environments try to ensure knowledge transfer, so project environments become increasingly popular forms of organisation. Developing a deeper understanding of such forms therefore has become a key academic task. Our work contributes by arguing the case for thinking in terms of routines which can be adapted, developed and crafted locally, but which are grounded in the repetition of common generic patterns. Investigating and understanding the form and nature of such patterns is required, if we are to understand both the efficacy of project based environments and the nature of innovation itself.

PART 3

TECHNOLOGICAL COMPETENCIES

Chapter 7

Technological Indicators of Performance

PARI PATEL

Introdution

The purpose of this paper is to review the considerable progress made in recent years to measure and understand the activities that generate technical change at the level of the firm. These activities are concerned with producing knowledge, the skills and experience necessary to create new products, and, processes and services which are now widely recognised as key factors both in economic growth and welfare at the national level and (more recently) in competitive performance at the firm level.

Since the beginning of the 1960s, there has been continued improvement in empirical understanding of the sources and patterns of technical change, especially at the level of the industrial sector and country. This reflects, in large part, the marked increase in resources devoted to the measurement of technological activities arising out of two very practical concerns. The first was the growing demand mainly from scientists, corporate managers and governments for more reliable information on the scientific and technological activities to which an increasing proportion of public, corporate and national resources were being allocated, often with the expressed intention of gaining competitive advantage. The second development has been in information technology, as a result of which major new possibilities for analysing scientific and technological activities are continuing to emerge.

However, it is only comparatively recently that progress has been made in measuring and analysing technological activities at the level of the firm. This has been partly the result of increasing awareness of the rapid growth in corporate expenditures on technology and related activities. In some cases, these exceed spending on investment in plant and equipment (Kodama, 1991). At the same time, there has been growing dissatisfaction with the way conventional theories and models treat the role of such activities in the modern business firm (Kay, 1979). Hence there is now a rapidly growing body of literature (both theoretical and practical), reviewed elsewhere in this book, concerned with analysing corporate competencies, of which technological activities are a major part.

The progress in the range, accuracy and availability of firm-level measures is due mainly to a mixture of public and private initiatives. The New York Stock Exchange made the public disclosure of R&D expenditures mandatory for quoted companies in the mid-1970s. Since then, *Business Week* has been publishing the results for the 600 largest US companies every year, and has recently started publishing comparisons of company patenting (*Business Week*, 1993). In the UK, the *Financial Times* publishes an annual "R&D Scoreboard" for British companies, but it also includes data for 300 of the world's largest R&D spenders. The initiatives by the US Patent Office at the beginning of the 1980's to computerise and disseminate information from patent records have also had a major impact. At the same time, private organisations have become a major source of information and analysis on patenting activities, particularly, the work of F. Narin and his colleagues (1987) at *Computer Horizons Inc.* in the USA.

The plan of this chapter is as follows. The next section contains a discussion of the main measures used together with their main strengths and weaknesses. In the third section, we review the state of our knowledge resulting from firm-level studies based on these data, which are grouped around three sets of issues:

(i) The impact of technological activities on corporate performance.
(ii) The relationship between firm size and technological performance.
(iii) The analyses of the nature and characteristics of firm-level technological competencies.

The last section highlights the conclusions and points to questions that remain, as yet, unanswered.

The Major Measures of Technological Activity

Table 7.1 lists the main measures of technological activities used in the various studies, their main strengths and weaknesses, as well as an indication of possible levels of comparison. The main message from the table and discussion below is that, in common with measures of most other important economic and social activities, there is not (and never will be) a single perfect or best measure of innovation.[1] Some indicators work well for certain classes of firm (for example, R&D for big chemical and electrical firms). Others work well for certain fields of technology (such as patents for mechanical technologies). Yet others for certain types of innovation outputs (such as product announcements for product innovations).

Research and Development (R&D)

The widely used R&D indicator is better at measuring technological activities in the science-based classes of technology (chemicals and electrical-electronic) than in the production-based and information-based classes (mechanical and software). As Freeman (1982) and Mowery and Rosenberg (1989) have pointed out, R&D activities have grown in importance as sources of technological change, following the

---

[1]For the most widely used indicator (GDP), there is very little consensus on how to measure output in service sectors which form a major part of the economy in most leading industrial countries.

Table 7.1. Strengths and weaknesses of measures of innovative activities.

Measure	Strengths	Weaknesses	Possible Levels of Comparison			
			Country	Industry	Tech Field	Firm
Research, and Development (R&D) activities	• Regular and recognised data on main source of technology	• Lacks detail (technical fields) • Strongly underestimates small firms, design, production engineering and software	√	√	X	√
Patents	• Regular detailed and long-term data • Compensates weaknesses of R&D statistics	• Uneven propensity to patent • Misses software (but now patentable in the US)	√	√	√	√
Significant innovations	• Direct measure of output	• Measure of significance • Cost of collection • Misses incremental changes	X	√	X	√
Innovation surveys	• Direct measure of output • Comprehensive coverage	• Variable definition of innovation • Cost	√	√	X	X
Product announcements	• Close to commercialisation	• Misses in-house process innovations and incremental product improvements	?	√	X	√

Table 7.1 (*Continued*)

Measure	Strengths	Weaknesses	Possible Levels of Comparison			
			Country	Industry	Tech Field	Firm
		• Possible manipulation by marketing and public relations				
Technical employees	• Measures tacit knowledge	• Lack of homogeneity of qualifications	X	√	√	√
Expert judgements	• Direct use of expertise	• Finding independent experts • Judgements beyond expertise	?	√	√	√

√ = Yes
X = No
? = Maybe

growing contribution of professionalised science (particularly chemistry and physics) to industrial technology and the spread of the functional organisational form, especially in the growing number of large firms. R&D has the following important limitations as a measure of inputs to technological activities:

First, it underestimates (mainly mechanical) technological activities related to production. This is because much technical change in production technologies takes place in and around the design, building and operation of complex capital goods and production systems. In such circumstances, technical change is generated in design offices and production engineering departments, as well as in R&D laboratories.

The second limitation of R&D statistics is that they capture only very imperfectly the development of technology in small firms, where technology-producing activities often do not have a separate functional and accounting identity (Kleinknecht, 1987). Nearly all manufacturing firms with more than 10,000 employees have R&D laboratories. Most with fewer than 1,000 employees do not (Pavitt *et al.*, 1989).

Third, R&D activities underestimate the development of (mainly software) technology related to information processing, in part because a proportion of such technology is developed outside R&D in Systems Departments; and in part because a growing proportion is developed by firms in the service sector, where the coverage of official R&D surveys is typically very weak.

Finally, the main practical difficulty with using R&D expenditure as a measure of firm-level competencies is that it cannot be classified according to areas of technology (or fields of knowledge), such as biotechnology or opto-electronics.

Patenting activity

Since they are a record of invention, many economists treat patents as an intermediate output of R&D activities. While this assumption has its potential uses, it also leads to puzzles and anomalies. Thus, the most sophisticated econometric analyses have detected no time lag between R&D "inputs" and patenting "outputs" at the level of the firm (Pakes and Griliches, 1984; Hall *et al.*, 1986). This raises the question of when patenting occurs in the R&D sequence — a subject which we have little precious direct empirical information. If it typically takes place early in the innovation process, it will be a poor measure of the output of development activities.

The main advantages of patent data are that they reflect the corporate capacity to generate change and improvement, are available at a detailed level of technology over long periods of time, are comprehensive in the sense that they cover small as well as large firms, and are used by practitioners themselves.[2] However, patent statistics also have their drawbacks.

First, there are major inter-sectoral differences in the relative importance of patenting in achieving its prime objective, namely, to act as a barrier to imitation. Thus, recent studies have shown patenting to be relatively unimportant in automobiles, but very important in pharmaceuticals (Arundel *et al.*, 1995; Levin *et al.*, 1987; Bertin & Wyatt, 1988). Moreover, patents do not yet fully measure technological activities in software since copyright laws are often used as the main means of protection against imitation (see Barton, 1993; Samuelson, 1993). Given this inter-sectoral variety in the propensity to patent the results of R&D, patent statistics are most reliable when normalised by sectoral totals.

Second, there are major differences among countries in the procedures and criteria for granting patents. For this reason, comparisons are most reliable when using international patenting or patenting in one country. The US patenting statistics are a particularly rich source of information, given its rigour and fairness of criteria and procedures for granting patents, the strong incentives for firms to get patent protection for world-class technology in the world's largest market (see Bertin & Wyatt, 1988), and the high quality of services provided by the US Patent Office. More recently, data from the European Patent Office are also becoming more readily available.

There is a further criticism of patenting as an indicator of technological activities which we think is not justified. We are not convinced that it is a drawback that patents differ greatly in their economic value (Schankerman & Pakes, 1986). The same is true of R&D projects (Freeman, 1982) for the same reasons. Technological activities involve

---

[2]See Aspden, H. (1983) Patent statistics as a measure of technological vitality, *World Patent Information*, 5, 170–173; Narin, F., E. Noma & R. Perry, (1987) Patents as indicators of corporate technological strength, *Research Policy*, 16, 143–155; *Business Week* (1993) The global patent race picks up speed, 9 August, 49–54.

cumulative learning under uncertainty. There are, therefore, bound to be failures, major successes and follow-up improvements, all of which are interdependent. Thus, we would expect both similar and large variations in the distribution of the value of R&D and patenting across all firms and countries.

Direct measurement of innovation

There are three different ways in which analysts have attempted to measure directly the inputs and outputs of innovative activities. First, they have attempted to measure directly the output of innovations through the identification of significant innovations and their sources (Freeman, 1971; Kleinman, 1975; Feinman & Fuentevilla, 1976; Townsend *et al.*, 1981). The main contribution of this tradition of analysis has been to identify important sources of innovation not satisfactorily captured by the R&D and patenting measures: in particular, the important contribution of small firms, suppliers and customers. Again, the relative importance of the various sources of innovation has been shown to vary systematically among sectors (Pavitt, 1984; Cesaratto & Mangano, 1993). The main disadvantage of this approach is that if undertaken comprehensively, it is labour-intensive and, therefore, costly and time-consuming. It also poses difficult conceptual and practical problems on how to classify the varying degrees of innovation, from the incremental, through the significant, to the epoch-making.

Second, more recently, analysts have begun to collect and analyse new product announcements in trade journals as a measure of innovation output (Acs & Audretsch, 1990; Kleinknecht & Bain, 1993; Coombs *et al.*, 1996; Santarelli & Piergiovanni, 1996; Tidd *et al.*, 1996). The main advantages of this approach are that it provides a direct indicator of the products which are close to commercialisation and the data can be collected relatively cheaply without contacting the company. Moreover, the data can be combined with other firm-level measures, such as R&D

and patenting, to expand the range of possible analyses that can be undertaken. The main drawback is that this method does not capture process innovations. Furthermore, for most purposes, the new product announcements need to be classified or weighted in some way to gauge their importance, a task which requires considerable technical expertise. The main contribution of this approach has been to show that small- and medium-sized firms account for a much higher share of technological activities than that shown by their share of total R&D (Acs & Audretsch, 1990; Kleinknecht & Bain, 1993).

The last method is the use of large-scale firm-level surveys undertaken in a number of EU countries to gather information about the inputs and outputs of innovative activities (OECD, 1992, 1996). These surveys provide a direct measure of the output of all the innovative activity within a firm: the proportion of total sales due to the introduction of new products. More importantly, they measure the total costs of innovation, including not just R&D, but design, testing, production engineering, start-up investment and marketing. They are comprehensive in coverage, including firms from all size classes and innovating, as well as non-innovating, firms. The major drawback of this approach is that it relies on the subjective assessment by a firm of its own level of innovative activities and the costs associated with them. This is most clearly illustrated by Calvert et al. (1996) who show that Spanish firms report, on average, a higher level of sales in new products across all industries compared to French firms. Another drawback of this approach is that there is no disclosure, at the firm-level, due to confidentiality requirements. Hence there is no possibility of combining these data with other firm-level indicators. The main contribution of these innovation surveys is that they have shown the importance of "non-R&D expenditures" in total technological activities and its variation across industries (Evangelista et al., 1997). Future improvements in the implementation of the surveys will open up many new possibilities of firm-level analyses, such as the relationship between the relative importance of internal and external sources of knowledge and innovation outputs.

Technical employees

Finally, another indirect measure used more recently is based on detailed statistics of the educational background of employees with higher educational qualifications in engineering and science. For example, using systematic data collected by the Swedish Association of Graduate Engineers, Jacobsson *et al.* (1995, 1996) have examined the fields of technological competencies of Swedish firms. The main advantages of this approach are that it captures tacit knowledge which, by definition, does not result in patents or publications, and it also captures "non-R&D" activities within large firms and the activities of small firms. The main conceptual problem is the assumption that there is a one-to-one correspondence between categories of scientists and engineers and categories of technological competencies. While this may hold for some cases, such as chemical engineers, it may not hold for others, such as physicists, who may be employed in solving a variety of different problems within a firm.

The main contribution of this approach has been to show that the level of technological diversity within firms is greater when using educational data than that shown when using patent data (Jacobsson *et al.*, 1996). In particular, educational data are much better at capturing the multi-disciplinary character of technological activities. However, the main drawback, at a practical level, is that such systematic information on the educational background of employees does not exist in other countries, especially those with a larger volume of scientists and engineers.

Technological Indicators of Performance: What We Know

In this section, we review some of the major firm-level studies which have used the indicators discussed above. The purpose is to highlight the methodology used and the main results rather than an attempt to present a comprehensive coverage of all the studies. In particular, we group our review around three sets of issues:

(i) The impact of technological activities on firm performance.
(ii) The relationship between firm size and technological performance.
(iii) The analysis the nature and characteristics of firm-level technological competencies.

A majority of the studies which address the first two sets of issues are based on R&D data, with the occasional use of patent data as additional information. More recently, data on new product announcements have been linked to firm performance by Tidd *et al.* (1996) and to firm size by Acs and Audretsch (1990), Kleinknecht *et al.* (1993), Coombs *et al.* (1996) and Santarelli and Piergiovanni (1996). The third group of studies are based on patent statistics and technical employees.

Impact of Technological Activities on Firm Performance

The studies concerned with measuring the impact of technological activities on some measure of firm performance were pioneered in the late 1970s and early 1980s by the group associated with Zvi Griliches[3] at the National Bureau of Economic Research (NBER) in the US in the 1980s. Amongst these majority are concerned with an econometric estimation of a production function (or cost function) using a measure of R&D capital stock as one of the independent variables, a smaller number are concerned with analysing the relationship between R&D and patenting and the stock market value of the firm. A small number of more recent studies have examined the relationship between ex-post profitability and technology. The main conclusion to be drawn from reviewing these studies is that although technological activities make a positive contribution to firm performance, it is very difficult to be precise about the magnitude of this contribution given the large element of "noise" in the data.

---

[3]See Griliches (1984) for a compilation of some of the early studies.

Production function approach

This approach consists of estimating a regression equation where the dependent variable is some measure of output — either sales[4] or value added — and the independent variables are labour (number of employees) and the measure of physical capital (plant and equipment) and "knowledge" capital, that is, a capital stock measure based on R&D expenditures. In some studies, this becomes a regression of labour productivity (sales or value added divided by the number of employees) on physical and R&D capital divided by the number of employees. In yet others, the relationship being tested that between the rate of growth of total factor productivity and R&D intensity. The aim of most of these studies is to arrive at a single estimate of the magnitude of the contribution of R&D to some measure of performance.

A thorough review of firm-level studies based on this approach is contained in Mairesse and Sassenou (1991). The majority are based on US firms and a smaller number on French and Japanese firms. There are a number of measurement problems involved in the estimations based on the production function approach. They include the following:

(i) A correct specification should have value added as the dependent variable. However, if sales are used instead, then materials need to be included in the list of independent variables. Usually, such data are not available (e.g. for US firms). Moreover, another serious measurement problem in the time series dimension is the lack of appropriate price indices to deflate sales or value added.

(ii) The construction of R&D capital stock by means of "perpetual inventory" method requires:

---

[4]If sales is used as the dependent variable, then some measure of materials need to be included in the list of independent variables.

(a) A long enough history of R&D expenditures.

(b) Appropriate R&D deflators.

(c) Some idea about a rate of depreciation.

In practice, each of these presents major measurement problems. These are avoided in some studies by using a specification that relates "total factor productivity" growth[5] directly to R&D intensity, with the coefficient on the latter being interpreted as a rate of return to R&D.

(iii) There needs to be a correction for double counting in the measures for capital and labour as they will include R&D equipment and R&D employees. Failure to do so will result in an underestimation of the contribution of R&D.

(iv) Given the discussion of inter-sectoral variability in R&D as a source of technology, the analysis needs to be sectorally based, which is the case in only some of the studies.

The main results of the studies reviewed in Mairesse and Sassenou (1991), together with the more recent work by Hall and Mairesse (1995, 1996) on US and French firms, can be summarised as follows.

Cross-sectional studies have shown that the elasticity of R&D capital, with respect to some measure of output, is between 0.05 and 0.20 (that is, a 1% increase in R&D capital stock increases sales or value added by between 0.05% and 0.20%), and statistically highly significant. Studies which report on sectoral results, such as Mairesse and Griliches (1984), show that the elasticity for the so-called science-based sectors is substantially greater than the average. However, the problem with some of the studies is that the reported estimates may be biased due to the omission of variables characterising firms or industries. Such biases may result in an overestimation of the value of the elasticity of R&D

---

[5]However, as Mairesse and Sassenou (1991) point out, such estimations are beset with problems of measurement and interpretation. For example, the construction of total factor productivity assumes that the data on the share of labour and capital in total output is readily available.

capital. Thus, in studies such as Mairesse and Cuneo (1985), the value of the R&D elasticity is reduced from 0.16 to 0.10 with the inclusion of industry-specific variables.

A number of studies use panel data (cross-sections over time) to include the influence of firm-specific characteristics by introducing firm-specific dummy variables or deviations of the variables from their individual firm means. It turns out that such regressions, using time series data, produce estimates of the elasticity of R&D capital which are much lower in magnitude (and, in some cases, close to zero) than those discussed above, and are also mostly statistically insignificant.

Finally, another interesting "stylised fact" emerges from the more recent work by Hall (1993b) and Mairesse and Hall (1996). By comparing their more recent estimates based on data for French and American firms in the 1980s to their earlier estimates based on data in the 1970s for the same countries, they show that the contribution of R&D to productivity has fallen in the 1980s compared to the 1960s and 1970s: from around 0.10–0.15 to 0.02. For US firms, Hall (1993b) shows that during this period (from 1970 to 1990), they increased the proportion of sales devoted to R&D. At the same time, the relative cost of R&D funds to these firms became lower with the introduction of R&D tax credit.

Market value approach

This approach is based on the idea that technological activities create "intangible capital" for the firm, which in turn generates future income and profits, and should show up in the valuation of the firm by the stock market. There are two types of studies based on this approach. The first examines the effect of changes in a firm's R&D or patenting on its stock market rate of return over time[6] (see Griliches et al., 1991;

---

[6]A variant on this is to examine the impact of public announcements on R&D expenditures on the change in the market value of the firm (see Chan et al., 1990).

Pakes, 1985). The second type of studies examine the relationship between market value and the value of all the other assets which belong to the firms, including a measure of R&D capital stock (see Hall, 1993a, 1993b).

The first set of studies use time series analysis to examine the dynamic relationship between patents, R&D expenditures and the stock market rate of return (measured as one period rate of return to holding a share of the firm). The idea is to examine how "unpredictable" changes in R&D and patenting are related to changes in the rate of return of firms. Thus, Pakes (1985) uses data for 120 US firms over a period of eight years (1968–85) to show that although there is a strong correlation between these three variables, very little of the variation in the stock market rate of return (only about 5%) has to do with the variations in the technology variables. Griliches *et al.* (1991), using a much larger sample of US firms (340 firms over the period 1973–80) and similar methodology, arrive at very similar conclusions. In particular, they emphasise that annual fluctuations in the number of patents account for a very small proportion of the variation in the market value of firms.

The second set of studies begin by specifying a "value function" of the firm, which is the sum of "physical" capital (mainly plant and equipment) and all the "intangible" assets that are valued by the market but are not included in the measured capital of the firm. The latter includes R&D capital (as defined above) as well as other factors, such as brand name and reputation, which are, in principal, not measured. The main problem with such analyses is that they *infer* the market's valuation of R&D capital and do not really *measure* it. Thus, any explanatory variable that is left out of the regression, but affects a firm's valuation and is correlated with R&D, will have its effects imputed to R&D.

Two major studies based on this approach are by Hall (1993a, 1993b) and use data on US firms from the 1960s to 1990. The dependent variable is the ratio of total market value (defined as debt plus equity) to the book value of physical assets (plant and equipment). The main independent variable is the R&D capital stock (as defined above), which is a proportion of the value of physical assets. Other variables included in some specifications are cash flow (as a measure of market power or profitability) and advertising expenditures.

In the cross-sectional dimension, the coefficient on the R&D variable is large and highly significant. It also explains a fair amount of variance in market value (Hall, 1993a). However, the most significant result of the two Hall studies is that estimating this coefficient in successive panels from 1970 to 1990 shows that its value declined very steeply during the 1980s: from around 1 in 1982 to 0.2 in 1990. This decline in the aggregate stock market value of R&D assets, relative to ordinary capital stock, is composed of two contrasting movements: an increase in the value of ordinary capital and a very steep decline in the absolute value of R&D assets. There are also major differences among industrial sectors: electrical-electronics (including computing) and instruments have seen the steepest decline; in chemicals, the relative valuation of R&D assets has risen; and in pharmaceuticals, it has remained high throughout. The implication of these results is that there has been a very high rate of obsolescence in technology-related assets in the US electronics and instrument industries, probably a result of rapid technological change.

More recently, a promising new avenue for future work has been opened up through a pilot study undertaken by Tidd *et al.* (1996). Using a sample of 40 UK companies, they link data on new product announcements and R&D expenditures to firm performance, as measured by the market-to-book value. Both technology variables have a positive and statistically significant effect on the ratio of market-to-book value.

Relationship between technology and profitability

A small number of studies have used regression techniques to measure the impact of technology on ex-post profitability. For example, Geroski *et al.* (1993) use matched data from company accounts and the SPRU

Innovation survey to examine this relationship for UK firms.[7] The dependent variable used is net profits before tax and interest payments as a proportion of sales. The list of independent variables include the number of innovations introduced as well as a number of industry-specific variables. They show that the number of innovations produced by a firm has a positive and statistically significant effect on its profitability, but, the effect is small. There are substantial "permanent" differences between the profitability of innovating and non-innovating firms which are not closely tied to the timing of the introduction of specific innovations. The profit margins of innovating firms are less sensitive to cyclical downturns than those of non-innovators.

Firm size and technological performance

Considerable progress has been made in the last 20 years in the conceptualisation of the relations between firm size and market structure on the one hand, and technological performance on the other. In particular, it has become more widely accepted that both are jointly determined by the degree of technological opportunity and appropriability (Dasgupta and Stiglitz, 1980; Nelson & Winter, 1982). These vary widely amongst sectors and explain most of the variance amongst them in market structure and the size distribution of innovating firms (Levin *et al.*, 1985; Geroski & Pomroy, 1990). Among other things, this has exposed the difficulty of isolating the influence of firm size and market structure on technological activities in cross-sectoral comparisons, where technological conditions vary greatly among industrial sectors.

At the same time, the last 20 years have shown that empirical results on the relationship between firm size and technology intensity are sensitive to the sample of firms and the measure used for technological activities. In the 1960s, an r-shaped relationship was established between

---

[7]They gather data for 721 large publicly quoted UK firms for the period 1972–83. Of these, 117 introduced at least one innovation.

technology intensity and size in large US firms, when patenting was used as an indicator of technological activities (Scherer, 1965): i.e. patent intensity increases more proportionately in smaller firms and less than proportionately in the largest ones. In the 1970s, systematic data on large US firms' R&D expenditures showed a linear relationship between technology intensity and size (Soete, 1979). In the 1980's, a U-shaped relationship was found — in UK firms covering all size categories — between size and technology intensity measured in terms of the number of significant innovations divided by employment (Pavitt et al., 1987): innovations per employee are highest in the smallest and largest firms.[8] Our own more recent work, which uses R&D and patent statistics for large (Fortune 500) firms, showed a linear relationship between firm size and the volume of technological activity (Patel & Pavitt, 1992).

At a more descriptive level, patent statistics also show that the relative importance of firms' technological activities in different size categories varies across product groups and technological fields (Patel & Pavitt, 1991). In broader terms, this means that large firms predominate in R&D-intensive sectors (chemicals, electrical-electronic and transport equipment) while small firms predominate in capital goods (machinery, processes, instruments and metal products).

Measuring and mapping technological competencies

The basic premise of the studies concerned with mapping and measuring firm-specific technological competencies is that they are major factors in explaining why firms are different, how they change over time, and whether or not they are capable of remaining competitive. There are two ways in which such competencies have been measured. The first uses patents granted in different technical fields for a given firm (Granstrand

---

[8]However, this may partly be a measurement error as some of the innovating units in this database were regarded as independent entities when, in fact, they were a part of large firms (see Tether et al., 1997).

et al., 1997; Patel & Pavitt, 1997; and Prencipe, 1997) and the second uses the different fields of educational qualifications of scientists and engineers employed by a firm (Jacobsson & Oskarsson, 1995); Jacobsson *et al.*, 1996). Most of the studies reviewed below are based on patent data and have focussed on the activities of large firms.

One of the main objectives of the research based on this approach is the measurement and analysis of the spread of firm-level technological competencies across different fields of technology (or technology diversification). Some analysts have explored the relationships between technology diversification and product diversification, growth of sales and of R&D (Oskarsson, 1993; Gambardella & Torrisi, 1998). Others have examined the extent to which firms are related to each other (both within the same industry and across different industries) in "technology space" in order to measure research "spillovers" (Jaffe, 1989). Narin and his colleagues (1987) have used these data for corporate and competitor analysis.

Characteristics of technological competencies

This section highlights our own systematic study of the technological activities of 440 of the world's largest firms classified according to one of 16 product groups (Granstrand *et al.*, 1997; Patel & Pavitt, 1997) and based on their US patenting activities, broken down into 34 technical fields. This shows that technological competencies have the following characteristics:

(i) They are typically *multi-field* with a substantial proportion of activities outside what would appear to be the core fields. For example:

    (a) *Elect./electronic firms* = ~34% outside broad elect./electronic fields, of which ~20% is in machinery.

    (b) *Chemical firms* = ~33% outside broad chemical fields, of which ~16% is in machinery.

    (c) *Automobile firms* = ~70% outside broad transport fields, of which ~46% is in machinery.

Thus, firms in all sectors are active in machinery technologies, where they often do not have a distinctive technological advantage, and where smaller firms are particularly active.

(ii) The range of technological competencies is broader than the range of products as shown in Table 7.2, which compares the number of firms with their principal activity in selected product groups with the number of firms active in their corresponding distinctive technologies. In all cases, the latter is considerably larger than the former.

Table 7.2. Number of active large firms in selected principal products, and in closely related technologies, 1985–90.

Principal Product	Number of Firms (Out of 440)	Technological Field (Out of 34)	Number of Active* Firms (Out of 440)
Computers	17	Calculators and computers, etc.	151
Electrical and electronic	56	Semiconductors	94
Instruments	21	Instruments and controls	288
Chemicals	66	Organic chemicals	190
Pharmaceuticals	25	Drugs and bioengineering	114
Mining and petroleum	31	Chemical processes	304
		Apparatus for chemical, food, etc.	234
Non-electrical machinery	58	General non-electrical industrial equipment	246
		Non-electrical specialised industrial equipment	241
		Metallurgical and metal working equipment	225
Automobiles	35	Road vehicles and engines	77
Aerospace	18	Aircraft	28

*With five or more patents granted, 1985–90.

(iii) Thus, each firm has a measurable *profile* of competencies with varying levels of commitment and competitive advantage in a range of technological fields. In general, firms' technological profiles are *highly stable* over time, thus reflecting the localised and cumulative nature of technological learning. Fewer than 10% of the 440 firms have no significant correlation between their profiles in 1969–74 and in 1985–90.

(iv) The technological fields in which firms have been acquiring an in-house capability most vigorously since the early 1970s — computers, biotechnology and pharmaceuticals, and materials — are also those where firms have increased most vigorously their external alliances for technological exchanges and joint developments.

(v) The technological profiles of large firms are *highly differentiated*, according to the products that they make. First, firms have significantly different profiles of technological competence to most others: only 15% (of the 440 firms) are similar. Secondly, in all sectors, firms have a higher probability of finding others with similar technological profiles *within* their own sector than those *outside*: from twice as high for machinery firms to more than 10 times as high for pharmaceutical firms. Thirdly, the frequency of technological proximity between firms in different industrial sectors is not spread out evenly or at random, but reveals three distinct groupings:

(a) Chemicals, pharmaceuticals, and mining and petroleum sectors.
(b) Machinery and vehicles.
(c) Eelectrical and computers.

These results:

(i) *Confirm* the importance of *path dependency* in the accumulation of firm-specific technological competencies.

(ii) *Confirm* the importance in technology strategy of integration (or "fusion") of different fields of technological competence.

(iii) *Challenge* much of the current conventional wisdom about technology strategies in large firms. In particular, they show the following:

(a) Large firms are heavily constrained in their choices about technology strategy.

(b) External alliances in technology complement internal competence-building, and not a substitute for it. In technology strategy, "make or buy" is not a feasible choice set.

(c) Radical technological breakthroughs are very unlikely to destroy all — or even the majority — of technological competencies in large firms. Indeed, they are more likely to augment the range of competencies that firms develop.

(d) In many sectors (particularly transportation), large firms do not focus their technological activities only on their "distinctive core competence", but also on technological linkages in their supply chain.

(e) Notions of "focus", normally applied to production and marketing strategy, do not necessarily apply to technology strategy.

Technology and product diversification and corporate performance

A number of recent studies have explored the relationship between technology diversification, product diversification and corporate performance. Gambardella and Torrisi (1998) use data on new subsidiaries, acquisitions, collaborative agreements and patents for 32 of the largest US and European firms in electronics to show that, in the 1980s and early 1990s, many firms focussed on fewer businesses, but not on fewer technical areas. They also show that corporate performance is positively associated with technological diversification and a greater focus in business operations.

Using data on sales, R&D and patenting for 57 large firms based in Europe, Japan and the US, Oskarsson (1993) shows that in the 1980s, there was a general increase in technology diversification within the sample, even in firms where product diversification decreased. Moreover, technology diversification is a significant variable in explaining the growth of corporate sales and corporate R&D.

Geographic spread of technological competencies within firms

Analysts have also examined the nature and extent of the geographic spread of technological activities within large firms using data on patenting[9] (Cantwell, 1992, 1995; Patel & Pavitt, 1991; Patel, 1995, 1996; Patel & Vega, 1997, 1998). The main "stylised facts" to emerge from comparisons of more than 500 large firms based in Europe, Japan and the US for the period 1980 to 1996 are as follows:

(i) Large firms continue to perform a high proportion of their technological activities in their home[10] countries although there are some differences among them, mainly according to nationalities, with Japanese firms continuing to concentrate their activities in Japan while the European firms locating more technology outside their home countries.

(ii) Within Europe, the share of corporate technological activities performed outside the home country is higher in those from small countries (more than 50% in firms from Belgium, the Netherlands and Switzerland) than in those from large countries (a third or less in firms from France, Germany and Italy). The main exceptions are large British firms with more than 50% outside the UK.

(iii) The geographic spread of foreign activities of these firms is uneven with the US, Germany and the UK accounting for the largest proportion and Japan very little.

(iv) According to Cantwell (1992), there is a statistically strong relationship between the share of large firms' technological activities

---

[9]They use the the country of residence of the inventor of a patent as a proxy measure for where the technological activity was performed.
[10]Country in which their headquarters is located.

performed outside their home country and their share of foreign production.

(v) The proportion of firms' technological activities performed abroad *decreases* with the technology intensity of the industry and the firm (Patel, 1995, 1996). Thus, the industries with the most internationalised firms are food and drink, building materials and mining and petroleum. The least internationalised include the aircraft, instruments and automobile industries.

(vi) Analysing the activities of the most internationalised large firms, Patel and Vega (1997) show that in a large majority of cases, these firms tend to locate their technology abroad in their core areas where they are strong at home and where the location has complementary strengths. In a small minority of cases, firms go abroad in their areas of weakness at home to exploit the technological advantage of the host country.

These results suggest that adapting products and processes and materials to suit foreign markets, as well as providing technical support to off-shore manufacturing plants, are major factors in the internationalisation of corporate technology. They are also consistent with the notion that firms are increasingly engaging in small-scale activities to monitor and scan new technological developments in centres of excellence in foreign countries within their areas of existing strength. However, there is very little evidence to suggest that firms routinely go abroad to compensate for their weaknesses at home.

Conclusions

The above review shows that considerable progress has been made over the last 20 years in the measurement and understanding of the activities that generate technical change at the firm level. In particular, the greatly improved coverage, range and accuracy of technology indicators have:

(i) Shown that although R&D statistics are important, they are not always a satisfactory measure for all those activities at the firm level directed towards knowledge accumulation and technical change.

(ii) Enabled more detailed and meaningful analyses of technological competencies within firms, especially in terms of their spread across technical fields and geographic space, the results of which have important implications for the management of technology.

(iii) Resolved some of the controversies surrounding the relationship between firm size and market structure on the one hand, and technological performance on the other.

Nevertheless, unresolved issues remain which are concerned with the establishment of a robust relationship between technology and economic performance at the firm level. While cross-sectional studies show that there is a statistically significant relationship, this becomes less robust over time and within specific industrial sectors. This points to the need for:

(i) More firm-specific data on both technological and financial performance over longer periods of time.

(ii) Wider set of approaches than those based on just the production function and market value function.

An interesting study in this context was carried out by Simonetti (1996) who uses data on 300 US firms in the Fortune list between 1963 and 1987 to show that firms which concentrate their technological activities in new fast-growing areas (as measured by their patenting) grow faster than their competitors in the same industry.

Finally, in the future, our understanding of the nature and economic impact of technical change will be greatly improved by studies based on the combined use of a range of publicly available measures, such as R&D expenditures, patents, new product announcements and the technical qualifications of employees. At the same time, new possibilities will be opened up by information from new innovation surveys currently being carried out in a number of EU countries.

Acknowledgement

In preparing this paper, the author has benefitted greatly from comments by Keith Pavitt.

Chapter 8

Assessing Technological Competencies

FRANCIS NARIN

General Introduction

The forecast of a company's probability of success is enormously complicated and depends on many financial, managerial and technological variables. In the financial realm, the analyst has a wide variety of quantitative financial indicators available to aid in the analysis. Until recently, however, the managerial and technological inputs to the models have been based on less objective, but more qualitative, data. The new Tech-Line® Technology Indicators system created by CHI Research is designed to address the technology part of the problem. It seeks to bring the quantitative indicators of company technological strength "out of the black box and onto the spreadsheets" and into the models.

Technological knowledge and innovation are central forces driving modern, high-tech companies. The quantitative indicators of company technological strengths will allow securities analysts, investment professionals and economists to explicitly include company technology strengths in their analyses.

The data in the first on-line Tech-Line® covers 1,139 companies (including top universities, agencies and organisations) in 26 industry groups and 30 technology areas over 10 years with nine technology indicators. This yielded approximately 4,000,000 data elements for analysing company performance.

Before the advent of technology indicators, analysts assessed the technological strengths of companies from R&D budgets, announcements by management, interviews with R&D managers, new products and other important, but qualitative, information. Occasionally, patent analysis was used as an input, especially by the economists. Otherwise, it was of not much use to the financial community because the data were of a low quality and inaccessible. Specifically, three major problems have restricted the production of this kind of indicator in the past: identification of company patents, allocation into usable categories, and identification of quality in the patent portfolio.

Tech-Line addresses all three problems. To produce Tech-Line®, CHI developed techniques which unify more than 19,000 variant names and subsidiaries of the 1,139 top patenting companies, regroup the patents into 30 technology areas and 26 industry groups familiar to analysts, and use advanced patent citation indicators to provide measures of the quality of the patents within each technology areas for each company in each year.

All these ideas will be discussed in greater detail in subsequent sections of this paper. For the moment, upon acceptance of the idea that company patents are correctly identified, that the technology areas make sense, and that citation analysis identifies quality in the patent portfolios, the following are a sample of questions which can be addressed with this kind of patent portfolio data:

(i) Which companies have the highest impact patents in semi-conductors?

(ii) In an M&A situation, which of the companies has the most valuable patent portfolio?

(iii) How concentrated is a company's R&D across different technology categories?

(iv) How much do patent portfolio properties add to the prediction of stock market prices? (Fig. 8.1 indicates that this may be quite a significant factor.)

(v) Which smaller companies have leading edge technology portfolios in biotechnology?

(vi) How similar are the technological profiles of the major pharmaceutical companies?

(vii) How completely has Monsanto shifted its research emphasis into agriculture?

(viii) Would the merger of Glaxo-Wellcome and SmithKline Beecham been a good one from the point of view of the technological leadership at Glaxo-Wellcome?

Tech-Line data can answer these and many other questions about the relationship of technology to economic and financial performance.

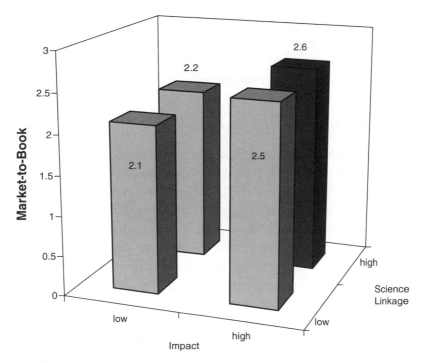

Fig. 8.1. Chemicals: median portfolio M/B ratio based on classifying firms by patent impact and science linkage in the previous three years averaged over six prediction periods.

The next section of this paper discusses the basic ideas behind the database and its application. This is followed by a review of the key research literature behind the database. The last section then defines and discusses each of the indicators used in Tech-Line. Detailed documents on all aspects of these technology indicators are available at www.chiresearch.com.

Technical Introduction

Tech-Line provides a series of quantitative indicators of company technological strengths based on patent portfolio analysis. All these indicators (and many more specialised ones) have been used internally by CHI Research, Inc. in its consulting practice, tracking the world's technology for industrial and public clients. However, these have not been made widely available to the financial, investment and economics communities before because of the difficulties in obtaining unified, clean company data to work with, technology definition and differentiation between run-of-the-mill and important patents.

Company identification and reassignments

Company identification requires a massive process of consolidation of company names. The 1,139 Tech-Line companies — where "companies" include some major research laboratories, government agencies, universities and other entities patenting in the United States (US) — exist in the US patent system under more than 19,000 different assignee names. For example, the patents of Bayer include patents from more than 150 different assignee names under which Bayer and its subsidiaries have patented in the US. The 1,139 Tech-Line companies include 460 US companies, 565 non-US companies, 66 universities, 30 government agencies and 18 research institutes. Together, they account for about 63% of all US patents.

In addition to company identification, hundreds of thousands of patents originally assigned to one company have been reassigned as a result of property or asset sales, mergers and acquisitions, various changes in corporate structure and so forth; those reassigned patents are assigned to their current corporate owners.

Technology categorisations

Classification problems have also bedevilled the use of patent data in strategic and financial analysis. The most obvious way to partition patents is by patent classification — the assignment of a patent by patent examiners. However, hundreds of major classes and many tens of thousands of sub-classes, covering all forms of technology, are used by the US Patent Office. Moreover, these classifications are invention-art-based, rather than application-specific. Hence, for example, a classification describing a blade for a rotating bladed member might cover both a desk fan and a jet engine. Thus, devising a way to partition patents by classification requires a high degree of knowledge and experience.

Tech-Line partitions patents based on the International Patent Classification (IPC) system, which has a somewhat more industrial orientation than US patent classifications. The 30 technology areas in Tech-Line (Table 8.1) are based on the first given IPC on each patent. (There can be more than one IPC-assigned, but the first is usually considered to be the main classification.) These categories should go a long way towards meeting the general needs of the non-technical community for patent data in categories which make sense from a corporate viewpoint.

Identifying important patents

The third major problem is the identification of important patents from the many tens of thousands of patents issued each year. For this, we use techniques developed from patent citation analysis to characterise a company's overall patent portfolio and within each of the 30 technology areas.

The basic idea of patent citation analysis is that highly cited patents — patents that are listed as "references cited" on many later

Table 8.1. Patent growth and concentration indicators for all Tech-Line® Companies, 1993–1997.

Technology Area	Number of Patents 1993–1997	Patent Growth Percentage in Area	Percentage of Company Patents in Area
1. Agriculture	4,542	6	1.3
2. Oil and gas	4,604	−19	1.3
3. Power generation and distribution	4,730	0	1.3
4. Food and tobacco	2,641	−18	0.8
5. Textiles and apparel	4,165	5	1.2
6. Wood and paper	2,035	8	0.6
7. Chemicals	40,828	4	11.6
8. Pharmaceuticals	12,610	23	3.6
9. Biotechnology	6,113	89	1.7
10. Medical equipment	8,348	43	2.4
11. Medical electronics	3,769	73	1.1
12. Plastics, polymers and rubber	20,117	2	5.7
13. Glass, clay and cement	2,880	−16	0.8
14. Primary metals	1,913	−15	0.5
15. Fabricated metals	4,879	1	1.4
16. Industrial machinery and tools	14,426	−4	4.1
17 Industrial process equipment	9488	−2	2.7
18. Office equipment and cameras	22,076	23	6.3
19. Heating and ventilation	2,211	22	0.6
20. Miscellaneous machinery	11,250	−5	3.2
21. Computers and peripherals	37,078	81	10.6
22. Telecommunications	33,350	44	9.5
23. Semiconductors and electronics	26,740	39	7.6
24. Measuring and control equipment	16,333	0	4.7
25. Electrical appliances and computer	17,132	12	4.9
26. Motor vehicles and parts	13,169	0	3.8
27. Aerospace and parts	1,996	−6	0.6
28. Other transport	2,518	−4	0.7
29. Miscellaneous manufacturing	15,477	2	4.4
99. Other	3,530	1	1
All	350,948	16	100

patents — are generally of much greater importance than patents which are never cited, or are cited only a few times. The reason for this is that a patent which contains an important new invention — or major advance — can set off a stream of follow-on inventions, all of which may cite the original, important invention upon which they are building.

The key indicators used in Tech-Line, summarised below, are:

(i) *Number of patents.* Indicating company technology activity, it is a count of Type 1 (regular, utility) patents issued in the US patent system from 1987 to the present.

(ii) *Cites per patent.* Indicating the impact of a company's patents, this indicator is based on cited year; for example, all 1990 company patents as cited in subsequent years.

(iii) *Current impact index (CII).* A Fundamental indicator of patent portfolio quality, it is the number of times the company's previous five years of patents, in a technology area, were cited from the current year, divided by the average citations received by all US patents in that technology area from the current year. Expected = 1.0.

(iv) *Technology strength (TS).* Indicating patent portfolio strength, it is the number of patents multiplied by the current impact index, that is, patent portfolio size inflated or deflated by patent quality.

(v) *Technology cycle time (TCT).* Indicating the speed of invention, it is the median age, in years, of the US patent references cited on the front page of the company's patents.

(vi) *Science Linkage (SL).* Indicating how leading edge the company's technology is, it is the average number of science papers referenced on the front page of the company's patents.

(vii) *Science Strength (SS).* Indicating how much the company uses science in building its patent portfolio, it is the number of patents multiplied by science linkage, that is, patent portfolio size inflated or deflated by the extent of science linkage. This is a count of the total number of science links in the company patent portfolio.

Research Background

In this section, we will review the evidence that indicators of company technological strength, based on patent portfolio analysis, provide a valid way of assessing the quality and value of a company's patented technology. We will do this by first reviewing the background research in science and patent citation analysis, as well as in economics. All these studies point to the conclusion that citation analysis provides significant measures of quality when assessing portfolios of publications or patents. In addition, there is emerging evidence that patent portfolio analysis, including citation indicators of the impact of the holdings in those portfolios, are indicative of — and in some cases predictive of — company technological, economic and stock market success.

Figure 8.1, for example, from some preliminary and ongoing research at New York University, indicated that companies which have highly science-linked and highly cited patents may have substantially higher stock market/book ratios than companies with less highly science-linked and less highly cited patents.

The main thrust of this section is that in both the scientific and technological realms, there is compelling evidence that high citation — to research papers in the scientific literature and to issued US patents in the technological literature — is associated with the importance of the scientific or technological discoveries being cited. Since this association is a statistical one, it does not guarantee that every highly cited paper or patent is of importance, or that a paper or patent that is not highly cited is not of importance. It does argue, however, that a company with a portfolio of highly cited and science-linked patents is more likely to be technologically successful than one that does not have such a portfolio.

Just having a strong intellectual property portfolio does not, of course, guarantee a company's success. Many additional factors do affect the ability of a company to move from quality patents to quality products, or even to high profits. The decade of troubles at IBM, for example, is certainly illustrative of this, since IBM has always had very high quality and highly cited research in its laboratories.

The key studies discussed in this section were selected to capture the parallel growth of the three disciplines behind Tech-Line: science citation analysis, patent citation analysis, and closely related economic and policy analysis. Each of those studies has an additional bibliography, from which the reader can get to literally hundreds of papers which provide the relevant background.

Science citation analysis

The origins of large-scale citation analysis are traced to the work of Eugene Garfield, who first proposed the *Science Citation Index* in the 1950s as a tool to increase the power of scientists to retrieve prior scientific papers (Garfield, 1955). Garfield also pointed out that in evaluating science, it is important to trace the impact that a given paper has had. This is because all scientific work builds on earlier scientific work. For a scientists to be able to fully understand the impact his own work is having, he should have a tabulation of its citation impact and all the later papers that cite it.

In the early 1960s Garfield created the *Science Citation Index*, which has since grown to a major resource for science covering more than 4,000 scientific journals, more than half a million papers a year, and more than five million citations annually.

Although Garfield and his colleagues were well aware of the potential use of citation data in measuring the impact of individual papers, the widespread acceptance of science citation data in evaluation is associated with the creation, by the National Science Foundation, of the first *Science Indicators* report in 1972. Narin and his colleagues at CHI Research (then called Computer Horizons, Inc.) utilised the *Science Citation Index* data for *Science Indicators* and created both national and international scientific performance indicators. They used counts of publications and, most importantly, counts of how frequently those publications were cited to create the first major indicators of national scientific performance used in that report.

The large-scale use of publication and citation techniques has continued in the subsequent *Science Indicators* reports issued every two years since the 1972 report. For example, the *Science and Engineering Indicators 1998* report contained many tables and graphs based on this kind of bibliometric data.

As part of the general development of *Science Indicators* techniques, CHI, under contract with the National Science Foundation, produced a monograph entitled *Evaluative Bibliometrics* (Narin, 1976), which reviewed the state-of-the-art of citation analysis techniques, and in particular their application to the evaluation of the performance of scientific institutions. In particular, in Chapter Five of *Evaluative Bibliometrics*, 24 different validation studies were summarised, all of which support the idea that high citation in the scientific literature is associated with positive peer opinions of the importance of scientific papers, with peer rankings of research institutions, and with other independent indicators of quality and the impact of sets of research papers.

One of the most fascinating and telling demonstrations of the importance of very high citation is the publication of a series of papers related to the bibliometric characteristics of Nobel laureates in science. In an early paper discussing the quality of research and Nobel prizes, Inhaber noted: "The quality of the work of Nobel laureates in physics, as measured by citations, is an order of magnitude higher than that of other scientists" (Inhaber & Prednowek, 1976: 34).

Garfield himself has written on this extensively and has published a relatively comprehensive table illustrating the very high citations received by papers of Nobel laureates. Specifically, he looked at 125 Nobel laureates in the fields of chemistry, physics, physiology and medicine. He found that 80% had published what he calls citation classics, that is, papers in the most cited 1,000 articles in the *SCI* between 1961–1982, or papers that are cited more than 300 times. This corresponds roughly to the top 4/10,000 of all published scientific papers (Garfield, 1986).

The area of citation analysis continues to be a vibrant one, with a steady stream of papers applying these techniques to the evaluations of groups of scientists, research departments, institutions and nations. This work is particularly active in Europe, with major bibliometrics research and education programmes in all the major European countries. The journal *Scientometrics*, edited in Hungary, is devoted almost entirely to this field, and is an important resource for anyone looking to update themselves on the many applications of citation analysis in science. Finally, in April 1998, Ron Kostoff placed an extensive monograph on various metrics of science on the Internet. This monograph may be accessed directly at **http://www.dtic.mil/dtic/kostoff/index.html**. Kostoff's monograph is self-contained and extensive, and contains more than 5,000 references to earlier works.

The early validation techniques covered the full range of studies still being used in research evaluation. They covered the correlations between the publication and citation measures of national, institutional, research group, and individual performance, and external rankings. At the national level, for example, an early policy analysis by Derek de Solla Price showed that nations publish research papers roughly in proportion to their Gross Domestic Product (GDP); that is, in proportion to their economic size, and not to their population or land area or anything else (Price, 1969). Much later, CHI showed that this also carries over into technology, and that other nations' inventors patent in the US patent system in general proportion to their national economic size as measured by the GDP (Narin, 1991).

At the institutional level, citation techniques have been applied extensively to the ranking of university departments. This had been done systematically in the US in a series of reports in which relatively large numbers of senior academics ranked major university departments. In a paper published in 1978, and reprinted in 1980, CHI showed that not only do these peer rankings of universities correlate well with publication rankings, but that the correlations are always increased substantially when citation data is included. That is, the rankings of university departments based on a combination of the number of papers and how frequently they are cited are much more highly correlated with peer rankings than those based on publication counts alone (Anderson *et al.*, 1978).

Basics of patent citation analysis

When a US patent is granted, it typically contains eight or nine "References Cited — US patents" on its front page, two references cited to foreign patents, and one to two non-patent references cited. These references link the just-issued patent to the earlier cited prior art and limit the claims of the just-issued patent. They point out where the essential and related art already exists, and delineate the property rights of the invention as determined by the US Patent and Trademark Office.

The "references cited" on US patents are a fundamental requirement of patent law. When a US patent is issued, it has to satisfy three general criteria: it must be useful, novel and not obvious. The novelty requirement is the primary factor which leads to the references that appear on the front page of the patent, since it is the responsibility of the patent applicant and his attorney — and of the patent examiner — to identify, through the various references cited therein, all of the important prior art upon which the issued patent improves. These references are chosen and/or screened by the patent examiner, who is "not called upon to cite all references that are available, but only the best" (Patent & Trademark Office, 1995).

When this referencing pattern is turned around, and all of the subsequent citations to a given patent are tabulated, one obtains the fundamental information used in patent citation analysis, namely, a count of how often a given patent is cited in later patents. These distributions tend to be very skewed: there are large numbers of patents that are cited only a few times, and only a small number of patents cited more than 10 times. For example, for patents issued in 1988 — and cited in the next seven years — half the patents are cited two or fewer times, 75% are cited five or fewer times, and only 1% of the patents are cited 24 or more times. Overall, after 10 or more years, the average cites/patent is around six.

As was the case with science citation analysis, there is, of course, no official standard by which the importance of a patent may be judged except, perhaps, for the Federal Court's designation of "pioneering patents". Therefore, most studies of citation frequency and patent importance are based upon the opinions of knowledgeable scientists or engineers, or correlations with non-patent measures. However, in the case of pioneering patents, we have a direct legal indicator of patent importance and, as will be shown in a moment, pioneering patents are cited, on average, six or more times as frequently as average patents issued at the same time.

The first paper of which we are aware that looked at patent citations as a way of finding important patents was an early study carried out by Reisner (1963) at IBM, who experimented with the use of citation analysis to find key patents. By tracing the references from one patent to another, Reisner found 43 of 60 patents she was looking for.

Computerised citation data covering all US patents first became available in 1975. In the following year, in the Sixth Technology Assessment and Forecast report, the Patent & Trademark Office tabulated the patents which were most highly cited and suggested that "the number of times a patent document is cited may be a measure of its technological significance" (OTAF, 6th Report, 1976).

In 1978, Ellis, Hepburn and Oppenheim in the UK experimented with citation networks, tracing from patents to identify key discoveries and turning points.

The first relatively formal study of patent citation analysis was carried out by CHI Research under the sponsorship of the National Science Foundation (Carpenter *et al.*, 1981). At the time the study was proposed, in the late 1970s, the Science Indicators Unit at the National Science Foundation was considering whether to add technology indicators, based on patent citations, to the stable of science literature indicators which were then being used in the *Science Indicators* reports. NSF commissioned CHI to do a study to see whether patents associated with important discoveries were more highly cited than average patents.

A set of 100 important patents and a set of 102 control patents were selected. The former was obtained by identifying a key patent underlying a product which had received the IR-100 award, which was established by the journal *Industrial Research & Development*. This award "honors the 100 most significant new technical products — and the innovators responsible for them — developed during the year" (*Industrial Research & Development*, **13**, pp. 3, December 1980).

Patents related to the 1969 and 1970 awards were used in order to ensure that there was sufficient time for the patents to be cited to their full potential.

The results of that study are summarised in the following tabulation:

	IR-100	Control
Total patents	100	102
Total cites	494	208
Cites/patent	4.94	2.04
Patents cited > 10 times	17	4

Clearly, the IR-100 patents are much more highly cited. This difference is due to the presence of highly cited patents in the IR-100 set.

Following this study, patent citation indicators were added to the *Science Indicators* report (by then called *Science and Engineering Indicators*) and their use has expanded over the subsequent years.

Another formal validation study, carried out by Carpenter and his colleagues at CHI in 1983, tested whether the citations from issued US patents could be used to measure the science dependence and foreign dependence of patented technologies. Rankings based on the number of citations per patent to the scientific literature and foreign-origin material were compared to peer rankings of the science and foreign dependence of the patents. Overall, a high degree of agreement was found between the expert opinions on the science and foreign dependence, as well as corresponding bibliometric rankings. For example, the eight technologies judged most science-dependent by experts averaged 0.92 cites per patent to scientific journal papers. Meanwhile, the eight technologies judged least science-dependent had only 0.05 references per patent to journal papers.

Another citation validation study was carried out by students at the Worcester Polytech Institute and the US Patent & Trademark Office. The abstract of that report succinctly summarises its contents:

> "This report, prepared for the United States Patent & Trademark Office, analyses the importance of patents frequently cited by patent examiners. Information regarding the commercial and technical significance of the 419 most highly cited patents from 1975 and 1980 was obtained through a survey of patent attorneys and patent examiners. The characteristics of an important patent were determined through the survey. The results were found to support the hypothesis that highly cited patents are important."
> (Worcester Polytech, 1988)

A quite formal validation study of patent citation importance within an industrial context was carried out by CHI Research in co-operation with Eastman Kodak Laboratories. Kodak was interested in the possibility of using patent citation data in an analysis of their own and some of their competitor's technology, and had desired to independently validate whether, within an industrial laboratory, high patent citation was associated with knowledgeable peer assessment of the importance of the patents. In that study, a collection of nearly 100 Kodak patents in their core area of Silver Halide Technology were divided into sets of 16 each. The sets were then given to senior laboratory staff for evaluation. Every patent was evaluated by three or four different people. As a result, the rankings of the patents could be cross-tabulated. The Kodak evaluators were senior intellectual property staff, the senior laboratory management and senior laboratory scientists. In the case of scientists, the patents they were given to rank were screened to make sure that they did not rank their own patents. Each person was asked to rank the patents based on how much each has changed the state-of-the-art in the field of the invention.

The results of that study were very well summarised in Fig. 8.2. It shows, quite clearly, that whether a patent is cited one, two or three times does not seem to make much difference in the peer ranking, but that patents cited more than five times, that is, relatively highly cited patents, were ranked far more highly by the Kodak staff. This finding is statistically significant, especially for group 8, the most highly cited patents. Of the 15 respondents in the study, eight gave group 8 patents

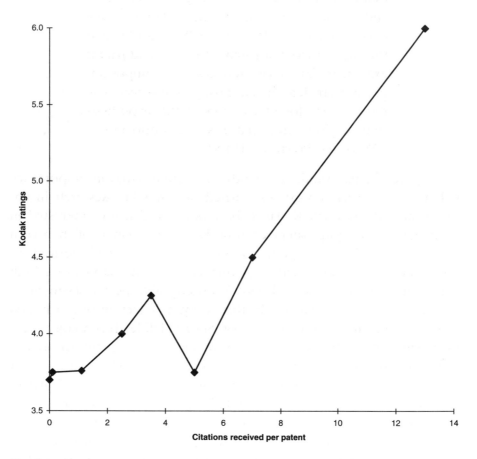

Fig. 8.2. Average rating versus average citations received for eight patent groups: Kodak highly cited patents are much more highly rated.

the highest average rating. Using the binomial model, the probability of this is 0.0002 (Albert *et al.*, 1991).

The most recent evidence for the importance of highly cited patents comes from within the Patent office itself: from the strong associations between citation frequency and Patent Office recognition, and in the extremely high citation to pioneering patents.

CHI has looked at the citation frequency of three different categories of patents: patents listed in the National Inventor's Hall of Fame; patents of Historical Significance in a list prepared by the US Department of Commerce for the US bicentennial; and patents that had been adjudged as pioneering patents by the Federal District Court.

A summary of this data is shown in Fig. 8.3, which plots citation indices for the three sets of patents: Pioneering, Hall of Fame and Historically Significant. Because the patents are distributed over a relatively long period of time, we divided the number of times each patent was cited by the expected number of times patents issued in the same year have been cited, counting citations in our database from

Patents granted between 1960 and 1995. Citations from 1971 to March 1995.

Fig. 8.3. Very high citation indices are found for selected patents.

1971 through March of 1995. The results were striking. Pioneering patents are cited almost seven times as often as expected; Hall of Fame patents are cited more than six times as often as expected; and Historically Significant, almost 2.5 times as often as expected! And, in fact, of all the patents looked at, only one was cited fewer times than expected. This is certainly a very direct validation of the idea that important patents tend to be cited much more heavily than on average.

A very recent paper, still in publication by F. M. Scherer of Harvard and colleagues in Europe and at CHI, has looked at a sample of US and German patented inventions on which profitability information — the private value of the patents — was obtained (Harhoff *et al.*, 1999). They considered only patents for which all the fees had been paid to keep the patents in force in Germany for the full 18 years of the patents, and then queried the owners of those patents as to the asset value of the patent — by essentially asking: what is the smallest amount which they would have been willing to sell this patent to an independent third party for in 1980? In the German patent system, the two patents in the highest value category were much more highly cited than the others; in the US patent system, the patent citation frequency of the patents with an estimated value of US$20 million or more were substantially more highly cited than those with lesser estimated values.

Economic and policy analysis

In this section, we review a few studies which support the idea that there is a positive relationship between important technological advances and economic outcomes. This is the so-called "linear model" of innovation: the idea that invention and innovations originate in basic and applied research before progressing into technological and economic benefit. This simple linear model has been supplanted by much more complex views of the process with many feedback loops, but the origins of technical knowledge in basic research still lie at the core of this process (Turney, 1991).

It is also, of course, widely accepted today that research makes an important contribution to economic growth. In his statement on technology for America's economic growth, President Bill Clinton has stated that

> "scientific advances are the well-spring of technical innovations. The benefits are seen in economic growth, improved healthcare and many other areas." (Clinton & Gore, 1993)

A recent paper of ours discussed quite extensively the increasing linkage between US technology and public science, and has demonstrated that the underlying citation by patents to research papers, used in Tech-Line as science linkage, has increased dramatically over the last decade (Narin *et al.*, 1997).

As far back as the late 1960s, systematic efforts were underway to trace the linkage between research and economically important innovations. A key study done then was the TRACES study (Technology in Retrospect and Critical Events in Science) performed under NSF's sponsorship at IIT Research Institute (Narin, 1968). It looked at five economically important innovations, including magnetic ferrites, video-recording and the contraceptive pill, and traced back to their origins in applied and basic research.

The key advance embedded in TRACES was the semi-quantitative approach. Although citation analysis was not utilised — partially because citation data was essentially inaccessible then — there was an attempt to classify, count and identify the key events leading up to the innovations.

By the early 1980s, it was possible to obtain reasonably large-scale patent data and Griliches and his colleagues at Harvard, as well as the National Bureau of Economic Research (NBER), began a long series of quantitative studies looking at the economic importance of patents. In a 1981 paper, Griliches found a significant relationship between the market value of the firms and its "intangible" capital. It was provided by past R&D expenditures and the number of patents (Griliches, 1981).

A particularly interesting paper in this sequence, by Ariel Pakes in 1985, *On Patents R&D and the Stock Market Rate of Return*, found that an unanticipated patent is associated with an increase in firm value of US$865,000.

In 1990, Griliches comprehensively surveyed the use of patent statistics as economic indicators (Griliches, 1990).

Those studies, and most of the economic studies up to recent time, were very aggregate. They were based on corporate identifications that were either not unified at all or not nearly as refined as those that are now available on Tech-Line, and without the augmentation that citation analysis adds.

In 1987, Narin and his colleagues studied a group of 18 US pharmaceutical companies and showed that the number of patents they obtained, and especially whether the companies had highly cited patents, were both correlated with the peer opinions of the companies and with increases in pharmaceutical company sales and profits (Narin *et al.*, 1987). That study showed quite clearly that highly cited patents tended to occur around economically important inventions such as Tagamet for SmithKline, and that these important technological events lead, in that industry, to increases in company sales and profits. In fact, the Tagamet patents that were highly cited in the 1980s are still the underpinnings of SmithKline Beecham today.

A somewhat different approach, with the same results, was taken in a study by Trajtenberg (1990) with the marvellous title *A Penny for Your Quotes* ("quotes" is the European term often used for citations). Trajtenberg analysed patent citation patterns associated with advances in CAT scanners and showed a close association between citation-based patent indices and independent measures of the social value of innovations for computed tomography scanners. Of particular significance is his finding that "the weighting scheme appears to be non-linear (increasing) in the number of citations, implying that the information content of citations rises at the margin" (p. 172). This directly supports the idea that highly cited patents are of particular technical importance.

In a broader study, Franko, at the University of Massachusetts, showed that the US and UK losses in global markets between 1960 and 1986 may have been caused by a lack of investment in technology when compared to their Japanese and continental European competitors. According to him,

> "The proportion of corporate sales revenues allocated to commercially oriented R&D emerges as a, perhaps the, principal indicator of subsequent sales growth performance relative to competition over 5–10 year periods. Insofar as many US and UK firms have lost global market share relative to Asian and European competitors over the past two decades, a significant contributory factor would appear to have been negligence on the part of many US and UK firms of investment in technology as a factor determining strategic, competitive advance." (Franko, 1989)

An interesting observation is that the superior technological performance of the US in the mid to late 1990s is associated with an increasing US inventor share of US patents, back up to over 50% of the patents granted in the US.

In a beautifully written general article in *Scientific America*, Rosenberg and Birdzel at Stanford put forth the thesis that the linkage of knowledge and technology, as well as the freedom to absorb and use it in industry, was the fundamental driving force behind the economic rise of the West. Specifically,

> "Close links between the growth of scientific knowledge and the rise of technology have permitted the market economies of the Western nations to achieve unprecedented prosperity." (Rosenberg & Birdzel, 1990)

A few years later, *Business Week* published the two Patent Scoreboards using CHI Research data to rank major companies across 10 different industries (Coy & Carey, 1992; Buderi *et al.*, 1993). These Patent Scoreboards were two of the first times when these ideas were introduced directly to the business community. Hence, analysts could look at the relationship between the business performance of companies and their technological strengths.

There is also a growing awareness of the value of intellectual capital — of which patents are a major component. This is reflected in a recent article in *Fortune*, " Your Company's Most Valuable Asset: Intellectual Capital", by Stewart (1994), which asserted that the modern company is really driven by knowledge, and not by bricks and structures.

The economists associated with the NBER are now using patent citation techniques in a wide variety of ways to study the following: the spillovers of research from company to company and from university to company, the characteristics of successful companies and, in general, the acceptance of the notion that patent citation is equivalent, in the statistical sense, to high impact technology. A paper by Jaffe *et al.*, (1993) provides a linkage to this literature.

Interest is also rapidly growing to find ways of valuing corporate intangibles for financial purposes. The intangibles research project, headed by Professor Baruch Lev at The Stern School of Business in New York University, is addressing the accounting treatment of corporate investment and intangibles such as R&D franchise and brand development. In particular, a study by Professor Lev showed that the accounting rule, which allows an acquiring company to set a value for the "in process" research and development assets and write off that amount immediately, significantly allows the acquirers to avoid future charges to earnings from goodwill. Thus, this tends to provide companies with a boost to their future earnings (Deng & Lev, 1998).

In a work that is still underway, Bronwyn Hall and her colleagues at the NBER are looking at market value and patent citations by using a new database that has been assembled by NBER for research purposes. Their research, while still preliminary, is quite advanced in its mathematical techniques and is being used to estimate how much citations to patents contribute to such indicators as the market value of a company. They found that "citation weighted patents do better, especially in the earlier years when the citation measure is more complete", and that "an increase of one citation per patent is associated with a 3–4% increase in market value at the firm level" (Hall *et al.*, 1998).

Finally, a relevant and important preliminary study by Professor Lev and his student, Zhen Deng, assisted by CHI, looked at the relationship between Tech-Line variables and various financial indicators, including R&D budgets and stock market performance (Deng *et al.*, 1999). In particular, they found that companies whose patents had above average current impact indices (CII's) and science linkage indicators (SL's) tended to have significantly higher market-to-book ratios and stock market returns, both contemporaneously and for a number of years into the future (Fig. 8.1). This finding is one of the key evidence that indicators of corporate technological performance, based on patents and patent citations, may provide significant new tools to securities and financial analysts.

Indicator Definitions

This chapter will cover, in some detail, the specific indicators used in Tech-Line, as well as the many decisions and unifications that must be undertaken to create a usable technology indicators database.

We will begin with the choice of patents to include and the identification of the company (assignee) which owns the patent currently before proceeding to the most basic indicator: the cites per patent received by a patent from subsequently issued patents. We will then define the Current Impact Index, a synchronous citation indicator which characterises the quality of a company's patents in the last five years, and then on to Technology Cycle Time, which characterises the rapidity with which companies invent, and finally,

Science Linkage, which shows whether a company's patents are linked to scientific research. In latter is a strong indicator of leading edge position across a wide range of science-based advanced technologies. A few composite indicators constructed from these basic ones will also be defined.

Number of patents

The number of patents indicates company technology activity. It is a count of a company's Type 1 (regular, utility) patents issued in the US patent system from 1987 to the present.

For its patent counts, Tech-Line considers only regular (Type I) US utility patents. Other categories of US patents, such as plant patents, design patents, reissues, continuations and so forth, are not counted in order to maintain the focus of the database on the key category of patents which contributes to corporate technological strengths.

Company name unification

When a US patent is issued, it is issued to the inventor and, if the inventor works for a company, the rights to the patent are normally assigned to the company. The latter is then identified as the assignee of that patent.

The first problem is that companies obtain their patents under many different names: companies may patent under divisional names; subsidiaries may obtain patents in their own names; companies' names may change over time; and so forth. CHI has gone through a massive unification of these various assignee names for the 1,100 companies covered in Tech-Line, which are constructed by combining more than 19,000 different original assignee names in a major attempt to identify correctly, the company to which patents are assigned in the first place. For example, the following shows a few names under which patents assigned to Hitachi were filed, and which have been unified in Tech-Line:

Step 1. Typographical unification

| Hitachi Maxell, Ltd.
Hitachi Maxell Ltd.
Hitachi Maxwell, Ltd. | $\longrightarrow$ | Hitachi Maxell, Ltd. |

Step 2. Company unification

| Hitachi Denshi KK, Ltd.
Hitachi Keiyo Eng. Co., Ltd.
Hitachi Seiko, Ltd.
Hitachi Kiden Kogyo KK
Hitachi Lighting, Ltd.
Hitachi, Ltd.
Japan Servo Co., Ltd.
Hitachi Maxell, Ltd. | $\longrightarrow$ | Hitachi, Ltd. |

Company restatement

The second problem related to the assignment of a patent to a company is mergers, acquisitions and divestitures, which CHI has attempted to take into account by restating all companies as at the end of 1997.

More specifically, insofar as we can tell which patents belong to a subsidiary or part of a divested or acquired company, these patents are moved with a merger/acquisition. For example, the patents of SmithKline Beecham not only include those under its name, but also those that were originally filed under SmithKline and French Laboratories, Beckman Instruments, Beecham, and so forth. This process is carried out by scanning a number of resources, but is by no means perfect, especially for the smaller companies. Hence, the corporate identification in Tech-Line, while better and more up-to-date than any database of which we are aware of, is certainly not perfect.

Reassignments

Another major attribute of the Tech-Line database is that we have attempted to account for the major reassignments of patents. When a merger and acquisition takes place, or a major area of technology is sold, it sometimes happens that a reassignment of patents is registered in the Patent Office from the original assignee to a new assignee. This reassignment is captured in a complex, as well as being extremely difficult to process, database produced by the Patent Office. CHI has processed this database and moved, via reassignment, hundreds of thousands of patents from the original assignees to their new assignees, including the many patents moved across Tech-Line companies. Some of the reassignments are not very important from a company strength's viewpoint, such as from one part of a company or one version of a company's name to another, while others are indicative of the genuine transfer of intellectual property from one company to another. As well as we could, the reassignments — which were recorded by the Patent Office — affecting the Tech-Line companies have been accounted for and the reassigned patents are, within Tech-Line, assigned to their current owners.

Restatement limitation

It is very important to mention, however, that companies do not, by any means, always reassign their patents, even when major divestitures and acquisitions occur. For example, the old patents of AT&T were not reassigned to Lucent by registration of the reassignment at the USPTO. However, there is a public record in SEC documents of which patents went to Lucent and NCR from AT&T; we have made use of those public filings to assign to Lucent the great majority of the patents which were originally assigned to AT&T. In cases where patents were not explicitly reassigned, and we have not found any public record of them, the patents stayed with the original company. For example, Imation, which was split off from 3M, and is now beginning to patent vigorously under its name, does not appear to have been reassigned back any 3M patents. Therefore, it does not yet have enough patents to be included as a Tech-Line company.

Choice of companies

The on-line Tech-Line database was built upon earlier CD-ROM versions of Tech-Line. The criteria for selecting companies in those earlier times were relatively large numbers of patents in the late 1980s and early 1990s, with each edition of Tech-Line adding to it companies that had newly emerged as major patenters. However, the earlier versions broke the data down into broad sets of chemical, electrical and pharmaceutical companies, and the coverage was not even across other areas. Thus, while most of the top 1,100 patenting companies are covered in Tech-Line, there may be a few companies with recent rapid increases in patenting which we have missed. We will attempt to get any that should be covered in future releases of Tech-Line, which may also be expanded to cover smaller companies.

The lists of all the companies covered in Tech-Line are given on the CHI homepage at www.chiresearch.com. The coverage is global; approximately one-half of all US patents are foreign-invented. This is reflected in the Tech-Line company proportions. More specifically, the first edition of Tech-Line in July 1998 covers the following:

(i) 48% are US organisations.
(ii) 52% are foreign organisations.

Specifically:

(i) 355 US parent companies.
(ii) 105 US subsidiaries.
(iii) 469 non-US parent companies.
(iv) 96 non-US subsidiaries.
(v) 30 government agencies (10 from US).
(vi) 18 research institutes (13 from US).
(vii) 66 universities (64 from US).

Patent growth percentage and percentage of company
patents according to area

Two indicators are based directly on the number and growth rate of patents. These are Patent Growth Percentage in Area and Percentage of Company Patents in Area. Patent Growth Percentage in Area, from one period to the next, is just the number of patents in the current period less the number of patents in the previous period and divided by the number of patents in the previous period expressed as a percentage. The percentage of company patents in area is, just as it says, 100 times the number of patents in the area divided by the total number of patents for the company. Both are illustrated for all Tech-Line companies in the first edition of Tech-Line On-Line in Table 8.1.

Note that the largest area is chemicals with 11.6% of all patents followed by computers and peripherals at 10.6%. It is also apparent the high-tech areas expand the fastest. The most rapidly growing area over the five-year period is biotechnology: with a growth rate of 89%. It is followed by computers and peripherals (80%) and medical electronics (73%).

Still growing at a rapid rate, but down from the top three, are medical equipment (43%), telecommunications (43%) and semiconductors and electronic components (38%). In addition, three other areas are growing faster than the patent system: pharmaceuticals (23%), office equipment and cameras (23%), and heating and ventilation (22%). The overall Tech-Line growth rate was 16%. The areas which seem to be shrinking in patenting most rapidly are oil and gas (19%), food and tobacco (18%), glass, clay and cement (16%) and primary metals (15%). Real differences exist, in the rates of growth of patenting within different areas. As mentioned before, it is important that comparisons be made within technology areas.

Cites per patent

Cite per patent indicates the impact of a company's patents. It is a count of the citations received by a company's patents from the front pages of subsequent patents. For example, the cites per patent in 1990 report the number of times a company's patents were mentioned.

In patent citation analysis, high citation counts are often associated with important inventions, which are fundamental to future inventions. Companies with highly cited patents may be more advanced than their competitors, as they will have more valuable patent portfolios. After six years, the average US patent is cited about five times.

When comparing cites per patent, one must be careful to do so within a given technology area and within a specific year. The next section will discuss variations in citations in different technology areas.

The reason that comparisons can only be made within a specific year is because citations accumulate over time. For the first on-line edition of Tech-Line, the cite count per patent were those received by a particular patent from all US patents issued through June 1998. The result is that a US patent issued in 1990 will have more than seven years of citation, whereas a patent issued in 1992 will have only five years of citations. This is illustrated in Table 8.2, which shows the

Table 8.2. Cites per patent received by all Tech-Line® patents.

Year	Cites Per Patent
1988	6.6
1989	5.9
1990	5.4
1991	4.8
1992	4.2
1993	3.4
1994	2.6
1995	1.6
1996	0.8
1997	0.1

Note: Citations counts through 16 June 1998 for US patents.

number of cites for each patent in Tech-Line in all technology areas between 1988 and 1997.

Current impact index (CII)

The current impact index (CII) indicates patent quality of the patent portfolio. It is the number of times a company's patents in the last five years have been cited during the current year, relative to the entire patent database. A value of 1.0 represents the average citation frequency; a value of 2.0 represents twice the average citation frequency; and 0.25 represents 25% of the average citation frequency within the technology.

The key characteristic of CII is that it is a synchronous indicator: it looks back to the last five years. As a result, it moves alongside financial indicators and is sensitive to a company's current technology. For example, 10 or 15 year-old patents that are highly cited will not affect the CII, except those that the company has issued within the last five years. Essentially, the CII is the sum of the citation ratios for each of the company's patents in the last five years and cited by all patents during the current year. The following illustrates the computation of the CII for a hypothetical company, ABC:

Number of patents issued in year.

	1986	1987	1988	1989	1990
World	71,662	72,860	81,954	76,542	95,530
ABC	104	250	125	180	285

Number of citations from 1991 to year.

	1986	1987	1988	1989	1990
World	35,321	36,854	50,765	40,970	52,635
ABC	62	130	65	102	165

Average cites per patent from 1991 to year.

	1986	1987	1988	1989	1990
World	0.49	0.51	0.62	0.53	0.55
ABC	0.60	0.52	0.52	0.57	0.58

For each of the last five years, we form a citation ratio, which is the ratio of average cites to ABC's patents divided by the average cites for all patents. For example, for each of the five years included in the table above, we obtain the following citation ratios:

ABC's citation ratios (ratio to world).

1986	1987	1988	1989	1990
1.22	1.02	0.83	1.07	1.05

The final step in calculating the CII is the sum of these ratios, which is weighted by the number of patents the company has in each of the previous five years. The following illustrates this:

$$CII = \frac{1.22 \times 104 + 1.02 \times 250 + 0.83 \times 125 + 1.07 \times 180 + 1.05 \times 285}{104 + 250 + 125 + 180 + 285}$$

$$= 1.03$$

The current impact index is a citing year indicator. It gives you the impact or quality of the company's patents based on citing from the current year backwards. This is the reverse of the standard cites per patent indicator. The latter is based on the year cited and the sum of all the citations received in subsequent years.

For the entire patent system, the expected CII is 1.0. This means that a company whose patents have a CII of 1.5 has patents which are cited 50% more than expected during the current year in the last five years.

Since the CII only takes into account the last five years, one of its important characteristics is that when a company begins to run out of bright, new, inventions, its CII will begin to fall relatively quickly. This gives the analyst a stronger picture of what is likely to happen to a company's technology in the near future. However, in some industries, such as the pharmaceutical industry, there is a long time lag between patents and products, this should, perhaps, be factored into the analysis.

However, the essence of all citation indicators is to capture the fundamental technological strengths and capability of a company, and not to identify exactly which products or discoveries are going to be commercially important. There is too much uncertainty in technology to do it with any kind of general indicator. To borrow a sports metaphor, it is virtually impossible to know which player on a team will score. However, by analysing the talents in both teams, you can greatly improve your prediction of which team will win.

The basic premise behind technology indicators is that they are a necessary, but not sufficient, condition for company success. While it is not sufficient for a company to have a strong, creative technological and inventive capability, it is necessary if it wishes to become competitive in any of the technology-driven fields. A company either has to have or develop that technology in-house. Alternatively, it can license it in. Otherwise, it will be at a grave disadvantage.

Table 8.3 shows the five-year CII, by technology area, compared against the entire patent system for all the Tech-Line companies combined.

Again, there are substantial differences in technologies. The highest CII is found for medical equpment (2.38) while the lowest, in agriculture, is only 0.64, thus roughly indicating that the former is almost four times as highly cited the latter.

A second important observation of the table is that the value for "All" is 1.14 and not 1.00. The reason for this is because CII is calculated against the entire US patent system, whereas the Tech-Line

Table 8.3. Current impact index by technology area for all
Tech-Line® Companies, 1993–1997.

	Technology Area	Current Impact Index
1.	Agriculture	0.64
2.	Oil and gas	0.84
3.	Power generation and distribution	0.90
4.	Food and tobacco	0.91
5.	Textiles and apparel	0.79
6.	Wood and paper	0.99
7.	Chemicals	0.79
8.	Pharmaceuticals	0.79
9.	Biotechnology	0.68
10.	Medical equipment	2.38
11.	Medical electronics	1.77
12.	Plastics, polymers and bubber	0.77
13.	Glass, clay and cement	0.78
14.	Primary metals	0.59
15.	Fabricated metals	0.82
16.	Industrial machinery and tools	0.77
17.	Industrial process equipment	0.89
18.	Office equipment and cameras	1.22
19.	Heating and ventilation	0.95
20.	Miscellaneous machinery	0.86
21.	Computers and peripherals	1.88
22.	Telecommunications	1.65
23.	Semiconductors and electronic	1.35
24.	Measuring and eontrol equipment	1.02
25.	Electrical appliances and computer	1.01
26.	Motor vehicles and parts	1.33
27.	Aerospace and parts	0.68
28.	Other transport	0.70
29.	Miscellaneous manufacturing	0.88
99.	Other	1.06
All		1.14

companies only account for 63% of US patents. The fact that this number is substantially higher than 1.0 indicates, just as one would expect, that the major companies covered in Tech-Line have patents which are more highly cited than the entire patent system. In fact, patents owned by individual inventors and not assigned to companies in the US system are cited much less frequently than those assigned to companies.

Technology strength (TS)

Technology strength indicates the strength of the patent portfolio. It is the number of patents multiplied by CII, that is, the patent portfolio size is either inflated or deflated by patent quality.

We have tried, using the technology strength indicator, to capture both the size of the company's technological activity through the number of patents, as well as quality through the CII. There is, we must admit, a slight inconsistency in the way technological strength is defined, in that the number of patents refers to those in the current year while the CII citation indicator is based on cites of the company's patents in the last five years. The implicit assumption of technology strength is that the company's newly issued patents will have a similar impact and quality as its other recent patents.

Technology cycle time

Technology cycle time (TCT) indicates the spead of innovation. It is the median age, in years, of US patent references cited on the front page of the company's patents.

Fast-moving technologies, such as electronics, have a life cycle that is as short as three to four years. Slow-moving technologies, such as ship and boat building, may have a technology life cycle that is as long as 15 years or more. Companies with a shorter life cycle than their competitors in a given technology area may be advancing more quickly from previous technology to current technology.

Technology cycle time captures some elements of the rapidity with which a company is inventing, since it measures, in essence, the time between the previous patent and the current patent. As mentioned earlier, it varies substantially from one technology area to another (Table 8.4). Technology cycle time also varies from country to country. For example, Japanese inventions patented in the US tend to have a much shorter technology cycle time than their American counterparts, which in turn, have a shorter life cycle than European inventions. This difference is particularly noticeable in technologies such as electronics. We interpret this as a sign that the Japanese companies are innovating very rapidly, and possibly making incremental but rapid changes in their technology and products, whereas the European companies tend to innovate at a much slower pace, particularly in electronics. The US companies straddle somewhere between the two.

Another interesting aspect of technology cycle time is that it can be used, alongside the rate of increase in patents, to identify areas in which a company is intensively active in. This is because if a company is increasing its patenting and is at the forefront of a technological area, it will tend to have a short technology cycle time. We found that companies which are relatively slow in their inventive cycles tend to be very fast in one area, which is often the area in which they are known to be technology leaders.

As with many of the other indicators, the computation of TCT is not totally straightforward. For one, we use the median, rather than the average, age of the cited references. This is because there are, very often, one or two classic references in a patent. If we were to use the average, these one or two references would distort the data. The actual computation is illustrated in Table 8.5, where we show the six US patent references given in US patent 5200004.

Next to the patent and the year, which is normally given in the reference, is the age of each of the references from the point of view of the patent issued in 1993. The problem is: what is the median since it falls between two patents, each of which appears to be of five years of age?

Table 8.4. Technology cycle time by technology area for all Tech-Line® companies, 1993–1997.

Technology Area	Technology Cycle Time (1993–1997), in years
1. Agriculture	10.2
2. Oil and gas	11.9
3. Power generation and distribution	9.0
4. Food and tobacco	11.9
5. Textiles and apparel	12.9
6. Wood and paper	12.3
7. Chemicals	9.0
8. Pharmaceuticals	8.1
9. Biotechnology	7.7
10. Medical equipment	8.3
11. Medical electronics	6.7
12. Plastics, polymers and rubber	10.2
13. Glass, clay and cement	10.1
14. Primary metals	10.3
15. Fabricated metals	10.1
16. Industrial machinery and tools	10.7
17. Industrial process equipment	11.1
18. Office equipment and cameras	6.7
19. Heating and ventilation	10.4
20. Miscellaneous machinery	12.3
21. Computers and peripherals	5.8
22. Telecommunications	5.7
23. Semiconductors and electronic	6.0
24. Measuring and control equipment	7.7
25. Electrical appliances and computer	8.3
26. Motor vehicles and parts	7.1
27. Aerospace and parts	13.2
28. Other transport	11.1
29. Miscellaneous manufacturing	10.1
99. Other	9.7
All	8.0

Table 8.5. Technology cycle time illustration.

Patent: 05200004
Application date: 16 December 1991
Issue date: 6 April 1993
Title: Permanent Magnet

	Year	Patent Number	Age
References to	1957	2810640	36
US Patents	1966	3241930	27
	1988	4722869	5
	1988	4770718	5
	1990	4925741	3
	1991	5043025	2

In order to approximate this, we make the assumption that when there are multiple references to the same age (in years), they are evenly distributed throughout the year. The technology cycle time, computed for that patent would then be 5.5 years.

Science linkage

Science linkage (Ω) indicates how leading edge the company's technology is. It is the average number of scientific papers referenced on the front page of the company's patents.

High science linkage indicates that a company is building its technology based on advances in science. Companies at the forefront of a technology tend to have higher science linkage than their competitors. This type of citation is growing rapidly, averaging roughly one per patent: drug and medicine patents often have five or more; leading edge biotechnology patents, 15 or more; and Genentech's patents, 25 or more.

Science linkage is a particularly interesting indicator and one that has received a lot of coverage in the press recently. This is because CHI's research has shown that some 75% of all scientific references cited on the front pages of US patents had their origins in public science; that is, they were based on research done at universities, government laboratories, various non-profit research institutions and so forth (Narin *et al.*, 1997). Thus, we established quantitative evidence as a major role for fundamental, mainstream basic research in support of leading edge industrial technology. This work has been reported in a number of papers, including *The New York Times* (Broad, 1997), and elsewhere.

The construction of the basic data for the science linkage indicator is rather complex and tedious. This is because we differentiate between scientific references — which are included — and other non-patent literature references — which are excluded. When a US patent is issued, in the category known as "other references cited", there is a great variety of materials, including publications that are clearly scientific and those that are not. For example, there are thousands of references to technology disclosure bulletins which we exclude from our science linkage calculations.

In order to make that distinction, we have, by combining computer matching, manual verification and correction, processed more than two million non-patent references since 1983. Currently, we are processing close to 14,000 per week. This means that there are currently more than 14,000 non-patent references per week on the front pages of US patents. Figure 8.4 illustrates how this choice is made. The particular patent, 5200001, for a permanent magnet, contains seven non-patent references. Of these seven, we considered five to be scientific references, that is, published scientific papers and papers presented at formal scientific meetings. We do not consider the third reference a scientific one since it refers to a manuscript which may or may not have been distributed at a scientific meeting. As for the fifth reference, which alludes to the Patent Abstracts of Japan, it is almost certainly not a scientific paper.

In highly science-dependent fields such as biotechnology, the great majority of non-patent references are, in fact, scientific references. However, in many other fields, including some areas of electronics and those in the mechanical fields, most of the non-patent references are not scientific references. This differentiation is likely to be important

Patent: 05200001

Application date: 29 November 1990

Issue date: 6 April 1993

Title: Permanent magnet

References to non-patent literature:

Science

1: M. Endoh, *et al.* (1987) Magnetic properties and Thermal stabilities of Ga substituted Nd-Fe-Co-B Magnets. *IEEE Trans. on Magnetics*, 23(5), 2290.

Science

2: X. Shen, *et al.* (1987) The effect of molybdenum on the magnetic properties of the Nd-Fe-Co-B system. *J. Appl. Phys.* 61(8), 3433.

Non-science

3: Liu Guozeng, *et al.* (1989) Effect of Mo addition on the magnetic properties and thermal stability of sintered (Prnd)-Fe-Co-Al-B Magnet. Paper distributed at Kyoto, Japan, in May 1989.

Science

4: W. Rodewald & P. Schrey (1989) Structural and magnetic properties of sintered Nd14.4Fe67.0-Xc011.8Moxb6.8 magnets *IEEE Transactions of Magnetics*, 25(5), 3770–3772.

Non-Science

5: *Patent Abstracts of Japan* (1988) 12(82), and Jp-A-62 (1987) 218543 (Seiko).

Science

6: A. Maocai, *et al.* (1985) Effects of additive elements of magnetic properties of sintered Nd-B-Fe magnet. *Proceedings of the Eighth International Workshop of Rare Earth Magnets*, pp. 541–552.

Science

7: S. Hirosawa, *et al.* (1990) High coercivity Nd-Fe-B type permanent magnets with less dysprosium. *IEEE Transactions on Magnetics*, 26(5), 1960–1962.

Fig. 8.4. Science reference illustration.

Table 8.6. Science linkage by technology area for all Tech-Line companies, 1993–1997.

Technology Area	Science Linkage (Science References/Patent)
1. Agriculture	3.3
2. Oil and gas	0.8
3. Power generation and distribution	0.7
4. Food and tobacco	1.3
5. Textiles and apparel	0.3
6. Wood and paper	0.9
7. Chemicals	2.7
8. Pharmaceuticals	7.3
9. Biotechnology	14.4
10. Medical equipment	1.1
11. Medical electronics	2.2
12. Plastics, eolymers and rubber	0.9
13. Glass, clay and cement	1.0
14. Primary metals	0.9
15. Fabricated metals	0.7
16. Industrial aachinery and tools	0.2
17. Industrial process equipment	0.7
18. Office equipment and cameras	0.4
19. Heating and ventilation	0.2
20. Miscellaneous machinery	0.1
21. Computers and peripherals	1.0
22. Telecommunications	0.8
23. Semiconductors and electronic	1.3
24. Measuring and control equipment	0.9
25. Electrical appliances and computer	0.4
26. Motor vehicles and parts	0.1
27. Aerospace and parts	0.3
28. Other transport	0.1
29. Miscellaneous manufacturing	0.6
99. Other	0.9
All	1.5

since it seems that the linkage to science is the driving force behind many important areas in technology.

The fact that science linkage varies widely from one technology to another is depicted in Table 8.6. It lists the average science linkage measures for the five years, 1993 to 1997, for all Tech-Line companies in each of the 30 technology areas.

Quite clearly, there is a wide range of science linkage with biotechnology which, at 14.4, is almost twice that of the next highest area, pharmaceuticals, which is 7.3. Interestingly enough, the third highest area is agriculture. This is almost certainly due to the biotechnology revolution and the many advances in plant and animal genetics which are revolutionising agricultural technology. The fourth most science-linked area is chemicals. Undoubtedly, this is due to the fact that chemistry is a science and some biologically active agents are classified as chemicals rather than pharmaceuticals. Finally, the fifth area is medical electronics.

The areas which are the least science-linked are those which one would expect — miscellaneous machinery, motor vehicles and parts, and other transport — each of which have an average, less than one-tenth of scientific references per patent.

Science strength

Science strength (SS) indicates how much the company uses science to build its patent portfolio. It is the number of patents multiplied by science linkage, that is the size of the patent portfolio being inflated or deflated by the extent of science linkage. This is a count of the total number of science links in the company's patent portfolio.

Conclusions

Taken together, the combination of unified patent counts and indicators of technology quality in Tech-Line® should go far towards providing analysts with new and detailed insights into company technological strengths and the prospects for future company success.

Chapter 9

The Complex Relations Between Communities of Practice and the Implementation of Technological Innovations*

DONALD HISLOP

Introduction

One of the benefits of the current growth of interest in the subject of knowledge and learning in organisations is that this work has produced a number of concepts which may significantly improve the understanding of a wide range of organisational processes. Lave and Wenger's (1991) "community of practice" idea represents one of the potentially most useful of these concepts, and is arguably the most enduring element of their theory of situated learning (Contu & Willmott, 2000: 272; Fox, 2000: 853). Its importance is indicated by the extensive way it has been used in the burgeoning knowledge literature (Baumard, 1999; Brown & Duguid, 1991, 1998; DeFillippi & Arthur, 1998; Fox,

*This chapter first appeared as a paper in the *International Journal of Innovation Management*, 2003, 7(2), 163–188.

2000; Hildreth *et al.*, 2000; Liedtka, 1999; McDermott, 1999; Pan & Scarbrough, 1999; Raelin, 1997).

This paper applies the "communities of practice" concept to analyse the implementation of IT based process innovations in a number of case studies, and suggests that it has the ability to provide fresh insights into the dynamics of innovation processes. The socio-technical perspective conceptualises the implementation of technological innovations as involving the blending and synthesis of new knowledge and artefacts with existing organisational practices, artefacts and knowledge (Clark & Staunton, 1989; McLoughlin, 1999). Thus if, as the communities of practice literature suggests, organisational communities of practice both shape the structure of the organisational knowledge base, and represent important reservoirs of organisational knowledge, they have the potential to play an important role in the implementation of technological innovations.

The paper considers how organisational communities of practice (CoP's), and innovation processes mutually impinge on each other. Thus the paper considers both how communities of practice affect innovation processes, as well as how the implementation of change affects organisational communities of practice. Specifically, this involves examining a number of questions, including: how did the existing CoP's shape the distribution of relevant knowledge; how did the sense of identity possessed by members of CoP's impact on the sharing of knowledge within and between existing CoP's during the change process; did the CoP's facilitate or inhibit the sharing and utilisation of relevant knowledge during the innovation processes; what effect did the changes examined have on the knowledge/practices of existing CoP's; and what effect did the changes examined have on the population size/character of existing CoP's.

The paper has two primary objectives, to empirically and theoretically examine the links between innovation processes and communities of practice. The empirical objective is addressed through utilising case study evidence from a number of companies. The data used is drawn from longitudinal, qualitative studies of comparable innovations in seven case study companies. While the companies examined are from a range of countries, and sectors of activity, the focal innovation in each organisation was similar: all the case companies researched were attempting to implement IT based, multi-site, cross-functional management information systems.

The theoretical objective is achieved by reflecting on what the empirical data presented says about the way innovation processes and communities of practice are linked, and the general way that the community of practice concept requires to be modified and reconceptualised to make it a more useful analytical tool. This is important, as while the terminology of "communities of practice" has been become widely used, it still remains a relatively poorly developed concept. Issues which arguably require to be more effectively addressed include: taking greater account of the difficulties involved in sharing knowledge between different communities of practice; and more fully taking account of the potential negative aspects of communities of practice. Such analyses are required as too much contemporary writing on communities of practice focuses narrowly on their benefits and advantages (for example, Brown & Duguid, 1991; McDermott, 1999).

The next section more fully conceptualises both innovation processes and communities of practice. Following this, the paper briefly describes the organisational context of the seven case study companies, as well as the type of innovation projects they were undertaking. This section of the paper also contains empirical evidence on the extent to which communities of practice existed in the case companies. The following section, which represents the empirical core of the paper, describes the empirical evidence on the inter-relationship between the organisational CoP's outlined and the innovation processes being carried out. The main body of the paper then closes by discussing the theoretical implications of the data presented.

Theorisation on Communities of Practice and Innovation Processes

The communities of practice concept is based on two central premises: the activity based nature of knowledge/knowing, and the group based character of organisational activity. The development of an activity based view of knowing in organisations, what Cook and Brown refer to as an "epistemology of practice" (1999), has been developed to overcome what are regarded as the limitations of traditionally static, objectified views of knowledge (Blackler, 1995; Brown & Duguid, 1991; Clark, 2000; Tsoukas & Vladimirou, 2000). While traditional, static views of knowledge are based on a dichotomy between thinking and doing, in stark contrast, the activity based perspective suggests that this represents a false separation. Thus thinking and doing are fused in knowledgeable activity, the development and use of embodied knowledge in undertaking specific activities/tasks. Secondly, these organisational activities are typically social/communal activities (Gherardi *et al.*, 1998; Hayes & Walsham, 2000; Lave & Wenger, 1991; McDermott, 1999; Raelin, 1997). Barnes (1977: 2) provides a concise summary of this idea in the following quote,

> "knowledge is not produced by passively perceiving individuals, but by interacting social groups engaged in particular activities. And it is evaluated communally and not by isolated, individual judgments."

Fox (2000: 854), and Contu & Willmott (2000: 272) reinforce this when they define communities of practice, as, respectively, a group of people involved in a shared practice, and a community which reproduces its knowleddeability through common, collective practice. Thus activity is embedded in the particular social-occupational-functional groups that people work within. Knowing and working are therefore, ultimately social processes involving an ongoing interaction among individuals working within the same context, or addressing similar issues. For example, DeFillippi and Arthur (1998: 131–132), in a study of film production showed that for apprentice technicians processes of learning by watching were crucial. Also, Brown and Duguid (1991), drawing heavily on Orr's (1990) study of photocopy repair engineers, also showed how knowing was an ongoing, development process, based in engaging with day to day, practical tasks.

Based on such insights, Baumard defines a community of practice as a "community of practitioners within which situational learning develops...", which results in the community developing "a system of relationships between people, activities and the world" (1999: 209–210). Communities of practice thus typically possess three primary characteristics. Firstly, participants in a community possess a stock of common, shared knowledge. Secondly, communities typically also develop shared values and attitudes. Finally, and equally importantly, participants/members of communities also possess a sense of collective/group identity (Brown & Duguid, 2001).

The relationship between communities of practice, and the implementation of innovations is potentially of great interest for a number of reasons. Firstly, the communities of practice which exist in organisations are likely to influence the implementation process. The socio-technical perspective considers the implementation of technological innovations as involving the mutual adaptation of the technological system being implemented, and the organisational context within which they are being introduced (Badham *et al.*, 1997; Bryman, 2000: 470; Fleck, 1997; Mcloughlin, 1999; Scarbrough & Corbett, 1992; Leonard-Barton, 1995; Orlikowski, 1992). From this perspective the integration of knowledge represents a key element of these processes, typically involving the customisation of "new" knowledge and artefacts and their integration with existing organisational structures, practices and knowledge (which will themselves require some level of customisation) (Barley, 1986; Hislop *et al.*, 1997; McCabe, 1996; Harris, 1997). Thus, if communities of practice both shape the distribution of knowledge in organisations, and are important reservoirs of knowledge, the specific character of an organisation's communities of practice may significantly influence the dynamics of technological implementation processes. Dougherty (2001), for example, suggests that one of the defining characteristics of successful innovating organisations is their effective cultivation, use and support for organisational communities of practice.

Another reason for examining the relationship between innovation processes and communities of practice is that the relationship between them is likely to be two way, and not simply unidirectional. Thus not only will an organisation's communities of practice influence the nature of innovation processes, but the changes being implemented may also have implications for the communities. Lave and Wenger (1991: 113–117) suggest that there is likely to be tensions and contradictions within any community of practice between continuity and change, i.e., between the sharing and utilisation of existing practices/knowledge, and the evolution, development and ongoing modification of these practices. The implementation of technological innovations such as those examined thus represent a potential discontinuity impinging upon the practices, knowledge and norms of existing communities of practice.

Finally, the community of practice concept can also supplement and enrich our understanding of the dynamics of innovation processes through providing a new analytical concept with which to more fully understand behaviour during the implementation of innovations. Thus, for example, while issues such as the dynamics of inter-functional and business unit relations are well developed in the mainstream innovation literature, the community of practice concept provides a potentially useful extra dimension with which to characterise and explain these dynamics.

Organisational Context: Organisation-Wide Innovations, Fragmented Knowledge, and Multiple Communities of Practice

This section of the paper describes the character of the organisations and innovations which are examined, outlining their cross functional, multi-site character, and concludes by outlining the range and types of community of practice which are affected by, and involved in the change projects examined. The data presented is from seven detailed longitudinal case studies, all of which were implementing similar, standardised, cross functional, multi-site information management systems. Each company was visited at least twice (typically there were 3–4 visits per company), with visits occurring over a time period of between one year and 18 months. The focus of the research was on the progress and dynamics of the implementation projects described, with the longitudinal nature of the research allowing each implementation project to be followed over a number of stages. The source of data in each of the companies was semi-structured interviews with a range of project, and general management representatives. Table 9.1 lists the general characteristics of the case companies, the innovations examined, and the number of sites involved in the changes.

One issue worth briefly commenting on is the organisational context to the focal innovations. In all seven companies, the stated managerial objectives from their innovation projects were extremely similar and

Table 9.1. Organisation and innovation characteristics.

Company	Company Details	Innovation Type	International Project	Number of Sites Involved in Innovation Project
UK-Cast	UK based international specialist castings and injection mouldings	ERP System (Enterprise Resource Planning)	Yes	12
UK-Pharm	Specialist, international pharmaceuticals corporation	ERP System	Yes	4
UK-Pen-Gem	UK pension and life assurance company	Sales Automation Tool	No	60
UK-Pen-Swin	UK pension and life assurance company	Telephone Service Centre	No	10+
France-Connect	French mechanical connectors	ERP System	No	6
Neth-Bank	Dutch based, international bank	Intranet	Yes	100+
Swed-Truck	Swedish based, international fork lift truck company	ERP System	Yes	11 divisions (20+ sites)

were concerned with the closely inter-related objectives of improving co-ordination levels (between sites, functions, business units), and/or developing greater levels of standardisation (see Table 9.2). This issue will be returned to later, as it had quite significant implications for many organisational CoP's.

From the research conducted, a number of general conclusions can be drawn regarding the communities of practice which existed in the case companies. One of the most striking common feature across all

Table 9.2. Objectives of change.

Company	Change Type	Stated Managerial Objectives of Change
UK-Cast	ERP System	♦ Standardisation of operating practices/IT systems
		♦ Improve cross business co-operation
UK-Pharm	ERP System	♦ Improve efficiency of manufacturing practices
		♦ Improve cross functional co-ordination
		♦ Improve inter-business co-ordination of manufacturing
UK-Pen-Gem	Sales Automation Tool	♦ Automation and standardisation of sales support processes
		♦ Improve co-ordination between sales offices and corporate centre
UK-Pen-Swin	Telephone Service Centre	♦ Improve customer service and business retention
		♦ Improve co-ordination of assurance and pensions business
France-Connect	ERP System	♦ Improve/introduce co-ordination across sites/businesses
		♦ Improve cross-functional communications
Neth-Bank	Intranet	♦ Create a "networked bank"
		♦ Improve co-operation across business units
Swed-Truck	ERP System	♦ Standardisation of business processes/IT systems in Europe

seven companies was the fragmented nature of their knowledge bases. To some extent this was related to their multi-site, multi-divisional character. However, in relation to the focus of this paper, one of the most important consequences of this fragmentation was that each organisation possessed a large number of separate, and distinct communities of practice. Further, because the innovations examined were organisation-wide in scope, this meant that in each of the case companies significant numbers of communities both possessed organisational knowledge of relevance to the innovations being implemented, and were also affected by the changes that were occurring.

Finally, not only did the case companies all contain large numbers of distinct communities of practice, there were also a number of different and distinctive types of community. The most typical focus for these communities were business units and functions. This was largely because within these organisations work activities tended to be sub-divided and separated along these lines. Thus, any individual, or group of individuals had responsibility for, and involvement with a specific range of work activities. These groups of individuals can be referred to as communities of practice, as they possessed, to differing degrees, all three of the characteristics of such communities outlined above (some common knowledge/practices, a shared sense of identity, and some element of common, work related values). Table 9.3 provides a brief summary of the characteristics of the main communities of practice in the case companies which were relevant to the innovation processes examined.

These characteristics can be more fully illustrated by describing one of the cases in detail. In the case of Swed-Truck, which sold, rented and serviced fork lift trucks, work was organised into small, discrete business units, which had responsibility for all business within specific geographic regions (typically nationally focused). Within this structure, there was, in general, little need for interaction between business units, and they operated as virtual stand-alone businesses. The structuring of work within Swed-Truck had historically been managed like this, and had, to some extent become institutionalised.

While each of the national business units in principle sold the same range of products and services, in reality they had significant autonomy

Table 9.3. Communities of practice.

Company	Common Identity	Common Knowledge	Share Values	Origin
UK-Cast	Business unit	Localised, specific business knowledge (products, markets, etc.).	Autonomy of business unit is positive (provides flexibility to respond to particular market/customer demands).	Corporate centre acted as holding company. History of relatively strict autonomy for BU's.
UK-Pharm	Business unit & function	Localised, specific business knowledge & specialised functional knowledge.	• Business — Localised autonomy is good. • Function — Collegiality within functions, but inter functional antagonism & rivalry for status.	Historical culture of functional and site/business isolation. Sites focussed on particular product lines. Lack of co-ordination between sites.
UK-Pen-Gem	Business unit & function	Localised, specific business knowledge & specialised functional knowledge.	• Business — Localised autonomy is positive. • Function — Collegiality within functions, but specialised nature of knowledge makes inter functional interaction difficult.	Strong historic culture of sales function autonomy. Also, dominant historical culture of product/business "silos" which operated in isolation.

(Continued)

Table 9.3 (*Continued*)

Company	Common Identity	Common Knowledge	Share Values	Origin
UK-Pen-Swin	Business unit & function	Localised, specific business knowledge & specialised functional knowledge.	• Business — Localised business autonomy is positive. • Function — Collegiality within functions, but specialised nature of knowledge makes inter functional interaction difficult.	Dominant historical culture of product/business "silos" which operated in isolation from each other. Isolation and independence of IT, administration and sales.
France-Connect	Function & geographic site	Specific functional knowledge.	Collegiality within functions, but inter functional antagonism & rivalry for status.	Dominant historical culture of functional isolation. Functional isolation reinforced by geographic separation of main functions (production, sales, IT).
Neth-Bank	Business unit & occupation	Localised, specific business knowledge & technical, occupational knowledge.	• Business — Localised business autonomy is positive. • Occupation (IT) — Sense of collegiality and commitment to help and share knowledge.	Dominant, historic culture of business unit autonomy. Antagonistic, competitive relations between BU's.
Swed-Truck	Business unit	Localised, specific business knowledge.	Autonomy of business unit is positive.	Historic culture of business unit autonomy. Limited interaction between BU's.

over how they did this. This was not only because the nature of the market, and character of customers varied significantly for each business, but that management in each business unit offered different levels of service and support to their customers. This resulted in the development of separate and somewhat specialised knowledge communities, which only had knowledge of their own customers and working practices. The autonomy of the business units was such that the evolution and development of their working practices, the upgrading of their IT systems etc., was done purely on the basis of local considerations, and issues of corporate wide compatibility were never considered. Thus, discrete and specific knowledge communities developed, with staff in each business unit possessing substantial amounts of specialised knowledge, relevant to their own localised working practices, and customer demands, which had limited transferability and relevance, in other business units.

The implementation of a corporate wide information management system into this context had a number of implications for these local, business unit focused communities of practice, as will be seen. Primarily, the introduction of greater levels of standardisation to some extent impinged on the autonomy of the communities over how they worked. Ultimately, the greater level of interaction between and knowledge sharing amongst local communities that the changes required to some extent threatened the local communities through (attempting) to create a larger, organisation-wide community. Thus, the technological innovation being implemented by Swed-Truck had quite significant implications for its traditional, business unit focused communities of practice.

Relations Between Communities of Practice and Innovation Processes

This section of the paper presents the main empirical evidence from the organisations/innovation processes examined. The richness of the qualitative data that was collected means that, within the space available in a paper, it is impossible to fully do justice to it. Thus, to address this, specific episodes/aspects from some of the case studies are presented to illustrate the diversity of ways in which the communities of practice and innovation processes interacted. This section is therefore structured thematically. A summary table (see Table 9.4) also draws these findings together. Finally, where other published data exists on the case companies, references are given, as they provide more detailed analyses of some of the case companies.

As illustrated in the previous section, the broad, typically organisation-wide scope of the innovation processes examined, combined with the fragmented nature of (all) the organisational knowledge bases meant that a diverse range of different communities of practice were involved. In fact, this arguably represents one of the defining characteristics of the innovation processes examined. These innovation processes thus required the co-ordination and management of personnel with significantly different knowledge bases, experiences, values and identities. As will be seen, this was an important aspect of these innovation processes, as one of the main ways in which the communities of practice affected them was through the character of the interaction between different communities.

The innovation processes examined provided evidence that the existence of communities of practice can act to either inhibit, or facilitate the utilisation and sharing of knowledge. Therefore while the existence of the communities of practice identified undoubtedly had a significant impact on the innovation processes examined, their overall effect was somewhat ambiguous. The rest of this section describes different episodes which illustrate key aspects of the relationship between the innovation processes examined, and the organisational communities of practice, involved in, or affected by these processes.

Ambiguous effects: Neth-Bank

The ambiguity referred to is well illustrated by the case of Neth-Bank, where communities of practice both inhibited, and facilitated processes of knowledge sharing in its attempts to develop a corporate wide intranet system. As with all other case companies, Neth-Bank had a strong historical culture of business autonomy. It had historically been structured into distinct and separate business units, which operated with complete autonomy from each other. This therefore influenced the development of distinct communities of practice within these business units, whose staff typically had little or no knowledge of the work carried out in other business units. Further, relations between these communities were typically antagonistic and competitive, rather than supportive (Newell *et al.,* 2000; Swan *et al.,* 1999).

The innovation that was studied within Neth-Bank, the development of its global intranet, was an attempt to overcome this, and develop a more co-operative culture. However, without exception, the various intranet (sub) projects that were developed were significantly inhibited by the reluctance of staff from different business units to collaborate and share knowledge with each other. The character of these business communities proved to be one of the major factors inhibiting the development of their global intranet, which required them to work together collectively to effectively implement it. In fact, what occurred in Neth-Bank was that each business unit developed its own, separate and distinctive intranet system. Thus, ironically, an innovation whose intention was to improve inter-business unit collaboration in the end had the effect of reinforcing rather than reducing business unit boundaries.

At the same time within Neth-Bank, however, another type of community of practice existed, a professional community of practice focused around their IT activities. While IT staff within Neth-Bank typically had a business unit focus, being employed by, and working within specific business units, there was evidence that a significant number of IT personnel also possessed a sense of identity as being part of an organisation-wide IT community, which to some extent transcended their narrower business unit identities. In contrast to the narrowly focused business unit communities, many IT staff, who were part of this community, had a positive, supportive impact on the development of the intranet. This was visible through the informal sharing of knowledge amongst IT staff, across business units, with business unit boundaries appearing not to inhibit these processes. These processes of knowledge sharing arguably supported the development of the global intranet through facilitating the dissemination of relevant, and important specialist knowledge. However, these communities were limited by the fact that they were typically partial, and highly localised, being based on the personal, informal networks of different IT staff. Therefore, their impact on the intranet projects was limited, and they were not able to counterbalance the knowledge hoarding of the business communities.

Inhibiting knowledge sharing: Clashes between functional communities

In two of the companies, UK-Pharm, and France-Connect, their communities of practice had a uniformly negative influence on their innovation projects. In both companies there had been a historical culture of autonomy and isolation between the main functions involved in and affected by the innovations examined (sales, manufacturing and IT in both cases). As with Neth-Bank's business units, relations between them had typically been competitive and antagonistic. Further, in both cases these functional groups could be described as communities of practice as they had developed their own specific specialist knowledge and values and had a coherent sense of identity. In both companies, these characteristics of their functional communities of practice significantly inhibited the progress of the innovation processes examined, as they failed to effectively work together and share relevant knowledge as was necessary for the success of the innovations. As a consequence, in both cases, not only were the implementation timetables extensively delayed, but the overall functionality of the innovations were also significantly compromised.

These cases are also of interest due to the way that the attitudes and behaviours of the functional communities of practice were shaped by the effect that the innovations processes had on them. The lack of co-operation and participation by the different communities of practice in both companies was due as much to the perception that they would be adversely affected by the innovations being implemented, as by any antagonism between the communities. In these companies different communities developed a perception that they would lose autonomy and power from the implementation of an organisation-wide information management system. These communities treasured their historical autonomy, and interpreted the proposed changes as being about reducing, attacking or undermining it through the development of (as they saw it) more standardised and centrally controlled working practices. Thus, in these two cases the two way nature of the relationship between innovation processes and communities of practice was clearly evident.

Local community loyalties: Resistance and transcendence

In UK-Cast and Swed-Truck, communities of practice were typically organised around business units, rather than functions. Further, while the innovations in both cases could be interpreted as reducing and undermining the historical autonomy of these communities, the communities of practice in these companies reacted quite differently to the changes that were being implemented. While in both companies, the innovations being implemented witnessed a move from highly autonomous and locally determined practices towards more constrained local autonomy and the use of more standardised practices, in Swed-Bank these changes were embraced, while in UK-Cast they were challenged.

In the case of Swed-Truck, whose innovation process was one of the most successful of the seven companies examined, the project management methods used played a significant role in encouraging staff from business communities of practice to transcend their traditionally localised senses of identity and embrace and support the changes being implemented (Hislop, 1999; Swan *et al.,* 1999). In the development phase of their innovation project, a cross-business unit project team was utilised. Further, the project team were able to create a sense of involvement and participation among local staff during the roll-out phase, as they were allowed to have an important role in local customisation activities. These project management methods had the effect of creating support for, and active involvement in the innovation process in Swed-Bank by staff from all but one business unit, and their project was deemed a success internally.[1]

These generally positive attitudes to change by Swed-Truck business communities contrasted starkly with the more generally negative reaction of staff in UK-Cast to an innovation with similar objectives. In UK-Cast the localised, business unit focused communities of practice were resistance to UK-Cast's proposed changes as they were interpreted as being against the interests of the local business unit communities. In this innovation process, a them-versus-us dynamic emerged between the corporate centre ("them"), who were interpreted as imposing change which would increase significantly levels of central control, and the local business units ("us") who the local communities interpreted as being the losers, through the dilution of their highly treasured autonomy. Thus, the innovation was seen to threaten existing and traditional communities of practice, which produced a negative reaction to the changes that corporate management in UK-Cast were attempting to implement.

The general findings, outlining the inter-relationship between the communities of practice and innovation processes, are detailed in Table 9.4.

Discussion

This section of the paper draws together the dominant themes and issues which emerge from the empirical data just examined, and links back to the theoretical issues touched on at the start of the paper. Before doing this, it is necessary to acknowledge the limitations of the empirical data utilised. Firstly, the case study based nature of the research, and the anecdotal nature of the evidence presented limits the generalisibility of the conclusions.

---

[1] The only resistance of any significance in Swed-Truck's case was by one local business unit. Interviewees were extremely divided about the source of this resistance. In the end their resistance was overcome by a combination of carrot and stick methods, where some of their concerns were deemed legitimate and addressed, while others were challenged, rejected and ignored.

Table 9.4. Effects of community of practice on innovation processes.

Company	Community Type	Effect of CoP's on Innovation Process
UK-Cast	Business	◆ Need to involve staff from range of business unit communities with knowledge of their processes-systems ◆ Strength of identity to BU's produced resistance to change. Change seen as threatening BU autonomy
UK-Pharm	Functional & Geographic	◆ Antagonistic functional communities inhibited co-operation ◆ Need to involve staff from range of business unit communities with knowledge of their processes-systems ◆ Production function/community highly resistant to change — Seen as challenging their power ◆ Site based identity overcome through careful selection and training
UK-Pen-Gem	Functional & Business	◆ Staff from sales function/community not involved in project development
UK-Pen-Swin	Functional & Business	◆ Need to involve staff from product area communities with knowledge of their processes/systems ◆ No significant resistance to change
France Connect	Functional & Geographic	◆ Antagonistic functional communities inhibited co-operation ◆ Cross functional nature of innovation required involvement of staff from all functions ◆ Strong resistance to change from sales function — Seen as challenging their power/autonomy
Neth-Bank	Occupational & Business	◆ Need to involve staff from range of business unit communities with knowledge of their processes-systems ◆ Management staff from BU's resistant to development of global intranet — Seen as undermining their autonomy ◆ Cross-BU co-operation of some IT staff supported intranet development
Swed-Truck	Business	◆ Need to involve staff from range of business unit communities with knowledge of their processes-systems ◆ Negligible resistance to change

Thus, further research is necessary to evaluate the generalisibility of the findings presented. For example, the research specifically examined innovations with organisation-wide implications, thus further research could be done of different types of innovation, which may involve and affect different ranges and types of communities in different ways.

After some general issues have been discussed regarding the nature of organisational activity and knowledge, the discussion will examine three focal themes in detail: the two way nature of the relationship between innovation processes and communities of practice; the (significant) difficulties involved in sharing knowledge between different communities of practice; and the potentially negative aspects of communities of practice.

The empirical evidence presented reinforced and supported the suggestions made earlier in the paper concerning both how knowledge/knowing in organisations is deeply embedded in practice/activity and further, how such organisational practice is typically collective in nature (Barnes, 1977; Brown & Duguid, 1998; McDermott, 1999). Thus the different communities of practice in each organisation developed their specialised and localised knowledge through the autonomy they had to structure, organise and carry out the (collective) tasks and activities they deemed necessary to meet the specific needs of their particular customers and market conditions. Thus the communities examined developed specialised knowledge both as a consequence of the autonomy they had, as well as the specificity of their customer/market conditions. Therefore, the communities of practice identified did provide an important social mechanism through which knowing and understanding developed, and further, they also represented important reservoirs of knowledge within the case companies.

The empirical evidence presented also reinforced arguments concerning the diffused, fragmented and highly differentiated nature of organisational knowledge (Clark, 2000: 255–257; Fox, 2000), and that organisations can be usefully conceived as distributed knowledge systems (Blackler et al., 2000; Grant, 1996; Tsoukas, 1996). All of the case companies examined contained large numbers of separate and distinct communities of practice, with their own specialist knowledge bases. Therefore, they require to be viewed as a "community-of-communities" (Brown & Duguid, 1991: 53), making one of the general tasks of management being to co-ordinate these diverse communities (Brown & Duguid, 2001; Cohen & Levinthal, 1990; Kogut & Zander, 1992).

Relations between communities of practice and innovation processes

In general terms, the data presented reinforces the mutuality of the relationship between innovation processes and communities of practice, thus, not only did the communities of practice affect the dynamics of the innovation processes researched, but the innovation processes has some quite significant consequences for the organisational communities of practice.

One of the most significant ways in which the communities of practice affected the innovation processes examined was through the way they influenced attitudes and behaviour of their members/participants. This was visible in two main ways. Firstly, the sense of identity workers had as being part of a community, combined with their interpretation of how their community was being affected by the innovations examined, significantly shaped their general attitude to the innovations. Thus, in Swed-Truck the business unit communities supported the changes being implemented, as did the IT based occupational community in Neth-Bank. Equally, the negative reaction of UK-Cast's business unit communities, and UK-Pharm and France-Connect's functional communities to their innovations could equally be explained in this way. These findings are also reinforced by another study which showed how scientific communities of practice in a UK research organisation resisted moves towards commercialisation as they interpreted this change as being fundamentally in contrast with the values of their community, which was related to developing scientific knowledge as an end in itself, rather than the commercial exploitation of scientific knowledge (Breu & Hemingway, 2002).

Secondly, the sense of identity that the workers in the case companies had in specific communities of practice also significantly shaped with whom they were willing to share knowledge. Thus, the antagonistic and competitive nature of relations between Neth-Bank's business unit communities, and UK-Pharm and France-Connect's functional communities of practice shaped their reluctance to share knowledge important to the innovations being implemented with each other.

The impact of these attitudes and behaviours on the innovation processes examined was significant, and crucially affected their degree of success. Thus the relative success of Swed-Truck's innovation and the relative failure of Neth-Bank's, UK-Pharm's and France-Connect's innovations to a significant extent shaped the willingness or reluctance of relevant communities to share their knowledge with each other. This therefore reinforces the socio-technical perspective on innovation processes (embodied most clearly in the work of Leonard-Barton, 1995; McLoughlin, 1999; Orlikowski, 1992), which considers the blending and integration of artefacts and knowledge as being a fundamental component of all technological innovation processes.

The type of innovations examined, which have impacts and relevance for a range of different CoP's can be referred to as boundary objects (Brown & Duguid, 1998). Boundary objects, which can be physical, symbolic, or linguistic, can be utilised to develop relations between the communities they impact on, through providing a common focus (Gherardi & Nicolini, 2002). The relative success of Swed-Truck's and UK-Pen-Swin's implementations is arguably because the project management methods utilised and emphasised this aspect of these innovations. This resulted in community members learning that the different communities had more in common than had historically been understood to be the case, with this realisation creating an element of willingness among people to collaborate in inter community collaboration.

The innovation processes examined also had significant consequences for the organisational communities of practice, which as illustrated, to some extent shaped their reaction and attitudes towards the innovations. The innovations examined were regarded by community members as presenting a potentially significant threat to the existence and viability of their traditional communities of practice. This was because these innovations potentially undermined the three core elements of these communities: their knowledge, identity and values.

The implementation of an organisation-wide information management system was regarded as threatening the values of independence and autonomy, which most communities treasured (see Table 9.3). This was because such systems, requiring a greater level of standardisation than had been historically traditional (see Table 9.2), were felt to reduce the ability of divisions to respond independently to the specific need of their markets and customers. Secondly, and relatedly, these innovations were perceived as threatening the common knowledge base of these autonomous communities through devaluing and making redundant the specific knowledge they possessed, and replacing it with more standardised knowledge and working practices developed at a corporate level. Thus the ability and need to develop local knowledge was regarded as being reduced. Finally, these innovations were also perceived to threaten and weaken the sense of identity possessed by community members. This sense of identity existed and was sustained because these communities had the ability to develop an independent body of common knowledge, shaped by the value of having local autonomy. Thus, by potentially undermining the values and knowledge of these communities, the innovations examined were also perceived as weakening the bonds which created a coherent and independent sense of identity.

Thus, overall the relationship between the implementation of innovations and CoP's can be seen as two way: not only do organisational CoP's affect the dynamics of innovation processes, but these innovation processes will impact on and affect the organisational CoP's. Separating cause from effect in such a relationship is thus likely to be difficult. This relationship is summarised in Fig. 9.1.

These findings reinforce the idea that communities of practice are dynamic rather than static, and that they evolve over time (Fox, 2000). Lave and Wenger (1991) suggested that there are likely to be tensions between continuity and change, as new practices, or changes in the constitution of communities may threaten or undermine existing practices and social relations. Such tensions are likely to occur on an ongoing basis, as members of communities grow old and their skills and

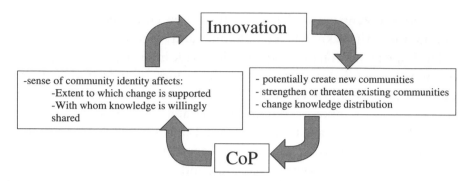

Fig. 9.1. Innovations and communities of practice.

competencies change, and through changes in the membership of communities, as some members of a community leave, and new ones join. What the research data presented suggests is that, if new organisational innovations introduce a significant discontinuity in working practices, then the conflict and tensions this produces may well result in organisational communities of practice not supporting these innovations.

The (not insignificant) difficulties of knowledge sharing between communities

One of the starkest findings from the research data presented was that the sharing of knowledge between different communities of practice was by no means straightforward. Thus, in Neth-Bank and UK-Cast there were problems in sharing knowledge between their business focused communities of practice, and in UK-Pen-Gem, UK-Pharm and France-Connect there were problems in knowledge sharing between their functional communities of practice. In fact, the research data suggests that there are a number of significant difficulties to such processes.

Acknowledging and examining the differences of sharing knowledge within and between communities, and the potential difficulties involved in sharing knowledge across communities requires to be addressed as they are issues which are neglected in much of the literature on this subject (see for example, Brown & Duguid, 1991; DeFillippi & Arthur, 1998; McDermott, 1999). Arguably, this is because much of the communities of practice literature focused narrowly on the dynamics of knowledge sharing within communities.

As has been well illustrated by the majority of the communities of practice literature, the existence of communities of practice facilitates the sharing of knowledge within a community, due to both the sense of collective identity, and the existence of a significant common knowledge base. However, the sharing of knowledge between communities is much more problematic, due to the lack of both these elements. Thus the dynamics of knowledge sharing within and between communities of practice are likely to be qualitatively different, with the sharing of knowledge between communities typically much more complex, difficult and problematic (Brown & Duguid, 1998).

Taking the issue of divergent identities first, the existent of different identities between different communities of practice arguably complicates the knowledge sharing process through the perceived or actual different interests between communities and the potential for conflict this creates. This was visible in the majority of the case companies, and, as illustrated earlier, one factor inhibiting knowledge sharing between communities examined was the perception that there were significant differences of interest. These findings are not unique to the case companies examined, as other research has shown that actual or perceived difference of interest has actively inhibited processes of knowledge sharing (Ciborra & Patriotta, 1998; Hayes & Walsham, 2000; Lazega, 1992; Storey & Barnett, 2000). In general terms, the communities of practice literature tends to play down, or neglect issues of power, politics and conflict, however, this represents a general weakness of much of the contemporary literature on organisational knowledge (Hayes & Walsham, 2000; Blackler, 1995; Swan & Scarbrough, 2001).

The other factor which arguably complicates the sharing of knowledge between communities of practice, is the distinctiveness of their knowledge bases, and the lack of common knowledge which may exist. Further, not only is the knowledge of these communities different, but their knowledge bases may also be based on qualitatively different assumptions, and interpretative frameworks (Tsoukas, 1996; Becker, 2001). Brown and Duguid (2001) referred to these as "epistemic differences", which significantly increase the difficulty not just of sharing knowledge between communities, but understanding the knowledge of another community and the assumptions it is based on, in the first place. Thus, the limited degree of common knowledge which can exist between different communities is likely to inhibit and complicate the sharing of knowledge.

Thus, paradoxically, the features which make communities of practice effective vehicles for the communication and knowledge sharing within a community, a shared common knowledge base, and a sense of collective community identity, may inhibit knowledge sharing across communities (Alvesson, 2000). For the type of cross-functional, multi-site innovation examined in this paper, which typically involved staff from a range of communities having to work together, this issue was extremely pertinent, as the innovation processes examined involved and required a substantial amount of knowledge sharing between communities.

The potential and unexplored dark side of communities of practice

While the period since the late 1990s witnessed an enormous growth of interest in the concept of communities of practice, the vast majority of the writing on the topic has been saturated in an almost suffocating optimism. Thus communities of practice have been variously argued to underpin levels of organisational innovativeness (Amidon, 1998; Brown & Duguid, 1991; Dougherty, 2001; Liedtka, 1999; Mitsuru, 1999), support and encourage organisational, individual and group learning (DeFillippi & Arthur, 1998; Iles, 1994; Lave & Wenger, 1991; Raelin, 1997), and facilitate processes of knowledge sharing (Brown & Duguid, 1998; Hildreth et al., 2000; McDermott, 1999; Ward, 2000). Connecting to the issue examined in the previous section, this bias may be a consequence of the fact that the communities of practice literature has typically focused rather narrowly on intra-community dynamics and knowledge sharing, rather than on inter-community dynamics. Arguably, however, through emphasising the positive aspects to communities of practice, this work has tended to neglect or overlook any potential negative consequences to them.

For the community of practice concept to be a useful analytical tool for understanding organisational processes and innovation dynamics, a more balanced perspective is needed which accounts for both the potential benefits and disadvantages of communities of practice. The data presented in this paper, for example, suggests that communities of practice are just as likely to resist as to support innovation processes, and that they have the potential to inhibit as much as facilitate knowledge sharing. Breu and Hemingway (2002) also show how communities of practice do not necessarily support innovations that are not deemed to be compatible with community interests.

Other work also suggests further ways in which communities of practice may have a dark side. Alvesson (2000), Baumard (1999: 211), and Brown and Duguid (2001) all suggest that if communities of practice have a particularly strong sense of identity, this may create a sense of exclusion and isolation which may inhibit communication or collaboration with the wider organisation. Leonard and Sensiper (1998) and Starbuck and Milliken (1998) also suggested that a potential negative aspect to any closed working group was the way they could blinker thinking, which can results in the exclusion or sidelining of relevant ideas.

Conclusion

As outlined earlier, the twin objectives of the paper were to firstly provide empirical evidence on whether and how communities of practice influenced the appropriation of innovations in a number of case study organisations, and secondly contribute to theory on innovation processes through utilising the community of practice concept. In general, the "communities of practice" concept proved useful and relevant for understanding the dynamics of the innovation processes examined. Not only were a wide range of communities of practice identified in all seven case companies, but they were also found to exert a significant influence in the innovation processes examined. Thus it is suggested that the communities of practice concept represents a potentially useful analytical tool for understanding the dynamics of innovation processes, and knowledge sharing practices more generally.

The data presented showed that for all of the case companies examined, organisational knowledge tended to be specialised, fragmented and highly diffused across sites, functions and business units. Further, this knowledge tended to be concentrated in specific communities of practice, with each community having responsibility for, and conducting a particular range of organisational tasks. This therefore reinforced Brown and Duguid's (1991) vision of an organisation as constituting a "community of communities". One of the major effects of this on the innovation processes examined was that they typically involved the collaboration of a wide range of different communities of practice.

Sharing and utilising knowledge between different communities of practice, which is an issue not adequately addressed in the large majority of the academic literature on the subject, was found to be a non-trivial issue. Firstly, the narrow specialist nature of knowledge which can develop within communities, may create problems of communication and understanding with individuals not in possession of this specialist knowledge, particularly as the knowledge of specialist communities may be based on very different assumptions and interpretative frameworks (Becker, 2001). Secondly, the sense of identity that individuals can invest in communities may act to inhibit the communication or sharing of their knowledge with individuals outside of the community of practice, particularly if there is a perception that the interests of different communities may be in conflict (Storey & Barnett, 2001).

While the majority of the communities of practice literature has typically emphasised their positive effects on knowledge sharing, the data presented here suggests that they had a more ambiguous impact. Thus, while there was evidence that communities facilitated the sharing of knowledge in some circumstances, in others, they actively inhibited it. Thus, while the communities of practice concept is useful in understanding and explaining the dynamics of innovation processes, such an analysis should be open to the possible negative aspects to communities of practice, to avoid the blinkered focus on their advantages which occurs when the concept is reified.

PART 4

ORGANISATIONAL COMPETENCIES

Chapter 10

Are There Any Competencies Out There? Identifying and Using Technical Competencies

DOROTHY GRIFFITHS and MAX BOISOT

The management of knowledge is increasingly being recognised as one of the major challenges facing the firm today. This challenge is not simply about the volume of knowledge which the modern firm must manage, but it is also about its nature, for knowledge is, ever more centrally, a source of competitive advantage in the global business environment.

This chapter will describe a model and a methodology which the authors have developed to assist companies on one aspect of this critical task: the identification, development and use of technologically-based knowledge assets or competencies.

We begin by exploring the concept of competence and explain how we have interpreted it. We review some of the literature on identifying and measuring competencies. We then describe a model developed by one of the authors (Boisot, 1994) and discuss its relevance to the exploration of competencies. Following this, we describe a methodology which we have been developing to apply Boisot's model to the exploration of knowledge-based assets. We conclude with some examples of its use as well as some lessons.

The Resource-Based View of the Firm

Traditional approaches to strategy have focussed on the analysis of products and markets as the key to competitiveness and successful performance. Strategic thinking and strategic analysis have evaluated competitor activities, market positioning, process costs, product life cycles, product differentiation and so on. The focus has been on how companies position themselves in relation to products, markets and competitors. The most well-known exponent of this approach is M. Porter. In *Competitive Strategy* (1980), he focussed on industrial structure and competitive positioning within industries. In it, he developed his — by now famous — Five Forces model for analysing competition within an industry: the power of suppliers; the power of buyers; the threat of substitutes; the threat of new entrants and the extent of the rivalry among existing firms. Firms could use this framework to understand their own position in their industry. Porter then went on to analyse a number of generic strategies, focussed on either cost or differentiation, which firms could adopt. In his 1985 book, *Competitive Advantage*, he introduced the concepts of the value chain and value chain analysis as a means for a company to understand and to ensure that it adds value at every stage of its processes. Much strategic analysis — albeit using a variety of models — has focussed on the issues of cost/quality and product/market.

This traditional approach to strategy dominated strategic thinking, analysis and activity from the 1960s to the 1980s and remains influential. For example, it provides the framework for most strategy courses in business schools. But the rise of global markets and of the global companies which serve them, together with an intensification of competition, deregulation and the rapid pace of technological change so characteristic of the end of the twentieth century, have posed a number of puzzles for this traditional approach For example, how does it explain a company like Canon which has managed to both move into and succeed in diversified markets? Rumelt (1984), through analysing diversification strategies, showed that of the nine potential strategies, the two which were most successful were those which built on an existing skill or resource base within the firm. Similarly, how does the traditional approach explain the significance of strategic asset stocks as opposed to flows? Dierickx and Cool (1989) for example, argued that while flows can be rapidly adjusted, stocks — representing as they do the accumulated flow of assets over a period of time — take longer to adjust. A traditional "portfolio" approach would tend to compare asset flows and ignore the potential significance of asset stocks. Yet, a new technology is likely to represent the flow of R&D (and other) resources over a number of years: an asset stock. Rumelt (1994) has further argued that the pressure for diversity, together with the toolkit of the traditional approach, has pushed responsibility further and further down diversified organisations. While this has produced what he calls a clarity of vision on products and profits, this vision has come at a cost: the ability to coordinate across functions, regions, products and times which is "at the heart of strategic advantage".

There has, however, long been an additional alternative perspective available to strategists and strategy scholars which can address these puzzles. This approach has, as its central theme, the view that *firm-specific* activities can also be a source of competitive advantage. Not surprisingly, this resource-based approach has been attracting increasing attention in recent years. Prahalad and Hamel (1990) have characterised the differences between the traditional and resource-based views as being between a "portfolio of competencies versus a portfolio of businesses". More dramatically, Stalk *et al.* (1992) have contrasted a "war of positions" with a "war of movement".

The origins of the resource-based approach can be traced — in different ways — to Selznick and to Penrose. In 1957, Selznick described the importance of "distinctive competencies" to the competitive success of firms. Penrose (1968), focussing on the growth of firms, emphasised the importance of considering resources from a broader perspective. She argued that it was not sufficient to just simply consider resources in and of themselves. It was also important to consider what they actually contributed to the organisation. Firm uniqueness follows from a particular configuration and utilisation of resources. Later, Wernerfelt

(1984) continued the theme (and probably coined the term the "resource-based view of the firm") in a paper in which he identified a whole range of resources which might, potentially, be available to a firm as a source of advantage. Among them, he included brand names, in-house knowledge of technology, the employment of skilled personnel, efficient procedures and capital. He also raised the question of strategies to develop new capabilities. At the heart of the resource-based approach is the recognition that firms within an industry are heterogenous (Barney, 1991).

There is as yet no agreement on what aspects of firm behaviour confer advantage. Different commentators have focussed on different factors. Bogaert *et al.* (1994) have reviewed some of the concepts used in the resource-based approach to strategic analysis. They begin with Wernerfelt and his concept of "resources" and subsequent emphasis on the analysis of "resource position barriers". Itami (1987) focussed on "invisible assets", which are often information-based resources. Barney discussed "firm resources", all the "assets, capabilities, processes, attributes, information and knowledge controlled by a firm". Grant (1991) distinguished between "resources" "inputs to the production process" and "capabilities" "the capacity to perform some task". Hall focussed on the importance of "intangible resources": "know-how" as opposed to "know what". Amit and Schoemaker (1993) discussed three key concepts of "resources", "capabilities" and "strategic assets". And, most famously, Prahalad and Hamel (1990) introduced the concept of "core competence", in which competencies are "the collective learning of the organisation".

The concept of capabilities is sometimes distinguished from that of competence. "Capabilities" tend to be used to describe more broadly-based business processes than "competence". Capabilities refer to the ability of a firm to deploy resources, while competence is used to describe the resources themselves. Teece *et al.* (1992) added the further dimension of "dynamic capabilities" to refer to capabilities which enable the firm to create new products and processes and to respond to changing market circumstances.

Henderson and Cockburn (1995) summarised this distinction as being between what they describe as "component" competencies and "architectural" competencies. The former refer to knowledge and skills and the latter, to their use.

The Concept of Core Competence

The most well-known and widely discussed vision of competence is that by Gary Hamel and C.K. Prahalad (1990). Their ideas serve as a referent for many in the field, including the present authors. Hence, it is worth describing their vision in more detail. In 1994, Hamel outlined their "working definition" of core competence as follows. First a core competence is an *integration* of skills and technologies. He argued that a core competence is unlikely to exist in a single skill or an individual team. Rather, they exist at an aggregate level: typically in the order of five to 15 in any large firm. Second, a core competence is a *product of learning* in the sense that it incorporates both tacit and explicit knowledge. Core competencies are, therefore, not assets in the usual accounting sense of the word. Third, core competencies deliver a *fundamental customer benefit*. Fourth, a core competence has longevity: they are sustainable because they are *difficult to imitate*. And fifth, core competencies must enable access to *new markets* through their incorporation into a range of the firm's products and services.

Prahalad and Hamel are, of course, not alone in stressing the importance of tacit knowledge to competitive advantage. Nonaka and Takeuchi (1995) criticise western management for its neglect of tacit knowledge in preference to explicit knowledge. Japanese success, in their view, follows from the capacity within Japanese companies to access and convert tacit knowledge into explicit knowledge (a point to which we shall return). Perhaps it is no coincidence that so many of Prahalad and Hamel's examples are drawn from Japanese firms.

According to Penrose (1959), companies grow in the direction set by their capabilities and these slowly expand and change. There is now a considerable literature, particularly in relation to technology, on the importance of learning and the consequent path dependency and cumulative nature of technological knowledge within firms (see for example, Nelson & Winter, 1977; Dosi, 1982; Teece & Pisano, 1994). What these authors demonstrate is the unique, firm-specific way in which firms approach technological development and use. Similarly Leonard-Barton (1992) and Teece *et al.* (1992) both stressed the significance of tacit knowledge within a firm as a source of advantage. In a related vein, Senge (1990) and others work on the "learning organisation", addresses the capture and use of tacit knowledge and experience. Thus, as Dierickx and Cool (1989) argue, strategic assets are built up over time. Their development is tied closely to a firm, its history, prior learning and investment and development activities, in a way which defies imitation and is non-tradable. Would be imitators are thwarted by the difficulty of discovering and re-enacting another firm's development trajectory.

Core competencies can, thus, be summarised as firm-specific, generic, sustainable skills and knowledge which are a product of learning. Hence they incorporate both tacit and explicit elements and offer some kind of value-based functionality to the customer.

Core competencies are not, of course, all of the same type. Hamel and Prahalad (1994) distinguish three types: market access, integrity-related and functionally-related. Market access competencies bring the firm into contact with customers; integrity-related competencies enable the firm to do things better/faster than its competitors; and functionally-related competencies confer distinctive — as opposed to incremental — customer benefits. They contend that the latter are becoming relatively more important for competitive success. This is because consolidation builds global businesses and all companies move to uniformly high standards of quality and service.

The resource-based approach to strategy, thus, offers firms a different framework to think about competitive positioning. In doing so, it raises a number of critical questions relating to the identification, development and management of core competence to which we now turn.

Identifying Core Competencies

At one level, the identification of competence appears to pose few difficulties. There are many cases which refer, for example, to the core competence of Honda in engines or Sony in minituarisation, and which explore why and how these firms have developed and maintain these competencies. But for core competence to be a tool of strategic analysis, what is also required is a means for firms to analyse, rigorously, their own and their competitors' competencies. One problem with this is that of causal ambiguity (Barney, 1991; Collis & Montgomery, 1995). Some commentators have argued that some sources of competitive advantage are so complex that the firm itself — let alone its competitors — does not understand them (Lippman and Rumelt, 1982).

Led by Prahalad and Hamel, a number of commentators on competence have developed what Knott *et al.* (1996) have described as the hierarchical model of competence. Influenced, they and others (Miyazaki, 1994) suggest, by Giger's (1984) concept of a technological bonsai, a hierarchical model of competencies has been produced in which *knowledge and skills* are integrated into *competencies.* These are incorporated into a variety of *core products* which serve a variety of *strategic business units* and their *markets.* Knott and his colleagues, in attempting to use this model empirically, criticised it on a number of grounds. First, they found examples which did not conform to the hierarchy. For example, they found end products based on individual skills and some service-based competencies which could be delivered directly to customers. Second, they found a blurring between skills and competencies which suggested that the later could not be expressed simply in terms of skills. Third, they found that they had to broaden the concept of core products to include core technologies. Finally, they found it difficult to consider competencies in isolation from other organisational factors and the linkages between them. Based on these problems, they proposed a holistic model of competence which

> "shows competence as an attribute of organisa-
> tion, influenced by the external environment,

organisational factors, and individuals, that delivers output of value ... competence is not a *subset* of the organisation, but a holistic, common *property* of it" 1996: 499, (original emphasis).

Knott (1997) has since gone on to try to develop and use this holistic approach. As yet, it remains at the developmental stage.

A number of academics have sought to identify core competencies by testing their characteristics against a set of empirical indicators. Barney (1991), for example, argues that for a firm resource to offer the potential of sustained competitive advantage, it must exhibit four attributes: value, rarity, imitability and sustainability. It must be valuable in the sense that it exploits opportunities and/or neutralises threats in a firm's environment; it must be rare among a firm's current and potential competition; it must be imperfectly imitable, and there cannot be strategically equivalent substitutes for it.

Similarly, Klavans (1994) distinguishes two trends in the core competence literature which he describes as the technological and the institutional. The technological view, which he believes owes its origins to Schumpeter (1984) and Penrose (1959), treats core competencies as "objective capabilities". The focus is on the ability of the firm to "create" (innovate) and then "capture" (own/control) scientific and technological knowledge. Such core competencies lend themselves, he argues, to objective measurement via various bibliometric techniques. The institutional view, rooted in Selznick (1957) and, more recently, Prahalad and Hamel (1990), focusses on the socio-political factors which influence the firm's definition of what it is and are amenable to identification through psycholinguistic techniques. They can be acessed through strategic language statements which can be interpreted as revealing the firm's image of its competency: a case of rhetoric reflecting perceived reality.

Empirical work on measuring competencies falls, according to Henderson and Cockburn (1995), into a number of types. There is research which explores the impact of competence at aggregate levels of performance (for example, Hitt & Ireland, 1985; Collis & Montgomery, 1995). There is research which explores the evolution of competence within individual firms (Iansiti & Clark, 1994, Leonard-Barton, 1992) and empirical studies, such as their own (Henderson & Cockburn, 1995), which attempt to link firm and sector level analyses.

Methodologies to identify and measure core competencies are a growth area in the strategic management literature. Yet, despite all the effort and attention, Coyne *et al.* (1997) writing in *The McKinsey Quarterly* (1997:41), noted how elusive core competencies remain:

> "Few managers we have talked to could claim to have utilised core competence to achieve success in the marketplace, and even fewer to have built a core competence from scratch. Indeed, most were uncertain as to exactly what qualifies a core competence ... it is like a mirage: something that from a distance appears to offer hope ... but turns to sand when approached."

Our own experience in working with the concept of core competence supports their view. Competencies disappear all too easily upon close examination. A careful scrutiny of competence claims reveals, all too often, that they are neither firm-specific nor sustainable, and that they convey neither functionality to the customer nor generic qualities to the firm. We feel that at least part of the problem rests with the process and consequences of accessing and exposing tacit knowledge. Tacit knowledge, almost by definition, is difficult to capture. Capture will almost certainly render it explicit. Rendering tacit knowledge explicit creates two potential problems: it either under-represents the knowledge or renders it imitable through description. Together, these have made us feel cautious about an empirical indicator approach to competence identification.

To help firms overcome the difficulties which we have described, we developed a methodology to assist them first to identify and, second, to hold an internal dialogue about technologically-based competencies or knowledge-based assets. It is based on the Boisot (1994) model of the movement of information within and between organisations, which we now describe.

The C-Space

The C-Space (culture-space) is a conceptual framework which focusses on the structuring and flow of information within and between organisations. It consists of two dimensions: *codification*, the extent to which data can be compressed and expressed on paper — simple text is typically more codified than images and quantitative information is more codified than discourse — and *diffusion*, the extent to which information is shared by a given population of agents. Agents can be either employees or firms. Boisot's theory describes the conditions under which new knowledge can be structured and shared both within and between firms, and integrates these into a dynamic model of learning.

The codification of knowledge involves taking information that human agents carry in their heads and which they find hard to articulate, and structuring it in such a way that its complexity is reduced. This enables it to be incorporated into physical objects or to be described on paper. Once this has occurred, it will develop a life of its own and can diffuse quite rapidly and extensively (Fig. 10.1).

Drawing on the resource-based perspective, a firm's technology can be viewed as information assets embedded in objects, documents and the minds of individuals, and is capable of generating value.

The social learning cycle

New knowledge moves around the C-Space in a cyclical fashion as shown in Fig. 10.2.

The social learning cycle (SLC) involves moving beyond codification and diffusion to embrace two other types of activities essential to effective learning: absorption and scanning. *Absorption* is a move down

Fig. 10.1. The C-Space.

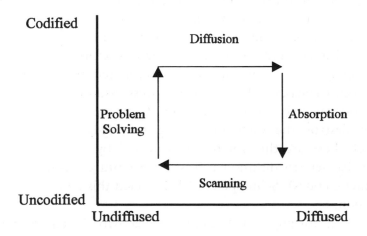

Fig. 10.2. The social learning curve.

the C-Space in which the codified knowledge picked up in the north-east corner is tested and used in a wide variety of contexts and is gradually internalised by learners. Over time, such learning-by-doing (or by using) builds a great deal of tacit knowledge. *Scanning* is a move to the left in the C-Space in which absorbed knowledge gives rise to unique insights. The integration of newly absorbed knowledge with an existing stock of uncodified tacit knowledge is something internal to the individual and, hence, highly personal. It is by no means automatic or trouble-free and individuals will vary in their ability to achieve it. Occasionally, these attempts at integration will give rise to unique insights or patterns. The extraction of unique patterns from generally available data creates new knowledge in a few individual heads, thus moving it from a tacit, yet diffused, state on the right of the C-Space to an equally tacit, but now undiffused, state on the left (Williamson, 1975). These patterns are indications of possible opportunities or threats that remain latent in the data and which have to be teased out through a process of creative problem-solving. If a given pattern appears promising enough to one or more individuals scanning the available data, it invites them to invest time and effort in giving it structure and to codify it in some way; a move up the C-Space on the left that initiates another round of the SLC.

If codification and diffusion eliminate scarcity rents, absorption and scanning, in contrast, might be considered the rent-generating, entrepreneurial phases of the SLC. The process ensures that new knowledge will continuously move up the C-Space and will sooner or later destroy the value of existing knowledge assets, no matter how well these are thought to be protected by barriers to diffusion. (Typical barriers to diffusion consist of patenting, economies of scale and esoteric codes). Schumpeter (1934) called this a process of creative destruction.

The social learning cycle is a purposive activity. It requires resources. Attention to the SLC can define what companies need to do over time to maintain and renew technologies and linkages in the lower left-hand corner of the C-Space, where knowledge is at its most tacit and new knowledge initiates problem-solving activities. The SLC illustrates the importance of integrating new and existing knowledge within the firm if knowledge creation is to be relevant to its needs (Iansiti & Clark, 1994).

Core competencies and the C-Space

Effective technology management is about knowing where to locate knowledge assets and the organisational linkages which integrate them together in the C-Space. The working hypothesis that has guided our research is that core competencies, if they exist within a firm, will occupy the lower left-hand region of the C-Space. In this context, competencies can be considered as technologies linked by organisational processes. Sometimes, the links bridge different parts of the organisation and, at other times, different technologies. Like the technologies which they integrate, organisational linkages are subject to the action of the SLC. One moment, they describe a tacit coordination among team members; the next moment, they are rigid organisation-wide rules or codified industry-wide regulations. Moving links up the C-Space gives them stability and facilitates their diffusion. That stability, however, can sometimes hinder. When it acquires the kind of inertia that blocks the future evolution of a competence, it becomes a competence trap which prevents the firm from adapting to new circumstances (Leonard-Barton, 1992).

The paradox of value: Creating value in the C-Space

A firm's effectiveness requires that its learning processes, that is, the particular SLCs it either generates or participates in, add value to its knowledge assets. We take value to reflect the blend of utility and scarcity embedded in a firm's product offerings and, in particular, in the knowledge base which generates these product offerings (Walrus, 1984; Boisot *et al.*, 1997).

In the C-Space, the utility of knowledge assets is a function of their degree of codification. The more an item of knowledge can be formalised, standardised or simplified, the more easily and reliably it can be manipulated and, subsequently, combined with other items of knowledge. The scarcity of knowledge assets, on the other hand, is a function of how close to the origin, along the diffusion dimension, such assets can be located. The lower the percentage of a given population in possession of a useful and sought-after knowledge item, the scarcer it becomes.

By this definition, therefore, maximum value is achieved by knowledge located at point MV in the C-Space in Fig. 10.3 (in this figure, the diffusion dimension is represented by the firms that make up an industry — other specifications are, of course, possible). Yet, point MV, because of the high degree of codification it implies, is located in the region in which knowledge reaches its highest degree of diffusibility. In other words, the point is unstable. This leads to a *paradox of value*: the greater the potential utility achieved by an item of knowledge, the more precarious and unstable the scarcity that it achieves becomes. More than anything else, perhaps, is the paradox of value that serves to demarcate the economic behaviour of firms, with respect to their *knowledge* assets, from that relating to their *physical* assets. Put starkly, an oil field cannot be photocopied; the formula for Coca-Cola can.

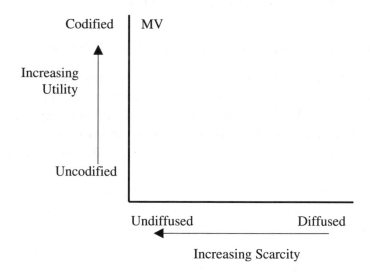

Fig. 10.3. The location of maximum value.

Being a knowledge asset, a core competence, is subject to this paradox of value. Firms have two quite distinct ways of dealing with it which we now explore.

Managing the Paradox of Value

In his discussion on adaptive processes, March (1987) distinguishes between exploitative and exploratory learning. Simplifying somewhat, exploitative learning pursues efficiency gains. It manifests itself in enterprise behaviour, primarily through a concern with things such as costs and prices. It tends to take the object of its learning for granted and aims to acquire a complete and detailed knowledge of it. One example of deliberate exploitation at work is provided by the experience curve in which product-related learning, whether secured through repetition or scale effects, is pressed into the service of driving down costs (Henderson, 1979).

Exploratory learning, in contrast, generates new options. At the enterprise level, this consists of identifying, often in a somewhat random and unstructured fashion, what new and value-adding possibilities are consistent with a given cost and price structure. Exploratory learning takes nothing for granted with respect to the objects of its learning and is more comfortable viewing them as a set of contingent and constructed representations. Thus, for example, Japanese car manufacturers in the 1980s were securing significant competitive advantages for themselves by incorporating, as standard items on their models, features that had hitherto been offered as expensive extras on car models in the west. There was nothing revolutionary in this: they had simply challenged a distinction between economy and luxury models which had become tacitly entrenched in the minds of Western automobile manufacturers as part of the way that the world works (Womack *et al.*, 1991).

In economic parlance, exploitative learning might be labelled equilibriating since, when applied to economic activity, it codifies and standardises the terms on which market competition can take place, thus allowing them to become visible and accessible to others. In such competition, initial cost and price advantages gradually get competed away through imitation and diffusion of best practice so that, over time, competition converges on an equilibrium price.

Exploratory learning, on the other hand, might be labelled disequilibriating since, with an open-ended specification of product or process attributes, it is impossible ever to fully codify the terms on which market competition is likely to take place, thus making it harder for market players to imitate each other. A firm's initial competitive advantages can therefore, be maintained by the continuous creation of novel, and often tacit, value-adding product or process attributes which are difficult for outsiders to cost and, sometimes, even to price. Although exploitative and exploratory learning will typically work in tandem, Levitt and March (1988), nevertheless, note a strong organisational preference for exploitative over exploratory learning.

The neo-classical theory of the firm assumes that effective organisational learning is essentially exploitative in nature and leads, over time, to market equilibrium — a process we label *N-learning*. A Schumpeterian perspective on the firm, on the other hand, takes organisational learning to be both exploratory and disequilibriating, as well as exploitative and equilibriating. It is viewed as a source of discontinuous novelty, as well as of efficiency gains, and under certain circumstances, also as a source of creative destruction. We label this second process *S-learning*. In the C-Space, N-learning comes to a halt in the north-east region following the diffusion of codified knowledge. S-learning, in contrast, involves moving beyond this region down the space through a complete SLC. N-learners, by focussing on the erosion of scarcity, tend to limit the diffusion of knowledge and to hoard it. S-learners, believing that diffusion can help them to renew their knowledge, are often quite happy to share it.

Applying the C-Space to the Exploration of Core Competencies: Our Methodology

The C-Space is a conceptual model. Our recent work has explored whether, and how, it can be operationalised to assist firms in discussions about their core competencies. In particular, we wondered whether it could be used to assist them in the recognition of significant tacit knowledge in such a way that this knowledge would not be made more vulnerable to diffusion to competitors. Our objectives and our claims are modest, but we believe that the methodology we have devised can assist firms in this way.

The methodology is workshop-based. The objectives of the workshops are twofold: first, to enable firms to map their technologies and the key linkages between them onto the C-Space; and second, to act as an elicitation device to facilitate a discussion about the meaning — in terms of core competencies and knowledge resources — of the data represented on this map.

There are a number of conditions which need to be met for a workshop to succeed. First, all its participants must be "literate" in the technology(ies) or "know-how" which are the subject of the workshop. Second, the participants must represent all the aspects of the technology(ies) or "know-how". Third, there must be sufficient time to complete all the stages.

Participants need to be "literate" in terms of the technology in order to be able to participate in the mapping exercises which place the technologies and linkages in the C-Space. As we shall see, divergent views about technology and linkage placement may represent valuable information. Hence it is important to ensure that such divergences are not simply a reflection of ignorance about the technologies.

Participants need to represent all aspects of a technology for the same reason. It is almost inevitable that the workshop participants will have different levels of experience and expertise about different aspects of a technology. These differences need to be reflected in the mix of participants who attend the workshop.

The workshops consist of five stages:

(i) Pre-workshop preparation.
(ii) Workshop introduction.
(iii) Identifying key linkages.

(iv) Mapping technologies and linkages.
(v) Discussion and interpretation.

To prepare for a workshop, we have typically worked with one or two internal champions. The champions undertake the pre-workshop preparation.

Stage one: Pre-workshop preparation

The following tasks need to be completed in this stage:

(i) Selecting the level of technology aggregation.
(ii) Breaking the technology down into relevant constituent elements.
(iii) Establishing the mapping orientation.
(iv) Selecting the workshop participants.

The level of technology aggregation

Technologies can be considered at different levels of aggregation. For example, a telephone, like the one sitting on your desk, could be considered as one technological element in a broader communication technology, of which other elements might include switches at an exchange. Or the telephone can be considered as the technology and be broken down into its constituent technological elements. The first step in a workshop is to decide what level of aggregation is appropriate. Core competencies, by definition, tend not to relate to disaggregated technologies. A clear, and shared, understanding of both the technology and its level of aggregation is critical. Our experience suggests that it is more relevant to consider technologies at a level where they constitute a process or a system.

Breaking the technology down into its constituent elements

Having established the level of technology aggregation, the next step is to break the technology into a number of constituent elements. Take, for example, a process. The process will consist of a number of elements.

Typically, each element consists, in turn, of a number of technologies. For example, the technology to make a fibre might consist of the following elements:

(i) Pulp
(ii) Mix
(iii) Dissolve
(iv) Filter
(v) Spin
(vi) Wash
(vii) Dry
(viii) Fibre
(ix) Purify
(x) Evaporate

We have found that, once the level of technology aggregation has been decided, those working with the technology within the firm do not find it either problematic or difficult to break the technology down into its constituent elements. It is important, however, that there is a consensus on the identity of these elements (see stage two).

Identifying the mapping orientation

The third task is to identify the mapping orientation. Is the workshop to consider technologies and the linkages between them at this moment in time, at a specified previous moment, or as they might become? Staff from different functions in a firm might have different perspectives on technologies and linkages. Is the workshop to represent a particular view, for example, research or marketing, or a cross-section of opinion? Failure to clarify these issues can subsequently give rise to unresolvable ambiguities.

Selecting the workshop participants

Workshop participants, as we have seen, need to be technologically literate and to represent all the elements of the technology(ies) or "know-how" which is/are to form the focus of the workshop. Since a key part of our claim for the C-Space focusses on its role as an elicitation device, there needs to be a sufficient number of participants to hold a discussion. We feel that there is probably a lower limit of about 12 participants for an effective workshop. Traditional problems of large numbers making for difficult discussions can be avoided by the use of groupware technologies. These enable small groups to hold simultaneous dialogues within a large group. Thus, they remove the problems of an upper limit on workshop size.

Stage two: Workshop introduction

The second stage consists of introductions to:

(i) The C-Space
(ii) The software, if a groupware-based facilitation system is to be used.

It is our experience that the majority of workshop participants find the C-Space model conceptually attractive. In order to participate fully in the discussion, participants need to be conversant with the C-Space and its core concepts. To do this, a fairly lengthy and detailed account of the C-Space, such as that described in this article, is required.

If Groupware is being used, participants need to familiarise themselves with the software before the workshop exercises begin.

Stage three: Identifying key linkages

The third stage is to identify the linkages between the elements of the technology. To do this:

(i) A consensus must be reached on the technology elements which were identified prior to the workshop.
(ii) The key linkages between these elements need to be identified and agreed upon.

First, a workshop champion needs to describe and explain the identification and selection of the technology elements. Workshop participants can then decide if they wish to modify the list in any way.

The next step is to identify the linkages between these technologies. Linkages refer to the relationships between technological elements. Some are significant while others are more distant. In C-Space terms, they are important because a competence may rest as much on how technological elements are related as in the technologies themselves. Linkages do not refer to the sequential relations between technological elements. Rather, they refer to the impact of one element on another. The balance between different feedstocks, for example, can affect the properties of a product. This is not a sequential relationship, but it is a linkage in our terms. Linkages may be mono-directional or involve feedback.

We access the significance of linkages by asking the workshop participants to identify and rank those which they believe to be most significant. One way to do this is to evaluate the impact of the linkage on performance. A linkage which has a critical impact on performance is more significant than one which has a more peripheral impact. This can be undertaken on an individual or group basis, depending on the size of the workshop. We have typically asked participants to complete a matrix where they can indicate of the impact of the technology elements on each other.

When the first round of responses are collated, a list of 10 to 12 of the most significant linkages can then be drawn up using some kind of consensus building. Numbers larger than 10 to 12 are only a problem in the sense that they extend the complexity of the mapping stage which follows.

Stage four: Mapping technologies and linkages

As with the other stages in the workshop, the four the stage involves a number of elements:

 (i) Locating the technologies and linkages in the C-Space.
(ii) Reviewing the results.
(iii) Agreeing upon a pattern.

As a first step, participants are asked to place each of the technologies and linkages identified in stage one and three onto the C-Space. This, they do so by placing each of them at a point on the codification and diffusion scales. The relevant population for diffusion needs to be defined: rather different data are generated when the diffusion population is the firm, as opposed to the industry, for example. For discussions about competence, it is often helpful to explore how widely knowledge about technologies and linkages are shared within the firm *and* within the industry. Comparing firm and industry level diffusion patterns can help firms to recognise that, while a particular technology may not be widely diffused within the firm, it is widely diffused among other firms in the industry. In this way, participants avoid the trap of believing that because something is new to them, it is also new to their competitors.

We have explored a number of different ways to manage the scaling of technologies and linkages onto the codification and diffusion scales. In the end, we have found it most helpful to provide participants with a framework, such as the following, to guide them. The scales need to be "tailored" to the context in which they will be used. An example of a codification scale used in a process industry is as follows:

Codified

Can be totally automated
Can be partially automated
Can be systematically described
Can be described and put down on paper
Can be shown and described verbally
Can be shown
Inside someone's heard

Uncodified

An example of a diffusion scale to be used at the industry level is:

Diffused

Known by all firms in all industries
Known by many firms in all industries
Known by many firms in many industries
Known by many firms in a few industries
Known by a handful of firms in a few industries
Known by only a handful of firms in one industry
Known only by one firm in one industry

Undiffused

Such scales may appear rather inexact but, for this purpose, they are exact enough. The C-Space is an heuristic and not an indicator or a measurement device.

Having completed the scaling on an individual basis, the next step is to feedback the results to participants in order to allow them to discuss differences. Quite often, differences reflect nothing more than different interpretations of the scales, and it is important that these be resolved so that more significant differences can be highlighted.

Groupware technology is very helpful in this context. Not only does it facilitate the rapid dissemination of the data, but the format of small groups clustered around a terminal lends itself easily to the discussion of differences. With large workshops, a further variant is to ask that the scaling itself be done in small groups.

On some occasions, however, the divergences between the scores of different individuals may require additional investigation (on occasion, beyond the workshop and involving additional resources). It is by no means uncommon to undertake some rescaling on an agreed upon interpretation.

Once this is completed, and agreed upon, the workshop participants have, before them, a series of C-Spaces into which the key technologies and key linkages have been mapped. Typically, there will be four: key linkages diffused at the firm level; key linkages diffused at the industry level; technologies diffused at the firm level; and technologies diffused at the industry level. These form the input for the final, and most critical, stage of the workshop: interpretation.

Stage five: Interpretation

This is the core of the workshop activity. Participants now have "maps" of the technologies and the key linkages in the C-Space, and can discuss what these data might signify in terms of core competence identification. To illustrate what these discussions can generate, we will briefly review the outcome of the use of the C-Space in three different contexts.

Each of our examples is drawn from an international company operating in a competitive environment. Company A was involved in a technology transfer situation with an overseas partner based in the host nation. Company B was bringing a new technologically-based product to the market. Company C was concerned with developing technologies to address particular operational problems. Collectively, the examples represent different issues in the management of technology-based knowledge assets.

The first example is the simplest. Company A faced a situation where its overseas partner was particularly anxious to gain access to a particular element of A's technology. A, however, believed that this technology constituted a core competence. Mapping A's technologies and linkages in the C-Space (Fig. 10.4) showed A, rather to its surprise, that the technology it was trying to protect was widely diffused within the industry. So, if its partner wanted access to this technology and A refused to share it, it could easily acquire access through A's competitors. A transferred the technology.

Company B is in the chemicals sector. It presented itself to us as a company which had demonstrated a consistent pattern of innovation, in relation to a type of product, over a long period of time. Since it had just brought a novel variant of the product to market, it believed that it had a core competence in relation to product development.

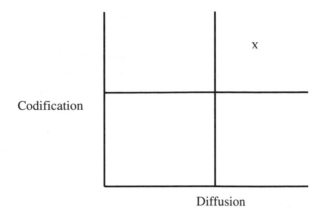

Fig. 10.4. Company A: Location of the key technology.

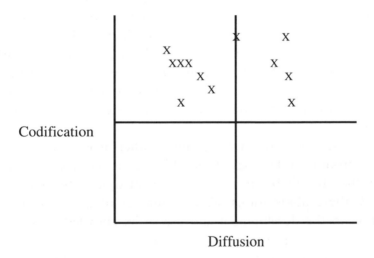

Fig. 10.5. Company B: Pattern of technologies of the new product.

The history of product group, in relation to Company B, suggested the importance — in C-Space terms — of scanning and tacit knowledge, and of a balance between exploitation and exploration. Company B took this to be evidence of a possible competence.

The workshop focussed on the new product. Diffusion was examined in terms of B's competitors, that is, at the industry level. The active workshop participants were staff with a good knowledge of the technology of the product and the history of its development within B.

The workshop produced a pattern of technologies and linkages in the C-Space as shown in Fig. 10.5. This pattern led to a number of observations. First, it is not immediately obvious that B has a core competence in product development. If it did, we would have expected to see some technologies and linkages located in the lower left quadrant of the C-Space. And, while challenged by some, the majority of the workshop participants shared our view.

Second, the pattern shown by B is typically that of the N-learner we described earlier, or — as we have described them elsewhere — a technology hoarder (Boisot, Griffiths and Mole, 1997). In common with all other actors in its sector B exploits technology. And in B's case it was seeking to exploit its new product by holding it in the region of maximum value via patents. The workshop suggested that the novel aspects of the manufacture of the new product were in the upper left quadrant of the C-Space, whilst longer established, more industry standard technologies were represented in the upper right quadrant.

Third, when — as we have explained earlier, it is a case of when — B's new product technology does diffuse to its competitors, it is not obvious that B will be in a position to introduce its successor.

For B, these observations raised a number of questions and issues in relation to the development and use of its knowledge assets. Some examples of these questions were as follows.

Company B operates in a sector which requires large capital investment in manufacturing plant in order to launch a new product. As such, B is involved in a tension between a rapid codification to permit exploitation and a less rapid codification to permit innovation. The workshop data suggested that B was placing more emphasis on the former than the latter. Might this prove to be short-sighted in the long term?

Having committed itself to the new product, B has invested a large amount of capital in the construction of the plant and the equipment to manufacture it — resources to "hold" it in the region of maximum value and marketing and sales resources. In short, B has made a huge commitment to its new product. Novelty, in the form of radical new products, driving out of the lower left-hand quadrant of the C-Space, is a potential threat to all this investment. Might B, then, no longer be interested in new knowledge assets?

Company C is a major petrochemical company. The focus of the workshop was a series of technologies to address a particular operational problem. In contrast to Company B, Company C believed that technology was subject to such rapid diffusion in their sector that there was no longer any point in trying to either regard or use it as a source of competitive advantage. Instead, they were seeking advantage through what they believed to be an organisationally-based competence relating to their ability to manage and use technology. They believed that they could utilise technological knowledge faster than their competitors and stated, explicitly, in internal documents, that they were developing a technology strategy based on the use, rather than the creation, of technology. Figure 10.6 indicates the pattern of technologies and linkages in Company C. (Again, diffusion was considered at the industry level.)

The pattern shown by Company C is more typical of the S-learner (or technology sharer) which we described earlier. Company C engages in exploratory learning. It actively searches for discontinuities in relation to technology and is open to processes of rapid and continuous technological change.

By reflecting on this pattern, C arrived at a number of conclusions. First, it became clear that technology generation remained important to them even though they no longer sought to exploit their knowledge assets by moving them through the region of maximum value. Second, they recognised that they continued to seek advantage in the way that they used technologies. Internal processes — many of them of an informal, uncodified nature — were important in this as they

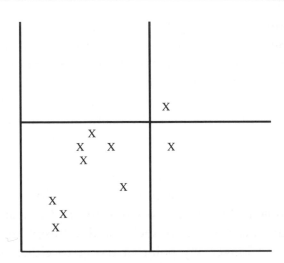

Fig. 10.6. Company C: Pattern of technologies.

enabled fast adoption and use which is critical to generating this advantage. Third, and related to this, they recognised the value of the tacit knowledge held in their employees' heads.

As with Company B, the workshop left C with a number of questions. Having highlighted the importance of the informal processes which operate in the lower part of the C-Space, C was left wondering how best to support them. Interestingly, it also left it wondering whether, in relation to the technologies in the extreme bottom left quadrant of the C-Space, it might, after all, wish to move them up towards the region of maximum value.

More importantly, too, the workshop challenged their self-image. Prior to the workshop, they had described their core competence in terms of internal processes which facilitated fast learning: they would seek and achieve advantage by bringing in technology developed elsewhere and to use it faster and more effectively than their competitors. The workshop data suggested, however, that this was only half the picture. The other half is C's continued creation of technology, which it then pushes out into the market to be developed (and which C subsequently brings back in and uses). C's creativity is actually driving its SLC. Hence C was left considering whether its self-image should more properly be that of a creator and user — but not a developer — of technology, with all that that implied (Griffths, Boisot and Mole, 1998).

Some Lessons

Taken together, these examples suggest a number of lessons. We believe it is no accident that it is much easier to discuss the identification of core competencies in the abstract than it is to identify them empirically. Nor do we find it some kind of intellectual game that so many terms are used to try to capture the key concepts of the resource-based view of competition. Nor is it surprising that, while firms can articulate what they believe their core competencies to be at a rather general level — such as "product development" in Company B for example — they experience much greater difficulty in articulating what the competence might constitute in any more detailed and strategically meaningful way. Yet, without some deeper insight, firms will face problems in the effective management of these crucial knowledge assets. Part of the difficulty, we have come to realise, relates to the capture of tacit knowledge. Perhaps it is not actually desirable for a firm to be able to articulate its tacit knowledge. Articulation involves description which, in turn, facilitates diffusion. But a crucial characteristic of a competence is its tacit nature and the element of learning which this represents. Company C clearly saw its winning advantage in the way it could use and absorb technologies — a lower C-space activity — the details of which they found hard to articulate. The use of the C-Space meant that they did not actually have to articulate these key processes: the C-Space facilitated both recognition and recognition without codification. It is this tacit element of competence which we believe provides inimitability and sustainability. We are not alone, of course, in pointing to the significance of tacit knowledge in the management of knowledge assets. Nonaka and

Takeuchi (1995), notably, have a model of knowledge creation which shares Boisot's recognition of the role and significance of tacit knowledge, as well as the type of organisational structures which might most appropriately support its development and management.

Perhaps the holy grail of core competence identification is an organisational litmus paper to test for their presence. In character, with its status as a holy grail, this litmus test has proven elusive. Our brief review of the extensive literature on core competencies indicated both the diversity of terms and concepts used to access core competence and some different approaches in their measurement. Our review left us puzzled over the difficulties experienced in the definition of such a central concept in a major strategic approach. The C-Space has enabled us to resolve a little of this puzzle. By providing a framework, through which the relative significance of tacit knowledge can be identified without having to render the knowledge explicit, the C-Space can facilitate the management of knowledge assets. As such, we offer it as a heuristic — as an elicitation device — which can be added to the strategic analyst's toolkit to identify and manage those aspects of knowledge-based resources which might constitute a core competence.

Chapter 11

The Organisation of "Knowledge Bases"*

JONATHAN SAPSED

Introduction

"**K**nowledge bases" within organisations are usually conceptualised as technical or functional disciplines, such as mechanical engineering, electronic engineering, marketing, accounts, project management and so forth. Typically management scholars analyse the knowledge bases profile of firms by proxy measures such as the patents or publications generated within these disciplines, where they are available.[1] Similarly, practicing managers often organise their firms' with the disciplinary categories in mind. Even where an organisation is designed to mix them up: such as in matrix or cross-functional management, knowledge assets are persistently thought of at the high level of functions.

This chapter argues that there is an inconspicuous sub-level of specialised knowledge base associated with tools, products, project experience and requirements that may hamper the intents of higher level organisation

---

*This chapter is based on the article, How should "knowledge bases" be organised in multi-technology corporations? *International Journal of Innovation Management*, Special Issue in honour of Keith Pavitt, 2005, **9**(1) 75–102.

[1]Exemplary studies of the patent analysis tradition include Granstrand *et al.* (1997), Patel and Pavitt (1997) and Brusoni *et al.* (2001).

design. The concept of "knowledge bases" is operationalised not as disciplinary fields or subfields but at the level of the team. The chapter shows how individual engineers share or do not share their knowledge with team members and their colleagues outside the team. By considering these dynamics, which are rooted in identity, career aspirations and learning paths, we gain a more complete understanding of knowledge bases, and how to organise them.

The chapter analyses two case studies of organisations attempting to manage transitions aimed at improved co-ordination processes. These are similar firms in high-tech, multi-technology, knowledge-intensive businesses. Both are project-based, in the same geographical region and about the same size, yet they have taken their organisations in contrary directions. The first has moved from organisation around functional disciplines to product-based, cross-functional teams, while the second has done the reverse. The chapter reviews the effects of these different organisational solutions on the processes of knowledge integration within the firms, the effects on communities of practice and the ways in which the systems have developed and adapted in response to the reorganisations.

The next section in the chapter reviews the literature on cross-functional teamworking pointing out the controversy over its purported advantages. It shows that there are tensions generated by cross-functional team structures. The third section addresses these tensions by looking at the received theory on social identification and the more recent work on communities of practice. Section four outlines the method for the study; an inductive approach based on grounded theory procedures that attempt to guard against tautological research. Section five outlines five categories that were common across the two companies: organisational change; knowledge integration; loss effects and problems; deployment of expertise and evolution. The conclusions follow in section six.

Cross-Functional Teamworking

It is a commonly found proposition in the management literature that cross-functional teams or matrix style organisation is associated with better knowledge sharing, and consequently better performance than pure functional forms (for example, Eisenhardt & Tabrizi, 1995; Cummings, 2004). But the discussion of functional organisation versus cross-functional organisation is not new. The distinction between functional and project-oriented organisation was well described by Sapolsky in 1972, in a military context:

> "A functionally specialised organisation is responsible for a particular organisational process or skill, e.g., aeronautical engineering, accounting, or typing, irrespective of the purposes to which those processes or skills are applied. A project-type organisation is responsible for a particular organisational purpose, e.g., strategic retaliation, conventional warfare, or counterinsurgency, and thus ties together all the process and skills necessary to accomplish that purpose." (1972: 62)

Indeed Sapolsky himself referred to "the classical statement" on the distinction by Luther Gulick in 1937. While the lineage goes back some time, in recent years cross-functional project teamworking has emerged as an important imperative for organisations and the subject of considerable managerial and scholarly attention. Empirical research suggests that most New Product Development (NPD) activity uses the cross-functional form (Griffin, 1997). Gobeli and Larson (1987) present data for a sample of 1,634 project managers in NPD, construction and new services and processes where less than 50% of managers used a pure functional structure, while 85% used some form of cross-functional matrix structure. As regards performance, Holland *et al.*'s (2000) review shows that inter-functional communication and transparency was correlated or associated with successful NPD projects.

Cross-functionality is only one type of diversity that is said to benefit teamworking outcomes, alongside age, gender, ethnicity, personal background, etc. Roberts (1987) asserts that diversity of technical background, age and values appears to heighten project team performance, as well as maintaining tension and challenge in the team. Too much similarity, comfort and familiarity reduces productivity and tends against the refreshment of technical knowledge through external contacts. Leonard and Sensiper (1998) argue that although diversity entails the management of divergent viewpoints, this "creative abrasion" can generate discussion and thought resulting in new ideas. Leonard and Sensiper suggest "...intellectually heterogeneous groups are more innovative than homogeneous ones." (1998: 118).

However, research on diverse teams also shows that group members tend to have lower job satisfaction, higher turnover and stress (Keller, 2001). By contrast to traditional functional silos, in terms of knowledge management there is a problem in co-ordinating a diverse set of areas of expertise (Denison *et al.*, 1996). While various authors argue that for systemic tasks like NPD, Cross-Functional Teams (CFTs) are more effective, Roberts (1987) and Allen (1984) claim functional organisations show best technical performance. This is contested by Gobeli and Larson's (1987) study, which shows that project managers generally felt that dedicated cross-functional project teams and project matrix type structures were judged most effective on criteria of technical performance, costs and schedule. More functional configurations were considered ineffective.

Roberts (1987) warns of the erosion of technical skills if a cross-functional project team is maintained over time. Engineers are removed from the disciplinary structure of their functions, and while matrix organisation is a noble ideal, usually one interest dominates. There is often tension and conflict. Members of cross-functional teams, which are typically temporary, working groups, often act as champions of their respective functions (Denison *et al.*, 1996). Donnellon (1993) refers to team members withholding their functional knowledge from the CFT as a means of defending functional territory. As a practical solution, Donnellon suggests shifting the role of the functional manager away from controlling the resources that are "made available" to CFTs, in favour of a "supplier" role; teams themselves should be responsible for delivery. This generally supports Gobeli and Larson's position above that recommends the balance of responsibility in favour of project team managers.

Teamworking, Identity and Communities of Practice

These tensions could simply be interpreted as the group-serving bias observed in behavioural decision-making research, which is shown to have an even greater effect than self-serving biases (Taylor & Doria, 1981). However, individual and group identity is another notion fraught with problems and factorial issues. Social identification theory suggests that the immediate group is often more salient for the individual, than an abstract, secondary organisation, as the immediate group is where interpersonal proximity and task interdependence is greatest (Ashforth & Mael, 1989). The immediate group can be a functional discipline or project team, but typically individuals have multiple, conflicting identities in the organisation. These are usually unresolved and are managed separately; "compartmentalised", sometimes giving rise to hypocrisy and "selective forgetting" (Ashforth & Mael, 1989: 35).

For the ethnomethodology field — the study of sense making in everyday life — the team context is not so much imposed by the external functions of the collected team members, as negotiated and achieved through the individuals' interactions in the team setting (Sharrock, 1974; Housley, 2000). Work on individual and group productivity bears this out, Roberts (1987) observes that in the innovation literature the nature of the immediate work group in terms of composition and supervision matter greatly to productivity among technical professionals, in addition to exogenous factors like the individuals' job maturity.

This somewhat dated debate becomes relevant again with the current interest in "communities of practice", as described by Lave and Wenger (1991) and Brown and Duguid (1991): "These groups of interdependent participants provide the work context within which members construct both shared identities and the social context that helps those identities to be shared." (Brown & Duguid, 2001: 202). These communities naturally emerge around local work practice and so tend to reinforce "balkanisation" around functions or occupation, but also extend to wider, dispersed networks of similar practitioners (van Maanen & Barley, 1984; Constant, 1987). Brown and Duguid's solution is "intercommunal negotiation" of differently practicing individuals, challenging and stretching each other's assumptions about ways of working. Cross-functional teamworking is an organisational setting that promotes this kind of intercommunal negotiation.

But the real value of cross-functional teamworking appears to be the channels it opens to the bodies of knowledge that are exogenous to the team. This is confirmed by recent research by Keller (2001), which shows that there is an important mediating variable between cross-functional diversity in a team and performance: external communications. By itself functional diversity had a strong, negative direct effect on budget performance, and no direct effect on schedules, but the presence of external communications affects improvement to technical quality, schedule and budget performance, but reduces group cohesiveness.

In general a high frequency of knowledge sharing outside of the group has long been established as positively related to performance, as gate-keeper individuals pick up and import vital signals and understanding (Allen, 1984; Ancona & Caldwell, 1992; Brown & Utterback, 1985). In particular, cross-functional composition in teams is argued to permit access to disciplinary knowledge bases outside (Sapsed et al., 2002).

From this discussion, several threads of research point to a view that cross-functional teamworking may be regarded as an organisational means of promoting the exchange of knowledge and practice across disciplines and communities. The literature suggests that this benefits creative activities such as new product development but there are associated penalties with regard to technical performance and professional career development. The picture that emerges is one of teamworking as organisational design (Galbraith, 1994; Mohrman et al., 1995) to promote the objectives of knowledge sharing, as well as the accustomed objective of efficiency in manufacturing operations (Tranfield et al., 2000).

Method

The empirical research presented here consists of two case studies of companies attempting to design and implement contrary organisational designs to manage essentially the same sorts of problems that arise in project-based, complex task environments. The two case study organisations, LandTraining Simulations and Visual Displays[2] both operate in high-tech project-based businesses in related sectors and provide differentiated products to many of the same customers. The products and solutions they develop require integrated contributions from several diverse knowledge fields and technical disciplines. Both development facilities are located within a mile of each other in the UK, although they have corporate affiliations in North America.

For these similarities the organisations make comparable case studies for comparison. Although one, LandTraining is a division of a much larger organisation and the other, Visual Displays is independent; LandTraining is quite autonomous in terms of its organisational operations and management. The two face similar structural constraints from country, region and industry, have similarly sized workforces with similar skill sets, and need to cope with the same problems of knowledge integration and uncertain, discontinuous business conditions. What is particularly intriguing for research purposes with these two case studies is that despite the resemblance, each has designed and implemented organisational changes that move in contrary directions. LandTraining Simulations has moved from project-based, cross-functional teams to a predominantly functional organisation, while Visual Displays has done the reverse.

The research was aimed at exploring and understanding the teamworking and knowledge dynamics and the effects of the reorganisations. The research process was influenced by the procedures and thinking of grounded theory (Glaser & Strauss, 1967; Strauss & Corbin, 1990). Grounded theory is an inductive approach to research that is concerned with avoiding preconceptions and the tautological confirmation of them. It is useful for research aiming at deep contextual understanding where labelling and analysis is tightly coupled to observed or recorded phenomena. In LandTraining Simulations the author conducted 15 face-to-face interviews with software team leaders, project managers, managers for systems engineering and purchasing, a systems

---

[2]These names are used instead of the actual companies' for reasons of confidentiality.

architect and a director for engineering and software. In Visual Displays 13 interviews were conducted with product team managers, technical development managers, programme managers, directors of sales and marketing, product strategy, operations and corporate organisation. The interviews had a modal length of one hour each.

Company documentation was also collected and analysed, including organisational diagrams, internal presentations used to support the initiatives and process and procedure documents such as work breakdown structures. The interviews were semi-structured but diversions from the "script" were also explored and recorded as respondents occasionally raised important issues that were unanticipated. The interviews were taped, transcribed and the data was systematically coded according to categories, properties and dimensional scales (Strauss & Corbin, 1990). For example, the following quote from one project manager:

> "...if you're designing a switch box then the electrical guys are designing all the wiring and the circuit, and the mechanical guy [is] designing the box to put it in and where on a particular piece of equipment this box is going to fit, so they work very closely together. And that has been a problem in the past; that the electrical guys go off and do their thing, the mechanical guys go off and do their thing and when you come to actually put this unit together it doesn't fit... that's improved now, it only happens once and its improved it, it is just a matter of banging heads together."

was coded as follows:

Category: Team Knowledge Requirement
Property: Product integration
Dimensional Scale: Cross-Discipline Interaction — No Interaction

All interviews were systematically coded in this way, building up a table of variables for each organisation. Relationships between these variables were then mapped, which allowed the subsuming of many of them, revealing five categories that were common to both organisations: organisational change; effects on knowledge integration; loss effects and problems; deployment of expertise and evolution.

Such grounded theory procedures intrinsically involve subjective interpretation but efforts are made to leave an audit trail and to validate the constructs with others to check for empirical reliability. The results were verified with the practitioners from the firms through interactive workshops and written reports, as well as academic colleagues. Finally follow-up interviews were conducted approximately one year after the initial interviews in order to check that the results were robust over time and not unduly affected by the "snapshot" approach. This follow-up phase revealed what had subsequently occurred in the firms and resulted in the fifth factor, evolution. The two firms are compared under each of the five key factors below.

The Case Studies

Organisational change and the role of boundary objects

The first category relates to the transitions in the two organisations; the motivations for them and the artefacts and tools — so called boundary objects — that were developed to facilitate the changes.

LandTraining Simulations

LandTraining Simulations' organisation structure was previously oriented around project-based, cross-functional teams, in which engineers worked for "heavyweight" project managers. This has changed to a functional system organised around technical disciplines called "resource groups", with project managers procuring pieces of work as deliverables from the functional managers. Groups from each discipline are assigned to the project with one engineer designated as the group leader for that project.

This is the form of organisation that Donnellon (1993) argues effectively relegates functional managers to the position of suppliers of resources, which should tend to encourage their co-operation from a

LandTraining Simulations

LandTraining Simulations is a provider of customised simulators and training solutions to military and civilian markets. It is based in a cluster of simulation firms in the UK, but is a division of a 5,000-employee international business headquartered in North America. Because of volatility in the defence industry and the project-based nature of the business, the division's workforce fluctuates from year-to-year from 60–200 staff. Its products support training of land-based military applications such as for air defence, artillery and tanks, and battle command and control simulation. Civilian applications include simulators to train airline pilots. The products are typically high value, highly customised or one-off units. They are complex products to develop, requiring the integration of various engineering disciplines; software, design, databases, production, electro-mechanical and electronic. In addition specialist knowledge of the applications is required, such as image generation or user-end knowledge such as the behaviour of artillery in the field.

Increasingly LandTraining Simulations has had to recruit and build capability in a new and different product area, microcomputer-based training (CBT), which is proving to be an effective and low-cost alternative to high-end customised simulators. In response, LandTraining Simulations has been trying to effect a shift in thinking away from technology and equipment to training needs and solutions.

Visual Displays

Visual Displays is a supplier of high-end screen displays and structures for a wide range of visualisation applications. These include corporate presentation and broadcasting, training devices and a growing range of applications in virtual reality for education and engineering, as well in entertainment. Visual was created in 1984 to take advantage of the trend towards outsourcing of subsystems in simulators. While the firm is developing markets for the newer applications, its core customer base remains that of simulators in the same way as their neighbour LandTraining, for whom they have supplied screen modules. The firm is organised around three core cross-functional teams that specialise in specific product lines. Although this permits a degree of standardisation, the workflow is project based and involves high degrees of customisation for each client. The production of these display systems requires the integration of knowledge bases in electronics, mechanical engineering, software, and structural design as well as specific know-how in optics, projectors and mirrors. Increasingly, Liquid Crystal Displays are being introduced to this product market.

The firm has been growing at a steady rate of around 20% for 10 years and is entering a stage of consolidation and maturity, as distinct from its early period as an entrepreneurial start-up. It currently has 170 employees, most of which are at the firm base in the same simulation cluster as LandTraining Simulations. Visual Displays also has sales and marketing branches and a spin-off Virtual Reality company in North America.

Fig. 11.1.

Table 11.1. Key factors in the case study organisations.

	Organisation Design	Knowledge Integration	Loss Effects	Deployment of Expertise	Evolution
LandTraining Simulations	From CF project teams to functional groups	Regular reviewing & integration of project pieces	Project Manager loses control	Niche experts & generalist systems architects	Project teams for novel projects
Visual Displays	From functional groups to CF product teams	Improved product lines. Inter-team knowledge breakdown	Engineers losing community & skills breadth	Generalists deployed on R&D	Functions co-locating. Middle tier emerging in teams

project management viewpoint. The reorganisation was motivated by two concerns; firstly management were aware that under the prior system an engineer with a particular skill may have been required on one project and "owned" by another team. The change was intended to make engineering resources more widely accessible and allocated more suitably. Secondly, engineers had been dissatisfied with the old project-based system because they were frequently working in isolation from their technical peers. The transition to functional groups was attempting to re-establish closer ties *within* the disciplines. The engineers took advantage of a move to a new building with large, open-plan space and set up their workspaces in functional tribal settlements.

To support the changes, representatives of all functions were involved in the creation of graphical process maps, showing linkages between the key players and groups in the new project process. These maps were devised by a cross-functional working group, effectively serving as boundary objects (Star & Griesemer, 1989), artefacts that embody and symbolise negotiated agreement between the different communities (Brown & Duguid, 2001; Carlile, 2002). By contrast Key Performance Indicators (KPIs) for the measurement of overheads, project completions,

Fig. 11.2. LandTraining Simulations.

overspend, etc., were developed at engineering development meetings and implemented within the functions. While the interfaces between communities are agreed at the boundaries and embodied in the process maps, the KPIs enable measurement within the functional communities.

Visual Displays

Visual Displays' reorganisation was antithetical to LandTraining Simulations'. Visual moved from a functional system into three cross-functional teams that specialise on three product lines; firstly, wide "panorama" style screens; second, wraparound, spherical screens with several projectors blending to generate the image; and third, special customised products with a rear-mounted projector. Each team has between 10 and 20 projects ongoing within the product line. Bids, sales and marketing and R&D functions were located outside of the product teams. Project managers were combined together with electronic, mechanical and commissioning engineers in the multidisciplinary teams, in order to achieve a greater customer focus and relationship. There was also a desire to promote learning across disciplines, as the firm's corporate organisation director explained, "ideally a display engineer is multidisciplinary, he is an expert in one technology but knows something about all of them. The idea of the teams was that engineers would pick up skills from the other disciplines."

To compensate for breaking up the functional disciplines, a new management role was introduced, the Technical Development Manager

(TDM). TDMs were appointed for electronic design, mechanical design and programme management and were intended to provide leadership for the functional discipline. Although "owned" by an individual team, the idea was that they would lead their functional communities across the organisation. This is a quasi-matrix device often recommended for project-based organisations (e.g., Hobday, 2000).

Visual Displays' reorganisation was a much more planned and deliberate strategy than LandTraining Simulations'. The perceived need for a more formal organisation design to improve communications came about because of the firm's growth of 30% per annum. The directors wanted to mix up disciplines, which they felt had become large enough to become too entrenched and internally focused. Similarly to LandTraining, this was an effect of the previous building which encouraged "groupishness" through its architecture of several small rooms, each of which housed a co-located functional group. The reorganisation preceded a move to a new building, which permitted large, open plan spaces.

There was a 12-month process of design, advocacy and planning during which all disciplines were consulted. The initiative was managed by a cross-functional working group involving strategic retreats, regular presentations on the new organisation structure, with consultation on details like job designs. The initiative was supported by internal publicity including a countdown poster campaign and T-shirts. A definite "D-Day" date was set when people would move desks and take up their new roles.

This long period of consultation served to span boundaries between the disciplinary communities, so that the new organisation design was built on a base of consensual legitimacy. Similarly to the process maps in LandTraining, an important boundary object developed in Visual Displays was a cross-team Work Breakdown Structure (WBS). This was intended to give an operational focus to complement the product focus achieved by the reorganisation. Previously projects and functions had their own spreadsheets, databases and time-cost reporting. The introduction of the WBS meant that they could now plan and measure against the same codes, and could begin using enterprise management tools. The WBS was based on a Product Structure, a hierarchical architecture of product subassemblies and components, negotiated jointly between engineers of all the disciplines.

The WBS is an effective boundary object, framed at a high enough level to allow discretion over the activities reported within the codes, but allowing for monitoring of overspending; code categories include, for instance, technical investigation, performance characteristics review, system testing and so on. This is an example of the distinction between the framing and content of complex management problems and solutions, as shown by Fiol (1994). Consensus is achieved with the framing of the problem; the need for accounting and accountability; the cash flow pressures of a project-based organisation; the need for common approaches to project management for better integration; but leaving sufficient scope for the inescapable content discrepancies and divergences within the agreed structure. In both companies boundary objects played an important role in facilitating the reorganisations through providing informational support and symbolising agreement between the communities.

Effects on knowledge integration

The second category refers to the task of integrating the diverse knowledge bases in the development and installation of products. This involves teamworking through consulting colleagues, reviewing, verifying and final integration both within and between the newly created teams.

Fig. 11.3.

LandTraining Simulations

The integration of knowledge resources is stressed as a key capability for turning the ownership of those resources into competitive advantage (Grant, 1991, 1996a, 1996b). For both LandTraining and Visual, the major problems of projects arise with integrating the pieces of the project together. These problems tend to occur late on in the production phase. Integration is complex and all about teamworking. But "teamworking" in this task environment is generally a matter of individuals independently completing their project pieces and validating these with others prior to the pieces being integrated "...most people can work largely in isolation, they are following their schedules that are laid down on the Gantt charts, but they're generally doing fairly individual things..."[3] or more bluntly "...people don't tend to talk to other people, they just sit and code their chunk."[4]

However communication becomes critical at the integration stage, as explained by this software team leader:

> "...you can still break it down into bits, and they go off and do their bit and then come back and say, 'I have finished'. And it's at that point that you've got to fit all the bits together and hopefully, they talked to each other whilst it has been going on, and then fitting all the bits together is a lot easier...in the end, if people have been speaking then it all comes together much more smoothly, it wastes a lot less time in trying to iron out problems."[5]

So although the teamworking in the company is not interdependent on a task level in the short term, in the sense that one team member cannot proceed without a colleague's actions, a high degree of communication is important in integrating the quite different knowledge

[3]Author's interview with software team leader A, LandTraining Simulations.
[4]Author's interview with software team leader C, LandTraining Simulations.
[5]Author's interview with software team leader B LandTraining Simulations.

bases together. Problems occur if validation and cross-checking has been insufficient and these problems are exacerbated if engineers are part-time players on a project. However, in general, managers in LandTraining reported a preference for the new functional system shortly after the change was made. They found that engineers were less tied-up than in the prior project-teamworking system.

Visual Displays

Meanwhile, combining technical disciplines in product teams had improved integration processes in Visual Displays. The firm had previously had problems that would only appear at the final stage of installation at the customer's site. Design and production engineers would only learn that their systems were not fitting together when the problem reached crisis-point. Following the reorganisation, commissioning engineers' feedback on integration problems is communicated directly to the designers and engineers in the product teams at an early stage. Engineers have a greater sense of the "big picture", understanding the issues and problems of their colleagues in other disciplines.

However, in spite of the improvement in knowledge integration in the product development teams, breakdowns in knowledge transfer continued to occur between the teams and the external services and functions. The non-technical bids and business development functions are dependent on the product teams engineering knowledge, and frequently need to interrupt their workflow. There are similar problems between R&D and the product teams where new product prototypes are passed over to the product teams at a stage they consider too early. These are typical problems that arise in complex organisations where knowledge integration is an inter-team, as much as an intra-team organisational problem (Grant, 1996a, 1996b, 2001; Sapsed *et al.*, 2002).

Loss effects and problems

The third common category was associated with various perceptions of loss and dispossession resulting from the reorganisations.

LandTraining Simulations

One objective of the change to functional organisation was to satisfy engineers' needs for exposure and organisational proximity to their disciplinary community.

> "...one of the problems that the guys found in the project teams and they were always moaning because...you might have three, four software engineers on a project where there were thirty or forty in the company and they got isolated over in their project group. They were always talking to the 'leccies [electrical engineers] and the clankies [mechanical engineers] and they never got to talk to their colleagues [laughs]. So they always felt a bit sort of isolated from their colleagues and felt they were missing out on the engineering chit-chat that goes on and the cross-fertilisation and in a way I think they felt a lack of technical leadership."[6]

Organisation into functional groups has effectively addressed this desire for regular contact with disciplinary peers. But there is a corresponding denuding of the project manager. Some complained of the loss of their previous pastoral role, where the project manager was responsible for all the team members' appraisals and personal development. Another frustration is the shift in authority between the project manager and the resource group manager:

> "I've got no-one in this company that works for me so I have not only got to manage people who are working for my project, I have also got dependent on them as well. I'm dependent on

---

[6]Author's interview with project manager A, LandTraining Simulations.

them to release the resources — the resources
that I want at the time I want them."[7]

This belies the view that this form of organisation relegates functional managers to mere "supplier" status as described by Donnellon (1993). The experience in LandTraining Simulations suggests commitment to release resources can be difficult to attain and that the balance of power favours the functional manager.

Visual Displays

Visual's shift from functional teams to cross-functional teams brought the equal and opposite effects to LandTraining's reversion to functions. One director commented, "I think we've lost some things. I think we've lost technical specialisms. When all the designers worked together, they learned a lot from each other."[8] Lack of regular exposure to technical peers has the effects of eroding the currentness of the individual engineers' skill sets and losing the benefits of disciplinary communities of practice. One product team manager explained:

> "...as a company although we're quite small, we've got quite a cross section of engineering skills, when you look at all three teams. When you look at them [the engineers] individually unfortunately, it tends to narrow them down a bit. That's not just my view... we're aware that their skill levels are very directed towards their own team, and really couldn't jump straight into another team and start working effectively. That would not happen."[9]

Although gaining a sense of the "big picture" for their team's product, the engineers lose the overall viewpoint of the organisation. A corollary

---

[7]Author's interview with project manager A, LandTraining Simulations.
[8]Author's interview with director A, Visual Displays.
[9]Author's interview with technical development manager A, Visual Displays.

of team specialisation on products is a tendency towards balkanisation on product lines rather than functions; "...it has almost set up three different companies", one technical development manager observed. The TDM role of maintaining technical community across the teams has proved difficult to achieve as the pressures of current projects in the product team take priority:

> "... unfortunately you're up against team leaders who control their own teams and they're not going to really want their staff to spend a lot of time doing for example, learning about another product, spending time with another team. If for example, Panorama is stuck for one design engineer, they need one from another team, that is their first port of call that's what they've got to say, 'well, I need another person, can these other teams supply him' and they'll immediately go on the defensive saying 'Oh no, we can't let anyone go' [laughs] I'm not suggesting that is the case but sometimes maybe it is. You may end up employing some contractor, get round it some other way. So that side of it is not so flexible, [if] we had all the design engineers in one group, it's just a case of moving work around between them, because the team environment was not an issue. It does tend to put up walls, there's no doubt about that. It's got its pluses and its minuses, if you ask my opinion it's got more pluses than minuses."[10]

This shows that in some respects knowledge sharing and teamworking was actually damaged as a result of introducing cross-functional team structure. In both cases there were significant loss effects as a result of the re-orientations of teams.

---

[10]Author's interview with technical development manager A, Visual Displays.

Deployment of expertise

The fourth category relates to expertise; how it develops and becomes specialised, the implications of this specialisation for the organisation, and how experts and gurus are deployed.

LandTraining Simulations

The software and engineering teams in LandTraining contain a diversity of specialised knowledge bases. Individuals within teams tend to develop specific know-how, for instance in image generation or user interfaces, and are then deployed on tasks in subsequent projects that draw on this same knowledge. Over time they accumulate an expertise and this specialisation is reinforced on successive projects. The downside of this is that this knowledge is uneven across the teams and the organisation. The one or two experts on a key technology or tool are not always available when their expertise is demanded, presenting a major resource-loading problem. This specialism may be in a particular engineering field, for example, all three software teams call upon an engineer with expertise in sound. Specific product knowledge is also rare and valuable. One software manager describes the dilemma associated with one engineer's rare knowledge of the DEC PDP product family[11] as well as the specific application:

> "...this particular guy who's been here a long time, and he has got excellent experience in a number of areas, and the thing is he is a major player on one of the current projects, and if we get this Skyfire [project] we will need him very badly for that one because he used to work on Skyfire many, many years ago and its an old PDP product. Most of us don't have any knowledge

---

[11]The DEC PDP was a line of minicomputers in the 1960s, which later evolved into micro or supermicro computers in the 1970s and 1980s.

of PDPs now; none of us know really how that product used to work apart from him... Generally our products now are PC-based, this one's in the days of PDP. So he's currently allocated ...But he is really needed on Skyfire as well, so if we win Skyfire, what the hell do we do? He's allocated up to his eyeballs so we are almost just hoping that he can finish that before we go on Skyfire, and I don't know how the hell you'd ever train up someone to pick up Skyfire. Yes, you might get someone who knows PDP and who knows Assembler and things like that, but they won't know the product."[12]

From a project-completion viewpoint, it makes more sense to deploy the specialists on tasks rather than the less-experienced:

"Most engineers are capable of doing all the tasks, it's just how efficient they will do those tasks ... you know that if you can get someone else to do it, but it's going to take twelve weeks, as opposed to someone who can do it in two weeks. You know, because they have got to be trained for eight weeks and then they make loads of mistakes and then that's got to be redone, and they have got to have all the training there and so on. So people are very much in their own little area and I don't think it is a bad thing I think that really does focus people's skills most of the time, and I think it does mean we get a much better product in my view..."[13]

However, there is also the recognition that this reinforcement of expertise tends to promote a teamworking structure around knowledge specialisms, which undermines the firm's organisational strategy:

---

[12]Author's interview with software team leader A, LandTraining Simulations.
[13]Author's interview with software team leader C, LandTraining Simulations.

> "... What we don't want in the company of
> course is an I[mage] G[eneration] team and a
> GUI [Graphical User Interface] team and a
> core services team. That's not the way the
> company has been structured, but effectively it
> is because we have one or two people who do
> GUIs, some of them do IGs and so on, and we
> keep those people in those areas of work.... I
> just think these people are in those specialist
> areas, so you almost have two levels of teams,
> in some respects."[14]

This admission illustrates how there are levels of "knowledge base" within an organisational structure. At a high, abstract level there are the technical disciplines (within which patenting activity can be observed and measured). Yet below this is a level of specialisation that relates to particular products, processes and tasks that is not so easily identifiable. Typically senior management organises at the first level, while project managers, engineering and resource managers find themselves organising at the second. The two levels may be, and frequently are in conflict from a knowledge sharing and development perspective. Often people are assigned to organisational units reflecting their broad profession, but in terms of how they allocate their time and attention they serve the pressing requirements of operations. Their "specialised expertise" is in knowing how to efficiently achieve results in a set of activities with high entry barriers of learning, rather than in a particular subfield of their engineering discipline.

In LandTraining, specialist experts do not appear to be affected by the reorganisation in terms of their everyday activities. However LandTraining also has a small group of generalist experts. These are the "Throbbing Heads", gurus who possess rare knowledge bases combining know-how from all the engineering domains that go into

---

[14]Author's interview with software team leader C, LandTraining Simulations.

producing simulators, albeit uneven. This expertise has accumulated over years of experience in the industry, and is complemented by insights into the idiosyncrasies of the business process, and the dynamics of competition.

LandTraining's management have deployed these experts as "systems architects" focusing their attention largely on the bid stage of the process. This design was attempting to provide an overview to more accurately cost bids and assess the feasibility of prospects. The functional teams could be seen to have a fragmented and "localised' perspective on bids and the systems architect role was introduced to provide overview, which is seen as critical to bid work. Previously, there was a perceived discontinuity from bid team to project team, which were typically entirely different sets of people. Under the new system, the systems architects work intensively on the bid, defining the engineering solution and cost framework. Following contract award their involvement tapers off, but is still available as a resource for consultation.

Visual Displays

Visual Displays also has a small number of highly experienced engineers named the "display gurus". One director explains:

> "There are a handful of people in the company that you can identify as a display guru. We can't go to the universities and take graduates who've taken a course in display systems, because of course those courses don't exist, so we've got to breed them ourselves, develop them and train them. They are very much a multi-disciplinary person — its electronics expertise, mechanical, design, optical, software; it's a mixture of all those things."[15]

---

[15]Author's interview with director A, Visual Displays.

But unlike LandTraining Simulations, these experts are deployed as a Research and Development (R&D) team, working on a variety of internal projects that address the applications that the market will want in years to come. This is consistent with the Visual organisation design in which the "erudite overview" should be less critical than in LandTraining, because of the compensating influence of the technical development managers and the cross-fertilisation in the teams. In practice the interface between the R&D team, bids and the product teams is problematic, the point at which prototypes are passed on to the more commercially-oriented teams is ambiguous. In addition the accumulated expertise of the display gurus is not easily accessible to the product engineers since they are organisationally and philosophically separate. R&D engineers nevertheless find themselves distracted from their R&D projects by bid work, in effect enacting the systems architects role in LandTraining. Both organisations find their specialists are deployed more or less on the same tasks as before the changes, while their generalists' time is spread thinly on support activities.

Evolution

This fifth category, evolution, was added following validation research visits one year after the initial fieldwork was conducted. It captures the subsequent adaptation to the new system, which to some extent might also be interpreted as "slippage" into the original state.

LandTraining Simulations

LandTraining's organisational structure has changed significantly since implementation of the changes. The previous section referred to the "teams within teams" that exist within LandTraining Simulations as an effect of knowledge specialisations. Subsequent to the reorganisation, the large software team of 25 people has been formally divided into three small teams, focusing on projects requiring three distinctive software competences, as well as some "floaters" who will work in all areas.

To some degree then, project-based team structure has re-emerged, which reintroduces the concern among engineers that they will become too embedded in one area of application. As one software team leader put it, "...I think people are a little bit unsure and unhappy about [it] because not everyone likes the category they're currently working on and the...thing is 'well, am I going to get stuck in this one?'"[16]

In addition, some cross-functional teamworking has been reintroduced. For projects that involve a high degree of novelty for the firm, project managers have asserted the need for a dedicated team of people drawn on a full-time basis from the resource groups. The resulting organisation is rationalised as CFTs for new, novel projects, functional organisation for familiar, "business as usual" work.

Visual Displays

Similarly, some of the old order is re-emerging in Visual Displays. Physical layout now resembles the previous structure, as team members of the same discipline have all moved their desks together. This is professedly because of the differing preferences for lighting and noise levels between the functions, but may also be interpreted as the tribal instinct returning.

Again similar to LandTraining, another management layer has formed in all three product teams. The original design was attempting to maintain as flat a hierarchy as possible, but the size of the teams was too large for one team leader to handle. In fact, the senior management of Visual is considering another reorganisation to address some of the deficiencies of the current system. These include the inter-team breakdowns of knowledge transfer noted above, e.g., making the product teams more responsible for bids work and trying to better integrate product team engineers and R&D engineers working on new product development.

---

[16]Author's interview with software team leader A, LandTraining Simulations.

Although the development from the original designs is categorised as evolution, correcting and adapting the system after intervention, it is interesting that both organisations have reverted to previous practice to some extent. This could also be viewed as the attraction to homeostasis, as described in Schön's (1971) *Beyond the Stable State*. Certainly this applies as regards the reaction of the disenfranchised elements; project managers needing to direct a dedicated team for a difficult project; the impulse for engineers to colocate with their peers. These issues are discussed more generally in the conclusions.

Conclusions

The chapter has outlined the recent literature debating the best way of organising technical disciplines in multi-technology corporations. It has shown how this discussion is long-standing and echoes debates in the past. The research presented followed a grounded theory approach to two case studies of firms re-organising in contrary directions. As such the research is subjective in its interpretation and limited in how the results may be generalised. As regards the first weakness, the author has collected data from multiple sources and attempted to validate the analysis with the practitioners from the firms involved and with academic colleagues to check that it was accurate. As for the second weakness, a follow-up stage was conducted a year after the initial research to mitigate the time-specificity of the reorganisation. However, the population of MTCs is extremely numerous and diverse and there would be a huge variety of outcomes from a range of reorganisations. The two cases here serve as powerful contrasting illustrations of cross-functional and functional organisational design. Bearing in mind the caveats we can make the following conclusions.

The antinomy of cross-functional diversity and specialisation

The contrasting experience of the two cases shows how the benefits of specialisation bring the converse disadvantages. While cross-functional teamworking brings some benefits from a product viewpoint, there is a corresponding loss in disciplinary collegiality. Organisation on functional lines tends to the antithetical problems of disempowered project managers and challenges the integrity of projects. This suggests there is no single "best practice" for teamworking organisation in complex task environments. Rather there appears to be an antinomy, a contradiction of equally valid principles between the advantages and drawbacks of cross-functional teamworking organisation. One seasoned project manager from LandTraining Simulations suggested the organisation design should be influenced by the external conditions prevailing at the time; if engineers are in demand then accommodate them in a favourable structure, whereas in lean times for the firm, deploy them for organisational benefit:

> "As long as I've been in the industry, it's never been resolved, there's always this movement, we've always been going backwards and forwards between one way or the other... I don't think there is an answer, if there is someone would have had it. We're stuck with it, the fact that we are always changing, people can recalibrate it. And again the priorities change you see, if the job market is tight [for] your project engineers you've got to be a bit more careful as to how you look after engineers, and how you feed their aspirations. If you're in a situation where, there's a shortage of people out there, or recessionary times, and also you haven't got much work you've got to do, got financial pressures, then perhaps you give less priority to that, you worry about other issues, just getting the job done, and again it's a lot of external influences that could factor in."[17]

---

[17]Author's interview with project manager B, LandTraining Simulations.

From the other side a Visual Displays director concurs on the pros and cons of functional versus cross-functional structures:

> "We have achieved a good part of what we wanted to achieve, we certainly have removed a lot of the barriers that we had, the internal walls, where problems were thrown over walls, what you do find is, you almost can't win in some respects, you knock down some walls and others emerge in other places. The issue is more one of wherever the walls pop up, trying to squash them down again, it's a constant battle. I don't believe there is any perfect ideal structures, the nature of our business is we're full of matrix structures in our organisation, and its not just one simple matrix, it's a number of multidimensional matrices going on. The challenge is trying to identify where the walls are happening and trying to do things to minimise them."[18]

Both firms were quite sensitive to the positive and negative effects of their teamworking designs. Various mechanisms and techniques were employed to mitigate the unfavourable consequences. Boundary spanning activities and objects were used and were important in promoting intercommunal negotiation, such as the process maps, Work Breakdown Structure and working groups. These helped to gain agreement and understanding of the new organisations.

Less successful were the attempts to compensate for the loss effects of the new structures, such as the technical development managers in Visual. The technical leadership role was not fulfilled as the same individuals were also assigned to specific product teams. This role may be more successful in better-resourced companies without the pressures

---

[18]Author's interview with director A, Visual Displays.

of project-based workflow. Yet accounts of large technical organisations show a remarkably similar pattern, for example, Jack Morton's book on the management of Bell Labs — perhaps the best resourced and most successful technical organisation of the twentieth century.

Morton, writing in 1971 about the previous three decades, shows that the concern over knowledge sharing and the co-ordination of specialisation is not a new one. He recounts the various organisational and spatial bonds that were introduced to couple Bell Labs and Western Electric, as well as AT&T and the operating companies. These bonds, such as relocation of personnel or assigning a common manager to separate units, were designed to balance the isolating effects of earlier separations. Barriers are sometimes desired to avoid domination and creativity in research and it is the job of the manager to adjust the system with bonds or barriers as is appropriate to the current situation. This recalibration, as our project manager above put it seems to be an endless task, as Morton says, "...the job never ends." (1971: 63) We can see then that even in large technical organisations, the antimony between diversity and specialisation is not easily remedied by organisational devices.

Organisation design and knowledge bases

Organisation design is a popular topic for theoretical literature and prescriptions for practitioners. The chapter outlined some often-cited ideas on designing for teamworking and for complexity. Galbraith (1972, 1994), for example, stresses the design of complex organisations. Wageman (2001) provides evidence to suggest that team design affects team performance significantly more than any subsequent coaching. The two cases here show some of the limitations of design, as an *ex ante* means of predictable control. In both cases the outcomes were quite different to the intended plan. Both showed some "slippage" to new hybrid forms. Similar to Mintzberg's (1994, 1996) observations of emergent corporate strategies, it may be that organisation designs are rarely implemented as they are conceived. They evolve and adapt and in a short space of time look quite different to the design. As illustrated by the two cases, they may exhibit self-organising properties as studied by work on complex open systems (see Lewin, 1999).

The cases show how natural "self-organisation" occurs and that received knowledge profiles and prior structures have a continuing influence. LandTraining Simulations' teams are actually more organised around specialised knowledge and skill sets than technical functions, as noted by one of the software team leaders, in spite of the pronounced reorganisation. While reorganisations tend to revolve around knowledge bases at the higher level of professional disciplines and functions, for convenience and efficiency engineers often find themselves deployed according to a lower level of specialisation, related to product knowledge, specific tools or non-codified ways of getting work done. The view of knowledge bases as observed through classes and subclasses of patenting activity would pick up on the first level, but probably not the second. Yet neglecting to attend to this lower level of knowledge base is an important factor why organisation design tends to have undesired effects, or no effect at all.

Acknowledgements

This research was supported by the UK's Engineering and Physical Sciences Research Council, grants M74092 and GR/R54132/01. I am grateful to Stefano Brusoni, Mike Hobday, Raphie Kaplinsky, Paul Nightingale, Jim Utterback and the anonymous referees for their comments and suggestions. Gratitude is also due to the practitioners in the study who gave their time and insights so generously.

Chapter 12

Assessing Performance in Supply

RICHARD LAMMING

Origins

During the twentieth century, many commercial and industrial organisations in a wide variety of sectors, which depend upon other organisations for inputs of materials, components and services, appear to have developed operational attitudes towards their "suppliers" that may be characterised by indifference, arrogance and naïveté. These are typified by the lack of formal strategic consideration given to the inputs to the organisation (in contrast to that given to the outputs in the form of "marketing"), by the calibre and cadre of employee assigned to purchasing, and by a lack of sophistication in the systems and procedures used in attempts to gain control over the costs and conditions of inputs (such as raw materials, components or semi-manufactures, services, consumables, sub-contracted activities and energy).

This situation may be traced to the development of mass production with its predilection for domination of processes (production, design and service) and markets (sales, labour and supply). The assumptions of mass production — that repeatability and standardisation, and thus market development, may be achieved through "top-down" control — appear to have been extended to encompass supply relationships, the place of the supplier of materials or services to the organisation being akin to that of the "below-stairs" servant in Victorian households (with the customer in the role of "Master of the house").[1]

The "roadblock to innovation" — exposed in the mid-century North American automotive industry by Abernathy (1978) — was evident in the supplier base as much as in the internal machinations of the "big three" oligopoly which dominated the vehicle assembly operations in that country — and heavily influenced firms in the rest of the world — for over half a century.[2] Moreover, the deficiencies of mass production exposed by the MIT International Motor Vehicle Programme in the 1980s were as clear in the manufacture and supply of components as they were in the production of passenger cars.[3]

Thus, innovation in suppliers to the automotive industry was curtailed by commercial and philosophical standpoints which cast the customer firm as the origin of all technical and commercial innovation. Meanwhile, the supplier is cast as a controllable and dispensable entity required to do its master's bidding without deviating from the specified path.[4] Subsequent work has revealed that similar situations exist in other industries.

With the development and popularisation of statistical quality control[5] came the idea that processes might be monitored and, thus, controlled by the collection and analysis of dimensional data. This is followed by

---

[1] It is important to remember that, for all its pivotal importance to the development of prosperity in the twentieth century, Taylor's system was based upon the premise of assumed stupidity (a word he actually used) in the worker and total obeisance to the manager, or planner. Ford appears to have taken up this line of thinking; its application to the proprietors of suppliers and contracting firms is surely one of the most astounding mysteries of the origins of mass production.

[2] The big three were General Motors, Ford and Chrysler. The third of these absorbed the fourth, smaller, player — American Motors — in the 1980s.

[3] See Womack *et al.* (1990).

[4] This is discussed at length in Lamming (1993).

[5] This is generally agreed to have been galvanised by the publication of Walter Shewart's book in 1931, *The Economic Control of Manufactured Products*, based on work at the Bell Laboratories in the 1920s. Both W. Edwards Deming and Joseph Juran were followers of Shewart.

judicious intervention in the process based upon or triggered by interpretation of the data. This development led to fundamental changes in manufacturing and underpinned the production of armaments in World War II (just as the Americans' requirements for World War I had accelerated the development of scientific management). This link with the defence sector (and, latterly, by association with the aerospace industry) led to the formalisation of quality standards for products, including components and materials, supplied for military customers. In the US and UK, the so-called "Military Specifications" and "Defence Standards" gave rise to the practice of formal assessment of suppliers for the purposes of accreditation as acceptable sources.

This assessment was, naturally, based upon the principles of statistical quality control (such as sample size, statistical inference, control charts and acceptable quality levels). The size and homogeneity of the defence customers (that is, goverment departments), as well as the standardisation of requirements, meant that suppliers could be reasonably expected to comply. The development of ideas in quality, however, and refinements in requirements, meant that frequent changes were made in specifications. Suppliers were also held responsible for keeping up-to-date with published documentation. In the customer organisations, meanwhile, the rule was often that business could not be placed with contractors who did not comply with Defence Standards (and were, thus, not "accredited"). The pressure for compliance was, therefore, placed jointly on contractors and on individuals within defence customers who were keen, for whatever reason, to engage those contractors. Responses to the latter pressure took the form of efforts within the customer to help the contractor/ supplier to become accredited — or schemes to "get round" the requirements in some way — by gaining dispensations or waivers for special circumstances (such as unique sources). The attitude that emerged, in terms of supply management, or procurement, was a modification of the *hauteur* in customers; the traditional, superior nature of the customer was combined with a common need (that is, in purchaser and contractor) for the supplier to succeed.

By the mid-1960s, two factors had led consumers in the West to expect higher quality in the products and services they purchased. The utilitarian nature of post-war consumerism in the 1950s had been replaced by the complacency and hedonism of the 1960s, fed by a developing concern for individually determined quality of life. Coupled with this was the emergence of international sources of supply, especially the availability of consumer products from the Far East. Japan, in particular, had learned lessons on total quality from its North American consultants and was applying them to its exported products, from transistor radios to automobiles (having grasped the strategy of entering markets at the low cost end and gradually increasing specifications, expectations, quality levels, market share, prices and margins). The exotic nature of the Japanese techniques, not fully explored until the 1980s, was nevertheless discussed by observers and would-be exponents — albeit in piecemeal fashion — in the 1970s, especially in respect of working practices. Key amongst these was the concept of quality, with practices such as "quality circles", "cost of non-quality" and "root cause problem solving" attracting much attention in the early 1970s.

In the West, as arguments between production (output-oriented) and quality (specification-oriented) managers raged in the factories of the 1970s, the consumers' call for improvements in product quality led to recrimination and blame in relationships within and between firms. The model provided by the Military Specifications and Defence Standards encouraged the development of similar schemes in other industries — notably the automotive sector. The concept of assessment of supplier performance, as a basic tenet of purchasing or supply chain management (as it was dubbed by consultants in the early 1980s), had arrived.

It is possible to trace the "professionalisation" of supply relationship management over the first half of the twentieth century, stemming from the introduction of scientific management and mass production thinking in manufacturing and service industries. Before mass production, there appears to have been a dynamic interaction between specialist firms which, in modern terms, might be seen as a network focused on delivering value to the eventual consumer. The massive expansion in the number of consumers was one driver for the development of marketing strategies based upon "push": planning products and then selling them.[6] The aphorism coined in retailing by H. Gordon Selfridge, that "the customer is always right", was transferred to industrial selling, thus launching millions of sales representatives upon the world, each knowing that a quarry that believed itself to be always right was a potentially very weak opponent in negotiation. In response to this, the function of purchasing was first developed as a job and, subsequently, as a "profession". Simple ideas, such as gaining multiple quotations for any requirement of the firm and then sourcing the business with the supplier/contractor offering the lowest price, became the tools of this new role. Since the imagination necessary was not extensive, the individuals filling the role were not typically as bright as their counterparts in sales, who plainly needed to survive on their wits.

When the notion of assessing the supplier's performance arose, therefore, it often fell to a combination of purchasing staff and quality control engineers to carry out the tasks: perhaps not the combination one would choose, with hindsight. In discussing this new "weapon in the buyer's arsenal", Lamberson et al. (1976) noted that each supplier could be advised on its shortcomings (discovered by the use of a formal system) and asked to discuss the performance target in the light of these problems. The supplier could then be penalised for non-conformance and, at the end of the contract, this non-conformance might lead to a loss of the customer's business. The supplier should be kept abreast of its performance and be expected to rectify any problems which affect performance. Lamberson's customer in the 1970s, who believed that he was always right, naturally assumed that faults in the supply chain were to be blamed upon the supplier, and had the data to do so.

---

[6]Both Taylor and Ford believed in an inexhaustible demand for the fruits of efficient labour and industry.

Ten years later, Gregory (1986: 25) reached similar conclusions; data obtained from performance measurement systems might, he observed, be used for a variety of purposes, ranging from managing the suppliers' average performance levels to supporting claims for legal remedies, such as liquidated damages and "breach of contract" penalty clauses. He also noted, however, that such systems might actually have a detrimental effect upon the buyer-supplier relationship; while the customer might see vendor assessment as a form of developmental co-operation, the suppliers may feel that they were faced with a range of coercive strategies from the customer. As Schonberger (1986: 169) points out,

> "... whether the supplier believes the benefits [of World Class Manufacturing] will flow downward does not matter much. Doing what the big customers want may be the only way to get a big contract."

Gregory (1986: 24) defines other problems which relate directly to the use of supplier measurement systems:

> "... many supplier evaluation techniques are either excessively time-consuming or so esoteric that a typical overworked manager cannot utilise them effectively from a practical point of view."

This is especially true when confronted with a complex technical or statistical analysis. While the act of analysing the relative importance of the evaluation criteria would in itself aid the validity of the selection process, doing so for each business transaction would be administratively demanding (this is also noted by Narasimhan, 1983 and Nydick & Hill, 1992). Problems with cost-based vendor assessment schemes, for example, centre around the validity of indirect performance costs, including issues such as how to derive accurate financial values for research and development activity, the maintenance of service levels and the development of the corporate image.

The Mechanisms

As we have seen, the development of supplier assessment began in the US and may be traced to Military Specifications there and elsewhere (for example, the British Defence Standards 0521/0524 in place in the 1970s.)

The techniques of statistical quality control (such as sampling, control charts and acceptable quality levels) were all evident in the early schemes. An audit trail for material (such as special steels) was often incorporated. This gave rise to an early focus on "house-keeping". In the automotive industry (an early adopter), the "safety critical" concept was well-established and its adaptation to focus on supplier performance was a simple matter.[7] The new schemes provided customers with the formal means to place the blame for supply problems upon the supplier.

The principles underlying supplier assessment include the following:

(i) Industrial customers should make purchases from, and only place contracts with, other firms which have been assessed formally with regard to their ability to provide timely delivery of goods and services to specification and in the manner required by the customer.

(ii) Performance in supply is the responsibility of the supplier. The supplier's efficiency or effectiveness may be assessed by the customer.

The application of the principles of total quality management to the performance of the supplier requires the integration of two quite distinct perspectives — the technical and the commercial. On the technical side, the monitoring of adherence to specification, inspection techniques and maintenance of standards may all be included. Early schemes embraced these factors naturally. They employed a variety

---

[7]The "safety critical" system assured an audit trail for any part in the vehicle which might lead to a death as a result of its failure (such as wheelnuts and braking assemblies). This entailed special documentation and physical facilities, such as secure storage and record-keeping.

of statistical analysis techniques based typically on the systematic and thorough collection of data, coupled with predetermined analyses and structured inference presentation using *pro forma* documentation constructed by the customer. In some cases, this was new to the supplier; in others, the suppliers themselves were already competent manufacturers and did not need the lessons that were foisted upon them by zealous customers. Inevitably, in the engineering industry, a supplier of technical products faced the assessment schemes of several customers, often with very different levels of requirements and methods for analysis.[8] The technical aspects of the assessment process, however, may be seen as reasonable dogma — after all, the customer is entitled to get what is requested, made to specification.

The commercial aspects of the assessment were less immediately justified. They were also more complex and took longer to evolve. A feature of this subject has always been the lack of a common and concise terminology as well as the nomenclature employed (in contrast to its progenitor, quality control, where terms such as "statistical process control" and "Ishikawa diagrams" quickly became universal standards). Early schemes were typically called "supplier quality assurance", thus reflecting the origins in quality control. As the perceived need to embrace business performance gained recognition, however, so the schemes became more adventurous in their character — and their names. In the mid-1980s, for example, General Motors launched its new scheme under the title "Targets for Excellence" (as an extension to its existing "Spear" programme). The complexity of TFE was so great that GM openly admitted it did not expect many suppliers (or, indeed, its own plants) to gain approval — the purpose was to create the goal.[9]

---

[8] By 1994, in the UK automotive industry, some suppliers were facing upwards of 20 different schemes. Elsewhere in Europe competitors in the industry had begun to band together to create joint schemes (Lamming, 1994).

[9] This is similar to the concept of "stretch" advocated a decade later by Hamel as a technique in strategic planning. See Hamel (1993).

In an early review of selection criteria, Dickson (1966) concluded that price was not seen as the most important — a remarkable result in view of the relationships that were perceived to exist at the time in North America. Dickson's list of common factors included product quality, on-time delivery and the supplier's performance history. Subsequent work (Lehmann & O'Shaughnessy, 1974; Gregory, 1986) showed the development towards the weight placed upon price as the world faced the competitive pressures of the 1970s and 1980s.

Monczka & Trecha (1988: 3) observed that the design, implementation and subsequent success of supplier measurement systems were based upon the way in which the overall effectiveness of purchasing is measured. They concluded that vendor assessment systems should generally concentrate on the areas of quality levels (such as the number of defects and the amount of rework), cost/price competitiveness, the type and level of technology and supplier responsiveness to purchaser problems and issues. Other writers at the time developed this line of argument further, as shown in Table 12.1.

Table 12.1. Criteria for supplier assessment.

Author	Selection Criteria
Dickson (1966)	Quality, on-time delivery, supplier performance history.
Lehmann and O'Shaughnessy (1974)	Price, quality, delivery, service.
Gregory (1986)	Proposal responsiveness, technical, quality, cost, general (qualifications of personnel, past delivery history).
Baily and Farmer (1990)	Quality, quantity, timing, service, price, financial stability, good management .
Presutti (1991)	Production scheduling and preventive maintenance, set-up time reduction, in-process quality control, sub-contracting.
Monczka Nichols and Callahan (1992)	Supplier quality performance, supplier delivery performance, total lead time to company by commodity, past price paid, engineering support/design service capabilities.

In practice,[10] formal systems usually break each factor down to give the sub-criteria against which scores and relative weightings are allocated. This allows potential suppliers to be measured. Most supplier selection methods rely on a ranking system[11] where each supplier is scored on the basis of a series of criteria and a "winner" is subsequently declared. Saaty (1986) points out that, in practice, these systems can become both excessively rigid and over-complicated, hence making it difficult for subjective criteria to be measured.

Dobler *et al.* (1990) conclude that the information gathering stage appears to cover a wide range of approaches, including the following items: general plant visits; the appropriateness of equipment; the effectiveness of production control, quality control and cost control systems; the competence of the technical and managerial staff; the morale of personnel in general; the quantity of back orders; the willingness of the supplier to work cooperatively with the company; and the quality of the key materials management activities.

Conceptualising the Techniques

During the 1980s, several management writers tried to capture the essence of this emerging technique. The American preference for the term "vendor" rather than "supplier", took a hold (although the term "supplier assessment" is still being used widely). A deterministic distinction became apparent between the vendor selection stage (vendor appraisal) and the vendor performance measurement stage (vendor rating). Some firms use both techniques separately; others only one; and yet others, a combination of both.

---

[10]For example, Courage's "PSI" system, Nissan's "QCDDM" and ICL's "Vendor Accreditation".

[11]These ranking systems tend to be simplistic and are often based on a derivative of the Analytical Hierarchy Process (AHP) developed by Saaty (1986). For further information on these techniques, refer to Zelany (1982), Saaty (1986) and Cousins (1994).

Gregory (1986) defined the process of vendor appraisal as the key initial stage of identifying potential firms for the supply of input products and services. It may be that no contract, nor the experience of dealing together, exists at this stage. Thus, vendor appraisal must be able to simulate the supply situation by dealing in terms such as control systems (which should ensure that the effective management of supply) and potential capacity (such as competence or capability assessment). Vendor appraisal, then, might be used to select firms which are to form part of a customer firm's "supply base".

Monczka and Trecha (1988) defined the second element of the vendor assessment process as vendor rating. It is specifically concerned with the measurement and assessment of an existing supplier's actual supply performance. Thus, vendor rating might be seen as

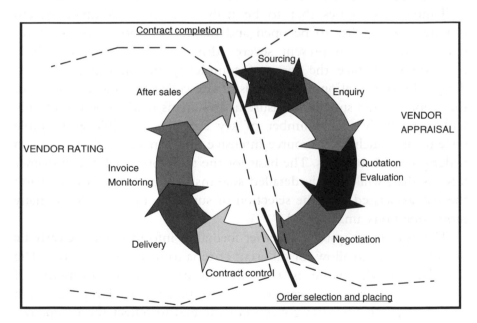

Source: Adapted from *Supplier Appraisal: A Technique to Aid Selection of Suppliers*, Briefing Publication, Chartered Institute of Purchasing and Supply, UK, 1990.

Fig. 12.1. The role of vendor assessment in the procurement cycle.

that part of vendor assessment which is conducted once supply has begun.

The model in Fig. 12.1 illustrates the respective roles that the vendor assessment and vendor rating systems play in the purchasing cycle. These two approaches may be used in conjunction with each other. The results of the latter can be used to feed back into the former, in what Timmerman (1986) refers to as a "vendor assessment system".

Timmerman provides a useful analysis of the techniques that were in use in the 1980s. It appears to be pertinent to today's developed approaches. His identification of the three types of measurement employed by customers — "categorical", "cost ratio" and "weighted point" — may be applied to basic, quality-oriented schemes or to the more commercially focused approaches of the 1990s. This is shown in Table 12.2.

Timmerman argues that to be truly accurate, a complex system requires the supplier to be open and helpful. He points out that restrictive systems can present severe administrative drawbacks. These restrictions can take the form of complexity and inflexibility in the design, implementation and analysis of the collected data. He observes that sophisticated supplier measurement systems tend to be useful only with a relatively small number of key suppliers. Flexible and simple systems are much less resource-intensive and can be used on a much wider group of suppliers. The basis for the trade-off which the customer faces is that, while highly detailed systems may be better for reducing the risk associated with the selection of suppliers, they may leave many more questions unanswered.

The assessment system (whether formal or informal) must clearly be flexible enough to allow for different criteria to be accommodated. The corollary to this issue is that the information requirements of the different purchasing categories must be reassessed regularly and changes made to the data collection strategies to reflect the company's developing information needs.

Schonberger (1986: vii) argues that if firms wanted to become "world-class" — presumably to capitalise on the benefits of management

Table 12.2. Measurement typologies.

Measurement Type	Description
Categorical	The customer categorises a supplier's potential or actual performance as "good", "neutral" or "bad" against a pre-defined list of criteria. This is primarily intuitive and relies upon judgement and experience. This approach is relatively cheap, requires few extra working procedures and lends some structure to the supplier measurement process. However, as it is so reliant upon subjective criteria, the results may be both variable and hard to validate.
Cost ratio	A direct comparison of the purchase cost and all of the consequential costs associated with that product. For example, the cost of any reworking or line stoppages due to a faulty part would be added to all the other hidden costs and calculated as a percentage of the purchase price. By doing this for the criteria of quality, delivery and service, the customer can arrive at the "real" cost of that part. This approach is extremely complex and requires an efficient cost accounting system to provide the necessary data. Without this, the values used to determine variables, such as stoppage costs, will only be arrived at subjectively. This will negate one thread of the rationale behind the systematisation of these approaches, namely, that they increase the objectivity of the supplier selection and evaluation process.
Weighted point	This is a fusion of the subjectivity of the "categorical" approach with the systematic techniques of the "cost ratio" method. Relevant performance criteria are identified and judgmental weighting are attached to each criterion.

Source: Timmerman (1986: 3).

practices — the mere adoption of the necessary tools and techniques to enable performance measurement, or, as he called it, "benchmarking", was simply not enough. He points out that it is the way in which these techniques are used to manage the supply base that is the vital issue:

"If suppliers have not met our needs, the customer is beginning to ask, what did we do wrong? And how can we foster good relations with our suppliers? Under World Class Manufacturing (WCM), adversarial relationships between customer and supplier are out, and a whole new set of buying and contracting practices are in ..."

The mid-1980s appeared to herald a significant change in conceptual thinking on performance measurement systems: it was realised that it was not necessarily what was being measured, with regard to a supplier's performance level, but how it was measured and, indeed, how the results were communicated back to the supply base. The literature and practice of the 1990s shows a move towards "partnership" strategies. These involve cooperation and measurement of the entire relationship, as opposed to the rating of one party by another. In such advanced situations, joint concern and responsibility for the efficacy of the value stream are recognised, along with the need to remove all waste and achieve a lean supply chain (Robertson, 1995). This is what Lamming (1993) refers to as "beyond partnership" and "relationship assessment".

In the UK, meanwhile, several vendor assessment schemes have been accorded almost seminal status. An example is the "QCDDM" scheme developed by Nissan in the UK, which monitors the supplier's management of Quality, Cost containment, Design competence, Development activity and Management approach. The feedback to suppliers is frequent and formal, and suppliers appear to accord it significant respect. The scheme itself has the innate problems of imposition, of course, but the pragmatism shown in its design appears to strike a chord with suppliers. It has now been used as a model for the UK automotive industry as part of the SMMT's "Industry Forum" initiative.[12]

---

[12]The SMMT is the Society of Motor Manufacturers and Traders in the UK. The Industry Forum, which has been widely acclaimed, was formed in 1995 out of a partnership between the SMMT and the Department of Trade and Industry, Vehicles Division.

The use of quantitative analysis techniques remains a part of assessment schemes. This is exemplified by the vendor management model (Cousins, 1994), which employs the OR techniques of multi-criteria decision-making and analytical hierarchy processing to enable the customer to build a profile of the supplier's attributes before and after placing an order.

Many firms tend to segment suppliers into different types: from being simply "suppliers" to "partners" or the like. Within this approach, the techniques of supplier assessment are usually subsumed, but are still present. The epithet, "co-maker", became popular in the manufacturing industry in the 1980s (like so many terms, the product of a consultancy campaign). However, the so-called co-maker arrangements typically contain both supplier assessment and development schemes in which the customer purports to have all the cards.

What Role do These Systems Play?

Bailey and Farmer (1990: 128) summarise the general role of investigations into suppliers' abilities in a helpful manner:

> "The extent of investigation into suppliers will be affected by the volume and value of possible expenditure. Unusual or first-time purchases, where the purchaser has little or no experience to call on, may justify extensive investigation. Parts made to purchaser's specification require more careful assessment of supplier capability than standard parts available off the shelf or from several satisfactory sources."

From the purchasing process described in Fig. 12.1, it appears that vendor assessment can play a part at two points in the cycle. The first stage, known as "vendor selection", clearly forms part of strategic supply marketing — identifying those firms with whom the customer wishes to align itself in the future. This requires the customer to develop a comprehensive list of potential suppliers (Plank & Kijewski, 1991) using a vendor appraisal scheme. Dobler *et al.* (1990) suggest that each prospective supplier should be evaluated individually, but Plank and Kijewski argue that comprehensive screening should only be conducted for the higher-value suppliers due to the costs of setting up such a system. This contradiction is resolved by Soukup (1987: 8) who suggests three situations to consider when introducing a formal measurement system:[13]

(i) *Homogeneous supply market.* The potential suppliers may be very similar in all performance criteria and under all foreseeable circumstances. Therefore, the chance of making a major mistake in choosing between suppliers is small and would be unlikely to have a great effect on overall performance. This selection could be routinely handled.

(ii) *Predictable differentiation.* The suppliers may differ greatly and one supplier may be clearly superior in all performance criteria and under all foreseeable circumstances. Therefore, the chance of making a major mistake in choosing the "wrong" supplier is unlikely as one is clearly superior to the others. This selection could be routinely handled.

(iii) *Unpredictable differentiation.* The suppliers may differ greatly under the different foreseeable conditions. The possibility of an error in the selection is, therefore, large and would risk serious consequences. This scenario warrants considerable effort and care.

Supplier development activities and the formation of supply strategies may be seen as attempts to reduce the unpredictability of differentiation and, thus, steer vendor assessment schemes towards "routinisation" — a feature of long-term relationships identified by Hakansson (1982). A dominant theme in these activities is the

---

[13]Category titles added.

reduction of the supplier base size. Schonberger (1986: 156) points out that: "Since too many suppliers means too little attention to each of them, supplier development starts with supplier reduction". This view is supported by Baily and Farmer (1990):

> "It is perhaps ironic that while some implementations rely upon these systems to reduce the supplier base by identifying key suppliers, a smaller supplier base is in itself viewed as essential in order to allow more time and effort to be spent with the remaining suppliers using rigorous performance evaluation techniques. The evaluation of all, or a large proportion, of a company's suppliers with anything but a small, flexible system would be an onerous and time-consuming task for even a large, well-resourced purchasing department."

Lamming and Oggero (1995), in a study of smaller manufacturing firms and their larger suppliers, conclude that a well-developed vendor assessment scheme helps the customer to gain the respect of the supplier and, thus, build relationships which may be mutually beneficial. They view the vendor assessment scheme as an important part of the purchasing strategy which, they reason, the smaller firm should develop.

The role of vendor assessment in purchasing may, therefore, be as an aid or guide in supplier base development and the strategies which surround such activity, as a feature of purchasing strategy itself, or as a tool in the operational process of buying goods and services. Such a broad remit calls for well-developed techniques and clear cost-benefit analyses.

The various conclusions of writers on vendor assessment are summarised in Table 12.3.

Table 12.3. Summary table of key points in the literature.

Authors	Summary of Findings
Dickson (1966)	The common criteria used by buyers in selecting suppliers were quality, on-time delivery and supplier performance history.
Lamberson *et al.* (1976)	Systems had been developed to provide information on the ability of the supplier to reach pre-arranged targets for performance improvements.
Sibley (1978)	Perceptions of organisational personnel differ. This will affect their perceptions of what constitutes a good supplier. This may have an effect on the supplier selection process.
Lehmann and O'Shaughnessy (1974)	Pricing considerations are the most important where the product was fairly simple. For more complex products, the other factors are more important.
Narasimhan (1983)	Increased importance of selecting the right supplier and managing their performance led to an emphasis on ensuring the validity and objectivity of these processes.
Gregory (1986)	Supplier measurement systems are simply data gathering, data formatting and information presentation tools which can only aid decision-making. Formal supplier measurement systems are frequently unwieldy and unfocussed.
Soukup (1987)	Changes in the market, or in the strategic environment, should be anticipated by adapting the formal supplier measurement systems. The effective use of these systems allows the bulk of purchasing transactions to be made routinely (see Plank & Kijewski, 1991).
Monczka and Trecha (1988)	The criteria used for the assessments are vital and should reflect exactly the underlying purpose of the system. Cost-based systems fulfil the important role of tying the assessment criteria to issues which the customer company generally considers of most importance. The drawback of cost-based approaches is that they cannot account for the importance of issues which are not directly or easily quantifiable, such as an effective and consistent R&D programme or the costs of non-performance.

Table 12.3 (*Continued*)

Authors	Summary of Findings
Monczka *et al.* (1992)	The information needs of the supplier selection process change in response to environmental changes and to the purchasing and company strategies being implemented. The systems being used to provide this information must, likewise, be flexible or the decision-making process will no longer match strategic reality. The information needs for different types of purchased goods/services vary — the supplier measurement system must reflect this. Problems with these systems arise when they are insufficiently linked to their strategic purpose and to the information needs of the purchasing process.
Dobler *et al.* (1990), Baily and Farmer (1990)	Detailed and resource-intensive systems need not be implemented across the board, but may be used selectively for strategically important suppliers. Less detailed systems could suffice for those suppliers who are less strategically important.
Nydick (1992), Cousins (1994), Lamming (1993), Macbeth (1994)	Recent moves towards closer and more long-term relationships with suppliers place an even greater emphasis upon the supplier selection and performance monitoring function as it becomes increasingly more difficult to obtain another suitable source of supply quickly.
Schonberger (1986), Womack *et al.* (1990), Ellram and Carr (1994)	The most current and influential manufacturing paradigms place a heavy emphasis on maximising the value which the supplier adds to a product or service in order to maximise a supply chain's value-adding capabilities. This, in turn, places heavy an emphasis on the assessment and selection of suppliers, and upon the monitoring of their performance in order to maximise their contribution to the supply chain.
Mandal and Deshmukh (1993)	Employing Interpretive Structural Modelling, an interactive learning process, the concept of "driver power" is derived for each criterion used in assessment. There is a differentiation between dependent and independent variables: the former are important for vendor selection whereas the latter are important for vendor development.

Table 12.3 (*Continued*)

Authors	Summary of Findings
Smytka and Clemens (1993)	The use of a financial modelling approach to supplier selection provides a "total cost" scheme, thus concluding that the costs of such a complex system are more than offset by the benefits which may be realised by the customer.
Purdy *et al.* (1994)	The supplier places importance on the presence of an improvement plan within the assessment process and deprecates the degree of formal documentation that is entailed. Suppliers may learn how to get a good score without actually becoming better suppliers.
Wilson (1994)	Price is less important a criterion than previously thought. Total product cost is now a major factor, naturally incorporating within it the impacts of quality and service.
Watts and Hahn (1994)	Supplier evaluation is linked intrinsically with supplier development, building on factors such as financial situation and reliability, rather than simple quality and delivery factors.
Lamming *et al.* (1996b)	Suggested that vendor assessment might be replaced by relationship assessment, in which neither party assesses the other, but both assess the relationship as a joint responsibility.
Lambert *et al.* (1997)	Healthcare industry work concludes that despite intense pressures on costs, price was not the most important criterion for vendor assessment, due perhaps due to the importance of product quality in this industry. Nevertheless, it was concluded that suppliers were not performing to buyers' requirements.
Krause and Ellram (1997), Chakraborty and Philip (1996), Krause (1997)	Positioned supplier evaluation as a part of supplier development.

Supply Performance Measurement in the Modern Context

The more recent literature has managed to reveal the process problems in implementing vendor assessment, perhaps culminating in the conclusion of Purdy *et al.* (1994) that suppliers were becoming better at achieving a good score in vendor assessment schemes without necessarily becoming better suppliers. This is a concept well-grounded in transaction cost economics, as the notion of payment for cheating (see, for example, Kogut, 1988).

The development of inter-firm relationships in the 1990s has suffered from public hyperbole and rhetoric to such an extent that genuine groundwork undertaken by firms, coupled with conceptual development conducted by researchers, has sometimes suffered from a sweeping and rather myopic dismissal of innovations as "fads". Nevertheless, there is documented evidence of real changes in the manner in which firms conduct business with suppliers and in the expectations on both sides.[14]

As a part of this development, it appears that vendor assessment has grown into vendor development — the approach to supply management based on the customer's assumed ability to help the supplier become a better company. The echoes of the origins of vendor assessment are clear: despite the supposed respect for the supplier's position and competence that is contained (at least implicitly) within the partnership concept, there is still the notion that the customer knows best, even to the extent of advising suppliers on how to run their own businesses. Supplier development may, therefore, be expected to suffer from all the problems of supplier assessment.

---

[14]Worthy of special note in this context are the cases researched and prepared by members of Partnership Sourcing Ltd., an initiative company set up within the Confederation of British Industry with funding from the Department of Trade and Industry, in 1991. This organisation has extensive evidence of firms which have conducted new ways of relating to suppliers in many sectors. See also Macbeth *et al.* (1994) and Akacum and Dale (1995).

The development of the lean supply concept (Lamming, 1993, 1996) includes several aspects of relevance to vendor assessment and development. The first of these was the observation that the so-called "open-book negotiation" was typically used as a lever by customers to force suppliers to forego some of their bargaining power by revealing details of their process costs and related matters. This was generally done on the premise of the customer's vaunted ability to "help" the supplier to reduce costs and, thus, improve its business position. Since the suppliers had become accustomed to distrust the customer, the response to this idea may be assumed to be to cheat[15]; the supplier will not trust the customer with such data and, instead, will develop ways of "playing the game". This leaves the customer with the quandary: to use the data or to fight harder for the actual figures.

In the theory of lean supply, balance and equity at the interface would only be possible if each side was prepared to disclose private information to the other for the purposes of improving the overall effectiveness of the relationship.[16] This is termed "cost transparency" — a state in which all necessary information is exchanged between the partners to the relationship in confidence, to the degree considered appropriate. Where this is not possible, due to lack of the necessary confidence, it is recognised that there is an opportunity cost borne by the relationship, which may be expected to result in higher total cost of the transaction.[17]

The next step from cost transparency is to develop relationship assessment as a replacement for vendor assessment. The principle here is similar to that of open-book negotiation: if one party to the relationship assesses the other for the purposes of strengthening their negotiation stance, the other party may be expected to retaliate by

---

[15]The research behind the author's 1993 book was in the global automotive industry, but subsequent research has shown that the picture is much the same in other sectors.

[16]For a discussion on effectiveness, see Ellis Gibbs (1997).

[17]Cost transparency was introduced in Lamming (1993: 214–5) and explored further in Lamming *et al.* (1996a).

becoming good at dealing with the assessment (c.f. Purdy *et al.*, 1994). This will be especially so if the supplier is dealing with several customers, each of whom imposes its own regime.

During the 1980s, some firms began to develop their vendor assessment schemes to encompass two-way evaluation, that is, they invited the supplier to offer judgements on them as customers. This seemingly honourable plan was, however, apparently sometimes executed more as a further tactic in the traditional relationship: the customer browbeats the supplier into giving a good report and then claims (sometimes publicly) to be a "preferred customer". Some schemes did achieve progress, however, and that developed by Macbeth and Ferguson (1994), known as the Relationship Positioning Tool, is worthy of note. In this approach, a third party is employed to conduct an assessment of each company in the relationship, using common criteria, following which a programme of reconciliation is followed in order to improve the situation.

Two-way assessment, then, was clearly a major change from the traditional matter of the customer finding a way to attribute all faults in the supply process to the supplier. In practice, however, it often led simply to two-way blame, albeit damped by the customer's power to cajole the supplier. In lean supply terms, the basic flaw lies in the focus upon the firm (that is, customer or supplier) rather than the actual conduit for value flow — the relationship. Lean supply, therefore, includes provision for both companies, customer and supplier to assess the relationship — hence "relationship assessment" (Lamming *et al.*, 1996b). In this process, each partner conducts a self-assessment, using matching criteria, and then the two discuss how the relationship might be improved through joint action. Since it is the relationship — an impersonal third party to the transaction — that causes either the success or shortfall in performance, there is no point in either side blaming the other. Clearly, this is a radical proposal, since blaming others may be seen as a basic human trait. In practice, however, the principle of relationship assessment has been embraced keenly by firms in several industries, with the Society of British Aerospace

Fig. 12.2. The relationship assessment process.

Companies (SBAC) adopting it within their supply chain improvement initiative, SCRIA, in 1998. The original conceptual model for the Relationship Assessment Process (RAP) developed by the author and colleagues at Bath is shown in Fig. 12.2.[18]

The third logical step in this part of lean supply is to move to mutual development between customer and supplier, that is, a situation in which the benefits of experience, expertise, knowledge and investment in either company may be shared with the other. Once again, the complexity caused by multi-customer activity for the supplier makes the concept of relationship development difficult to

---

[18]Subsequently, the model was sold to a major strategy consulting firm to form part of their supply management approach. Please note that RAP and Relationship Assessment Process are now the Copyright of A. T. Kearney Inc., Chicago.

implement; the opportunity cost of not taking advantage of potential benefits must, once again, be included in calculations.

Summary

The radical approaches to measuring performance in supply relationships demand a different perspective on what is going on at the interface. The traditional view was that the interface represented one company deciding what it needed to buy, in order to satisfy its customers, and specifying to the chosen supplier how it should be supplied. This expanded to a customer role that included telling the supplier how to make the item and how to run the business that surrounded the manufacture (the same applies, of course, to the provisions of services).

Many business situations do not reflect this, however. Procurement managers in one large manufacturer of personal computers, when asked recently how their supplier of microchips viewed them, said: "As an important customer". The chip supplier, however, actually views the personal computer manufacturer not as a customer at all, but as a distributor. This is reflected, of course, in the popular common practice of enquiring first what chip a new PC has in it and, secondly, which brand of PC it is.

If innovation is about creative destruction and renewal, then the management practice of measuring suppliers' performance is currently undergoing a major innovation: old perspectives will be destroyed and the customer's role will change to one of partner, not overlord. The very terms "customer" and "supplier" may be redundant in some supply relationships before long. Naturally, not all supply situations will reflect this — cases where either side represents a monopoly (or part of an oligopoly) will distort the situation (although it is still likely that suppliers will learn how to deal with assessment schemes rather than take on developments which they themselves do not feel appropriate). In many cases, the supplier has more power than the customer. Hence the traditional approach will not work: relationship assessment may still be appropriate, however, since it is not dependent upon one side calling all the shots. In any case, what is important, it appears, is that the responsibility for effective supply is seen as the shared responsibility of both customer and supplier: measuring schemes that do not reflect this may cost their users dearly.

Acknowledgments

This research includes that conducted during a project funded by a grant (GR/J23769 — the *RAP* project) from the Engineering and Physical Sciences Research Council. In presenting this chapter, the EPSRC's support is gratefully acknowledged, as is the work of my colleague, Dr Paul Cousins, and research officers, Dorian Notman and Sam Hogan.

PART 5

IMPROVING COMPETENCIES

Chapter 13

Innovation: A Performance Measurement Perspective

PERVAIZ K. AHMED and MOHAMED ZAIRI

Introduction: Performance Management in the Modern Business Context

As competition intensifies and business gears itself up for the challenges of the 21st century, performance management continues to be in the spotlight. Increased consumerism, business globalisation and new management practices have raised questions about the way in which performance is measured. Clarity on the terms performance measurement, performance measures and performance measurement systems is a pre-requisite to establishing what impact, if any, practices have made on bottom-line business results.

In order for companies to achieve goals they have to measure. Measurement is the basis through which it is possible to control, evaluate and improve processes:

> "When you can measure what you are speaking about and express it in numbers, you know something about it. (Otherwise) your knowledge is a meagre and unsatisfactory kind; it may be

the beginning of knowledge but you have scarcely in thought advanced to the stage of science." (Lord Kelvin, 1824–1904, quoted in Heim and Compton, 1992: 1)

This point is also emphasised by the Foundation of Manufacturing Committee of the National Academy of Engineering

"World Class Manufacturers recognise the importance of metrics in helping to define the goals and performance expectations for the organisation. They adopt or develop appropriate metrics to interpret and describe quantitatively the criteria used to measure the effectiveness of the manufacturing system and its many interrelated components." (Quoted in Heim and Compton, 1992: 6)

Performance Measurement

The complex nature of performance measurement has resulted in a plethora of definitions and has prompted the view that it is "a mystery ... complex, frustrating, difficult, challenging, important, abused and misused" (Sink, 1991). Practitioners, including strategists, accountants, psychologists and human resource managers, have their own definition of performance measurement. Each requires its application either for internal reporting, such as individuals performance appraisal, or for external reporting, such as financial accounting ratios. The issue is further complicated by the notion that performance measures may be either individual or organisation-wide. Thus, it is hardly surprising that different definitions exist.

One simple definition which largely overcomes the above problems is the systematic assignment of numbers to entities. This has both a universal application and satisfies the requirements of various stakeholder groups. Zairi (1994) also defines the function of measurement as "to develop a method for generating a class of information that will be useful in a wide variety of problems and situations". This functionality is important as many performance measures are capable of information generation, but unless they are useful, they are meaningless.

In the context of individual performance, performance measurement provides the organisation with a "device through which to focus and enunciate accountability" (Sharman, 1993) and "an objective, impersonal basis for performance evaluation" (Sloma, 1980).

Some authors stress the importance of considering performance measurement as " the process of determining how successful organisations or individuals have been in attaining their objectives" (Evangelidis, 1983). This process approach to performance measurement recognises the existence and importance of inputs and outputs in the development of the performance measurement system.

Many authors have defined performance measurement in terms of the attributes of performance: "What is measured is rarely performance itself, but some specific attribute relating to the performance" (Euske, 1984). It is often the desired behavioural attributes which are the focus for measurement and they provide "feedback on activities that motivate behaviour leading to continuous improvement in customer satisfaction, flexibility and productivity" (Lynch & Cross, 1991).

Performance Measures

Performance measures have been defined as the "characteristics of outputs that are identified for purposes of evaluation" (Euske, 1984) while others have defined them as a "tool" to compare actual results with a pre-set target and to measure the extent of any deviation (Fortuin, 1988). It has also been suggested that performance measures "reflect the contribution of each team or process to the organisation's goal" (Turney, 1993).

Juran (1992) applied a TQM-focussed definition by stating that it is "a defined amount of some quality feature that permits evaluation of that feature in numbers". Clearly, to measure all the characteristics

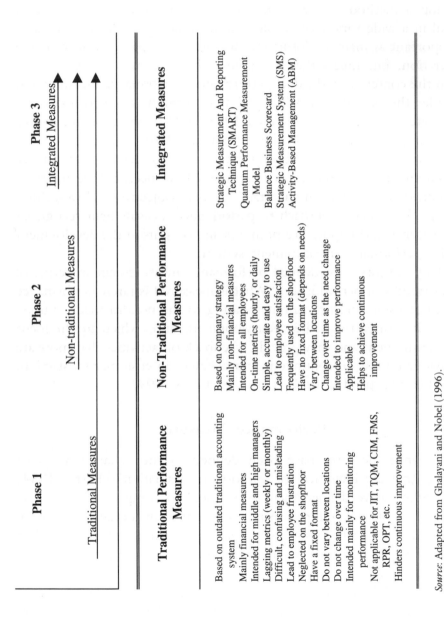

Phase 1	**Phase 2**	**Phase 3**
Traditional Measures	Non-traditional Measures	Integrated Measures

Traditional Performance Measures	**Non-Traditional Performance Measures**	**Integrated Measures**
Based on outdated traditional accounting system	Based on company strategy	Strategic Measurement And Reporting Technique (SMART)
Mainly financial measures	Mainly non-financial measures	Quantum Performance Measurement Model
Intended for middle and high managers	Intended for all employees	Balance Business Scorecard
Lagging metrics (weekly or monthly)	On-time metrics (hourly, or daily)	Strategic Measurement System (SMS)
Difficult, confusing and misleading	Simple, accurate and easy to use	Activity-Based Management (ABM)
Lead to employee frustration	Lead to employee satisfaction	
Neglected on the shopfloor	Frequently used on the shopfloor	
Have a fixed format	Have no fixed format (depends on needs)	
Do not vary between locations	Vary between locations	
Do not change over time	Change over time as the need change	
Intended mainly for monitoring performance	Intended to improve performance	
Not applicable for JIT, TQM, CIM, FMS, RPR, OPT, etc.	Applicable	
Hinders continuous improvement	Helps to achieve continuous improvement	

Source: Adapted from Ghalayani and Nobel (1996).

Fig. 13.1. Evolution in measurement approaches.

of an output would be impractical and undesirable. Therefore, it is the "vital signs which quantify how well activities within a process or the outputs of a process achieve a specified goal" that are the measures selected (Hronec, 1993).

Performance measures will have a range of hierarchical levels — corporate, business and functional (Hax & Majluf, 1991) — depending

Table 13.1. Performance measures.

Fitzgerald *et al.* (1991): Performance service businesses	1 Financial performancemeasures for 2 Quality of service 3 Flexibility 4 Resource utilisation 5 Innovation
Maskell (1991): Performance measures for world-class manufacturing	1 Delivery performance 2 Process time 3 Production flexibility 4 Quality 5 Financial performance 6 Social issues
Lynch and Cross (1991): "The performance pyramid"	1 Market 2 Financial 3 Customer satisfaction 4 Flexibility 5 Productivity 6 Quality 7 Delivery 8 Cycle time 9 Waste
Kaplan and Norton (1992): " The balanced scorecard"	1 Financial perspective 2 Internal business perspective 3 Customer perspective 4 Innovation and learning perspective
Hronec (1993): The vital signs	1 Quality 2 Cost 3 Time

on the output and "customer" being considered. The line manager, process manager, general manager, customer and shareholder will each have different requirements. An integrated set of performance measures will take into account all these factors. At an individual level, the performance measures "should be important causal factors related to managerial and employee behaviour" (Hendricks, 1994). Performance measures, therefore, "communicate how an activity is meeting the needs of internal or external customers" (Turney, 1992) and reflect the contribution of each team or process to the organisation's goals.

The biggest barrier to comparing performance measures is the inconsistency applied to its definition (see Fig. 13.1). For example, productivity may be a quality measure, a financial performance measure or it may be given a separate classification. This apparent inconsistency can adversely impact on benchmarks and reinforces the need for precision when benchmarking with external organisations.

Authors who have attempted to prescribe performance measures (Table 13.1) have done so without any indication of the applicability of the measurement frameworks. The measures are, therefore, anecdotal. However difficult it may be, some have achieved success. For instance, the Toyota Motor Company has operated their non-financial measurement system for more than 35 years and is integrated to its continuous improvement commitment (Brancato, 1995). Kelloggs Australia has also introduced a quality-based management system. Although many of the measures are non-financial, they have found them to be more predictive about the future of the company (Brancato, 1995).

Phases of Performance Measurement

Ghalayini and Noble (1996) propose that measurement has undergone phases in development. Three stages can be discerned (Fig. 13.1).

The first phase, which is deemed to have started in the 1980s, focussed heavily on financial measures such as profits, ROI and productivity. Within this system, measures are based on the traditional system of management accounting. Unfortunately, this perspective is handicapped by a number of shortcomings:

 (i) *Traditional accounting measures.* Traditional measures are based on a system of accounting, which was developed to primarily attribute costs, rather then use, in decision-making.

 (ii) *Lagging metrics.* Financial data report on historic events and, therefore, are not useful for operational assessment.

 (iii) *Corporate strategy.* Traditional measures do not take into account aspects derived from corporate strategy

 (iv) *Relevance to practice.* Traditional measures quantify performance only in financial terms, yet improvement efforts (such as customer satisfaction and adherence to delivery time) are difficult to translate into strict currency terms.

 (v) *Inflexible.* Traditional measures are used in fixed formats across all departments and parts of the business. Often, what is relevant to one section is not relevant to others, thus making the information somewhat redundant in many cases.

 (vi) *Expensive.* The collation of extensive amount of data is often a difficult and expensive process.

 (vii) *Continuous improvement.* The setting of standards for performance can often go against the grain of continuous improvement since it can lead to the establishment of norms of output and behaviour, rather than to motivate improvement. For instance, workers may hesitate to improve their performance if they think that the standard for the forthcoming period is to be revised upwards on the basis of current results.

 (viii) *Customer requirements and management techniques.* In an environment where customer requirements are of a higher quality, shorter lead time and lower costs have led to empowered decision-making on the shopfloor. Traditional financial reports, which are used by middle managers, do not reflect the organisational reality of more autonomous management approaches.

These problems provided the impetus for the development of non-financial measures. This is exemplified by the second stage of development. The second stage of measurement is characterised by non-financial measures. Characteristically they are:

(i) Measures which relate to manufacturing strategy and are primarily non-financial in nature, such as those pertaining to operational matters which facilitate decision-making for managers and workers.
(ii) Foster improvement rather than just monitor performance.
(iii) Change with the dynamics of the marketplace.

The third stage is characterised by an integrated use of financial and non-financial measures. These integrated systems, by examining performance from multiple angles and the trade-offs openly, attempt to guard against sub-optimisation.

Performance Measurement Systems

A performance measurement system has been defined as a "tool for balancing multiple measures (cost, quality and time) across multiple levels (organisation, processes and people) (Hronec, 1993). It is a "systematic way of evaluating the inputs, outputs, transformation and productivity in a manufacturing or non-manufacturing operation".

The performance measurement system is an object whose purpose is to measure, via a set of rules and procedures, using some form of yardstick (Ijiri & Jaedicke, 1981). It should also focus on continuous improvement. The data provided by the performance measurement system needs to be "relevant, factual information on core business processes and key activities" (Miller, 1992).

A systems perspective as exemplified by a TQM approach, stresses the need for measurement through the Deming continuous improvement cycle of Plan Do Check Act. Essentially, what gets measured gets done. Feedback is a central theme which runs through most TQM activities, and a performance measurement system provides the vehicle for this process to operate in an objective way. Within benchmarking, for example, identification of the performance gap requires a robust performance measurement system to be effective. Processes within a TQM environment are reviewed across functional barriers and, therefore, the performance measurement system is required "to integrate organisational activities across various managerial levels and functions".

Kaplan (1991) states that an effective performance measurement system "should provide timely, accurate feedback on the efficiency and effectiveness of operations". Within the dynamic marketplace, accurate information ahead of the competition may result in the difference between survival and non-survival. Dixon *et al.* (1990) identify five characteristics of successful measurement systems:

(i) Be mutually supportive and consistent with the business's operating goals, objectives, critical success factors and programmes.

(ii) Convey information through as few and as simple a set of measures as possible.

(iii) Reveal how effectively customers' needs and expectations are satisfied. Focus on measures that customers can see.

(iv) Provide a set of measurements for each organisational component that allows all members of the organisation to understand how their decisions and activities affect the entire business.

(v) Support organisational learning and continuous improvement.

Traditional performance measurement systems have focussed on the shareholder and top management with an overview of how the company operated in the previous financial year. They provide an element of consistency in that the common denominator is always impact on the bottom line, but these measures are retrospective and often produced a long time after the year has ended. According to Kaplan and Norton (1992), however, the real battle is for the hearts and minds of customers rather than the shareholder and top management in the fight for business survival. This dimension is not well represented in the traditional performance measurement system.

Line managers require accurate performance measures on a much more regular basis to enable effective process management. Whether the traditional measures provide shareholders and top management with the information they require is open to debate, as data which is required on tactical performance is used to assess the firm's current level of competitiveness and direct its efforts in attaining a desired competitive position in order to survive and prosper in the long run (Kaplan, 1991).

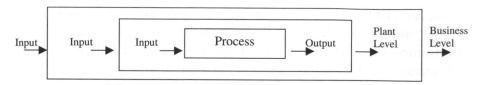

Fig. 13.2. Systems-level view of measurement.

Performance Measurement and Innovation

A key to maintaining competitive success is the ability to repeatedly and successfully commercialise new products. However, measuring innovation success is riddled with several problems. One of the key problems is due to the multi-dimensionality surrounding innovation outcomes. This is further compounded by the fact that measurement confusion often arises in the hierarchical level of assessment, which varies from one individual product to a portfolio of products to the firm. For instance, for most firms, the issue is one of financial performance and is defined in hard terms, whilst the metric for project success often has time as a primary focus, and so forth.

Moreover, while it is widely accepted that developing new products is important in ensuring success and profitability, to date there has been no common set of performance measures for the innovation function. Proposed measures are often a mixture of input and output measures together with some measures for evaluating the process used (see Fig. 13.2).

Often, measures are defined at the micro level, identifying success metrics for individual projects. This creates a gap between discrete/unique projects and firm performance at the industry level. Loch *et al.* (1996) propose that this gap has to be closed in delineating three performance measurement levels:

(i) *Firms business performance.* It measures the firm's success in the market.

(ii) *Development output performance.* It measures the development function's contribution to the firm's business objectives.

(iii) *Development process performance.* It measures the quality of development execution (competencies) which drives the performance.

As Loch *et al.* point out, it is well to note that while process performance is an important driver of output, it is not directly so for business performance. For instance, development processes are a determinant of costs, speedy product development and quality. However, new products must be taken together with other factors, such as cost position, excellence in marketing strategies and sales to determine business profits and growth. Thus, it may be possible for a process to be capable of excellent delivery in terms of new products to the marketplace, but if the market values other types of performance, say technical performance over innovation, then the company is still likely to fail. Hence the right performance dimension must be chosen (a point which we return to discuss in the section on strategy and innovation), and only after this can the appropriate definition and selection of process drivers be made.

The problem of defining the correct measure is not a new one. There exists a vast body of literature which deals with the diverse ways in which performance can be measured (Biggadale, 1979; Booz *et al.*, 1982; Bourgeois, 1980; Hitt & Ireland, 1985; Johne & Snelson, 1988; Ventkatraman & Ramanujan, 1986). For example, Venkatraman and Ramanujan develop a two-dimensional approach to the measurement of business performance:

(i) *Dimension 1.* It is concerned with the use of financial (profit, sales, growth, turnover and ROI) versus operational criteria (innovativeness, market standing and social responsibility).
(ii) *Dimension 2.* It is concerned with alternate data sources (primary versus secondary). Dess and Robinson (1984) conclude that subjective perceptual measures can be used when accurate objective measures are unavailable. This is better than the alternative of removing performance measurement altogether. Hart (1993) and Pearce *et al.* (1987) provide further support for utilising indirect and proxy measures by suggesting that they can be fruitfully applied in place of direct measures.

New product development is one aspect of company performance and, therefore, what has been written about business performance is just as pertinent to innovation measurement. However, some researchers, have examined this issue much more directly.

At the project level, Marquis (1969), in what is considered a classic case study, identified a number of drivers of success. The important ones were defined as:

(i)   Understanding user needs.
(ii) Internal communication.
(iii) External communication.

Rothwel *et al.* (1974), in project SHAPPO, added the following:

(i)   Attention to marketing.
(ii) Efficiency of development.
(iii) Authority of R&D.

Cooper (1979) and Cooper and Kleimschimdt (1987), in examining how new product success could be measured, highlighted other possible additions:

(i)   Project definition.
(ii) Product superiority.
(iii) Synergies with marketing.

Cooper (1979) utilised eight performance measures which, after a factor analysis yielded, three independent dimensions of new product development success. These were:

(i)   *Impact.* The impact or importance of the programme on a company's sales and profits.
(ii) *Success rate.* The success rate of the programme, assessing the track record of the company's products.
(iii) *Relative performance.* Capturing the relative performance of the programme in relation to objectives and competitors in terms of profits and success.

Cooper's (1979) study is important for several reasons. First, it highlighted that success along one dimension does not imply success in the other two dimensions. Secondly, it highlighted that different types of strategies need to be considered, and that these necessitate different interpretations and measurements of success. Cooper advocates that companies must first define the type of success they are searching and then select the most appropriate strategy. Subsequently, Cooper and Kleimschimdt (1987) reinforce the proposition that success is not a simple uni-dimensional concept.

Cordero (1990) identified three measures. These are:

(i) Overall performance:

    (a) Pay-out period.

    (b) The percentage of sales as compared to the industry average.

    (c) The sales of new products developed in the last five years as a percentage of current sales.

(ii) Technical performance:

    (a) Business opportunity, which is the monetary value of the total market created by technical inputs.

    (b) The number of patents.

    (c) The number of publications and citations.

(iii) Commercial performance:

    (a) Cash flow.

Griffin and Page (1993), as part of the PDMA taskforce in 1990, provide a structure to the variety of measures which deal with product development success. After interviewing academics and practitioners, they identified 14 most commonly used performance measures and categorised them into four categories. They also defined measures which are considered to be the "most desirable", but often remain under-used or even unused. The reasons cited for the poor deployment of these measures include poor systems, adverse company culture and lack of accountability.

Source: Griffin and Page (1996).

Fig. 13.3. Performance measures according to business category.

Strategy and Measurement

Companies pursue innovation for different reasons, and any measurement must be cognizant and aligned to this fact. As Griffin and Page (1996) note, research shows that interactions exist between innovation format and strategy, such that:

(i)   The factors which produce project success differ by project strategy.
(ii) Different strategies produce different kinds of success.
(iii) The project strategy mix pursued differs across more and less successful firms.

A good way of picturing the inter-relationship between strategy and innovation is through an extension of the Ansoff product-market matrix. This matrix-type approach was first adapted and introduced by Booz *et al.* (1982). It is a three-by-three matrix with six distinct categories:

(i) *New to the world (NTW)*. New products which create an entirely different market.
(ii) *New to the company (NTC)*. New products which, for the first time, allow a company to enter an established market.
(iii) *Additions to existing product lines (AEL)*. New products which supplement a company's established product lines.
(iv) *Improvement in/revisions to existing products (IM)*. New products which provide improved performance, or greater perceived value, and replace existing products.
(vi) *Repositioning (RP)*. Existing products targetted to new markets or market segments.
(vi) *Cost reductions (CR)*. New products which provide similar performance at lower cost.

Newness to the market

	Low		High
High	New to the company		New to the world
Newness to the firm	Product improvement	Add to existing lines	
Low	Cost reductions	Repositionings	

Source: Griffin and Page (1996).

Fig. 13.4. Innovation project-strategy framework.

The market/company framework is a useful way to interlink different types of measures to different formats of innovation. Griffin and Page (1996) identify the most useful measure according to project type. These are presented in Fig. 13.5 below.

Newness to the market

	Low		High
High	**New to the company** Market share Revenue or satisfaction Met profit goal Competitive advantage		**New to the world** Customer acceptance Customer satisfaction Met profit goal or IRR/ROI Competitive advantage
Newness to the Firm	**Product improvements** Customer satisfaction Market share or revenue growth Met profit goal Competitive advantage	**Additions to existing lines** Market share Rev./Rev. Growth/Satis./Accept. Met profit goal Competitive advantage	
Low	**Cost reductions** Customer satisfaction Acceptance or revenue Met margin goal Performance or qualit	**Product repositionings** Customer acceptance Satisfaction or share Met profit goal Competitive advantage	**Project strategy** Customer measure #1 Second customer measure Financial measure Performance measure

Source: Griffin and Page (1996).

Fig. 13.5. The most useful success measures by project strategy.

Furthermore, since different strategies produce different types of emphasis upon product development, it is unlikely that one set of measures can capture all facets of innovation across different strategies. Miles and Snow (1978) propose a generic typology of strategy on the basis of the speed of the response to changes in the product-market environment. The four categories are:

(i) *Prospectors.* Companies which respond early and are sensitive even to weak signals from the market. They attempt to be "first" with new products, markets and technologies.

(ii) *Analysers.* These companies are rarely forerunners, but through a process of carefully monitoring changes in the marketplace, especially competitors, they become fast followers. Often, they can build advantages through cost efficiencies by utilising a variety of market penetration strategies.

(iii) *Defenders.* They attempt to find and protect niche segments in relatively stable market conditions. They attempt to do so by offering higher quality, better service or lower prices. They tend to be insensitive to changes in the environment, which have little impact on their current operations.

(iv) *Reactors.* They respond only when forced to do so by environmental pressures. They tend to be very passive companies.

Research in the strategy field (Slater & Narver, 1993; Lambkin, 1988; McDaniel & Kohlari, 1987) has found evidence linking these four strategy types to product development differences. The key differences are:

(i) Prospectors and analysers place greater emphasis on growth through new product development than defenders and reactors.

(ii) Prospectors will tend to be pioneers, whilst analysers will tend towards imitation of new products. Analysers focus attention on business processes that allow them to rapidly add product lines to their existing portfolios.

(iii) Defenders are likely to emphasise product line extension strategies than "new" product market development.

(iv) Reactors are likely to be very inconsistent in their approach to innovation and product development.

On the basis of this framework, Griffin and Page (1996) recommend that:

(i) Prospector firms consider using some combination of:

   (a) The percentage of profits from new products less than "n" years old.

   (b) The degree today's new products lead to future opportunities.

   (c) The percentage of sales from new products less than "n" 2 years old.

(ii) Analyser firms should consider using some combination of:

   (a) The degree of new product fit to business strategy.

   (b) The development programme ROI.

   (c) The percentage of profits from new products less than "n" years old.

   (d) The success and failure rate.

(iii) Defender firms should consider using:

   (a) The development programme ROI.

   (b) The degree of new product fit to strategy.

(iv) Reactor firms should consider using some combination of:

   (a) The development programme ROI.

   (b) The success rate/failure rate.

   (c) The degree of new products fit to business strategy.

   (d) The subjective appraisal of the overall programme success.

Effective Performance Measurement Systems

Companies often describe their strategy in terms of customer service, innovation and the quality and capabilities of their people but then fail to measure these variables (Eccles, 1991). While strategies are often focussed simply on "enablers", in order to drive these there is a need to measure performance. To reiterate, measurement is important for the following reasons (Zairi, 1992):

(i) Because you cannot manage what you cannot measure.
(ii) To determine what to pay attention to and improve.
(iii) To provide a scoreboard for people to monitor their own performance levels.
(iv) To give an indication of the cost of poor quality.
(v) To give a standard for making comparisons.
(vi) To comply with business objectives.

Generally, organisational environments are committed to continuous improvement, but "traditional summary measures of performance are generally harmful and incompatible with improvement measures" (Zairi, 1992). Performance measures need to promote and encourage the right behaviours within an organisation, that is, those behaviours which assist the organisation to achieve its goals. They need to reflect a positive image which encourages involvement and ownership within a non-threatening environment if it is to succeed in the development of a continuous improvement ethos.

The characteristics of good performance management are (Zairi & Letza, 1995):

(i) Performance is reflected at various levels of organisational systems. It is measured at the strategic, tactical and operational levels.
(ii) Performance measurement is a distributed activity reflecting various levels of ownership and control.
(iii) Performance measurement reflects a blend of measures for individual tasks/activities to manage processes.
(iv) Performance measurement highlights opportunities for improvement in all areas with leverage points.

Often, measurement of soft aspects is neglected. However, as experience appears to suggest, it is often the case that by developing the soft aspects of measurement that the hard measures will naturally follow. Therefore, a holistic approach to measurement is required which includes both hard and soft measures. Kaplan (1991) has suggested that "companies should concentrate on internal performance improve-ment with the expectation of positive impacts on financial performance".

Traditional performance measures have focussed on outputs whereas there is a need to look towards the drivers of outputs — leadership, strategy, communication and so forth. It is from these that benefits will flow from improvement to the drivers or enablers. Although managers understand the concepts and the need for measurement, many organisations fail to develop performance measurement systems to support their development due to:

(i)   Failure to operationally define performance.
(ii) Failure to relate performance to the process.
(iii) Failure to define the boundaries of the process.
(iv) Misunderstood or misused measures.
(v)   Failure to distinguish between control and improving measures.
(vi) Measuring the wrong things.
(vii) Misunderstanding/misuse of information by managers.
(viii) Fear of distorting performance priorities.
(ix) Fear of exposing poor performance.
(x)   Perceived reduction in autonomy.

The needs and reasons for the failure of many performance measurement systems are evident. Clearly an inappropriate performance measurement system can act as a barrier to its implementation (Zairi, 1992).

Grafting new measures on to an existing system, which will reflect this change, is not the answer. Neither is making slight adjustments to an existing system. Enhanced competitiveness depends on starting from scratch and asking: "Given our strategy, what are the most important measures of performance, how do the measures relate to one another, and what measures truly produce long-term financial success in our business?" (Johnson, 1990).

Today's organisations compete on opportunity recognition, learning speed, innovation, cycle time, quality, flexibility, reliability and responsiveness. Financially orientated systems are outdated and too rule-bound for a business environment where competition is often based on how managers think about their business and how they invest their time and resources. A real strategic measurement system is one that is balanced, integrated and designed to highlight the firm's critical inputs, outputs and process variables (Eccles, 1991).

Models of Integrated Performance Measurement

The dynamics of today's marketplace require effective performance measures to assist managers in making decisions and taking actions. This enables organisational survival and prosperity. Effective performance measurement systems utilise traditional financial measures, but supplement them with non-financial measures to give a much more fuller picture and a more relevant management information system.

Historically, performance measurement has been designed for the benefit of shareholders and senior management rather than line managers and employees. Furthermore, the standard approach to calculating the measures and defining the terms as prescribed by the accounting bodies has enabled inter-company comparisons and reluctance by many to challenge their effectiveness. Consequently, measures which indicate return on capital, profitability and liquidity have dominated most performance measurement systems.

A more holistic approach to performance measurement asks: what is it that drives the top-line performance measures? Is it the process, people, leadership or resource utilisation? If so, are these performance measures included? Investment in knowledge, process improvement and people development will have a payback and impact on financial performance in future accounting periods, but there is a need for interim performance measures to check progress.

Many performance measurement systems fail to be effective because they are disparate, often measuring activities that are of local or individual interest to a manager rather than a key activity for the business.

Measurement requires medium to long-term commitment from senior management and all staff with potentially little impact on the financial performance measures in the short run. The drivers which underpin the financial performance measures, such as teamwork, process design, communication, tools and techniques, require non-financial performance measures to ensure that progress is being made and corrective actions are taken.

A linkage between strategy, actions and measures is essential and, unless companies adapt their measures and measurement systems to facilitate their introduction, implementation will fail to reap the expected benefits (Dixon *et al.*, 1990). Adoption of the wrong measures and performance measurement can be a potential obstacle. In the discussion which follows, we present a select set of frameworks for integrated measurement.

Strategic measurement and reporting technique (SMART)

SMART is a new approach to measurement developed by Wang Laboratories in 1989 (Dixon *et al.*, 1990). The aims of SMART are to integrate financial and non-financial reporting and to concentrate measurement on satisfying customer needs. SMART also provides a link between manufacturing and the company's strategic goals, together with a commitment to continuously improve the process by promoting constant evolution.

The operation of SMART (Fig. 13.6) begins with the corporate vision at the top of the pyramid and defines the markets in which the company competes, the services provided and the scope of the products. The vision leads to goals for the marketplace. Detailed financial goals lead to the business operating system objectives of customer satisfaction, flexibility and productivity. These objectives are achieved by cross-functional processes and the removal of functional boundaries. The final level in the pyramid is the departmental level, where the criteria includes quality, delivery, process time and waste.

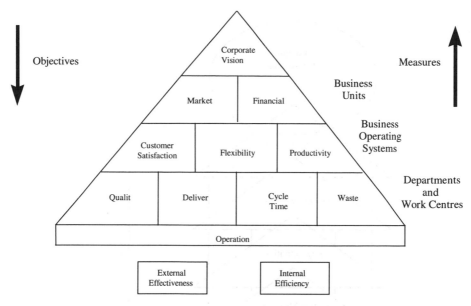

Source: Lynch & Cross (1991).

Fig. 13.6. The performance pyramid.

For each goal, the objective and criterion of at least one measure is used. The implementation of SMART resulted in 40% of the existing measures being discarded. Many were redefined and new measures added (Dixon *et al.*, 1990).

Quantum performance measurement model

The quantum performance measurement model (Fig. 13.7) suggests that superior performance is the result of an integrated planning and control system (Bemouski, 1994). Within the quantum performance measurement model, measures are distinguished between process (the activity) and output (the output from the activity). The measures that are used are divided between quality, cost and service (Hronec, 1993).

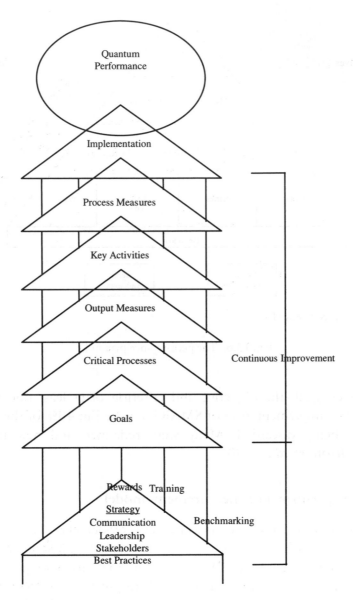

Source: Hronec (1993).

Fig. 13.7. Quantum performance measurement.

Balanced business scorecard

Kaplan and Norton (1992) reinforced the view that a balance between financial and non-financial measures is important to modern business:

> "Managers should not have to choose between financial and operational measures ... No single measure can provide a clear performance target or focus attention on the critical areas of the business. Managers want a balanced presentation of both financial and operational measures."

Following a year-long research project with 12 companies at the leading edge of performance management, they developed the Balanced Scorecard which does not dispense with financial measures, but integrates them with complementary operational indicators on "customer satisfaction", "internal processes" and "innovation and improvement" activities as key measures of future financial performance. The Scorecard seeks to minimise the amount of information that is presented, but maximise the effectiveness and usefulness of the presentation. This is done by a careful selection of "critical" indicators that really drive the business.

From the "customer" perspective, the Scorecard requires the translation of strategic statements at the level of service to specific measures which really matter to the customer, such as quality and delivery time. From the "internal process" perspective, the Scorecard focuses upon critical internal operations that are necessary to satisfy customer requirements fully. It also identifies core competencies which are the key to the maintenance of competitive position within the market. The "innovation and improvement" perspective measures the degree to which a business is able to continually improve products and processes to meet the requirements of an increasingly dynamic market.

This balanced approach to performance measurement has a number of significant advantages:

(i) *Strategic focus.* Most importantly, the Scorecard focusses on the strategic objectives of the business and measures the degree to which the business is performing satisfactorily to meet these objectives. It also indicates the future direction which should be followed. Apple executives (one of the 12 companies in the study) viewed the Scorecard approach as being essential in expanding discussions beyond gross margin, return on equity and market share.

(ii) *Clear and concise.* Most organisations will derive a whole range of indicators for business performance, mainly for individual operating activities. The Balanced Scorecard, being selective in its choice of indicators, forces senior managers to focus on key measures that are of strategic importance to the business. This provides a crucial balance between short-term and long-term activities.

(iii) *Cross-functional.* The Scorecard provides an integrated, or cross-functional, analysis of the business. It can provide information to finance, production, sales, marketing, distribution, administration and so forth on key functional indicators, but may also act as a focus to the entire organisation on what must be done to improve performance. This integrated approach is crucial to the need to remove perceptions of the business as existing in the form of a series of independent divisions or departments.

Strategic measurement systems (SMS)

Strategic measurement systems (SMS) was developed to assist management in defining and gaining clarity on their strategies and priorities. It provides managers with data which they may need to support investment proposals, or where R&D backing is required, based on non-financial measures (Vitale *et al.*, 1994). The steps in the development of a SMS are:

(i) Specify the goal — what are we trying to accomplish?

(ii) Match the measure to the strategy — what is most important to us? The firm's critical success factors will provide the focus for critical business functions.

(iii) Identify the measures — what would we measure? Feedback will be required from three audiences — customers, investment analysts and industry experts.

(iv) Predict the results — what will change? All aspects of the measure both positive and negative, need to be considered.

 (v) Build commitment and inspire action — who is on board? Commitment from the top management is required.

(vi) Plan the next step — where do we go from here? This may take the form of setting targets and integration into a formal incentive scheme or communication system.

Thus far, we have reviewed the pertinent theoretical aspects and frameworks of measurement. In the discussion that follows, we present a select group of case studies which serve to highlight the type of innovation measurement and metrics used by companies. The case studies presented highlight the different levels of maturity in measuring innovation, ranging from naïve and *ad hoc* systems to comprehensive approaches utilising a variety of measurement methodologies and metrics.

Measurement and Metrics in Practice

Case study one: ICL

Product-based measures

(i) *Cost reduction.* ICL measures its performance in cost reduction by percentage[1] and value-added terms.[2] Regular reviews are held on a periodic basis (monthly) involving customers. The products concerned are examined in relation to the following criteria:

   (a) Cost forecasts against targets.
   (b) Impact of exchange rates.

---

[1] ICL's cost reduction in percentage terms.
[2] ICL's cost reduction in value-added terms.

(c) Material price changes.
(d) Joint activities to reduce cost by design changes.

In addition, ICL uses value engineering workshops during the early stages of the product development process in order to examine the potential for reducing costs before production starts. The assumption is that at least 80% of product costs should be factored in before the manufacturing phase starts. In previous years, ICL had been setting itself a target of approximately 10% in cost reduction every year. This figure is reliant on two activities:

(a) The ability of the purchasing function to negotiate lower price contracts with suppliers.
(b) The continuous effort to try and reduce manufacturing costs through innovation, quality improvements and other means.

Process-based measures

(i) *Time to market.* ICL operates in a vulnerable market where, in some categories product lifetimes could be as little as six months. In line with the company's vision, a process of reducing the introduction times of new circuit boards was started in 1986.[3,4]
(ii) *Manufacturability assessment.* Manufacturing and design engineers work together in the early stages of new product development. They use design tools based on DFM principles to optimise design so that it will be right the first time. No printed circuit board is allowed to go into production with attributes that would compromise quality or increase manufacturing cycle time.[5-7] The following are some of the benefits achieved from cycle time reduction:

---

[3] Design to manufacture cycle time — manufacturing development build.
[4] Design to manufacture cycle time (PCBs) — design release to product general release.
[5] Engineering planning cycle time at ICL (PCB assembly planning).
[6] Engineering planning cycle time at ICL (final product assembly planning).
[7] Engineering change cycle time.

(a) Printed circuit product introduction cycle time reduced to three months.
(b) High data integrity.
(c) Faster and automated take-on of OEM design detail (electronic- and data-based).
(d) Common standards between design and manufacturing.
(e) Electronic trading of design and commercial data.
(f) Automated processing of design information for manufacture.

Case study two: Hewlett–Packard

Designer-customer interactions

(i) Understanding customer needs $= \dfrac{\text{Visit to customers}}{\text{Number of designers}}$

This measure is to promote more interaction between designers and customers by calculating the amount of contact.

Overall effectiveness of product development

(i) Staffing level effectiveness

$$= \frac{\text{Staff initially forecast as needed for a project}}{\text{Staff actually needed by project}} \times 100$$

This measure monitors how close the projections for the staff needed on a project matched the actual staffing required by the project.

(ii) Stability of the design

$$= \frac{\text{Number of design changes in a project}}{\text{Total cost of project}} \times 100$$

This measure tracks the number of design changes made. As large projects might need more changes simply because they are larger, this metric, by dividing against the project's costs, adjusts for the size of the project.

Overall effectiveness of the innovation process

(i) Innovation effectiveness

$$= \frac{\text{Number of projects finishing development}}{\text{Number of projects started development}} \times 100$$

Other measures

(i) Progress rate of project

$$= \frac{\text{Months late}}{\text{Total months initially scheduled for project}}$$

(ii) Cost estimation $= \dfrac{\text{Actual cost of phase}}{\text{Projected cost of phase}}$

(iii) Milestone progress rate

$$= \frac{\text{Number of milestones reached during month}}{\text{Number of milestones scheduled that month}} \times 100$$

Case study three: Exxon Chemical

In-process measures

(i) Penetration: Percentage of NPD budget utilising innovation process.
(ii) Percentage of new projects utilising innovation process.
(iii) Focus/Culling: Percentage of NO/GO or HOLD by gate two.

Results-based measures

(i) Speed of innovation: Elapsed time, stage one through four.
(ii) Performance: Second year EBIT (Earning before Interest and Tax) versus gate four.
(iii) Percentage of revenue from products more than five years old.

Definitions

(i) *Penetration*. The number of projects managed through the innovation process.

(ii) *Focus*. Reflected by early CULLING. Percentage of No Go or hold decision made during a period of time by the end of stage two (detailed assessment).

(iii) *Speed*. Average period (in months) of average development time for projects approved for commercial launch (stage five) during a specific year.

(iv) *Performance*. NPD/NBD Payout (NBD = new business development). Percentage of actual/projected IBIT Ratio in a particular year for projects in their second full year of operation after gate four: "Go Ahead".[8-12]

Case study four: Measurement of R&D at Dupont

Measures developed by the Imaging Systems Department (Research and Development Division) at Dupont are based on a series of key processes:

(i) R&D core processes:

    (a) Human development.

    (b) Technology planning and development.

    (c) Customer-focussed innovation.

    (d) Product and process design.

    (e) Competitive intelligence.

    (f) Business team partnership.

---

[8]Fig. 13.1. Overall number of projects being managed at each stage of the innovation process.

[9]Fig. 13.2. Number of new projects to stage one

[10]Fig. 13.3. Number of GO/NO GO decisions.

[11]Percentage of NO GO or Hold decisions made during each year at each stage of the innovation process.

[12]Percentage of sales of products for more than five years — new products as a percentage of revenue.

(ii) Customer needs groups:

   (a) People.
   (b) Standard R&D.
   (c) OSHA.
   (d) Just in time (JIT) manufacturing.
   (e) Process.
   (f) Product.
   (g) Innovation.

Measures related to the R&D process are referred to as *internal measures* while those related to customer needs are known as *external measures*.

Internal measures

(i) Human development

   (a) Percentage of courses taken per person.
   (b) Percentage of accomplishment awards.
   (c) Percentage of awards received (externally); organisation's perception of appraisal system.
   (d) Percentage of people actively involved in external professional organisations.
   (e) Percentage of department and local initiatives.
   (f) Percentage of attendance at committee meetings.
   (g) Ratio of courses approved to courses submitted.
   (h) Percentage of degrees earned after employment.
   (i) Percentage of formal university courses.
   (j) Percentage of courses conducted on site.

(ii) Product and process design

   (a) Yield of vendors.
   (b) Mill cost of formal complaints and raw materials/product type.
   (c) Percentage of clean runs.
   (d) Manufacturing cycle time (receipt of order to shipping).

(e) Relative product quality — percentage of product line rated first or second by customers.

(f) Dollar sales of new products in last three years — profits.

(g) Time spent "fire-fighting" new products and process ("hand holding").

(h) Percentage of coater downtime due to product/process problems of process/product simplifications.

(i) Longevity of product versions.

(j) Effort before versus effort after controlled sale.

(k) Shipping limits of material returned (how much was within specifications versus outside specificatons).

(iii) Business team partnership

(a) Percentage of people involved in business teams (horizontal integration).

(b) Percentage of new product/process proposals.

(c) Percentage of team awards; survey of business teams — how they treasure R&D participation.

(iv) Technology planning and development

(a) Percentage of long-term research programmes — need to define timing (active involvement in developing the programmes).

(b) Percentage of patents issued.

(c) Percentage of "core tech" programmes; average time from idea conception (marketing/manufacturing request) to commercialisation.

(d) Percentage of new or modified products and processes delivered.

(e) Percentage of technical publications and presentations external to IMG R&D.

(v) Customer-focussed innovation.
The lab programme cycle time:

(a) Percentage of SEED projects applied for.

(b) Percentage of successful SEED projects.

(c) Percentage of milestones achieved on time.

(d) Percentage of patent proposals.

(e) Percentage of new ventures initiated.

(f) Percentage of close customer partnerships.

(g) Percentage of new initiatives started.

(h) Percentage of differentiated products commanding price premium.

(vi) Competitive intelligence

(a) Percentage of competitive products analysed.

(b) Product technology concepts.

(c) Percentage of patent and literature searches requested (need variable feedback loop).

(d) Comprehensive Competitive Intelligence reports generated/updated (business).

External key measures

(i) People

(a) Percentage of people actively participating in external professional societies.

(b) Percentage of external awards received (from groups outside IMG R&D).

(ii) Innovation

(a) Percentage of successful SEED projects.

(b) Percentage of new ventures initiated.

(iii) Product

(a) Percentage of raw materials.

(b) Percentage of vendors.

(c) Dollar sales of new products.

(d) Percentage of formal complaints.

(iv) Standard R&D

(a) Number of patents issued.

(b) Number of publications/presentations outside IMG R&D.

(c) Number of new products/processes.

(d) Time from product/process conception to commercialisation.

(v) OSHA

(a) Volume of hazardous waste (solid, liquid and gaseous) plantwide.

(vi) Just in time (JIT) manufacturing

(a) Combined with process and product categories.

(vii) Process

(a) Yield.

(b) Mill cost.

(c) Manufacturing cycle time (raw materials shipping).

(d) Percentage of clean runs (defect free).

Business level measures: Financials

(i) *Profitability ratios.* These measure the returns generated on sales or investment, often in comparison with industry standards. Examples include:

(a) Profit margin on sales = Net profit after taxes/sales

(b) Return on total assets = Net profit after taxes/total assets

(ii) *Activity ratios.* These measure the use of resources and are best used in comparison with industry standards. Examples include:

(a) Fixed asset turnover = Sales/net fixed assets

(b) Total asset turnover = Sales/total assets

(c) Average collection period = Receivables/average sales per day

(d) Inventory turnover = Sales/inventory

(iii) *Project evaluation and comparison.* These methods help to select competing projects for the utilisation of funds. They are particularly important to commercialisation decisions as new products or processes are often easily conceptualised as the implementation of a project. The following are the two most commonly used techniques:

(a) The payback method calculates and compares the time to pay back initial investments for project alternatives. The more rapid the payback, the more desirable the project. The payback period is the time it takes a company to recover its original investment through net cash flows from the project.

(b) Discounted cash flow finds the present value of the expected net cash flows of an investment, discounted at the cost of capital. Net present value and internal rate of return project evaluation and comparison are types of discounted cash flow analysis. The advantage of these approaches is that they account for both the company's marginal cost of funds and the time profile of expected returns.

Leaning Points from the Case Studies

The case studies presented highlight that while there is a variety of approaches to measuring innovation, the measures can be categorised under three broad headings. These are:

(i) *Process-focussed measures*. These are measures which are concerned with speed, cost and quality. They are taken on a regular basis to address aspects of the innovation process which need optimising so that costs are kept to a minimum, time is reduced and quality is enhanced.

(ii) *Product-based measures*. These consist of all the measures concerned with:

(a) The performance of the product in terms of market share.
(b) Its worthiness in terms of leading to a competitive advantage — differentiation.
(c) Its cost in relation to the benefits achieved.
(d) Its financial worthiness.

(iii) *Business-level measures*. These are primarily financial measures, and present an aggregated picture of the performance of the organisation. Their use to drive innovation has to be guarded carefully because they can lead to a focus on short-term gains, rather than, account for the gains in the long run.

Generally, we can say that:

(i) Process-based and product-based measures are interrelated. Process-based measures are, however, on-line measures. They often lead to immediate action to deal with the problem and optimise those aspects concerned with the innovation process. Hence bottlenecks do not occur.

(ii) Product-based measures are, however, very often *retrospective* in nature. They can only be compiled once the information is made available, once the project has been complete and the product is performing in the marketplace.

(iii) Being overly concerned with product-based measures early in the innovation process appears to often distract teams from doing the right things (that is, moving the project forward). By imposing these types of measures early on in the process only encourages a mentality of 'let's work on less risky projects', 'let's play safe'. This leads to the achievement of small results without any significant leaps and real impact in the marketplace.

(iv) The whole idea of focussing on the innovation process and its improvement is to allow:

(a) A continuous flow of projects.
(b) A fast track development process.
(c) Low cost through improvements and optimising (organisational entitlement) — capability of the process.
(d) A mixture of large and small projects to reflect a healthy portfolio which incorporates short-term, medium- and long-term business needs.

It also aims to secure the following:

(a) Profit improvement.
(b) Customer satisfaction (Market Share).
(c) Consistent growth.
(d) Competitive supremacy in the business categories concerned.

(v) The optimisation of the projects *internally* to justify costs and make accurate financial predictions will lead to a "play safe culture" and a product-based culture.

(vi) Optimisation externally is, however, the most recommended route. This necessitates the company to start with its *raison d'être*, the customer and to align the organisational drivers from then onward.

Final Comments

Performance measures are vital for companies to ensure that they are achieving their goals. Measurement provides an important mechanism to evaluate, control and improve upon existing performance. Measurement creates the basis for comparing performance between different organisations, processes, teams and individuals.

Performance measurements have traditionally focussed on financial measures designed to benefit the shareholder rather than the line manager. Innovation managers require data and information which assist them in making business decisions. For example, if the innovation process is beginning to become inefficient, the sooner the manager is made aware of this, the faster the corrective action can be taken. Performance measures are an important means of providing managers with the information they require in order to innovate both effectively and efficiently. Financial information is received much too late by the line manager and will not assist in identifying the cause of the problem. Innovation success is built by having the right approach to measurement, as well as the appropriate metrics to act as vehicles for continuous improvement towards the goal of efficient and effective innovation.

Chapter 14

Learning and Continuous Improvement

JOHN BESSANT

Introduction: The Importance of Learning

Knowledge management within organisations is becoming an issue of strategic concern. This is linked to models of core competence and strategic advantage; whilst the terminology varies and often confuses, the underlying message is that firms should seek to identify what they are distinctively good at and then develop and deploy this to gain a competitive advantage. And because competence has to be accumulated gradually over time, it is hard for others to copy and, thus, the strategic advantage is more defensible (Kay, 1993; Prahalad & Hamel, 1994).

The key message in this discussion is that competence has to be learned and accumulated over time. Thus, there is growing interest in the mechanisms which firms utilise to enable this process (Pavitt, 1990). Here, the discussion is focussed on "capability" — again, a loosely used "humpty dumpty" word which often means whatever the authors want it to mean (Stalk *et al.*, 1992). But the underlying theme is one which focusses attention on how firms go about the process of building competence. For example, Teece and colleagues (1992) look at the ways in which firms frame and reframe "dynamic capability" while Nonaka (1991) focusses on knowledge capture and

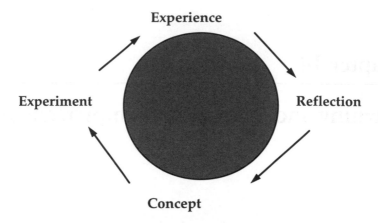

Experience

Experiment

Reflection

Concept

Fig. 14.1. Experiential learning cycle (Kolb, 1975).

sharing routines. Rush *et al.* (1997) and Keliner and Roth (1997) look at ways of capturing learning from projects. Increasingly, companies are reporting on how they have approached the problem. Other writers — for example, Senge (1990), Leonard-Barton (1991) and Garvin (1993) — provide different integrated models of pro-active learning in organisations, indicating the set of capabilities required.

It is clear from this that there is no generic solution. Instead, each firm has to work out its own approach; learning capabilities are as firm-specific as competencies. But it is also clear that there is some commonality of experience — certain classes of approach to the learning problem are used regularly. The examples include benchmarking, collaboration, structured project review and staff development through training.

All these approaches can be mapped onto a basic model of the learning process. For example, Fig. 14.1 shows the well-known experiential learning cycle originally put forward by David Kolb. It views learning as involving a cycle of experiment, experience, reflection and concept development.

Where an individual or firm enters is not important (though there is evidence for different preferred styles of learning associated

Table 14.1. Learning mechanisms and their relationship to the learning cycle.

Learning Approach	Position on Learning Cycle	Examples
Benchmarking — Learning by comparison	Aids structured reflection	Camp (1989), Womack *et al.* (1991)
Collaboration — Learning by working with others	Shared experience and experiment	Dodgson (1993), Coombs *et al.* (1992)
Strategic challenge	Structured and challenging reflection	Francis (1994)
Training/Developing the learners	New concepts Shared experience	Pedlar *et al.* (1991)
Project capture — Learning from reflection	Reflection	Kleiner *et al.* (1997), Rush *et al.* (1997)
Experiment — Learning from fast failure	Experiment and reflection	Pisano (1996)

with particular entry points). What does matter is that the cycle is completed — and incomplete cycles do not enable learning. Viewed in this way, each of the modes in Table 14.1 can be linked to one or more stages in the learning cycle; this argues for a multiple approach.

Organisational Routines to Enabling Learning

When talking about learning "capability" in this way, we are really concerned with clusters or patterns of behaviours which have become refined and rehearsed, and which are increasingly and repeatedly used to enable the learning process. In other words, they are "routines" which have been learned and embedded in the organisational culture — the underlying mixture of values and beliefs which drive the "way we do things around here" (Schein, 1984).

There is growing interest in routines and learning as a way of understanding organisational behaviour (Pentland and Rueter, 1994).

Winter, for example, defines routines as "... a relatively complex pattern of behaviour ... triggered by a relatively small number of initiating signals or choices and functioning as a recognisable unit in a relatively automatic fashion ..." (Winter, 1986). This is not to say that routines are mindless patterns. As Giddens points out "... the routinised character of most social activity is something that has to be 'worked at' continually by those who sustain it in their day-to-day conduct ..." (Giddens, 1984). It is rather the case that they have become internalised to the point of being unconscious or autonomous

One such cluster of routines is associated with improving learning at the organisational level by multiplying the number of people actively involved in the process. "Continuous improvement" (CI) is the generic label given to routines that involve a significant proportion of the work force in incremental problem-finding and solving on a continuing basis. This chapter looks at CI in terms of its potential as a strategic capability which firms are increasingly using to help them develop and sustain competencies.

Continuous Improvement

Continuous improvement (CI) can be defined as "... an organisation wide process of sustained and focused incremental innovation ..." (Bessant *et al.*, 1994). It is not a new concept — examples of systematic attempts to establish CI routines can be traced to the early 19th century — but rose to prominence in recent years as a result of Japanese experience (Robinson, 1991). The idea of employee involvement in improvement programmes was originally introduced to Japan as part of the post-war TWI initiative operated by the US and its allies, but internalisation and the development of a Japanese model — *kaizen* — soon followed (Schroeder and Robinson, 1993).

Kaizen evolved over an extended period and became a keystone of Japanese success in manufacturing. It represents a potent force for improving various aspects of organisational performance. For example, much of its original application was in the domain of quality, where a reputation for poor and shoddy products was turned to one in which world standards, measured in defective parts per million or less, were set. But *kaizen* has been applied with equal effect in other areas, such as increasing flexibility (through set-up time reduction), increasing plant availability (through total productive maintenance) and cost reduction (in particular, keeping pace with a highly valued Yen) (DTI, 1994).

The scale of CI activity in large Japanese firms is impressive. For example, Toyota regularly receives in excess of two million suggestions a year (equivalent to 35 per worker) and Toshiba in excess of four million (= 77 per worker) (Schroeder and Robinson, 1993). Figure 14.2 provides a further illustration of the extent to which CI represents a potent mechanism for securing high involvement in regular incremental innovation within Japanese firms. The average participation rate among these firms was 70% of the work force and the average adoption rate of their suggestions was 87%.

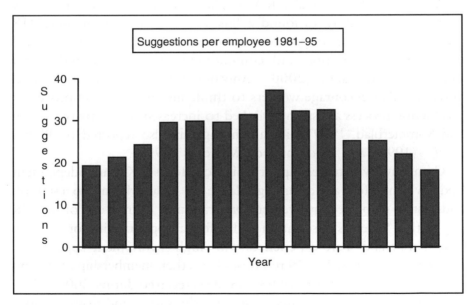

Source: Japanese Human Relations Association (1996).

Fig. 14.2. Average suggestions in Japanese companies (based on a sample of 600 firms).

During the past 20 years and driven by concerns around total quality management and "lean production", CI has increasingly been deployed in other countries with similar success. A study of UK experience (Richardson and Thompson, 1999) carried out for the Chartered Institute of Personnel and Development collected evidence to support the contention that in the 21st century "Tayloristic task management gives way to knowledge management; the latter seeking to be cost-efficient by developing an organisation's people assets, unlike the former which views labour as a cost to be minimised" (CIPD, 2001). They observe that although the task of convincing sceptical managers and shareholders remains difficult, "….more than 30 studies carried out in the UK and US since the early 1990s leave no room to doubt that there is a correlation between people management and business performance, that the relationship is positive, and that it is cumulative: the more and the more effective the practices, the better the result..." (Caulkin, 2001).

Analysis of the national UK Workplace Employee Relations Survey by Guest and colleagues found a link between the use of more HR practices and a range of positive outcomes, including greater employee involvement, satisfaction and commitment, productivity and better financial performance (2000). Another UK study concludes that "practices that encourage workers to think and interact to improve the production process are strongly linked to increased productivity" (Stern and Sommerblad, 1999). Similar findings are also reported by Blimes *et al.* (1997) and Wood and de Menezes (1998).

Company level studies support this view. Ideas UK is an independent body which offers advice and guidance to firms wishing to establish and sustain employee involvement programmes. It grew out of the UK Suggestion Schemes Association and offers an opportunity for firms to learn about and share experiences with high involvement approaches. A recent survey (based on 79 responses from their membership of around 200 firms) indicated a total of 93,285 ideas received during 2000–2001. Not every idea is implemented, but from the survey and from previous data it appears that around 25% are — and the savings which emerged as a direct consequence were reported as being £88 million for the period.

A major survey involving over 1,000 organisations in a total of seven countries provides a useful map of the take-up and experience with high involvement innovation in manufacturing (Boer *et al.*, 1999). Overall, around 80% of organisations were aware of the concept and its relevance, but its actual implementation, particularly in more developed forms, involved around half of the firms.

The average number of years which firms had been working with high involvement innovation on a systematic basis was 3.8, supporting the view that this is not a "quick fix" but something to be undertaken as a major strategic commitment. Indeed, those firms which were classified as "CI innovators" — operating well-developed high involvement systems — had been working on this development for an average of nearly seven years.

Similar patterns can be found in individual case studies explored in greater detail elsewhere (Gallagher and Austin, 1997).

CI and Learning/Competence Building

The strength of CI as a learning capability is that it embeds a high frequency learning cycle across much of the organisation. For example, in producing their millions of suggestions every year, the employees of Toshiba, Toyota and others are involved in problem-finding and-solving on a daily basis. In the process, they use links to all stages in the learning cycle. The underlying learning behaviours associated with CI have become rehearsed and reinforced to the point where they are now "the way we do things around here". In other words, learning is part of the culture embedded in a cluster of CI routines. In particular:

(i) CI mobilises more learners across the organisation in a formal sense. Instead of innovation being primarily the province of few specialists, it now becomes the responsibility of many.

(ii) It embodies a standardised learning process, usually involving some form of explicit problem-finding, -solving and review of methodology, which can be shared and adapted.

(iii) It deals with easily digestible increments of learning which can be absorbed through many frequent, small cycles rather than occasional, disruptive big ones.

(iv) With its emphasis on display and measurement (but also on understanding of those measures by users), it formalises and makes available knowledge which hitherto was in the tacit domain, such as critical process variables. This has close links with the management model suggested by Nonaka (1991).

(v) Through the involvement of non-specialists, it opens up the possibility for challenges to the accepted solutions. Such naive, but often penetrating, questions can enable "unlearning" to take place.

Typically, CI activities include systematic search, controlled experiment, structured reflection and capture and sharing of learning. In many cases, this is enshrined in a simple problem-solving model such as that propounded by Deming (1986) (the Deming wheel of "plan, do, check, act", or variations). Table 14.2 indicates this correspondence.

Within the total quality literature, two themes can be detected: the need to eliminate variation (through a variety of statistical measurement and monitoring techniques applied to the processes themselves) and the need to introduce controlled variation (via experiments designed to improve and extend process capability or performance). Again, this pattern maps well onto a learning cycle; it also explains one of the difficulties in the current pursuit of standardisation to ISO 9000. As Melcher *et al.* (1990) observe, the elimination of variation and standard maintainance is only half the battle; the complement of innovative experimentation is also required.

There is some empirical support for the view of CI as a mechanism for organisational learning. For example, Sirkin and Stalk (1990), in their description of the turnaround of a US paper mill, identify four

Table 14.2. Links between CI and stages in the learning cycle.

Stage in learning cycle	Examples of CI-enabling activities
Experiment	Design of experiments Brainstorming Taguchi methods
Experience	Structured brainstorming Nominal group techniques Data collection and presentation via seven simple tools of quality management Display and charting Statistical process control
Reflection	Root cause analysis Flowcharting and process mapping tools Video analysis CEDAC
Conceptualisation	Capture into new procedures Statistical process control tools

learning loops. Leonard-Barton (1991) also explains the successful innovative performance of a US steel mill in terms of learning loops, again based on building a deep understanding of the key process parameters and extending it through a process of experimentation and consolidation (Bateman & David, 2002; Bessant, 2003).

Garvin (1993) lists several features common to "learning organisations". These can be mapped, in a similar fashion, onto CI practice. The next section provides some examples linked to his headings.

Characteristics of Learning Organisations

Training and development emphasis

CI focusses on the formal development of problem-solving skills through tools and techniques. It also emphasises the importance of individual thinking, as well as doing, and seeks to develop this through formal skills training, background personal development and so forth.

For example, at the UK plant of Perkins Engines, the diesel engine manufacturer, around 60% of its staff were actively involved in CI across some 530 projects. To prepare them for this, it provided a minimum of three days' training for every employee, giving them the basic platform for CI understanding and establishing the process in people's minds. Additional inputs — such as for those responsible for facilitating CI — were also made. Its initial investment in training during the 18-month start-up period was of the order of 16,000 person days. Another producer of automotive components, LDS was able to save £850,000 a year from its extensive CI activities. In building its Process Improvement Teams, it provided three days of training for each team member to establish the basic process and concepts of CI. It extended the training to its LIFE (Little Improvements from Everyone) programme involving 500 staff (= 60% of the workforce). In one of the major UK energy companies, each employee of National Power receives a minimum of 10 days' CI training. Interestingly, in addition, they give every employee £100 worth of training vouchers, which can be in anything — from gardening or sewing to work-related topics. The aim is to encourage a learning culture in which more work-specific inputs can take root. Similar programmes are in operation at Ford (where demand for training far exceeded expectations) and at Baxi, where employees can study a wide range of courses at local colleges with the company paying the fees and providing some time release.

Establish a formal process

CI revolves around a shared and formalised model of problem-finding and -solving. These vary from Deming's PDCA to company-specific variants.

For example, the large computer manufacturer ICL was involved in total quality development in the early 1980s and had a well-embedded Crosby-type system for error cause detection and removal. Their CI programme evolved from this but moved the emphasis from teams and project task forces to individual improvement suggestions, many of which could be quickly implemented by the individuals themselves. Later additional techniques were introduced linked to the six sigma approach pioneered by Motorola and GE. Another company in the process industries spent extensively on the training and development of its staff prior to commissioning and operating a major new plant. In the short run, the CI activity led to significant enhancements. For example, the complex automated plant was soon running at 100% of the design efficiency and then was "stretched" to perform at up to 125%. But this relied on an informal problem-solving process which had been developed through intensive preparatory training of the original staff teams. Over time, with employee movements and other changes, this sense of process had become diluted and, in some places, disappeared altogether. The result was a decline in CI activity despite the company's support and campaigns for such improvement.

Measurement

Most CI involves some component of measurement — from simple tally charts and data collection through to sophisticated statistical process control techniques. Measurement also focusses attention on getting *information* about process activities and, in doing so, learning about them and what good performance means. Spreading this awareness across the whole workforce, rather than confining it to specialists, is important. For many people, one of the barriers to effective CI is simply not knowing why improvements are important. Inevitably, this moves measurement away from being an instrument for control and towards a tool which people can use to guide improvement — and it poses major challenges for conventional measurement systems and targets.

For example, a major UK boiler manufacturer has developed a system for measurement derived from activity-based costing. With this system, it is possible to measure the effects of CI improvements on the overall business and to track the ways in which the company has learned over time. It also provides a background against which to assess improvements in repeated activities, such as new product development. Many other companies make use of "policy deployment" approaches, linking overall, broad strategic targets through divisional and departmental objectives to individual activities, perhaps as part of an appraisal system. Within such arrangements, suitable measures can be agreed and used to monitor learning and development — for example, through skills acquisition or the achievement of particular improvement targets. Other also use agreed key performance indicators (KPIs), often displaying them prominently and drawing attention to progress. Such systems provide a good indication of overall performance and the extent to which CI activities can affect it. But they also offer the chance to identify where, how and how effectively learning is taking place along key dimensions (Akao, 1991; Bessant and Francis, 1999).

Document

Closely associated with measurement is the capture of information resulting from experiments in trying to solve problems. Whether successful or otherwise, there is a high risk of re-inventing the wheel unless information is captured and displayed for others to use. Organisations do not have memories as such, but they do have libraries, databases, procedures, drawings and other storage mechanisms for information and knowledge. The challenge in effective CI is to transfer the experiences of individuals to a form in which it can be more easily shared and communicated to others. For example, in one of the ICI operating divisions, the project team responsible for commissioning new plants built up a problem register which detailed not only the incidence of problems, but also the approaches used in trying to solve them.

Another IT equipment maker runs the dELTA system, which is effectively a company-wide suggestion scheme based on electronic mail, offering the opportunity to capture some learning and to draw attention to possible applications, or extensions of ideas, implemented in one area.

People are asked to code their ideas as they put them into the system if they think that others might benefit. Over time, a large database is built up that is available to the rest of this global business and provides a valuable resource for dealing with recurrent problems.

In the LIFE system mentioned earlier, individuals are encouraged to identify and implement changes themselves rather than wait to present them to the management. In order to capture learning from this, they are all issued with a small "policeman's notebook" on which they write down brief details of what they did. At present, a copy of this is given to the programme managers or the supervisor to help keep track of the number of suggestions. Although this represents a possible way of capturing and extending learning, the volume of ideas likely to emerge as the programme takes off may make this impossible.

With the larger-scale process improvement team (PIT) activities, the company makes use of a simple visual matrix which systematically looks at where else solutions generated in one area, or towards one kind of problem, might be applied. Such systematic search processes can reduce the dangers of different groups re-inventing the wheel.

Experiment

Central to successful CI is a climate which allows for extensive experimentation and does not punish failures if those experiments go wrong. This approach of continuing experimentation is essential to improving and developing new processes.

Finding out the limits of processes, or possible new ways of managing them, is one of the tasks traditionally carried out in R&D and engineering departments. But mobilising the resource to do this across the whole organisation would take a great deal of effort if it were handled by specialists; CI offers an alternative by giving the responsibility and authority to everyone to undertake experiments.

An example of the kind of climate which encourages experiment can be seen at Baxi (Gallagher & Austin, 1997). The culture, which has been developing, emphasises empowerment: employees are encouraged not only to make suggestions, but to implement them, and are equipped with the resources they need to do so. One employee identified a possible improvement by substituting a painted metal part with a cheaper, unpainted part. In the event, the change was not effective. But the culture of the company was such that it did not punish the employee, but instead used the opportunity to capture extra learning — in this case about what would not work. Similar patterns are reported in several cases in the US by Leonard-Barton (1991).

Challenge

In order to maintain momentum, CI programmes often include not only stretching targets, but also continually re-set them. In his account of how Toyota reduced set-up times on presses, Shingo describes the relentless re-setting of targets to drive the times down from several hours to, eventually, single minutes (Shingo, 1983). A wide range of CI tools and techniques have been developed to assist this process of systematic challenge, from simple "five why" approaches to complex analysis.

Doing this requires a systematic approach to experiment and challenge, as well as a refusal to accept that anything cannot be improved. As one commentator puts it, "... best is the enemy of better ...". Another motto, reported by Leonard-Barton and descriptive of this approach, is: "if it ain't being fixed, it's broke"?

Thorn Lighting has an interesting variant on this theme: "... if you always do what you've always done, you'll always get what you've always got ...". Rosemount Engineering makes active use of what they term "stretch goals" — targets which are deliberately set as being very challenging and almost unattainable. An example might be "on time delivery whenever the customer wants"; the point is that even if the targets are not reached, the efforts expended in aiming at them will probably have moved the organisation a long way forward. In this particular case, the stretch target became "90% delivery with a two week lead time to customers" — a significant leap from the initial situation of 55% within a 12-week lead time, but one which they have already come close to achieving.

Reflect — learn from the past

A common problem in establishing learning cycles within organisations is the absence of time, space and structure for reflection. CI programmes are often characterised by regular meetings, during which progress is reviewed and new problems are identified for work. In many cases, this cycle is a daily affair — a brief five-to-10-minute meeting before the shift starts — while in others, it is a longer weekly session. In each case, there is a high frequency reinforcement of CI and an institutionalised and structured approach to reflection and review. Again, many of the tools and techniques in CI are designed as structured aids to this process — from simple benchmarking, fishbone and other analytical tools through to more complex aids.

Use multiple perspectives

Another powerful mechanism for enhancing and encouraging learning is to bring different perspectives to bear on a problem. This can be done in a number of ways, ranging from bringing different groups together in cross-functional teams to broadening individual experience and outlook through training, rotation, secondment or visiting. It is also here that benchmarking plays an important role: it provides an opportunity to review and explore how other organisations tackle particular issues and problems.

There is a second reason for emphasising the movement of people and perspectives within the organisation; such mobility helps to spread knowledge around the organisation and builds up a shared "organisational memory". With a traditional functional and departmental organisation, it is often possible to reach a situation where the left hand doesn't know what the right is doing. This can lead, in turn, to re-inventing the wheel, duplication of effort, failed attempts to solve problems because the key skills or knowledge are missing, and so forth. In contrast, moving people around the organisation and giving them a chance to see things in new ways or from different perspectives can be a powerful resource. There is considerable evidence to suggest the value of a multi-perspective approach. For example, several companies encourage their shop floor staff to make visits to customers and suppliers. This has a twofold effect: it generally acts as a powerful motivator, but it also helps throw new light on problem issues. By bringing customer or supplier perspectives back into the plant, this can often lead to improvements.

Cross-functional teams are now widely recognised as a critical element in new product development, particularly in those cases where speed is the essence. By employing such an approach in the design and development of the "Discovery", Land Rover was able to reduce the development time from the typical five years plus to just 28 months. Location is also important.   At the Wakefield plant of Coca-Cola–Schweppes, there are several small canteen areas located next to the main plant. Here, the shift teams can stop off and have a coffee or a snack, smoke and otherwise relax. It is also a powerhouse for discussions and suggestions for continuous improvement. In several cases, discussions have led to immediate action back in the plant, trying out solutions developed over coffee or in other informal exchanges.

Display

Closely linked to documenting the results of CI is the need to display and communicate them. This serves several purposes: it provides a powerful motivator for the teams or individuals responsible for them, and it also serves to carry over ideas which might find application elsewhere in the organisation. Display via storyboard and other approaches may capture the dynamics as well, such that others can learn from the process which the groups went through as well as the results which they achieved. Perkins Engines, for example, equips all its teams with standard sheets to facilitate such activity.

This can be helpful in maintaining motivation. For example, in one company, the newsletter regularly carried features about success stories. A suggestion was made that this was sometimes discouraging because it implied that those groups which have less success were failures. By adjusting the coverage to a "warts and all" review, including the discussion of problem, other groups began to learn about the process and the overall result was an increase in activity.

In summary, it can be argued that CI represents a powerful approach to competence building because it has the potential to develop and embed a continuous learning capability across the organisation. Fulfilling this potential is, however, not easy to achieve and we must now turn our attention to the problems of acquiring and developing CI capability.

Developing CI Capability[1]

Much of the reported experience of implementing CI indicates difficulties, particularly in sustaining the process (Boer *et al.*, 1999; Bessant, 2003).

---

[1] It will be helpful to describe the research base underpinning this discussion. Concern over the implementation problem led us to embark on a major five-year research programme called CIRCA — Continuous Improvement Research for Competitive Advantage. CIRCA was an "action research" project which worked with a range of user firms to try and understand the dynamics of CI implementation. In particular, the programme involved in-depth research with a small number of core case study companies and experience sharing, as well as "snapshot" case study work with a wider network of around 100 firms. A broader perspective was gained through participating in a European Network for research on CI (EuroCINET) established under the EUREKA programme, which has been running a large sample survey of CI experience and practice. In the UK, we surveyed (in conjunction with *Work Management* magazine) a sample of 142 firms. The results have been published and are now being collated with those from other countries (Boer *et al.*, 1999). The main objectives of CIRCA were to deliver a basic methodology for implementing and maintaining CI, as well as a toolbox of resources to support this (Bessant *et al.*, 1992). The original plan for the network was to offer access to these research results to a wider community via a series of dissemination workshops, but it has evolved into a much more extensive system which continues to operate. Membership has also grown from a planned group of 20 firms to over 70 organisations participating in some aspect of the Network's activities. A full description of the programme appears in Bessant (2003).

For many firms, the implication of this is that CI adoption remains a "fashion" item which they try, find difficult and move on from. The corollary of this can be seen in the examples of firms which have succeeded in obtaining strategic advantage — where efforts have been made and sustained over decades. (For example, many of the major Japanese firms began their CI activities in the 1950s and have been systematically refining and developing them since.)

Our research suggests that there is a correlation between the extent of what can be termed CI *performance* — its contribution to reduced costs, improved quality, faster response, and so forth — and the extent to which the *practice* of CI is developed and embedded in the organisation.

Our research suggests that it is possible to identify a number of key behaviours which have to be learned and reinforced to establish CI capability. These behaviours cluster together and are integrated and built upon to acquire capability in a hierarchical process. (The analogy can be drawn to the process of learning to drive. This involves a progressive acquisition of basic control skills, their

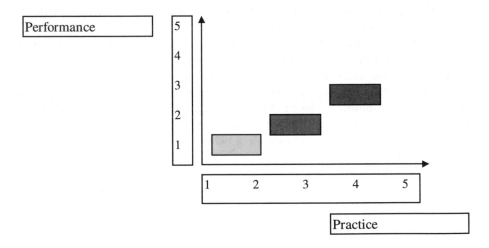

Fig. 14.3. Developmental model of CI.

integration into increasingly complex suites of behaviour, and gradual development of capability. With time and experience, the capability can be stretched — from simple competence to pass the driving test through to driving different cars, on different roads, under different conditions, and so forth. Eventually, a state is reached where driving becomes a near automatic capability, going on in the background whilst conscious attention is given to other tasks.)

The theoretical underpinnings of this approach lie in the concept of "routines" (Bessant and Caffyn, 1996). As noted by several authors, the development of firm-specific routines is an important determinant of successful innovative performance (Nelson, 1991; Pentland and Rueter, 1994). While the generic routines can be specified in terms of particular new behaviours which must be learned and reinforced — for example, systematic problem-solving through some form of learning cycle or monitoring and measuring to drive improvement — the particular ways in which different organisations actually achieve this will vary widely. Thus, routines for CI are essentially firm-specific. This is one reason why simply imitating what was done successfully within Japanese firms has proven to be such a poor recipe for many UK firms. There is no short cut in the process; CI behaviours have to be learned, reinforced and built upon to develop capability. (Details of the behavioural model and the constituent routines can be found in Bessant (2003).

The idea of increasingly skilful practice of the basic CI behaviours, and the notion that improved results (both in terms of business benefits and increased involvement in the CI process) follow from higher levels of such practice, enables us to posit a framework for mapping the evolution of CI capability. (This has much in common with other models such as the Capability Maturity model of software development or the EFQM Business Excellence model) (Paulk *et al.* 1993; Povey, 1996). Using this framework, it is possible to position an organisation in terms of the extent to which it has managed to develop and embed CI behaviours. This can be done through observation and examination of artefacts which result from consistent and repeated patterns of behaviour.

A Reference Model for CI Capability

Analysis of the process of CI development in a wide range of organisations suggests that there is a common pattern of stages of development. (To use the hackneyed metaphor of development of CI being a journey, these would represent milestones along the way.) Associated with each is the articulation and acquisition of particular behaviours: as the process develops, so the challenge lies not only in acquiring and embedding behaviours, but in integrating them into a systematic framework. This progress can be represented on a simple two-dimensional "reference model" which maps out stages in the development of both performance and practice.

Competence Development Through CI

Earlier, we saw that competence building is related to learning capability and, thus, the more developed the CI practice, the greater the impact we might expect to see. This is borne out in empirical data where firms which can demonstrate strategic performance advantage can also link this to the extent of the development of CI practice.

At low levels of practice development, the emphasis in CI development is primarily on "getting the habit" — articulating and experimenting with CI behaviours and gradually linking them into a structured and systematic framework. In terms of competence development, most activities are concerned with making tacit knowledge explicit — for example, by describing and defining procedures and then improving on them. As the organisation develops higher levels of CI practice, there is a shift towards more experimental forms of learning — from what Melcher and colleagues (1990) call standard-maintaining to continuously improving systems. At high levels, the kind of autonomous experimentation, sharing and open-ended learning behaviour typified -by descriptions of "the learning organisation" becomes the norm.

Table 14.3. The basic performance and practice dimensions of the model.

Level	Performance	Practice
0 = No CI activity	No impact from CI.	Random problem-solving.
		No formal efforts or structure.
		Occasional bursts punctuated
	by inactivity and non-	
participation.		
		Dominant mode of problem-solving is by specialists.
		Short-term benefits.
		No strategic impact.
1 = Trying out the ideas	Minimal and local effects only.	CI happens as a result of learning curve effects associated with a particular new product or process, and then fades out again. Or it results from a short-term input — a training intervention, for example — and leads to a small impact around those immediately concerned with it. These effects are often short-lived and very localised.
	Some improvements in morale and motivation.	
2 = Structured and systematic CI	Local level effects.	Format attempts to create and sustain CI.
	Measurable CI activity, such as the number of participants and ideas produced.	Use of a formal problem-solving process.
		Use of participation.
		Training in basic CI tools.
	Measurable performance effects confined to projects.	Structured idea management system.
		Recognition system.
	Little or no "bottom line" impact.	Often parallel system to operations.
		Can extend to cross-functional work, but on an *ad hoc* basis.

Table 14.3 (*Continued*)

Level	Performance	Practice
3 = Strategic CI	Policy deployment links local and project level activity to broader strategic goals. Monitoring and measurement drives improvement on these issues which can be measured in terms of the impact on the "bottom line" — for example, cost reductions, quality improvements and time savings.	All of the above, plus the formal deployment of strategic goals. Monitoring and measurement of CI against these goals. In-line system.
4 = Autonomous innovation	Strategic benefits, including those from discontinuous, major innovations and incremental problem-solving.	All of the above, plus responsibility for mechanisms, timing and so forth devolved to problem-solving unit. High levels of experimentation.
5 = The learning organisation	Strategic innovation. Ability to deploy competence base to competitive advantage.	CI as the dominant way of life. Automatic capture and sharing of learning. Everyone is actively involved in the innovation process. Incremental and radical innovation.

Learning to Learn

Our research also suggests that learning CI is a bimodal activity. Within any stage in the above model, there is much adaptive learning to be done in terms of refining the process and improving the ways in which behaviours can be articulated and embedded — for example, through fine-tuning reward systems. Much of this activity is concerned with finding particular problems — "blocks" — and deploying

Table 14.4. Enablers for continuous improvement.

Behaviour/Routines	Blockage	Enablers
"Getting the CI habit" — Legitimating and embedding basic problem-solving behaviour	Lack of suitable starting point/project to move from concepts into action. No formal process for finding and solving problems. Ideas are not responded to. Lack of skills in problem-solving. Lack of motivation. No structure for CI. Lack of group process skills.	Simple CI activities focussed on the workplace — for example, 5S techniques. PDCA or similar structural model plus tranining Simple idea management system based on rapid response. Training in simple CI tools — brainstorming, fishbone techniques and so forth. Recognition system. Simple vehicles based on groups. Facilitator training.
"Focusing CI" — Getting strategic benefit from CI	No strategic impact of CI. Lack of measurable benefit.	Policy deployment techniques — to focus problem-solving on strategic targets. Hoshin kanri tools. Introduce training in monitoring and measurement. Statistical process control. Process mapping and ownership.
"Spreading the word" — Extending CI beyond the local level	Lack of co-operation across divisions. Lack of inter-firm CI. Lack of process orientation.	Cross-functional CI teams. Inter-firm development initiatives. Process modelling tools and training.
"Walking the talk"	Conflict between espoused and practised values.	Articulation and review.
The learning organisation	No capture of learning.	Post-project reviews. Story-board techniques. Encapsulation in procedures.

Table 14.4 (*Continued*)

Behaviour/Routines	Blockage	Enablers
Continuous improvement of continuous improvement	Lack of direction. Running out of steam.	Formal CI steering group and strategic framework. Regular CI review and relaunch.

solutions — "enablers" — to deal with them. Over time, it has become clear that many of these "blocks" are commonly experienced. Similarly, many of the "enablers" have widespread applicability (although they will need tailoring to particular circumstances). Table 14.4 gives some examples; it follows from this that there are real possibilities for learning from others in developing CI capability (Nelson, 1991).

While much of the task in building CI capability is concerned with refining and improving the suite of activities in what is essentially an *adaptive learning* cycle, it is also clear that at certain stages of CI development, there is a need for what Senge (1990) terms "*generative*" learning and Argyris and Schon (1978), "*double loop*" learning. That is, the need for reframing the problem and finding new classes of solution. This is particularly associated with moving from one level in the reference model to the next, and is typically the result of the experience of reaching the limits of performance within a particular practice level. For example, "level 2" performance would see regular activity and local level impacts, but no real contribution to strategic goals. The reframing is necessary to develop routines which link the business strategy to the CI activity — through policy deployment, monitoring and measuring behaviours. Once again, there is some commonality of experience of blocks and the use of enablers here.

A Methodology for Developing CI

The model framework described above can be used to help explain and guide the development of CI capability. It can be linked to a classical

Table 14.5. Outline organisational development methodology for developing CI.

Basic Stages in OD	CI Stages	Support Tools
Audit — survey and feedback	Position against reference model.	CI assessment tool, a diagnostic instrument based on the reference model.
Target areas for action	Identify next stages in development with respect to reference model. Identify potential blocks and enablers.	Strategic review of CI — workshop. Reference model and description. Blocks and enablers "catalogue". Archetypes of CI — "firms like us" to provide guidelines.
Implement		"Toolbox" of resources — enablers. Action-learning network.
Review and repeat cycle		

OD methodology, as indicated in Table 14.5. Much of our current work is in exploring and testing this proposition, and in developing the tools to support this.

Conclusions

Arguably, the development of CI is a critical task for 21st century knowledge-based organisations, since it opens up possibilities for high involvement in developing strategic competencies. The embedding of a high frequency cycle of problem-finding, problem-solving, review, sharing and capture of learning is likely to be a critical issue. But it poses major challenges in terms of not only learning new behaviours, but also in forgetting — "unlearning" — many old ones which have traditionally excluded the majority of the workforce from participation in the problem-solving activities that characterise the true learning organisation.

Bibliography

Abernathy, W.J. (1978) *The Productivity Dilemma: Roadblock to Innovation in the Automobile Industry.* Baltimore, MD: John Hopkins University Press

Abernathy, W.J. & Utterback, J. (1978) Patterns of industrial innovation. *Technology Review*, **80**, 40–47

Acs, Z. & Audretsch, D.B. (1988) Innovation in large and small firms: an empirical analysis. *American Economic Review*, **78**, 678–690

_____, (1990) *Innovation and Small Firms.* Cambridge, MA: MIT Press

Akacum, A. & Dale, B.G. (1995) Supplier partnering: case study experiences. *International Journal of Purchasing and Materials Management*, Winter, 38–44

Akao, Y. (1991) *Hoshin Kanri: Policy Deployment for Successful TQM.* Cambridge, MA: Productivity Press

Albert, M.B., Avery, D., McAllister, P. & Narin, F. (1991) Direct validation of citation counts as indicators of industrially important patents. *Research Policy*, **20**, 251–259

Allen, T.J. (1984) *Managing the Flow of Technology: Technology Transfer and the Dissemination of Technological Information within the R&D Organization.* Cambridge, MA: MIT Press

Altman, E.I. (1971) *Corporate Bankruptcy in America.* Lexington Books

_____, (1983) *Corporate Financial Distress.* New York: Wiley

Alvesson, M. (2000) Social identity in knowledge-intensive companies. *Journal of Management Studies*, **37**(8), 1101–1123

Amit, R. & Schoemaker, P.J.H. (1993) Strategic assets and organisational rent. *Strategic Management Journal*, **14**, 33–46

Amidon, D. (1998) The evolving community of knowledge practice: the Ken awakening. *International Journal of Technology Management*, **16**(1/2/3), 45–63

Ancona, D. & Caldwell, D. (1992) Bridging the boundary: external activity and performance in organizational teams. *Administrative Science Quarterly*, **37**, 634–665

401

Anderson, R.C., Narin, F. & McAllister, P.R. (1978) Publication ratings versus peer ratings of universities. *Journal of the American Society for Information Science*, 29, 91–103. Reprinted in *Key Papers in Information Science*, ed. B.C. Griffith. Knowledge Industry Publications, Inc. (1980)

Angle, H. & Van de Ven, A. (1989) Managing the innovation journey. In *Research on the Management of Innovation*, ed. A. Van de Ven, H. Angle & M. Poole. New York: Harper & Row

Archibugi, D. (1992) Patenting as an indicator of technological innovation: a review. *Science and Public Policy*, 19(6), 357–368

Argenti, J. (1976) *Corporate Collapse*. New York: McGraw-Hill

Argyres, N. (1996) Capabilities, technological diversification and divisionalization. *Strategic Management Journal*, 17, 395–410

Argyris, C. & Schon, D.A. (1978) *Organisational Learning: A Theory of Action Perspective*. Wesley Publishing Company

Arnold, J. & Moizer, P. (1984) A survey of the methods used by UK investment analysts. *Accounting and Business Research*, Summer

Arundel, A., van de Paal, G. & Soete, L. (1995) Innovation strategies of Europe's largest industrial firms (PACE report). MERIT, University of Limbourg, Maastricht

Ashforth, B.E. & Mael, F. (1989) Social identity theory and the organisation. *Academy of Management Review*, 14(1), 20–39

Atuahene-gima, K. & Patterson, P. (1993) Managerial perceptions of technology licensing as an alternative to internal R&D in new product development: an empirical investigation. *R&D Management*, 23(4), 327–336

Augsdorfer, P. (1996) *Forbidden Fruit*. Aldershot: Avebury

Bacon, F. (1620) *The New Organon and Related Writing*

Bacon, G., Beckman, S., Mowery, D. & Wilson, E. (1994) Managing product definition in high-technology industries. *California Management Review*, 36(3), 32–56

Badham, R., Couchman, P. & McLoughlin, I. (1997) Implementing vulnerable socio-technical change projects. In *Innovation, Organizational Change and Technology*, ed. I. McLoughlin & M. Harris. London: Thomson

Baily, P. & Farmer, D. (1990) *Purchasing Principles and Management*. Pitman

Barclay, I. (1992) New product development process: past evidence and future practical application. *R&D Management*, 22(3), 255–264

Barley, S. (1986) Technology as an occasion for restructuring: evidence from observation of CT scanners and the social order of radiology departments. *Administrative Science Quarterly*, **31**, 78–108

Barney, J. (1991) Firm resources and sustained competitive advantage. *Journal of Management*, **17**, 99–120

Barnes, B. (1977) *Interests and the Growth of Knowledge*. London: Routledge and Kegan Paul (Routledge Direct Editions)

Barton, J. (1993) Adapting the intellectual property system to new technologies. In *Global Dimensions of Intellectual Property Rights in Science and Technology*, ed. M.B. Wallerstein, M.E. Mogee & R.A. Schoen. Washington, DC: National Academy of Sciences Press

Bateman, N. & David, A. (2002) Process improvement programmes: a model for assessing sustainability. *International Journal of Operations and Production Management*, **22**(5), 515–526

Baumard, P. (1999) *Tacit Knowledge in Organizations*. London: Sage

Baxter, W.T. (1984) *Inflation Accounting*. Deddington: Philip Allan

Becker, M. (2001) Managing dispersed knowledge: organizational problems, managerial strategies and their effectiveness. *Journal of Management Studies*, **38**(7), 1037–1051

Beer, M. & Eisenstat, R.A. (1996) Developing an organisation capable of implementing strategy and learning. *Human Relations*, **49**(5), 597–619

Bellon, B. & Whittington, G. (1996) *Competing through Innovation*. Dublin: Oak Tree Press

Berry, M.M.J. & Taggart, J.H. (1994) Managing technology and innovation: a review. *R&D Management*, October

Bertin, G. & Wyatt, S. (1988) *Multi-Nationals and Industrial Property*. Hemel Hempstead: Harvester-Wheatsheaf

Bessant, J. (1995) Networking as a mechanism for technology transfer: the case of continuous improvement. In *Europe's Next Step*, ed. R. Kaplinsky, F. den Hertog & B. Coriat. London: Frank Cass

Bessant, J. (2003) *High Involvement Innovation*. Chichester: John Wiley and Sons

Bessant, J. & Francis, D. (1999) Developing strategic continuous improvement capability. *International Journal of Operations and Production Management*, **19**(11), 1106–1119

Bessant, J. & Caffyn, S. (1996) High involvement innovation. *International Journal of Technology Management*, **14**(1), 7–28

Bessant, J., Caffyn, S. & Gilbert, J. (1996) Learning to manage innovation. *Technology Analysis and Strategic Management*, **8**(1), 59–69

Bessant, J., *et al.* (1994) Rediscovering continuous improvement. *Technovation*, **14**(1) 17–29

Bessant, J.R., Levy, P., Sang, B. & Lamming, R.C. (1993) Managing successful total quality relationships in the supply chain. *European Journal of Purchasing and Supply Management*, **1**(1) 7–17

Bettis, R.A. & Hitt, M.A. (1995) The new competitive landscape. *Strategic Management Journal*, **16**, 7–19

Bettis, R.A., Bradley, S.P. & Hamel, G. (1992) Outsourcing and industrial decline. *Academy of Management Executive*, **6**(1), 7–21

Blackler, F. (1995) Knowledge, knowledge work and organizations: an overview and interpretation. *Organization Studies*, **16**(6), 1021–1046

Blimes, L., Wetzker, K. & Xhonneux, P. (1997) *Value in Human Resources*. London: Financial Times

Blundell, R., Griffith, R. & Van Reenen (1993) Knowledge stocks, persistent innovation and market dominance. Paper given to SPES discussion group, Brussels, September

Boer, H., Berger, A., Chapman, R. & Gertsen, F. (1999) *CI Changes: From Suggestion Box to the Learning Organisation*. Aldershot: Ashgate

Bogaert, I., Martens, R. & Van Cauwenbergh, A. (1994) Strategy as a situational puzzle: the fix of components. In *Competence-based Competition*, ed. G. Hamel & A. Heene. Chichester: Wiley

Bogner, W., Thomas, H. & McGee, J. (1999) Competence and competitive advantage: towards a dynamic model. *British Journal of Management*, **10**, 275–290

Boisot, M.H. (1995) Is your firm a creative destroyer? Competitive learning and knowledge flows in the technological strategies of firms. *Research Policy*, **24**, 489–506

Boisot, M., Griffiths, D. & Mole, V. (1997) The dilemma of competence: differentiation versus integration in the pursuit of learning. In *Strategic Learning and Knowledge Management*, ed. R. Sanchez & A. Heene. Chichester: Wiley

Boisot, M., Lemmon, T., Griffiths, D. & Mole, V. (1996) Spinning a good yarn: the identification of core comptencies at Courtaulds. *International Journal of Technology Management, Special Issue on the Fifth International Forum on Technology Management*, **11**(3/4), 425–440

Boisot, M.H. (1994) *Information and Organisation: The Manager as Anthropologist.* London: Harper and Collins

Booz, Allen & Hamilton (1982) *New Product Development for the 1980s.* New York: Booz, Allen and Hamilton Inc.

Bowen, K. (1994) *The Perpetual Enterprise Machine: Seven Keys to Corporate Renewal through Successful Product and Process Development.* New York: Oxford University Press

Breu, K. & Hemingway, C. (2002) The power of communities of practice for subverting organisational change. Paper presented at 3rd European Conference on Organizational Knowledge, Learning and Capabilities, Athens, Greece, April 5–6

Briggs, P. (1994) Vendor assessment for partners in supply. *European Journal of Purchasing and Supply Management,* 1(1), 49–59

Broad, W.J. (1997) Study finds public science is pillar of industry. *The New York Times, Science Times,* Tuesday, 13 May

Bromwich, M. (1990) The case for strategic management accounting. *Accounting Organisations and Society,* February

Brown, S. (1998) Manufacturing seniority, strategy and innovation. *Technovation,* 18(3), 111–132

Brown, J.S. & Duguid, P. (1991) Organization learning and communities of practice: towards a unified view of working, learning and innovation. *Organization Science,* 2(1), 40–57

_____, (1996) Organisational learning and communities of practice. In *Organisational Learning,* ed. M.D. Cohen & L.S. Sproull. London: Sage

_____, (1998) Organizing knowledge. *California Management Review,* 40(3), 90–111

_____, (2001) Knowledge and organization: a social practice perspective. *Organization Science,* 12(2), 198–213

Brown, J. & Utterback, J. (1985) Uncertainty and technical communication patterns. *Management Science,* 31(3), 301–311

Brown, S.L. & Eisenhardt, K.M. (1995) Product development: past research, present findings and future directions. *Academy of Management Review,* April

Browning, J.M., Zabriskie, N.B. & Heullmantel, A.B. (1983) Strategic purchasing planning. *Journal of Purchasing and Materials Management,* Spring

Brusoni, S., Prencipe, A. & Pavitt, K. (2001) Knowledge specialisation, organisational coupling, and the boundaries of the firm: why do firms know more than they make? *Administrative Science Quarterly,* 46, 597–621

Bryman, A. (2000) Telling technological tales. *Organization*, 7(3), 455–475

Buderi, R., Carey, J., Gross, N. & Lowry-Miller, K. (1992) Global innovation: who's in the lead? *Business Week Patent Scoreboard*, 3 August

Budworth, D.W. (1993) Intangible assets and their renewal. Foundation for Performance Measurement, UK National Meeting, London, October

Burgelman, R.A., Maidique, M.A. & Wheelwright, S.C. (1995) *Strategic Management of Technology*, 3rd edn. Homewood: Irwin

Business Week (1993) The global patent race picks up. 9 August

Buzell, R.D. & Gale (1987) *The PIMS Principle*. New York: Free Press

Caffyn, S., Bessant, J. & Silano, M. (1996) Continuous improvement in the UK. *Works Management*, July

Calvert, J., Ibarra, C., Patel, P. & Pavitt, K. (1996) Innovation outputs in European industry: results from the CIS. EIMS Publication Number 34, European Commission — DG XIII, Luxembourg

Camp, R. (1989) *Benchmarking — The Search for Industry Best Practices that Lead to Superior Performance*. Milwaukee, WI: Quality Press

Campbell, R.S. & Levine, L.O. (1984) *Technology Indicators Based on Patent Data*. Washington: National Science Foundation

Cantwell, J. (1992) The internationalisation of technological activity and its implications for competitiveness. In *Technology Management and International Business: Internationalisation of R&D and Technology*, ed. O. Granstrand, L. Hakanson & S. Sjolander. Chichester: Wiley

——————, (1995) The globalisation of technology: what remains of the product cycle model. *Cambridge Journal of Economics*, **19**, 155–174

Cardinal, L.B. & Opler, T.C. (1993) Corporate diversification and innovation efficiency. Working Paper No. 93-0504, Edwin Cox School of Business, Southern Methodist University

Carlile, P.R. (2002) A pragmatic view of knowledge and boundaries: boundary objects in new product development. *Organization Science*, 13(4), 442–455

Carpenter, M.P. & Narin, F. (1983) Validation study: citations as indicators of science and foreign dependence. *World Patent Information*, 5(3), 180–185

Carpenter, M.P., Narin, F. & Woolf, P. (1981) Citation rates to technologically important patents. *World Patent Information*, **4**, 160–163

Caulkin, S. (2001) *Performance through People*. London: Chartered Institute of Personnel and Development

CBI/NatWest (1992) *Innovation Trends Survey*. London: CBI

Cesaratto, S. & Mangano, S. (1993) Technological profiles and economic performance in the Italian manufacturing sector. *Economics of Innovation and New Technology*, **2**, 237–256

Chakraborty, S. & Philip, T. (1996) Vendor development strategies. *International Journal of Operations and Production Management*, **16**(10), 54–65

Chan, S.H., Martin, J.D. & Kensinger, J.W. (1990) Corporate research-and-development expenditures and share value. *Journal of Financial Economics*, **26**(2), 255–276

Chandler, A.D. (1966) *Strategy and Structure*. Cambridge: MIT Press

Chaney, R., Devinney, T. & Winer, R. (1992) The impact of new product introductions on the market value of firms. *Journal of Business*, **64**(4), 573–610

Channon, D. (1973) *The Strategy and Structure of British Enterprise*. London: MacMillan

Chen, S. (1997) Core capabilities and core rigidities in the multi-media industry. Unpublished PhD Thesis, The Management School, Imperial College, University of London

Christenson, C. (1997) *The Innovator's Dilemma*. Cambridge, MA: Harvard Business School Press

Chusil, M.J. (1978) How much to spend on R&D. *PIMS Newsletter*, No. 13

Ciborra, C. & Patriotta, G. (1998) Groupware and teamwork in R&D: limits to learning and innovation. *R&D Management*, **28**(1), 43–52

CIMA (1993) *Performance Measurement in The Manufacturing Sector*. Chartered Institute of Management Accountants

CIPD (2001) *Raising UK Productivity: Why People Management Matters*. London: Chartered Institute of Personnel and Development

Clark, K. & Griliches, Z. (1984) Chapter 19. In *Patents, R&D and Productivity*, ed. Z. Grilliches & A. Pakes. Chicago: University of Chicago Press

Clark, K.B. & Fujimoto (1991) *Product Development Performance*. Boston: Harvard University Press

Clark, P. (2000) *Organizations in Action: Competition Between Contexts*. London: Routledge

Clinton, W.L. & Gore, Jr., A. (1993) *Technology for America's Economic Growth: A New Direction to Build Economic Strength*. Office of the President of the United States

Cohen, M.D. (1996) Individual learning and organizational routine. In *Organisational Learning*, ed. M.D. Cohen & L.S. Sproull. London: Sage

Cohen, W. & Levin, R. (1989) Empirical studies of innovation and market structure. In *The Handbook of Industrial Organisation*, Vol. 1, ed. R. Schmalensee & R. Willig. Elsevier

Cohen, W. & Levinthal, D. (1990) Absorptive capacity: a new perspective on learning and innovation. *Administrative Science Quarterly*, **35**, 128–152

Collinson, S. (1999) Developing and deploying knowledge for iInnovation: British and Japanese corporations compared. Paper presented at 15th EGOS colloquium, University of Warwick, 4–6 July

Collis, D.J. & Montgomery, C.A. (1995) Competing on resources: strategy in the 1990s. *Harvard Business Review*, **73**, 118–128

Company Reporting Ltd. (1993) *The 1993 UK R&D Scoreboard*. London: Company Reporting

Constant, E.W. (1987) The social locus of technological practice: community, system or organisation. In *The Social Construction of Technological Systems: New Directions in the Sociology and History of Technology*, ed. W. Bijker, T. Hughes & T. Pinch. Cambridge, MA: MIT Press

Contu, A. & Willmott, H. (2000) Comment on Wenger and Yanow. Knowing in practice: a "delicate flower" in the organizational learning field. *Organization*, 7(2), 269–276

Cook, S. & Brown, J. (1999) Bridging epistemologies: the generative dance between organizational knowledge and organizational knowing. *Organization Science*, **10**(4), 381–400

Cook, S.D.N. & Yanow, D. (1996) Culture and organisational learning. In *Organisational Learning*, ed. M.D. Cohen & L.S. Sproull. London: Sage

Coombs, R., Narandren, P. & Richards, A. (1994) An innovation output indicator for the UK economy. Report to the ESRC. Manchester, UMIST

——————, (1996) A literature-based innovation output indicator. *Research Policy*, **25**, 403–413

Coombs, R., Saviotti, P. & Walsh, V. (1992) *Technological Change and Company Strategies*. London: Academic Press

Cooper, R. (1994) Third-generation new product processes. *Journal of Product Innovation Management*, **11**(1), 3–14

Cooper, R.G. & Kleinschimdt, E.J. (1987) New products: what separates winners from losers. *Journal of Product Innovation Management*, **4**, 169–187

Cousins, P.D. (1994) A framework for the implementation, measurement and management of relationship sourcing strategies. Unpublished PhD Thesis, University of Bath

Coy, P. & Carey, J. (1993) The global patent race picks up speed. *Business Week Patent Scoreboard*, 16 August

Coyne, K.P. (1986) Sustainable competitive advantage — what it is and what it isn't. *Business Horizons*, January/February, Indiana University

Coyne, P., Hall, S.J.D. & Clifford, P.J. (1997) Is your core competence a mirage? *The Mckinsey Quarterly*, No. 1

Craig, A. & Hart, S. (1992) Where to now in new product development research? *European Journal of Marketing*, 26(11), 1–47

Crepon, B. & Mairesse, J. (1993) Innovation and productivity — the contribution of SESI's innovation survey to econometric analysis. Paper given to SPES discussion group, Brussels, September

CSO (1992) *UK Balance of Payments (Pink Book)*. HMSO

_____, (1992) *UK National Accounts (Blue Book)*. HMSO

Cummings, J.N. (2004) Work groups, structural diversity, and knowledge sharing in a global organization. *Management Science*, 50(3), 352–364

Dale, B. (1992) Total quality management — what are the research challenges? In *Proceedings of the Seventh Operations Management Association Conference*. Elsevier

Damanpour, F. (1991) Organisational innovation: a meta-analysis of the effects of determinant and moderators. *Academy of Management Journal*, 34, 555–590

Dasgupta, P. & Stiglitz, J. (1980) Industrial structure and the nature of innovative activity. *Economic Journal*, 90, 266–293

Davenport, T. (1992) *Process Innovation: Re-engineering Work through Information Technology*. Boston, MA: Harvard University Press

Davies, M., Paterson, R. & Wilson, A. (1991) *UK GAAP*. Middlesex: Longman

DeFillippi, R. & Arthur, M. (1998) Paradox in project based enterprise: the case of filmmaking. *California Management Review*, 40(2), 125–139

de Gues, A. (1996) *The Living Company*. Boston, MA: Harvard Business School Press

De Solla Price, D.J. (1969) Measuring the size of science. In *Proceedings of the Israel Academy of Science and Humanities*

Deming, W.E. (1986) *Out of the Crisis*. Cambridge, MA: MIT Press

Deng, Z. & Lev, B. (1998) The valuation of acquired R&D. Working Paper.

Deng, Z., Lev, B. & Narin, F. (1998) Science and technology indicators as predictors of stock performance. Draft paper

Denison, D.R., Hart, S.L. & Kahn, J.A. (1996) From chimneys to cross-functional teams: developing and validating a diagnostic model. *Academy of Management Journal*, **39**(4), 1005–1023

Devinney, T.M. (1993) How well do patents measure new product activity? *Economics Letters*, **41**, 447–450

Dickson, G.W. (1966) An analysis of vendor selection criteria and methods. *Journal of Purchasing*, **2**(1), 28–41

Dierickx, I. & Cool, K. (1989) Asset stock accumulation and sustainability of competitive advantage. *Management Science*, **35**, 1504–1514

Dixon, J.R., Nanni, A.J. & Vollmann, T. (1990) *The New Performance Challenge: Measuring Operations for World-Class Competition*. London: Irwin

Dobler, D.W., Burt, D.N. & Lee, L. (1990) *Purchasing and Materials Management: Text and Cases*. McGraw-Hill

Dodgson, M. (1993) *Technological Collaboration in Industry*. London: Routledge

Dodgson, M. & Rothwell, R. (ed., 1995) *The Handbook of Industrial Innovation*. London: Edward Elgar

Donnellon, A. (1993) Cross-functional teams in product development: accommodating the structure to the process. *Journal of Product Innovation Management*, **10**, 377–392

Dosi, G. (1982) Technological paradigms and technological trajectories. *Research Policy*, **11**, 147–162

Dougherty, D. (2001) Reimagining the differentiation and integration of work for sustained product innovation. *Organization Science*, **12**(5), 612–631

Drazin, R. & Schoonhoven, C.B. (1996) Community, population and organisation effects on innovation: a multi-level perspective. *Academy of Management Journal*, **39**(5), 1065–1083

Drejer, A. (1996) Frameworks for the management of technology: towards a contingent approach. *Technology Analysis and Strategic Management*, **8**(1), 9–19

Drury, C. (1992) *Management and Cost Accounting*, 3rd edn. London: Chapman & Hall

DTI (1994) *Learning from Japan*. Department of Trade and Industry

Dunphy, D. (1996) Organisational change in corporate settings. *Human Relations*, **49**(5), 541–552

Eccles, R. (1991) The performance measurement manifesto. *Harvard Business Review*, January/February

The Economist (1994) The vision thing. 3 September

Eden, C. & Huxham, C. (1996) Action research for the study of organisations. In *Handbook of Organization Studies*, ed. S. Clegg. London: Sage

Edmondson, A. & Moingeon, B. (1996) When to learn how and when to learn why. In *Organisational Learning and Competitive Advantage*, ed. B. Moingeon & A. Edmondson. London: Sage

Edwards, K.L. & Gordon, T.J. (1984) Characterisation of innovations introduced on the US market in 1982. Report to the US Small Business Administration, Connecticut, Futures Group

EIRMA (1986) Developing R&D strategies. Working Group Report

Eisenhardt, K.M. (1989) Agency theory: an assessment and review. *Academy of Management Review*, **14**(1), 57–74

Eisenhardt, K.M. & Tabrizi, B. (1995) Accelerating adaptive processes: product innovation in the global computer industry. *Administrative Science Quarterly*, **40**(1), 84–110

Eiteman, D.K. & Stonehill, A.I. (1989) *Multi-national Business Finance*. New York: Addison-Wesley

Ellis Gibbs, J.G. (1997) Effective relationships for supply — attributes and definitions. *European Journal of Purchasing and Supply Management*, **4**(1), 43–50

Ellis, P., Hepburn, G. & Oppenheim, C. (1978) Studies on patent citation networks. *Journal of Documentation*, **34**(1), 12–20

Ellram, L.M. & Carr, A. (1994) Strategic purchasing: a history and review of the literature. *International Journal of Purchasing and Materials Management*, Spring

Evangelista, R., Sandven, T., Sirilli, G. & Smith, K. (1997) Innovation expenditures in European industry. STEP Report 5/97, Oslo, Norway

Feinman, S. & Fuentevilla, W. (1976) *Indicators of International Trends in Technological Innovation*. Washington: National Science Foundation

Fiol, C.M. (1994) Consensus, diversity, and learning in organizations. *Organization Science*, **5**(3), 403–420

Fiol, C.M. (1996) Squeezing harder doesn't always work: continuing the search for consistency in innovation research. *Academy of Management Review*, **21**(4), 1012–1021

Fleck, J. (1997) Contingent knowledge and technology development. *Technology Analysis and Strategic Management*, **9**(4), 383–397

Fox, S. (2000) Practice, Foucault and actor-network theory. *Journal of Management Studies*, **37**(6), 853–868

Francis, D. (1994) *Step by Step Competitive Strategy*. London: Routledge

Franko, L.G. (1989) Global corporate competition: who's winning, who's losing, and the R&D factor as one reason why. *Strategic Management Journal*, **10**, 449–474

Freeman, C. (1971) The role of small firms in innovation in the United Kingdom since 1945. Committee of inquiry on small firms, Report No. 6, HMSO, London

———, (1982) *The Economics of Industrial Innovation*. London: Pinter

Frumau, C.C.F. (1992) Choices in R&D and business portfolio in the electronics industry. *Research Policy*, **21**, 97–124

Gallagher, M. & Austin, S. (1997) *Continuous Improvement Casebook*. London: Kogan Page

Galbraith, J.R. (1972) *Designing Complex Organizations*. Reading, MA: Addison-Wesley

Galbraith, J.R. (1994) *Competing with Flexible Lateral Organizations*. Reading, MA: Addison-Wesley

Gambardella, A. & Torrisi, S. (1998) Does technological convergence imply convergence in markets? Evidence from the electronics industry. *Research Policy*, **27**, 445–463

Garfield, E. (1955) Citation indexes for science. *Science*, **122**, 108–111

———, (1980) Are the 1970 prizewinners of Nobel class? *Current Comments*, **38**, 609

———, (1986) Do Nobel Prize winners write citation classics? *Current Comments*, **23**, 182

Garvin, D. (1993) Building a learning organisation. *Harvard Business Review*, July/August, 78–91

Georghiou, L., Metcalfe, J., Gibbons, M., Ray T. & Evans, J. (1986) *Post-Innovation Performance*. Middlesex: Macmillan

Geroski, P., Machin, S. & van Reenen, J. (1993) The profitability of innovating firms. *RAND Journal of Economics*, **24**, 198–211

Geroski, P. (1991) Innovation and the sectoral sources of UK productivity growth. *Economic Journal*, **101**, 1438–1451

———, (1994) *Market Structure, Corporate Performance and Innovative Activity*. Oxford: Oxford University Press

Geroski, P. & Pomroy, R. (1990) Innovation, and the evolution of market structure. *Journal of Industrial Economics*, **28**, 299–314

Gherardi, S. & Nicolini, D. (2002) Learning in a constellation of interconnected practices: canon or dissonance. *Journal of Management Studies*, **39**(4), 419–436

Gherardi, S., Nicolini, D. & Odella, F. (1998) Towards a social understanding of how people learn in organizations: the notion of situated curriculum. *Management Learning*, **29**(3), 273–297

Gibbons, M., Limoges, C., Nowotny, H., Schwartzman, S., Scott, P. & Trow, M. (1994) *The New Production of Knowledge: The Dynamics of Science and Research in Contemporary Society*. London: Sage

Giddens, A. (1984) *The Constitution of Society*. Berkeley, CA: University of California Press

Giger, M. (1984) Les bonzais de l'industrie Japanaise. *CPE Publication*, **40**, French Ministry of Industry and Research, Paris, July

Glaser, B.G. & Strauss, A.L. (1967) *The Discovery of Grounded Theory: Strategies for Qualitative Research*. New York: Aldine de Gruyter

Gobeli, D.H. & Larson, E.W. (1987). Relative effectiveness of different project structures. *Project Management Journal*, **XVIII**(2), 81–85

Goodacre, A. (1991) R&D expenditure and the analysts' view. *Accountancy*, April

Gouldner, A. (1970) *The Coming Crisis of Western Sociology*. London: Heinemann

Granstrand, O., Patel, P. & Pavitt, K. (1997) Multi-technology corporations: why they have "distributed" rather than "distinctive core" competencies. *California Management Review*, **39**, 8–25

Granstrand, O.P., Bohlin, E, Oskarsson, C. & Sjorberg, N. (1992) External technology acquisition is large multi-technology corporations. *R&D Management*, **22**(2), 111–333

Grant, R.M. (1991) The resource-based theory of competitive advantage: implications for strategy formulation. *California Management Review*, **33**, 114–135

——————, (1996a) Towards a knowledge based theory of the firm. *Strategic Management Journal*, **17**(Winter Special Issue), 109–122

——————, (1996b) Prospering in dynamically-competitive environments: organizational capability as knowledge integration. *Organization Science*, **7**(4), 375–387

——————, (2001) Knowledge and organization. In *Managing Industrial Knowledge: Creation, Transfer and Utilization*, ed. I. Nonaka & D.J. Teece. London: Sage

Gray, R. (1993) *Accounting for the Environment*. PCP

Green, K., Jones, O. & Coombs, R. (1996) Critical perspectives on technology management. *Technology Analysis and Strategic Management*, **8**(1), 3–7

Gregory R.E. (1986) Source selection: a matrix approach. *Journal of Purchasing and Materials Management*, Summer

Griffin, A. & Page, A.L. (1993) An interim report on measuring product development success and failure. *Journal of Product Innovation Management*, **10**, 291–308

—————, (1996), PDMA success measurement project: recommended measures for product development success and failure. *Journal of Product Innovation Management*, **13**, 478–496

Griffiths, D., Boisot, M. & Mole, V. (1998) Strategies for managing knowledge assets: a tale of two companies. *Technovation*, **18**(8/9), 529–539

Griliches, Z. (1981) Market value, R&D and patents. *Economics Letters*, **7**, 183–187

—————, (1984) In *Patents, R&D and Productivity*, ed. Z. Griliches & A. Pakes. Chicago: University of Chicago Press

—————, (1990) Patent statistics as economic indicators: a survey. *Journal of Economic Literature*, **28**(4), 1661–1797

Griliches, Z., Hall, B.H. & Pakes, A. (1991) R&D, patents and market value revisited. *Economics of Innovation & New Technology Journal*, **1**(3), 183–202

Guest, D., Michie, J., Sheehan, M. & Conway, N. (2000) *Employment Relations, HRM and Business Performance: An Analysis of the 1998 Workplace Employee Relations Survey*. London: CIPD

Hakansson, H. (ed., 1982) *International Marketing and Purchasing of Goods: An Interaction Approach*. Chichester: Wiley

Hall, B. (1993a) The stock market value of R&D investment during the 1980s. *American Economic Review*, **83**, 259–264

Hall, B. (1993b) Industrial research during the 1980s: did the rate of return fall? *Brookings Papers on Economic Activity*, 289–343

Hall, B. & Mairesse, J. (1995) Exploring the relationship between R&D and productivity in French manufacturing firms. *Journal of Econometrics*, **65**, 263–293

Hall, B., Griliches, Z. & Hausman, J. (1986) Patents and R&D: is there a lag? *International Economic Review*, **27**(2), 265–283

Hall, B.H., Jaffe, A. & Trajtenberg, M. (1998) Market value and patent citations: a first look. Paper prepared for the Conference on Intangibles and Capital Markets, New York University

Hall, E.H. & St. John, C.H. (1994) A methodological note on diversity measurement. *Strategic Management Journal*, **15**, 153–168

Hall, R. (1992) The strategic analysis of intangible resources. *Strategic Management Journal*, **13**, 135–144

_____, (1993) A framework linking intangible resources and capabilities to sustainable competitive advantage. *Strategic Management Journal*, **14**, 607–618

_____, (1994) A framework for identifying the intangible sources of sustainable competitive advantage. In *Competence-based Competition*, ed. G. Hamel & A. Heene. Chichester: John Wiley & Sons

Hamel, G. (1991) Competition for competence and inter-partner learning within international strategic alliances. *Strategic Management Journal*, **12**, 83–103.

_____, (1994) The concept of core competence. In *Competence-based Competition*, ed. G. Hamel & A. Heene. Chichester: Wiley

_____, (2000) *Leading the Revolution*. Boston, MA: Harvard Business School Press

Hamel, G. & Prahalad, C. (1993) Strategy as stretch and leverage. *Harvard Business Review*, March/April.

_____, (1994) *Competing for the Future*. Cambridge, MA: Harvard Business School Press

Harhoff, D., Narin, F., Scherer, F.M. & Vopel, K. (1998) Citation frequency and the value of patented inventions. *The Review of Economics & Statistics*, **81**(3), 511–515

Harris, M. (1997) Power, knowledge and social process in technology analysis: the case of CAD/CAM. *Journal of Information Technology*, **12**, 61–71

Harrison, E.F. & Pelletier, M.A. (1993) A typology of strategic choice. *Technological Forecasting and Social Change*, **44**(3), 245–264

Hartley, J.L. & Jones, G.E. (1997) Process-oriented supplier development: building the capability for change. *International Journal of Purchasing and Materials Management*, Summer, 24–29.

Hauor, G. (1992) Stretching the knowledge base of the enterprise through contract research. *R&D Management*, **22**(2), 177–182

Hauschildt, J. (1992) External acquisition of knowledge for innovations — a research agenda. *R&D Management*, **22**(2), 105–110

Hax, A.C. & Maijuf, N.S. (1991) *The Strategy Concept & Process: A Pragmatic Appraoch*. Prentice-Hall International Inc.

Hay, D.A. & Morris, D.J. (1991) *Industrial Economics and Organisation*. Oxford University Press

Hayes, N. & Walsham, G. (2000) Safe enclaves, political enclaves and knowledge working. In *Managing Knowledge: Critical Investigations of Work and Learning,* ed. C. Pritchard, R. Hull, M. Chumer & H. Willmott. London: MacMillan

Hayes, R.H., Wheelwright, S.C. & Clark, K.B. (1989) Measuring manufacturing performance. *McKinsey Quarterly,* Winter

Henderson, B. (1979) *On Corporate Strategy.* Cambridge, MA: Abt Books

Henderson, R. & Cockburn, I. (1995) Measuring competence? Exploring firm effects in pharmaceutical research. *Strategic Management Journal,* 15 (Special Issue), 63–84

Henderson, R.M. & Clark, K.B. (1990) Architectural innovation: the reconfiguration of existing product technologies and the failure of established firms. *Administrative Science Quarterly,* 35(1), 9–30

Hendry, C. (1996) Understanding and creating whole organisational change through learning theory. *Human Relations,* 49(5), 621–641

Hildreth, P., Kimble, C. & Wright, P. (2000) Communities of practice in the distributed international environment. *Journal of Knowledge Management,* 4(1), 27–38

Hislop, D. (1999) The Movex project: knowledge management at Brightco. In *Case Studies in Knowledge Management,* ed. H. Scarbrough & J. Swan. London: IPD

Hislop, D. (2003) The complex relations between communities of practice and the implementation of technological innovations, *International Journal of Innovation Management,* 7(2), 163–188

Hislop, D., Newell, S., Scarbrough, H. & Swan, J. (1997) Innovation and networks: linking diffusion and implementation. *International Journal of Innovation Management,* 1(4), 427–448

Hitt, M.A. & Ireland, R.D. (1985) Corporate distinctive competence, strategy, industry and performance. *Strategic Management Journal,* 3(3), 273–293

Hobday, M. (2000) The project-based organisation: an ideal form for managing complex products and systems? *Research Policy,* 29, 871–893

Holland, S., Gaston, K. & Gomes, J. (2000) Critical success factors for cross-functional teamwork in new product development. *International Journal of Management Reviews,* 2(3), 231–259

Hood, N. & Young, S. (1979) *The Economics of Multinational Enterprise.* Longman

Housley, W. (2000) Category work and knowledgeability within multidisciplinary team meetings. *Text,* 20(1), 83–107

Huber, G.P. (1996a) Organisational learning: a guide for executives in technology-critical organisations. *International Journal of Technology Management*, 11(7/8), 821–832

_____, (1996b) Organisational learning: the contributing processes and the literatures. In *Organisational Learning*, ed. M.D. Cohen & L.S. Sproull. London: Sage

Iansiti, M. & Clark, K.B. (1994) Integration and dynamic capability: evidence from product development and automobiles and mainframe computers. *Industrial and Corporate Change*, 3, 557–606

Iles, P. (1994) Developing learning environments: challenges for theory, research and practice. *Journal of European Industrial Training*, 18(3), 3–9

Inhaber, H. & Przednowek, K. (1976) Quality of research and the Nobel Prizes. *Social Studies of Science*, 6, 33–50

Isaksen, S. & Tidd, J. (2006) *Meeting the Innovation Challenge: Leadership for Transformation and Growth*. Chicester: Wiley

Itami, H. (1987) *Mobilising Invisible Assets*. Cambridge, MA: Harvard University Press

Jacobsson, S. & Oskarsson, C. (1995) Educational statistics as an indicator of technological activity. *Research Policy*, 24, 127–136

Jacobsson, S., Oskarsson, C. & Joakim, P. (1996) Indicators of technological activities. *Research Policy*, 25, 573–585

Jaffe, A., Trajtenberg, M. & Henderson, R. (1993) Geographic localisation of knowledge spillovers as evidenced by patent citations. *Quarterly Journal of Economics*, 108(3), 577–598

Jaffe, A.B. (1986) Technological opportunity and spillovers of R&D: evidence from firms patents, profits and market values. *The American Economic Review*, 76, 948–999

_____, (1989) Characterising the "technological position" of firms, with application to quantifying technological opportunity and research spillovers. *Research Policy*, 18, 87–97

Jelinek, M. & Litterer, J. (1994) Organizing for technology and innovation. In *Managing New Technology Development*, ed. W. Souder & J. Sherman. New York: McGraw Hill

Jensen, E. (1987) Research expenditures and the discovery of new drugs. *Journal of Industrial Economics*, XXXVI(1), 83–96

Kaplan, R.S. (1983) Measuring manufacturing performance. *Accounting Review*, LVIII(4), 686–705

Kaplan, R.S. & Norton, D.P. (1992) The balanced scorecard — measures that drive performance. *Harvard Business Review*, January/February, 71–79

Kay, J. (1993) *The Foundations of Corporate Success*. Oxford: Oxford University Press

Kay, N. (1979), *The Innovating Firm*. London: McMillan

Keller, R.T. (2001) Cross-functional project groups in research and new product development: diversity, communications, job stress, and outcomes. *Academy of Management Journal*, **44**(3), 547–555

Klavans, R. (1994) The measurement of a competitor's core competences. In *Competence-based Competition*, ed. G. Hamel & A. Heene. Chichester: Wiley

Kleiner, A. & Roth, G. (1997) How to make experience your company's best teacher. *Harvard Business Review*, September/October, 172–177

Kleinknecht, A. & Reijnen, J.O.N. (1993) Towards literature-based innovation output indicators. *Structural Change and Economic Dynamics*, **4**(1), 199–207

Kleinknecht, A. & Bain, D. (1993) *New Concepts in Output Measurement*. London: St. Martin's Press

Kleinman, H. (1975) Indicators of the output of new technological products from industry. Report to the National Science Foundation, National Technical Information Service, Department of Commerce, Washington

Klevorick, A.K., Levin, R.C., Nelson, R.R. & Winter, S.G. (1995) On the sources and significance of inter-industry differences in technological opportunities. *Research Policy*, **24**, 185–205

Knott, P. (1997) Internal processes influencing organisational-level competence. Unpublished PhD Thesis, University of Manchester

Knott, P., Pearson, A.W. & Taylor, R. (1996) A new approach to competence analysis. *International Journal of Technology Management*, **11**, 494–503.

Kodama, F. (1991) *Analysing Japanese High Technologies: The Techno-Paradigm Shift*. London: Pinter

Kogut, B. & Zander, U. (1992) Knowledge of the firm, combinative capabilities, and the replication of technology. *Organization Science*, **3**(3), 383–397

Kolb, D. & Fry, R. (1975) Towards a theory of applied experiential learning. In *Theories of Group Processes*, ed. C. Cooper. Chichester: John Wiley

Krause, D.R. (1997) Supplier development: current practices and outcomes. *International Journal of Purchasing and Materials Management*, Spring, 12–19

Krause, D.R. & Ellram, L.M. (1997) Critical elements of supplier development. *European Journal of Purchasing and Supply Management*, **3**(1), 21–31

Lamberson, L.R., Diederich, D. & Wuori, J. (1976) Quantitative vendor evaluation. *Journal of Purchasing and Materials Management*, Spring

Lambert, D.M., Adams, R.J. & Emmelhainz, M.A. (1997) Supplier selection criteria in the healthcare industry: a comparison of importance and performance. *International Journal of Purchasing and Materials Management*, Winter, 16–21

Lamming, R.C. (1994) *A Review of Relationships Between Vehicle Manufacturers and Suppliers*. Department of Trade and Industry, Vehicles Division and Society of Motor Manufacturers and Traders, London

————, (1993) *Beyond Partnership — Strategies for Innovation and Lean Supply*. London: Prentice-Hall

————, (1996) Squaring lean supply with supply chain management. *International Journal of Operations and Production Management*, **16**(2), 183–196

Lamming, R.C. & Oggero, D. (1995) Purchasing and supply relationship management between small customers and their larger suppliers (SCuLS). In *Proceedings of the Fourth International IPSERA Conference*. Birmingham

Lamming, R.C., Cousins, P.D. & Notman, D.M. (1996b) Beyond vendor assessment: relationship assessment programme. *European Journal of Purchasing and Supply Management*, **2**(4), 173–181

Lamming, R.C., Jones, O.A. & Nicol, D.J. (1996a) Cost transparency: a source of supply chain competitive advantage? In *Proceedings of the 1996 IPSERA Conference*. Eindhoven University

Lave, J.C. & Wenger, E. (1991) *Situated Learning: Legitimate Peripheral Participation*. Cambridge: Cambridge University Press

Lazega, E. (1992) *Micropolitics of Knowledge: Communication and Indirect Control in Workgroups*. New York: De Gruyter

Lehmann D.R. & O'Shaunessy J.O. (1974) Differences in attribute importance for different industrial products. *Journal of Marketing*, **38**, 36–42

Leifer, R. (2000) *Radical Innovation*. Boston, MA: Harvard Business School Press

Leonard-Barton, D. (1988) Implementation as mutual adaptation of technology and organization. *Research Policy*, **17**, 251–267

————, (1991) Core capabilities and core rigidities: a paradox in managing new product development. *Strategic Management Journal*, **13**, 111–125

————, (1992) The organisation as learning laboratory. *Sloan Management Review*, Fall

_____, (1995) *Wellsprings of Knowledge: Building and Sustaining the Sources of Innovation*. Boston, MA: Harvard Business School Press

Leonard, D. & Sensiper, S. (1998) The role of tacit knowledge in group innovation. *California Management Review*, **40**(3), 112–132

Lev, B. & Sougiannis, T. (1996) The capitalisation, amortisation, and value relevance of R&D. *Journal of Accounting & Economics*, **21**, 107–138

Levin, R., Cohen, W. & Mowery, D. (1985) R&D, appropriability, opportunity, and market structure: new evidence on the Schumpeterian hypothesis. *American Economic Review*, **75**, 20–24

Levin, R.C., Klevorick, A., Nelson, R. & Winter, S. (1987) Appropriating the returns from industrial research and development. *Brookings Papers on Economic Activity*, **3**, 783–831

Levitt, B. & March, J.G. (1988) Organisational learning. *Annual Review of Sociology*, **14**, 319–340

_____, (1996) Organisational learning. In *Organisational Learning*, ed. M.D. Cohen & L.S. Sproull. London: Sage

Lewin, A.Y. (1999) Application of complexity theory to organization science. *Organization Science*, **10**(3), 215

Liedtka, J. (1999) Linking competitive advantage with communities of practice. *Journal of Management Enquiry*, **8**(1), 5–16

Lippman, S. & Rumelt, R. (1982) Uncertain imitability: an analysis of interfirm differences in efficiency under competition. *Bell Journal of Economics*, **13**, 418–438

Loch C., Stein, L. & Terweisch (1996) Measuring development performance in the electronics industry. *Journal of Product Innovation Management*, **13**, 3–20

Luchs, B. (1990) Quality as a strategic weapon: measuring relative quality, value and market differentiation. *European Business Journal*, **2**(4), 34–47

Macbeth, D.K. & Ferguson, N. (1994) *Partnership Sourcing: An Integrated Supply Chain Approach*. UK: Pitman Publishing

Machin, S. & Van Reenan, J. (1993) Economic impact of innovation. Paper given to SPES conference, IFS, London, January

Mahajan, V. & Wind, J. (1992) New product models: practice, shortcomings & desired improvements. *Journal of Product Innovation Management*, **10**(4), 273–290

Mairesse, J. & Hall, B. (1996) Estimating the productivity of research and development in French and United States manufacturing firms: an exploration of simultaneity issues with GMM methods. In *International Productivity Differences*, ed. K. Wagner & B. van Ark. Amsterdam: Elsevier

Mairesse, J. & Sassenou, M. (1991) R&D and productivity: a survey of econometric studies at the firm level. *OECD STI Review*, **8**, 9–44

Mairesse, J. & Cueno, P. (1985) Recherche-devloppement et performances des enterprises: une etude econometrique sur donnees individuelles. *Revue Economique*, **36**, 1001–10042

Mandal, A. & Deshmukh, S.G. (1994) Vendor selection using interpretive structural modelling. *International Journal of Operations and Production Management*, **14**(6), 52–59

Mansfield, E. (1984) Chapter 6. In *Patents, R&D and Productivity*, ed. Z. Griliches & A. Pakes. Chicago: University of Chicago Press

——————, (1990) *Managerial Economics*. WW Norton Company

March, J.G. (1987) Exploration and exploitation in organisational learning. *Organisation Science*, **2**, 71–81

March, J. (1998) Introduction: a chronicle of speculations about organizational decision making. In *Decisions and Organisations*, ed. J. March. Oxford: Blackwell

McCabe, D. (1996) The best laid schemes of TQM: strategy, politics and power. *New Technology, Work and Employment*, **11**(1), 28–38

McDaniel, S.W. & Kolari, J.W. (1987) Marketing strategy implications of the Miles and Snow strategic typology. *Journal of Marketing*, **51**, 19–30

McDermott, R. (1999) Why information technology inspired but cannot deliver knowledge management. *California Management Review*, **41**(1), 103–117

McGarth, M.E. (1992) *Product Development: Success Through Product and Cycle Time Excellence*. Butterworth-Heinemann

McGee, J.E. & Dowling, M.J. (1994) Using R&D co-operative arrangements to leverage managerial experience. *Journal of Business Venturing*, **9**, 33–48

McLoughlin, I. (1999) *Creative Technological Change: The Shaping of Technology and Organizations*. London: Routledge

Melcher, A., et al. (1990) Standard maintaining and continuous improvement systems: experiences and comparisons. *Interfaces*, **20**(3), 24–40

Mintzberg, H. (1994) Rethinking strategic planning. *Long Range Planning*, **27**(3), 12–30

——————, (1994) *The Rise and Fall of Strategic Planning*. Herts: Prentice-Hall

Mintzberg, H., Pascale, R.T., Goold, M. & Rumelt, R.P. (1996). The "Honda effect" revisited. *California Management Review*, **38**(4), 78–117

Mitsuru, K. (1999) Strategic innovation in large companies through strategic community management: an NTT multimedia revolution case study. *European Journal of Innovation Management*, 2(3), 95–108

Miyazaki, K. (1994) Search, learning and accumulation of technological competences: the case of optoelectronics. *Industrial and Corporate Change*, 3, 631–654

——————, (1995) *Building Competencies in the Firm: Lessons from Japanese and European Optoelectronics*. New York: St. Martin's Press

Mohrman, S.A., Mohrman, Jr., A.M. & Cohen, S.G. (1995) Organizing knowledge work systems. In *Advances in Interdisciplinary Studies of Work Teams Vol. 2: Knowledge Work in Teams*, ed. M.M. Beyerlein, D.A. Johnson & S.T. Beyerlein. Greenwich, CT: JAI Press, Inc

Mole, V., Griffiths, D. & Boisot, M. (1996) Theory and practice: an exploration of the concept of core competence in BP Exploration and courtaulds. Paper delivered at British Academy of Management Conference, September

Monczka, R.M. & Trecha, S.J. (1988) Cost-based supplier performance evaluation. *Journal of Purchasing and Materials Management*, Spring

Monczka, R.M., Nichols, E.I. & Callahan, T.J. (1992) Value of supplier information in the decision process. *Journal Of Purchasing and Materials Management*, Spring

Morton, J.A. (1971) *Organizing for Innovation: A Systems Approach to Technical Management*. New York: McGraw-Hill

Mowery, D. & Rosenberg, N. (1989) *Technology and the Pursuit of Economic Growth*. Cambridge

Murphy, S. & Kumar, V. (1997) The front end of a new product development. *R&D Management*, 27(1), 5–15

Narasimhan, R. (1983) An analytical approach to supplier selection. *Journal of Purchasing and Materials Management*, Winter

Narin, F. (1976) Evaluative bibliometrics: the use of publication and citation analysis in the evaluation of scientific activity. Contract NSF C-627, National Science Foundation. 31 March, Monograph: 456pp. NTIS Accession #PB252339/AS

——————, (1969) Principal investigator. TRACES — technology in retrospect and critical events in sciences. IIT Research Institute. Prepared for NSF under Contract NSF C-535. Vol. 2

—————————, (1991) Globalisation of research, scholarly information and patents — ten-year trends. In *Proceedings of the North American Serials Interest Group (NASIG) Sixth Annual Conference*, 14–17 June

Narin, F. & Noma, E. (1987) Patents as indicators of corporate technological strength. *Research Policy*, 16, 143–155

Narin, F. & Olivastro, D. (1988) Patent citation analysis: new validation studies and linkage statistics. In *Science Indicators: Their Use in Science Policy and Their Role in Science Studies*. ed. A.F.J. van Raan, A.J. Nederhoff & H.F. Moed. The Netherlands: DSWO Press

Narin, F., Noma, E. & Perry, R. (1987) Patents as indicators of corporate technological strength. *Research Policy*, 16, 143–155

Narin, F., Hamilton, K.S. & Olivastro, D. (1998) The increasing linkage between US technology and public science. *Research Policy*, 26(3), 317–330. Reprinted in the AAAS Science and Technology Yearbook

National Science Foundation (1973) Science indicators, 1972. Report of the National Science Board and subsequent biennial Science and Technology Indicators reports

NEDC (1974) *Industrial Performance in the Longer Term*. NEDC, University of Sussex

Nelson, R. (1991) Why do firms differ and how does it matter? *Strategic Management Journal*, 12, 61–74

Nelson, R. & Winter, S. (1990) In search of a useful theory of innovation. *Research Policy*, 5, 36–76

—————————, (1992) *An Evolutionary Theory of Economic Change*. Cambridge, MA: Harvard University Press

Newell, S., Scarbrough, H., Swan, J. & Hislop, D. (2000) Intranets and knowledge management: de-centred technologies and the limits of technological discourse. In *Managing Knowledge: Critical Investigations of Work and Learning*, ed. C. Pritchard, R. Hull, M. Chumer & H. Willmott. London: MacMillan

Nixon, W., Sundgaard, E. & Sinclair, D. (1993) Industry and the city: is R&D the key? *Accountancy*, January

Nonaka, I. (1991) The knowledge-creating company. *Harvard Business Review*, November/December

—————————, (1994) A dynamic theory of organisational knowledge creation. *Organisation Science*, 5(1), 14–37

Nonaka, I. & Takeuchi, H. (1995) *The Knowledge-Creating Company*. New York: Oxford University Press

Nonaka, I., Takeuchi, H. & Umemoto, K. (1996) A theory of organisational knowledge creation. *International Journal of Technology Management*, **11**(7/8), 833–845

Nooteboom, B. (1996) Globalisation, learning and strategy. Paper delivered at EMOT Workshop, Durham University, 28–30 June

Nydick, R.L. & Hill, R.P. (1992) Using the analytic hierarchy process to structure the supplier selection procedure. *Journal of Purchasing and Materials Management*, Spring

Oakland, J. (1989) *Total Quality Management*. London: Pitman

Oakly, R., Rothwell, R. & Cooper, S. (1988) *Management of Innovation in High Technology Small Firms*. London: Pinter

OECD (1992) *OECD Proposed Guidelines for Collecting and Interpreting Technological Innovation Data — Oslo Manual*. OECD/GD(92)26, Paris

——————, (1996), *Innovation, Patents and Technological Strategies*. OECD, Paris

Ohlson, J. (1993) Accounting data and the economics of the value of the firm. Paper presented to The Management School, Imperial College, 3 November

Orlikowski, W. (1992) The duality of technology: rethinking the concept of technology in organizations. *Organization Science*, **3**(3), 398–427

Orr, J. (1990) Sharing knowledge, celebrating identity: war stories and community memory in a service culture. In *Collective Remembering: Memory in a Society*, ed. D. Middleton & D. Edwards. London: Sage

Oskarsson, C. (1993) Diversification and growth in US, Japanese and European multi-technology corporations. Mimeo, Department of Industrial Management and Economics, Chalmers University of Technology, Gothenburg

Pakes, A. (1985) On patents, R&D and the stock market rate of return. *Journal of Political Economy*, **93**, 390–409

Pakes, A. & Griliches, Z. (1984) Patents and R&D at the firm level: a first look. In *R&D, Patents and Productivity*, ed. Z. Griliches. Chicago: University of Chicago Press

Pan, S. & Scarbrough, H. (1999) Knowledge management in practice: an exploratory case study. *Technology Analysis and Strategic Management*, **11**(3), 359–374

Partington, D. (2000) Building grounded theories of management action. *British Journal of Management*, **11**, 91–102

Patel, P. (1995) Localised production of technology for global markets. *Cambridge Journal of Economics*, **19**, 141–154

—————, (1996) Are large firms internationalising the generation of technology? Some new evidence. *IEEE Transactions on Engineering Management*, **43**, 41–47

Patel, P. & Pavitt, K. (1991) Large firms in the production of the world's technology: an important case of "non-globalisation". *Journal of International Business Studies*, **22**, 1–21

—————, (1992) The innovative performance of the world's largest firms: some new evidence. *Economics of Innovation and New Technology*, **2**, 91–102

—————, (1997) The technological competencies of the world's largest firms: complex and path-dependent, but not much variety. *Research Policy*, **26**, 141–156

Patel, P. & Vega, M. (1998) Technology strategies of large European firms. Draft final report for "Strategic Analysis for European S&T Policy Intelligence" project funded by EC Targetted Socio-Economic Research Programme. Brighton, February 1998

—————, (1999) Patterns of internationalisation of corporate technology: location versus home country advantages. *Research Policy*, **28**, 144–155

Patent and Trademark Office (1976) Technology assessment and forecast. US Department of Commerce. Sixth report, June

—————, (1995) *Manual of Patent Examining Procedures*. Section 904.02, 6th edition. US Department of Commerce

Paulk, M., *et al.* (1993) *Capability Maturity Model for Software*. Software Engineering Institute, Carnegie-Mellon University

Pavitt, K. (1988) Uses and abuses of patent statistics. In *Handbook of Quantitative Studies of Science and Technology*, ed. A.F.J. Van Raen. Amsterdam: North-Holland

Pavitt, K. & Patel, P. (1988) The international distribution and determinants of technological activities. *Oxford Review of Economic Policy*, **4**(4), 35–55

—————, (1987) The elements of British technological competitiveness. *National Institute of Economic Review*, November, 72–83

Pavitt, K. (1984) Sectoral patterns of technical change: towards a taxonomy and a theory. *Research Policy*, **13**, 343–373

—————, (1985) Patent statistics as indicators of innovative activities: possibilities and problems. *Scientometrics*, **7**, 77–99

—————, (1990) What we know about the strategic management of technology. *California Management Review*, **32**, 17–26

—————, (2000) *Technology, Management and Systems of Innovation*. London: Edward Elgar

Pavitt, K., Robson, M. & Townsend, J. (1987) The size distribution of innovating firms in the UK: 1945–1983. *Journal of Industrial Economics*, **35**, 297–316

—————, (1989) Technological accumulation, diversification and organisation in UK companies, 1945–1983. *Management Science*, **35**(1), 3–26

Pawson, R. (2001) The promise of a realist synthesis. Working Paper, Evidence Network, Queen Mary College, London

Pedler, M., Boydell, T. & Burgoyne, J. (1991) *The Learning Company: A Strategy for Sustainable Development*. Maidenhead: McGraw-Hill

Penrose, E.T. (1968) *The Theory of the Growth of the Firm*. London: Basil Blackwell

Pentland, B. & Rueter, H. (1994) Organisational routines as grammars of action. *Administrative Science Quarterly*, **39**, 484–510

Peters, T. & Waterman (1982) *In Search of Excellence*. New York: Harper & Row

Pfeffer, J. & Salancik, G.R. (1978) *The External Control of Organisations: A Resource Dependence Perspective*. New York: Harper & Row.

Pike, R., Meerjanssen, J. & Chadwick, L. (1993) The appraisal of ordinary shares by investment analysts in the UK and Germany. *Accounting and Business Research*, **23**(92), 489–499

Pisano, G.P. (1990) The R&D boundaries of the firm: an empirical analysis. *Administrative Science Quarterly*, **35**, 153–176

—————, (1996) *The Development Factory: Unlocking the Potential of Process Innovation*. Boston, MA: Harvard Business School Press

Plank, R.E. & Kijewski, V. (1991) The use of approved supplier lists. *Journal of Purchasing and Materials Management*, Spring

Porter, M.E. (1983) The technological dimension of competitive strategy. In *Research on Technological Innovation, Management & Policy*, Volume 1, ed. R.S. Rosenbloom. Connecticut: JAI Press

—————, (1985) *Competitive Advantage: Creating and Sustaining Superior Performance*. The Free Press

Povey, B. (1996) Business process improvement. University of Brighton

Prahalad, C.K. & Hamel, G. (1990) The core competence of the corporation. *Harvard Business Review*, May/June, **68**, 79–91

——————, (1994) *Competing for the Future*. Boston, MA: Harvard University Press

——————, (1996) Keynote address at the strategic management society conference, Phoenix, 10–13 November

Prencipe, A. (1997) Technological competencies and product's evolutionary dynamics: a case study from the aero-engine industry. *Research Policy*, **25**, 1261–1276

Presutti, W.D. (1991) Technology management: an important element in the supplier capability survey. *Journal of Purchasing and Materials Management*, Winter

Prokesch, S. (1997) Unleashing the power of learning. *Harvard Business Review*, September/October, 147–168

Purdy, L., Astad, U. & Safayeni, F. (1994) Perceived effectiveness of the automotive supplier evaluation process. *International Journal of Operations and Production Management*, **14**(6), 91–103

Raelin, J. (1997) A model of work based learning. *Organization Science*, **8**(6), 563–578

Rappaport, A. (1986) *Creating Shareholder Value: The New Standard for Business Performance*. London: MacMillan

Reid, W. & Myddleton, D. (1988) *The Meaning of Company Accounts*. Gower

Reisner, P. (1965) A machine-stored citation index to patent literature experimentation and planning. In *Proceedings of Automation and Scientific Communications Annual Meeting*, ed. H.P. Lunh. Washington, DC: American Documentation Institute

Richardson, R. & Thompson, M. (1999) *The Impact of People Management Practices on Business Performance: A Literature Review*. London: CIPD

Roberts, E.B. (1987) Introduction: managing technological innovation — a search for generalizations. In *Generating Technological Innovation*, ed. E.B. Roberts. Oxford: Oxford University Press

Robins, J. & Wiersema, M.I. (1995) A resource-based approach to the multi-business firm. *Strategic Management Journal*, **16**(4), 277–300

Robinson, A. (1991) *Continuous Improvement in Operations*. Cambridge, MA: Productivity Press

Rosenberg, N. & Birdzell, Jr., L.E. (1991) Science, technology and the Western miracle. *Scientific American*, **263**(5), 42–54

Rothwell, R. (1992) Successful industrial innovation: critical success factors for the 1990s. *R&D Management*, **22**(3), 221–239

Rothwell, R. & Gardiner, P. (1984) Invention and re-innovation — the case of the Hovercraft. SPRU Working Paper, University of Sussex.

Rumelt, R.P. (1974) *Strategy, Structure and Economic Performance*. Boston: Harvard Business School

——————, (1984), Towards a strategic theory of the firm. In *Competitive Strategic Management*, ed. R.B. Lamb. Englewood Cliffs, NJ: Prentice-Hall

——————, (1991) How much does industry matter? *Strategic Management Journal*, **12**, 167–185

——————, (1994) Foreword. In *Competence-based Competition*, ed. G. Hamel & A. Heene. Chichester: Wiley

Rush, H., Brady, T. & Hobday, M. (1997) *Learning Between Projects in Complex Systems*. Centre for the Study of Complex Systems

Saaty, T. (1980) *The Analytical Hierarchy Process: Planning, Priority Setting, Resource Allocation*. London: MacGraw-Hill

Samuelson, P. (1993) A case study on computer programs. In *Global Dimensions of Intellectual Property Rights in Science and Technology*, ed. J. Wallerstein, M. Mogee & R. Schoen. Washington, DC: National Academy Press

Sanchez, R. (1997) Managing articulated knowledge in competence-based competition. In *Strategic Learning and Knowledge Management*, ed. R. Sanchez & A. Heene. Chichester: Wiley

Santarelli, E. & Piergiovanni, R. (1996) Analysing literature-based innovation output indicators: the Italian experience. *Research Policy*, **25**, 689–711

Sapolsky, H.M. (1972) *The Polaris System Development: Bureaucratic and Programmatic Success in Government*. Cambridge, MA: Harvard University Press

Sapsed, J.D. (2005) How should "knowledge bases" be organised in multi-technology corporations. *International Journal of Innovation Management*, **9**(1), 75–102

Sapsed, J, Bessant, J., Partington, D., Tranfield, D. & Young, M. (2002) Teamworking and knowledge management: a review of converging themes. *International Journal of Management Reviews*, **4**(1), 71–85

Scarbrough, H. (1999) Knowledge as work: conflicts in the management of knowledge workers. *Technology Analysis and Strategic Management*, **11**(1), 5–16

Scarbrough, H. & Corbett, M. (1992) *Technology and Organization: Power, Meaning and Design*. London: Routledge

Schankerman, M. & Pakes, A. (1986) Estimates of the value of patent rights in European countries during the post-1950 period. *Economic Journal*, **96**, 1052–1076

Schein, E. (1984) Coming to a new awareness of organisational culture. *Sloan Management Review*, Winter, 3–16

Scherer, F. (1965) Firm size, market structure, opportunity and the output of patented inventions. *American Economic Review*, **55**, 1097–1125

————————, (1983) The propensity to patent. *International Journal of Industrial Organisation*, **50**(1), 107–128

Scherer, F.M. & Revenscraft, D. (1982) *Applied Economics*. Boston: Brookings Institution Press.

Scholes, P. (1974) *The Concise Oxford Dictionary of Music*. London: Oxford University Press

Schön, D.A. (1971) *Beyond the Stable State: Public and Private Learning in a Changing Society*. London: Maurice Temple Smith

Schonberger, R.J. (1986) *World-Class Manufacturing: The Lessons of Simplicity Applied*. London: The Free Press

Schroeder, M. & Robinson, A. (1993) Training, continuous improvement and human relations: the US TWI programs and Japanese management style. *California Management Review*, **35**(2), 35–57.

Schumpeter, J. (1984) *The Theory of Economic Development*. Cambridge, MA: Harvard University Press

Sciteb/CBI (1991) *R&D Short-termism? Enhancing the R&D Performance of the UK Team*. ORBIC.

Selznick, P. (1957) *Leadership in Administration*. New York: Harper & Row

Senge, P. (1990) *The Fifth Discipline: The Art and Practice of the Learning Organisation*. New York: Doubleday

Sharrock, W.W. (1974) On owning knowledge. In *Ethnomethodology: Selected Readings*, ed. R. Turner. Harmondsworth: Penguin

Shingo, S. (1983) *A Revolution in Manufacturing: The SMED System*. Cambridge, MA: Productivity Press

Sibley, S.D. (1978) How interfacing departments rate vendors. *Journal of Purchasing and Materials Management*, Summer

Silberston, A. (1989) *Technology and Economic Progress*. London: Macmillan

Simmonds, J. (1981) Strategic management accounting. *Management Accounting*, **59**(4), 26–29

Simon, H.A. (1996) Bounded rationality and organisational learning. In *Organisational Learning*, ed. M.D. Cohen & L.S. Sproull. London: Sage

Simonetti, R. (1996) Technical change and firm growth: "creative destruction" in the fortune list, 1963–1987. In *Behavioural Norms, Technological Progress, and Economic Dynamics*, ed. E. Helmstadter & M. Perlman. Ann Arbor: University of Michigan Press

Sirkin, H. & Stalk, G. (1990) Fix the process, not the problem. *Harvard Business Review*, July/August, 26–33

Smith, K. (1992) Technological innovation indicators: experience and prospects. *Science and Public Policy*, **19**(6), 383–392

Smytka, D.L. & Clemens, M.W. (1993) Total cost supplier selection model: a case study. *International Journal of Purchasing and Materials Management*, Winter, 42–49

Soete, L. (1979) Firm size and inventive activity: the evidence reconsidered. *European Economic Review*, **12**, 319–340

Soukup W.R. (1987) Supplier selection strategies. *Journal of Purchasing and Materials Management*, Summer

St. John, C. & Young, S. (1991) The strategic consistency between purchasing and production. *International Journal of Purchasing and Materials Management*, Spring

Stacey, R.D. (1993) *Strategic Management and Organisational Dynamics*. Pitman Publishing

Stalk, G., Evans, P. & Shulman, L. (1992) Competing on capabilities: the new rules of corporate strategy. *Harvard Business Review*, March/April, 57–69

Star, S.L. & Griesemer, J.R. (1989) Institutional ecology, "translations" and boundary objects: amateurs and professionals in Berkeley's Museum of Vertebrate Zoology, 1907-39. *Social Studies of Science*, **19**, 387–420

Starbuck, W. & Milliken, F (1988) Challenger: fine tuning the odds until something breaks. *Journal of Management Studies*, **25**(4), 319–340

Stern, E. & Sommerblad, E. (1999) *Workplace Learning, Culture and Performance*. London: CIPD

Steward, F. (1994) Innovation strategies of UK pharamceutical companies. Paper presented at the International Conference on Management of Technology, March, Miami

Stewart, T.A. (1994) Your company's most valuable asset: intellectual capital. *Fortune*, 3 October, 68–74

Stoneman, P. (1983) *The Economic Analysis of Technological Change.* Oxford: Oxford University Press

——————, (1989) Working paper, University of Warwick

——————, (1990) The adoption of new technology — theory and evidence. ESRC dissemination conference. London, 4 December

—————— (ed., 1993) *Handbook of the Economics of Technical Change.* Oxford: Basil Blackwell

Storey, J. & Barnett, E. (2000) Knowledge management initiatives: learning from failure. *Journal of Knowledge Management,* 4(2), 145–156

Strauss, A. & Corbin, J. (1990) *Basics of Qualitative Research: Grounded Theory Procedures and Techniques.* Newbury Park, CA: Sage

Swan, J., Newell, S., Scarbrough, H. & Hislop, D. (1999) Knowledge management and innovation: networks and networking. *Journal of Knowledge Management,* 3(4), 262–275

Swan, J. & Scarbrough, H. (2001) Editorial: knowledge management: concepts and controversies. *Journal of Management Studies,* 38(7), 913–921

Taffler, R.J. (1982) Forecasting company failure in the UK using discriminant analysis and financial ratio data. *Journal of the Royal Statistical Society, Series A,* 145(3), 342–358

——————, (1983) The Z-score approach to measuring company solvency. *Accounts Management,* March

——————, (1991) Z-scores: an approach to the recession. *Accountancy,* 108(1175), 95–101

Taylor, D.M. & Doria, J.R. (1981) Self-serving and group-serving bias in attribution. *Journal of Social Psychology,* 113, 201–211

Teece, D.J. & Pisano, G. (1994) The dynamic capabilities of firms: an introduction. *Industrial and Corporate Change,* 3, 537–556

Teece, D.J., Pisano, G. & Schuen, A. (1992) Dynamic capabilities and strategic management. Working Paper, University of California, Berkeley

——————, (1992) *Dynamic Capabilities and Strategic Management.* University of Berkeley.

Tether, B.S., Smith, I.J. & Thwaites, A.T. (1997) Smaller enterprises and innovation in the UK: the SPRU innovations database revisited. *Research Policy,* 26, 19–32

Thompson, K.N. (1991) Scaling evaluative criteria and supplier performance estimate weighted point pre-purchase decision models. *Journal of Purchasing and Materials Management,* Winter

Tidd, J. (1995) The development of novel products through intra- & inter-organisational networks. *Journal of Product Innovation Management*, 12(4), 307–322

_____, (1997) Complexity, networks and learning: integrative themes for research on innovation management. *International Journal of Innovation Management*, 1(1), 1–22

_____, (2002) Innovation management in context: environment, organizational and performance. *International Journal of Management Reviews*, 3(3), 169–184

Tidd, J. & Bodley, K. (1999) The affect of project complexity on the new product development process. *IEEE Transactions on Engineering Management,*

Tidd, J. & Hull, F. (2003) *Service Innovation: Organizational Responses to Technological Opportunities and Market Imperatives.* London: Imperial College Press

Tidd, J. & Izumimoto, Y. (2002) Knowledge management and learning through international joint ventures: an Anglo-Japanese experience. *Technovation*, 22(3), 137–145

Tidd, J. & Taurins, S. (1999) Learn or leverage? Strategic diversification & organisational learning through corporate ventures. *Creativity and Innovation Management*, 8(2), 122–129

Tidd, J. & Trewhella, M. (1997) Organisational and technological antecedents for knowledge acquisition and learning. *R&D Management*, 27(4), 359–375

Tidd, J., Bessant, J. & Pavitt, K. (1997) *Managing Innovation: Integrating Technological, Market and Organisational Change.* Chichester: John Wiley & Sons

_____, (2001) *Managing Innovation: Integrating technological, market and organisational change*, 2nd edn. Chichester: John Wiley & Sons

_____, (2005) *Managing Innovation: Integrating technological, market and organisational change*, 3rd edn. Chichester: John Wiley & Sons

Tidd, J., Driver, C. & Saunders, P. (1996) Linking technological, market and financial indicators of innovation. *Economics of Innovation and New Technology*, 4, 155–172

Timmerman, E., (1986) An approach to vendor performance evaluation. *Journal of Purchasing and Materials Management*, Winter

Tonkin, D. & Skerrat, L. (1988) *Financial Reporting 87–88*. London: Institute of Chartered Accountants

Townsend, J., Henwood, F., Thomas, G., Pavitt, K. & Wyatt, S. (1981) Innovation in Britain since 1945. SPRU Occasional Paper No. 16, Science Policy Research Unit, Sussex University

Trajtenberg, M. (1990) A penny for your quotes: patent citations and the value of innovations. *Rank Journal of Economics*, **21**, 11

Tranfield, D. & Smith, S. (1998) The strategic regeneration of manufacturing by changing routines. *International Journal of Operations and Production Management*, **18**(2), 114–129

Tranfield, D., Smith, S., Foster, M. & Parry, I. (2000) Strategies for managing the teamworking agenda: developing a methodology for team-based organization. *International Journal of Production Economics*, **65**, 33–42

Tranfield, D., Young, M., Partington, D., Bessant, J. & Sapsed, J.D. (2003) Knowledge management routines for innovation projects: developing an hierarchical model. *International Journal of Innovation Management*, 7(1), 27–50

Tsoukas, H. (1996) The firm as a distributed knowledge system: a constructionist approach. *Strategic Management Journal*, 17(Winter Special Issue), 11–25

Tsoukas, H. & Vladimirou, E. (2000) On organizational knowledge and its management: an ethnographic investigation. Paper presented at Knowledge Management: Concepts and Controversies, University of Warwick, 10–11 February

Turney, J. (1991) What drives the engines of innovation? *New Scientist*, 40

Utterback, J. (1994) *Mastering the Dynamics of Innovation*. Boston, MA: Harvard Business School Press

Van Maanen, J. & Barley, S.R. (1984) Occupational communities: culture and control in organizations. In *Research in Organizational Behaviour*, ed. B.M. Staw & L.L. Cummings. Greenwich, CT: JAI Press, Inc

Van de Ven, A., Angle, H. & Poole, M. (1989) *Research on the Management of Innovation*. New York: Harper and Row

Wageman, R. (2001) How leaders foster self-managing team effectiveness: design choices versus hands-on coaching. *Organization Science*, **12**(5), 559–577

Walker, W.B. (1979) *Industrial Innovation and International Trading Performance*. New York: JAI Press

Walleck, A.S. (1991) Benchmarking world-class performance. *McKinsey Quarterly*, No. 1

Walrus, L. (1984/1926) *Elements of Pure Economics or the Theory of Social Wealth*. Philadelphia: Orion Editions

Ward, A. (2000) Getting strategic value from constellations of communities. *Strategy and Leadership*, **28**(2), 4–9

Ward, K. (1992) *Strategic Management Accounting*. Middlesex: Butterworth-Heinemann

Watts, C.A. & Hahn, C.K. (1993) Supplier development programmes: an empirical analysis. *International Journal of Purchasing and Materials Management*, Spring, 11–17

Weber, C.A., Current, J.R. & Benton, W.C. (1991) Vendor selection criteria and methods. *European Journal of Operations Research*, **50**(1), 2–18

Wernerfelt, B.A. (1984) A resource-based view of the firm. *Strategic Management Journal*, **5**, 171–180

Wieters, C.D. (1976) Influences on the design and use of vendor performance rating systems. *Journal of Purchasing and Materials Management*, Winter

Williams, I. & Miller, M. (1993) *US GAAP Guide* HBJ

Williamson, D. (1975) *Markets and Hierarchies*. Glencose: The Free Press

Wilson, E.J. (1994) The relative importance of supplier selection criteria: a review and update. *International Journal of Purchasing and Materials Management*, Summer, 35–40

Wind, J. & Mahajan, V. (1997) Issues and opportunities in new product development: an introduction to the special issue. *Journal of Marketing Research, Special Issue on Innovation and New Products*, **34**, 1–12

Winter, S. (1986) The research programme of the behavoural theory of the firm: orthodox critique and evolutionary perspective. In *Handbook of Behavioural Economics, Behavioural Microeconomics*, ed. B. Gilad & S. Kaish. Greenwich, CT: JAI Press

Womack, J.P., Jones, D.T. & Roos, D. (1990) *The Machine that Changed the World*. New York: Rawson Associates

Wood, S. & de Menezes, L. (1998) High commitment management in the UK: evidence from the Workplace Industrial Relations Survey and Employers' manpower and skills practices survey. *Human Relations*, **51**, 485–517

Worcester Polytechnic Institute (1988) Analysis of highly cited patents: are they important? Report prepared for the US Patent Office, 16 December

Zeleny, M. (1982) *Multiple Criteria Decision-Making*. New York: McGraw-Hill

Index

Alliances 13, 25, 178, 179
AT&T 209, 311, *see also* Lucent

Bayer 187
Benchmarking 32, 84, 86, 111,
    131, 325, 345, 347, 379,
    380, 392
Bibliometrics 193, 194
Biotechnology 16, 163, 178, 186,
    189, 211, 216, 219–221, 223,
    224
Brands 84, 87–89, 94–97, 99,
    100, 116, *see also* reputation

Canon 23, 254
Capabilities 14, 20, 34, 38, 39, 43,
    46, 52, 53, 60, 92, 133, 142,
    256, 257, 321, 331, 357, 379,
    see competencies
Chemicals 105, 118, 160, 173,
    175, 177, 178, 186, 189, 211,
    216, 219, 223, 224, 277
Collaboration 26, 238, 245, 250,
    251, 379, 380, *see* alliances
Competencies 1, 12–20, 22, 23,
    26–36, 39, 40, 44, 55, 60, 83,
    84, 101, 134, 135, 155, 157,
    159, 160, 163, 167, 168, 175,
    176, 178–180, 247, 252, 253,
    256, 257–261, 269, 270, 281,
    282, 339, 350, 364, 379, 381,
    402

Complexity 20–22, 26, 85, 109,
    110, 124, 125, 131, 262, 273,
    311, 320, 324, 337
Customers 19, 20, 34, 35, 37,
    38, 40–43, 59, 66, 67, 73,
    78, 85, 87, 92, 121, 135,
    142, 165, 236, 243, 246,
    258, 259, 289, 315, 318–320,
    324, 334, 335, 348, 366, 368,
    372, 391, 393

Delphi 41
Differentiation 36, 37, 110, 120,
    121, 123, 131, 187, 221, 254,
    328, 331, 375, *see* market
    differentiation
Diversification 13, 16–18, 26,
    28–31, 176, 179, 180, 254

Electronics 16, 18, 19, 28–30,
    106, 124, 130, 140, 173, 179,
    189, 211, 216–219, 221, 223,
    224, 292, 305
Ericsson 23

Financial performance 26, 27, 101,
    104, 111, 112, 123,
    125, 132, 182, 186, 344, 345,
    359–361, 383

General Electric (GE) 84
General Motors (GM) 314, 320

Hewlett Packard 365
Hitachi 30, 207, 208
Honda 16, 259

IBM 106, 191, 196
ICI 389
ICL 322, 366, 367, 387
Information technology 159
Innovation 13, 15–20, 22, 27, 33,
    42, 58, 61–63, 65–69, 73, 74,
    76, 78–80, 84–111, 115–118,
    121–126, 130–134, 136–139,
    142–144, 146–148, 151–156,
    160, 161, 163, 165–167, 174,
    182–184, 196, 197, 201, 210,
    217, 225–227, 229–231, 233,
    236–246, 249–251, 277, 279,
    281, 283, 287, 314, 337, 340,
    344, 349–351, 353–357, 359,
    366, 367, 369, 370–373,
    375–377, 381, 382, 384, 399
Intellectual property 24, 32, 86,
    87, 89, 92, 99, 191, 198, 209,
    see also patents

John Lewis Partnership 37

Knowledge 13, 14, 16, 19, 20, 23,
    25, 26, 31–33, 46, 48–53, 55,
    133–137, 139–142, 146,
    151–156, 158, 159, 162, 163,
    166, 167, 182, 184, 188, 201,
    204, 205, 225–230, 233–239,
    242–251, 253, 256–269, 274,
    276, 278–286, 288–291,
    296–298
  Codification 50, 51, 262,
    264–266, 274, 279, 282

Distribution 24–26, 31, 43, 92,
    114, 165, 174, 189, 216, 219,
    223, 226, 229
Kodak 198, 199

Learning 15, 22–25, 36, 39, 40,
    48, 50–55, 68, 135–138, 153,
    156, 165, 178, 225, 228,
    229, 245, 249, 256–258, 262,
    264, 265, 267, 268, 284, 294,
    301, 304, 331, 344, 359,
    378–381, 384–391, 397, 399
Lucent 209, see also AT&T

Market
  Attractiveness 85, 86, 121
  Differentiation 121
  Pull 20
  Share 21, 22, 36, 68, 88, 89,
    92, 105, 112, 120, 121, 204,
    316, 365, 375, 377
Motorola 30, 31

NEC 30
Nissan 322, 326

Organization
  Culture 32, 39, 45, 51, 55, 57,
    65, 234, 237–239, 380
  Learning 13, 24–26, 32, 33,
    268, 348, 385
  Structure 18, 26, 27, 31, 35, 60,
    291, 295

Patents 16–18, 27, 29, 38, 43,
    103–105, 107–110, 117, 123,
    131, 132, 160, 161, 163, 164,
    167, 172, 176, 177, 179, 183,
    185, 187–191, 195–215, 217,

218, 220, 221, 224, 278, 283,
    352, 372, 373
Pharmaceuticals 18, 19, 105, 118,
    164, 173, 177, 178, 189, 211,
    216, 219, 223, 224, 231
Philips 30
PIMS 84–89, 91–98, 100, 118,
    119, 121, 131
Proctor and Gamble 27
Productivity 85, 86, 93, 104–107,
    120, 130, 131, 169, 170, 171,
    286, 287, 344, 347, 361, 383
Profitability 103, 104, 110, 111,
    116, 120, 121, 149, 168, 173,
    174, 201, 349, 360, 374, *see
    also* financial performance
Publication counts, *see* bibliometrics
    194

Regulation 92, 261
Reputation 32, 38, 43, 45,
    47–49, 55, 57, 89, 90, 92, 98
Research and Development 16, 27,
    102, 104, 114, 123, 127–130,
    132, 160, 205, 306, 318, 370

Semiconductors 30, 31, 106, 177,
    189, 211, 216, 219, 223
Services 13–15, 17, 28, 30, 33,
    42, 46, 76, 85, 93, 115, 123,
    127, 144–146, 158, 164, 233,
    257

SmithKline Beecham 186, 203, 208
Software 16, 24, 31, 103, 140, 142,
    144, 150, 160, 161, 163, 164,
    272, *see also* information
    technology
Strategic business units (SBU) 27,
    28, 35, 259
Strategy, *see also* competencies
    Implementation 60, 68, 71,
    153, 166, 225, 226, 229–231,
    236, 239, 240, 246
    resource-based 14, 35, 60,
    254–256, 258, 262, 281
Success, probability 13
Suppliers 16, 19, 32, 34, 38, 43,
    44, 59, 67, 88, 135, 165,
    254, 291, 313–315, 318, 320,
    322–324, 326–334, 338, 367,
    393

Technological
    employees 32, 37, 136, 162, 163,
    167–170, 183, 262, 280
    opportunity 18, 19, 25, 68, 79,
    105, 106, 128, 131, 135, 151,
    174
    push 63, 100
    spillover 106, 107, 122
Telecommunications 189, 211,
    216, 219, 223, *see also* AT&T
Toshiba 30, 31, 382, 384
Transaction costs 25